Property in East Central Europe

Property in East Central Europe

Notions, Institutions and Practices of Landownership in the Twentieth Century

Edited by Hannes Siegrist and Dietmar Müller

berghahn
NEW YORK • OXFORD
www.berghahnbooks.com

Published in 2015 by
Berghahn Books
www.berghahnbooks.com

Library of Congress Cataloging-in-Publication Data

Property in East Central Europe: notions, institutions and practices of landownership in the twentieth century / edited by Hannes Siegrist and Dietmar Müller.
pages cm
Includes bibliographical references and index.
ISBN 978-1-78238-461-8 (hardback: alkaline paper) – ISBN 978-1-78238-462-5 (ebook)
1. Land tenure--Europe, Eastern--History--20th century. 2. Land tenure--Poland--History--20th century. 3. Land tenure--Romania--History--20th century. 4. Land tenure--Yugoslavia--History--20th century. 5. Right of property--Europe, Eastern--History--20th century. 6. Real property--Europe, Eastern--History--20th century. 7. Post-communism--Europe, Eastern--History--20th century. 8. Europe, Eastern--Social conditions--20th century. 9. Europe, Eastern--Economic conditions--20th century. 10. Europe, Eastern--Politics and government--20th century. I. Siegrist, Hannes. II. Müller, Dietmar, 1969-
HD590.7.P76 2014
333.309437'0904--dc23

2014018765

British Library Cataloguing in Publication Data
A catalogue record for this book is available from the British Library

ISBN 978-1-78238-461-8 (hardback)
E-ISBN 978-1-78238-462-5 (ebook)

Contents

Tables

Acknowledgements

We are grateful to the Volkswagen Foundation for supporting our research project on landownership in Eastern Europe, which was conducted from 2005 to 2009 at the Institute for the Study of Cultures at the University of Leipzig. We followed up with a research group on legal cultures in East Central Europe at the Leipzig Centre for the History and Culture of East Central Europe (GWZO) from 2009 to 2013. We thank the German Federal Ministry of Education and Research for financing this second research project.

We are also grateful to colleagues who have enriched our work through critique and useful comments. Hartmut Kaelble, Wolfgang Hildermeier, Bogdan Murgescu and Stefan Troebst were intellectually supportive in the incipient phase of the research, the latter two also, along with Hannes Siegrist and Dietmar Müller, constituting the leadership of the project. For numerous inspiring discussions along the way we owe thanks to Chris Hann, Claudia Kraft, Dieter Gosewinkel and Philipp Ther. All our efforts would have been futile without close collaboration with our East Central and South-Eastern European colleagues, whose expertise was instrumental in identifying relevant research questions and promising young colleagues. We would therefore like to thank Zoran Janjetović, Dubravka Stojanović, Milan Ristović, Bogdan Murgescu, Vlad Naumescu, Daniel Barbu, Elżbieta Kosćik and Jacek Novak.

We also wish to acknowledge several institutions that hosted discussions as part of the project: the Chair for Social and Cultural History of Modern and Contemporary Europe, Faculty of Social Sciences and Philosophy, University of Leipzig; the GWZO; the Centre for Comparative European History, Berlin; the Willy Brandt Centre in Wrocław and the history departments of the Universities of Belgrade and Bucharest.

Several people worked with patience and accuracy to turn our manuscript into the present book. Nick T. Emm, Jaime Taber and Philip Thomas respectively translated and copy-edited the volume, and Andrei Avram, Marie-Thérèse Mrusczok and Arno Trültzsch formatted and checked the texts and put together the bibliography and index. We are grateful for their help in this process.

Introduction

Property in East Central Europe

Notions, Institutions and Practices of Landownership in the Twentieth Century

Hannes Siegrist and Dietmar Müller

The epoch-making events of 1989 led to a spectacular renaissance of private property rights as a value and institution in the societies of Eastern Europe. In the minds of post-communist elites, shifting away from the statist socialist system would, in addition to changing the political system to parliamentary democracy, deeply affect the socio-economic and cultural sphere by restructuring society as the domain of private property owners. This great expectation indicates that the issue of property rights remains key to understanding the history of modern states and societies.[1] In the present volume, historians, lawyers and cultural anthropologists analyse the issue of landownership in twentieth-century East Central Europe to understand and explain how and why Poles, Romanians and Serbs shape and use proprietary institutions in projects of social, political, economic, cultural and legal 'modernization'. Their contributions show why societies that were largely dependent on agriculture well into the twentieth century have adapted traditional forms and developed hybrid and new types of property.[2] Special attention is devoted to the years around 1918, 1945 and 1989, when concepts of property and the role of property rights in the social and political sphere changed fundamentally.

This volume analyses the social, cultural, economic, legal and political meanings and functions of property rights in East Central Europe, investigating processes, structures, institutions, practices and mentalities in short-, mid- and long-term historical perspectives and at the macro-, meso- and micro-levels. Through comparative analyses of cases from three different countries, and of the institutional transfers between them, it aims to improve understanding of differences and similarities between nations, sub-national regions and transnational property cultures, and to help overcome some of the idiosyncrasies of single-nation historiographies, which rarely look across borders. At the same time, it challenges certain stereotypes in the international and Western historiography of East Central Europe.

The volume re-examines meanings and functions of property and similar exclusive rights in East Central Europe – an area whose extent, characteristics and definitions have varied significantly over centuries – and addresses the question of whether East Central Europe can be regarded as a distinctive area with regard to concepts of property and property relations.

The regional focus is on the territories of present-day Poland, Romania and Serbia (formerly part of Yugoslavia). Through comparative examination of societies, states, economies and legal cultures, the volume aims to identify regional, national and transnational similarities and differences, convergences and divergences, and transfers across borders.[3] Were East Central Europe's forms and regimes of property distinct because its peoples and states had to cope with specific economic and social conditions? Because its institutional, legal and political heritage was particular? Because its societies and states selected and adapted 'universal' or so-called Western property patterns in particular ways? Did the countries of East Central Europe develop specific types of property, property regimes and related institutional strategies in the twentieth century because of the particular challenges they faced in the process of nation building and state building? Or was this the case because wars, occupational regimes, violence, destruction and population dislocation were more calamitous than they were elsewhere in Europe?

Indeed, many common and similar structures, processes, strategies, experiences and challenges have characterized the development of property in East Central European countries. In the twentieth century, this development was determined by, for example, agrarian reforms after the First World War; reconstruction of the societies by People's democracy governments immediately after the Second World War; membership in the Soviet bloc, Comecon (Council for Mutual Economic Assistance) and the Warsaw Pact; de-collectivization and the turn away from communism after 1989; and entry to the European Union. A further common trait of Romanian, Yugoslavian and Polish histories is that, after the First World War, the nation-states incorporated provinces that had hitherto been part of the Habsburg Empire: Galicia became part of Poland, Vojvodina part of Yugoslavia, and Transylvania and Bukovina part of Romania. The three states thereby inherited legal customs, institutions and organizational patterns such as Austrian civil law, cadastres and land registration. Yet the new nation-states of Poland, Yugoslavia and Greater Romania (as defined in the interwar period) varied considerably in their approaches to this quite 'liberal', 'modern' legacy within their territory. Comparison of historical regions within these nation-states shows that, after both world wars, the respective western provinces that had had been part of the Habsburg Empire before 1918 were areas of particularly intense political interference with regard to the restructuring of landownership. A very similar situation prevailed in the eastern provinces of Poland after the First World War.

In the twentieth century, some of the older historical differences between the three countries persisted, while others faded away or became less distinct. Meanwhile, new differences and distinctions emerged. The Polish agrarian reform of the interwar period was far less radical than that in neighbouring countries. The communist regimes in Poland and Yugoslavia abandoned collectivization early on, whereas the regime in Romania imposed one of Comecon's highest collectivization quotas. Many more such processes of re-differentiation within East Central Europe are analysed in the present volume.

In what follows we shall first discuss concepts, practices, problems and historical narratives of landholding in East Central European history. Second, we introduce a conceptual framework for comparative analysis of social processes and relations regulated by proprietary institutions and norms. This aids in the analysis of different programmes, strategies and processes of 'propertization', which tend to conceive of social relationships increasingly and primarily as property-based relations but also distinguish between rival concepts of property rights – for example, individual versus collectivist. Finally, we summarize the central findings of the volume and present a critical interpretation of the history of property regimes in twentieth-century East Central Europe.[4]

Concepts and Historiographies of Landownership after 1989

This volume re-examines certain classical historical narratives and timeless myths about property and property regimes in East Central Europe, some of which were revived and widely diffused after 1989. A central feature of the political and scientific debates accompanying changes in property relations after 1989 was the almost unlimited expectation that a property regime based on a liberal-individualistic concept of property would solve many problems at once.[5] The restitution and rehabilitation of private property rights was intended to be the basis for rebuilding the economy by way of free interaction between property owners. The new legal and economic order would prepare the ground for a society of private property owners and guarantee the autonomy of the individual and the existence of the liberal economy, state of law and civil society. In many respects this referred directly to the 'Western' concept of liberal-individualistic property,[6] which defines property as a bundle of strong and absolute exclusive rights pertaining to an individual – irrespective of whether he or she belong to a particular local, regional or national community or a particular denomination, ethnic group, occupational category, gender and so on. A comprehensive and absolute property concept would establish and guarantee the rights of access, monitoring, use, exploitation and alienation by a natural or a legal person, and therefore standardize social relations and expectations in the economy and society by unambiguously assigning a comprehensive bundle of property rights to an individual. The property regime institutionalized and organized in this way would provide for an effective allocation of economic resources while aiming for the political effects of strengthening individuals in their social relations, and developing a society of active, self-conscious, autonomous citizens.[7]

Hence, the bulk of the so-called 'transition' literature published after 1989 in the economic, legal and political sciences claims that East Central European countries should adapt their legal norms and institutions to liberal Western standards, and thereby return to the constitutional and institutional path of democracy, market economy and private property.[8] Similar trends are visible in highly specialized disciplines and sub-disciplines like the agricultural sciences and economic history, which rid themselves of so-called Marxist ballast after 1990.[9]

Meanwhile, the recent revival of private property in East Central Europe was often embedded in the historical master narrative of the 'return to Europe', which contended that liberal and democratic values – including individualistic concepts and institutions of property – were already so widespread and deeply rooted in pre-communist East Central European nations that they merely had to press the restart button after 1990.[10] Sometimes references to the institutional and legal heritage of the interwar period were motivated by particular material and moral interests; sometimes they were part of general rhetorical strategies in the search for a new order.

Now, twenty-five years after the end of communism, both the history of the interwar period and the years from 1989 to 2010 can and should be investigated from a more distant, more critical historical perspective. Since then, Poland and Romania have become members of the European Union, which defines both the institutional standards and the borders of Europe. In the last decade, their accession to the EU has provoked and in some cases revived another historical debate over the thesis that, in centuries past, modernization and property regimes in East Central and South East Europe were characterized by a sequence of deficits and failed projects.[11] Thus, their history is interpreted in terms of 'divergence' and 'deviation' from an idealized 'Western' path that represents a 'standard' or 'normal' path of successful modernization. Ever since the nineteenth century, this narrative has periodically been spread in the historiography, collective memories and mentalities of both Western and Eastern Europeans, and it still inspires some Western historiography on Eastern Europe. Yet it also belongs to the much broader, periodically revived discourse of East Central European 'exceptionalism'.

The present volume re-examines these controversial historical narratives and ideologies in the light of new empirical and critical research, taking a comparative approach from a twenty-first-century perspective. It aims to historicize, contextualize and compare the evolution of concepts, institutions and practices of landholding in East Central European countries. The chapters analyse how particular social actors and states in Eastern Europe have conceived and used property rights in different contexts. They show and explain why cultural patterns, social institutions and legal norms and procedures – both indigenous and exogenous – were adapted, implemented or rejected in particular historical and social contexts.

Societies, states and hegemonic powers used and adapted proprietary institutions and similar exclusive rights in order to regulate roles and relationships in their territories. They varied practices, customs, laws and institutions concerning land and property, and embedded them in the institutional strategies of local, regional, national and international elites and counter-elites. Thus, property patterns varied considerably in both theory and practice. From the standpoint of an empirical comparative historiography, it is unsurprising that the chapters in this volume confirm that regional and national particularities existed, and that the neighbouring nations and regional communities of East Central Europe sometimes conceived of themselves as distinct from each other in particular ways. Yet they also exhibited similarities and convergences, periodically becoming more homogeneous in certain respects before differences emerged again.

The chapters of the present volume show that, first, the differences between different countries, sub-national areas and transnational regions in East Central Europe were often more gradual than fundamental; second, their borders were porous, their territorial extent subject to change and their histories interwoven; and third, their evolution was embedded in general European trends and connected with global processes that shaped the territorial and social order not only in East Central Europe but also in other regions, nations and transnational spaces of Europe. These general or universal trends include the transitions from an agricultural and rural to an industrial and urban society; from a traditional to a modern legal culture; from a pre-national society to a homogenized national society; from an aristocratic to a liberal and democratic society; from a liberal to an authoritarian society; from an occupied to an independent society; from a pre-communist to a communist society, and finally back to a post-communist society, and so on. With each shift, proprietary rules were adapted to specific aims and strategies, and embedded in complex institutional settings. These changes in proprietary laws, rules and customs were determined by institutional traditions and mentalities, contemporary interests and visions of the future.

Sometimes the problems, challenges and perspectives of Romanians, Poles and Yugoslavs were particular; at other times or in other respects they resembled those in other European societies. With regard to the forms of property rights and property regimes in the rural world, differences between East and West – in some respects and regions – became more fundamental in the late 1940s, that is, after the rise of communism. The history of property and property relations reveals that East Central Europeans adapted, reassembled, reinterpreted and rejected

Western patterns of modernity and property in manifold ways. Twentieth-century East Central Europe was the setting of more or less radical experiments in making and re-making proprietary institutions. What remains to be shown and explained here is why East Central European societies conserved and mixed older patterns in particular ways to establish new types of property.

Institutions, Norms, and Practices: Towards an Integrated Analysis of Property Regimes

The contributions to the present volume analyse the legal history of property rights and legal cultures in the context of the institutionalization of social relations in societies characterized by sometimes particular, sometimes similar conflicts and tensions in processes of modernization and traditionalization.[12] The heuristic framework for cross-disciplinary analysis of proprietary institutions is grounded in sociological and historical research on institutions, institutional change and institutional transfers.[13] Historical analysis of proprietary institutions in social, cultural, economic and political relationships relies on the central concepts of 'institutionalization' in general, and 'propertization' in particular.

Institutionalization refers to the social, cultural and legal processes that construct, implement and embed 'institutions', which themselves are defined as collective rules of operation that standardize, normalize and sanction social and cultural action. As fixed symbolic regulations, institutions (such as property, family, nation) provide a reliability of expectations in social relationships. When actors internalize social, cultural and legal rules in the framework of socialization and acculturation, the rules become 'subjective settings', elements of a 'social habit' or group-specific 'mentality'. In modern societies and cultures, institutional change is characterized by acceleration, the dissolution of borders and delimitation. Tensions between traditional and innovative as well as indigenous and foreign institutions become permanent and occasionally intensify. 'Institutional knowledge' – that is, knowledge about possible ways of regulating social relationships – is expanded and differentiated. Institutions such as land ownership and corresponding property rights become polyvalent and multifunctional due to their use in various social constellations and cultural contexts. Conflicts over their meaning and function thus increase periodically.

The historical and analytical concept of 'propertization' harks back to a particular type and mode of institutionalization in the nineteenth and twentieth centuries, when social relationships were increasingly understood as ownership relationships and regulated with the help of property rights, and proprietary institutions' increased importance fundamentally marked institutional and legal dynamics in turn. In general, 'propertization' means that claims to exclusive entitlements to, control over and use of material and immaterial goods are established and sanctioned with reference to theories, concepts and norms of property. Alternative rules and rights are devalued, displaced or repressed, while the territorial reach and temporal validity of proprietary rights and rules expand. In the course of the overall process of propertization, distinctive, variously exclusive or inclusive concepts of property – liberal-individualistic, cooperative, ethno-national and state socialist – compete with each other.[14]

The chapters here do not assume that processes of property creation are uniform and irreversible. On the contrary, the authors attempt to comprehend the dialectic of propertization, reversal and re-creation processes in their respective contexts. For that reason, they start by examining competition among actors, interests, ideas and institutions, asking how and why various property-related rules become widespread and assert themselves in the 'conflict of institutions' and in 'institutional fashions',[15] and how claims based on property can be embedded in general institutional settings and legal structures.

Our analysis of institutions and institutional change follows W. Richard Scott, who distinguishes analytically between the regulative, normative and cognitive dimensions of institutions.[16] In relation to property, this differentiation gives rise to three levels of institutional analysis: regulative, normative-social and cognitive-cultural. At the regulative level, the legal fixing of a property concept is regulated in the constitution, the civil law code and other individual laws. The normative-social dimension of analysis encompasses the whole array of rights of disposal and exploitation of land, as well as concrete dealings with actors in rural areas – in other words, strategies of buying and selling, leasing, inheriting and exploiting land. Arising at the interface between the regulative and normative-social dimensions is the question of how to handle the norms in organizations such as the cadastre, land registry and notarial system, staffed by geodesists, cadastral officials, notaries and lawyers. The cognitive-cultural dimension comprises general moral principles on the one hand, and on the other the particular meaning that local actors and communities, for instance, assign to landholding. It reflects the symbolic function of property in the social and cultural construction of a person and the family within a community. In this regard, morally charged rules play a special role in determining who may buy or inherit land, and how.

This kind of institutional analysis of property is only conceivable as an interdisciplinary form of propertization research that goes beyond the disciplinary property research of lawyers, economists, political scientists and philosophers. It opens up new opportunities for critical reflection on the institutions, practices, myths and ideologies of modern property cultures and property-owning societies. The chapters in this volume form a multidimensional analysis of property as an institution, leading to findings that point beyond any one individual case.

Property Law, Legal Cultures and Social Order

What abstract concept or historical type of property should be taken as a starting point or common reference point in comparative research on landownership and property regimes in East Central Europe? For reasons both current and historical, we have decided to present the history of property relations in rural East Central Europe primarily from a liberal-individualistic perspective on property. We acknowledge that Eastern Europeans' historical experiences were periodically heavily determined by concepts of collective, common or state property. But in the nineteenth and early twentieth centuries, the idea of economic liberalism based on the liberal-individualistic property concept also prevailed periodically, and South East European states like Serbia and Romania anchored individual property rights in their early constitutions, civil codes and legal practices.[17] In certain respects, these general principles were adapted to local legal and moral customs.[18]

However, the interwar period saw a dramatically intensified disengagement from the ideal of individual absolute title. In the new states of East Central and South East Europe, this ideal was deemed an unsuitable basis for the process of accelerated modernization that would bring these societies and economies into parity with Western Europe. Essentially, the elites in Warsaw, Belgrade and Bucharest had no particular confidence in either an unrestrictedly liberal property concept and free market forces on the one hand, or in the skills and decisions of small farmers on the other. From a national perspective, the risk that familial strategies, incompetence on the part of farmers and other eventualities would waste the economic potential of private property rights outweighed the promise of economic efficiency under individual absolute title. This critique of the liberal-individualistic property concept and its promises resulted in an 'ethno-national' concept of property enshrined in the constitutions of all East Central and South East European states.[19]

Whereas the ethno-national critique of liberalism and its universal property concept aimed to re-embed private property in the institutional order of a particular national order and type of economy, the rival Marxist critique was inspired by a universalistic, teleological theory of institutional, social and economic progress. Marxism viewed the historical development of mankind as aspiring towards a classless society in which no means of production would be privately owned: all productive resources would instead be publicly owned and controlled by society.[20] In parallel with the ethno-national perspective on property issues, the socialist critique of private property was widespread in manifold variations by 1945. In the second half of the twentieth century, the Marxist concept of property became the basis of socialist regimes in Eastern Europe.[21] Hence there developed a hierarchical order with state property at the top, followed by collective social property, and finally personal property as a residual category.

The ethno-nationalist conceptualization of property restricts the liberal-individualistic property concept in order to accommodate national and ethnic concerns. The socialist concept aims to change social stratification and rationalize processes of cooperation and planning in a centralized, planned economy. Though they spring from different ideologies, both concepts claim to set general wealth above private interests. Arguing in the name of society, and relying on assumptions of human and social evolution, they insist that the rights and the wealth of citizens are better served when represented by the state.

The foregoing considerations and the resulting forms of property led to three ideal types of legal culture, or socio-political regimes, in twentieth-century East Central Europe, namely, the liberal-individual, ethno-national and socialist orders. Table I.1 encapsulates their manifestations in different times and territories.

Individual property rights are conceived as a basic institution of a liberal free market society. Ethno-national concepts reshape property rights to optimize their social and economic functions on behalf of the nation, or an ethno-national majority. Socialist concepts of 'class-conscious handling of property' aim to

Table I.1 Law and property: periods, forms and types of property rights in twentieth-century East Central Europe

Periods	Forms and types of property rights
Interwar period (1918–1939)	Liberal-individualistic, with strong ethno-national bias in the new provinces
Wartime and occupation regimes (1914–1918; 1939–1945)	Formally liberal-individualistic, with strong ethno-national or racist bias
People's democracy (1945–1949)	Liberal-individualistic, with ethno-national and class bias
Stalinist regimes in the 1950s and 1960s	Communist-universalist In cooperatives, residual formal property rights for individuals In large state farms, property rights for the state
National particularities under state socialism	Poland: persistence of individual property Romania: collectivist property with ethno-national bias Yugoslavia: social property with widespread property rights
Post-socialism (after 1989)	Liberal-individualistic regime of private property rights with dwindling remnants of ethno-national and collectivist elements

shrink the bundle of exclusive individual property rights while strengthening exclusive rights of disposal in the name of the state, the people and the political avant-garde. Yet in the case of landownership, the implementation of such normative concepts, as formulated by East Central European elites, came up against great difficulty and resistance. The three legal property concepts discussed here and their corresponding pure or mixed property regimes all conceive of property as a means serving clearly definable purposes. They structure the social relations and moralize the social actions of individuals and organizations in distinct ways. Thus property rights vary according to their function in processes of social and cultural exclusion and inclusion, economic steering and political governance.

Politics and Property: Conditions, Motives and Strategies

The handling of issues and ideas by twentieth-century East Central European elites was far more arbitrary, incoherent and pragmatic than we might surmise from contemporary lawyers' and politicians' ideological legitimizations and retrospective rationalizations. Here, space permits explanation of only a few key considerations out of a broad range of reasons for these elites' decisions. Table I.2 summarizes their political conditions and motives, as well as the relevant meanings and functions of property.

Firstly, the circumstances of the two world wars significantly limited the elites' scope of action, both during hostilities and after the conclusion of peace.[22] Regardless of their preferences for specific property concepts and property regimes, in wartime the elites violated farmers' property rights through forced cultivation and forced surrender of products at regulated low prices. Furthermore – as Jacek Kochanowicz, Bogdan Murgescu and Jovica Luković show in this volume – countries particularly affected by hostilities and occupying forces experienced enormous post-war demand for the rebuilding of pre-war structures. In addition to the need for material reconstruction, Kochanowicz, Murgescu and other authors point to the enormous challenge of integrating new provinces, gained as a result of war and peace treaties, into the structures of the state.[23] For Poland, Romania and Yugoslavia, this was especially the case after the First World War, when their borders were either drawn up completely anew or considerably expanded in territorial terms. After the Second World War as well, it was necessary to reintegrate areas that for many years had partly come under the authority of various occupying regimes. Poland also had to cope with a westward shifting of its territory.

The aforementioned political conditions relating to property ideologies and regimes in the context of wars have hitherto been treated as constraints, but they also represented a source of opportunity. In this light, the need for

Table I.2 Politics and property: conditions, motives and strategies in twentieth-century East Central Europe

Period	Conditions, motives and strategies
Interwar period (1918–1939)	Reconstruction and integration after war and unification Agrarian reform and nation building
Wartime and occupation (1914–1918; 1939–1945)	Wartime economy with forced cultivation and sale at low prices Requisitions Ethnic cleansing and expulsion
People's democracy (1945–1949)	Reconstruction and integration after war Popularization of communist parties in the countryside Expulsions
Stalinist regimes in the 1950s and 1960s	Extensive industrialization Forced collectivization
National particularities under state socialism	Economic and political diversification in Comecon/Warsaw Pact Third Way in Yugoslavia Uprisings in Poland National communism in Romania
Post-Socialism (after 1989)	De-collectivization and re-privatization Opportunity for EU integration

reconstruction and integration was a welcome opening for political elites to reconstruct economic and legal systems on new foundations, in which changes in the concept of property and property regime were often accorded a very important function. But whereas this motivation structure predominated in the wake of the Second World War, during the period of People's democracy governments and the early communist regimes, a national-protectionist bias had prevailed at the time of the First World War.[24] The agrarian reforms of the years after 1918 – as indicated above all by Dietmar Müller, Christhardt Henschel and Srđan Milošević – contained political elements that, in the aforementioned sense of the state's perspective, fluctuated between constraint and opportunity. Parcelling out land to farmers generally increased the number of property owners, who tended to cling to their property, but at the same time, all this land was issued with a significantly reduced bundle of rights regarding inheritance, sale, mortgaging and exploitation.

This limiting of exclusive property rights to land was prompted not only by the elites' negative evaluation of farmers' qualifications and capacities, as mentioned above, but also by ethno-national considerations. In the new provinces, the distribution of land, and thus of the long-term chances for upward social mobility, was regulated to the advantage of the members of the titular nations – Poles, Romanians and Southern Slavs – and to the disadvantage of the new minorities, especially Germans, Hungarians and Jews, as well as Ukrainians in Poland. This ethno-national protectionism was implemented by means of expropriation and land distribution quotas that distinguished between certain regions and population groups of countries, and additionally by means of special colonization projects for government officials, soldiers, veterans and war-disabled persons and their families.[25] On a conceptual level, these dealings with landholding in the course of agrarian reform reflect how the liberal-individualistic concept of property, which was retained in the first constitutions of Poland, Romania and Yugoslavia during the interwar period, was gradually adjusted to further the social functions and nationalist strategies of the time.

After the Second World War, the scope of action of elites in the three countries fluctuated even more dramatically between constraint and opportunity. The presence of the Red Army clearly constricted East Central European elites' political scope of action more than the Paris Peace Treaties had done after the First World War. Meanwhile, the People's democracy governments and the communist regimes strove for much greater, revolutionary changes. In many respects, the aftermath of the Second World War, from which Poland, Romania and Yugoslavia again emerged on the side of the victors, now offered these countries' elites a second chance to address structural problems that earlier agrarian reforms had not radically resolved. These included agricultural inefficiency – the result of low levels of arable acreage, mainly cultivated by subsistence farmers – as well as the presence of significant minority groups. The brutal occupation by the Third Reich and its allies had disrupted the population and property structure of Poland and Yugoslavia by previously unknown means of dispossession and mass murder. However, it had also opened a morally safeguarded window of opportunity to partisan and People's democracy governments, which then tied the structural reorganization of Yugoslavia's rural areas and agricultural sector to an 'ethnic cleansing that displaced large parts of the German population and a smaller Hungarian group'.[26]

Another land redistribution in the late 1940s resembled the one implemented during the interwar period but took a more acute form, in the sense that significant amounts of the land issued in each case had previously been the property of minorities. This, together with the fact that the land was issued as private property, makes the agrarian reforms of the People's democracy governments seem like a more radical version of the interwar agrarian reforms. Not all expropriated land was redistributed, however; the state retained considerable amounts of land as its own property, and made it available for the founding of state farms and cooperatives, especially in Vojvodina, West Prussia and Silesia. Western Poland and north Yugoslavia could almost be characterized as laboratories of the new regimes.[27] In these cases, the agrarian reforms of the People's democracy governments pointed unambiguously to a future under a socialist property concept and property regime.

Changes in the elite, then, also warrant consideration in relation to the structural opportunities they enjoyed during the years after the Second World War, when local communist parties, backed by various levels of support from the Red Army and the Soviet Union, also used agrarian reform to boost their extremely low popularity in rural areas. Whether and to what extent the communist regimes of Poland, Romania and Yugoslavia were a concealed form of Soviet foreign rule, or to all intents and purposes systems whose supporters and structural problems were home-grown, has been the subject of intense debate in national historiographies and political publications since 1989.[28] In any case, here it can be asserted that the political legitimacy of the socialist property concept and its associated property regime was not the result of free elections but mainly due to the Soviet-dominated military and political situation in East Central Europe. Yet the question of the appeal of socialist property rights and rights of disposal should also be weighed against the background of the interwar period, when the elites monumentally failed to solve structural problems in rural areas with their agrarian reforms and subsequent agrarian policy, which can be described as agrarian modernization.

The designation of and grounds for the triad of state, collective and personal property throughout the socialist camp followed the Soviet model, although there were considerable deviations from the Moscow model at both the ideological and political levels.[29] The extent of the ultimately tolerated varieties can be gauged from the experience of the three countries examined in the present volume. Jovica Luković presents the case of the Yugoslavian Third Way, which was based not least on a critique of the Soviet management of property rights and rights of disposal. Third Way theoreticians did not deem the nationalization and socialization of property in the Soviet Union a viable way towards a classless and state-absent society, but considered it a veiled form of exploitative capitalist relations in which the state, or a class of technocrats acting in the name of the state, had usurped the role of owner of the means of production.[30] Despite considerable resistance to the collectivization and forcible state purchase of agricultural products endured by (former partisans turned) farmers in Vojvodina, the general shift in Yugoslavian property policy, which was known to have occurred as early as 1950, was not implemented until after Stalin's death in 1953, even in agriculture. Romania followed the Soviet agricultural model very closely in law, policy and practice. Collectivization in Poland and Yugoslavia, however, began with the same vigour but was abandoned in the 1950s – not on the basis of ideological dissent, but as a political reaction to social unrest, escalating even into insurrection, in both the countryside and cities in the mid 1950s. As a result, the proportion of collectivized land in Poland and Yugoslavia amounted to about 20 to 30 per cent, whereas in Romania the figure was 90 per cent.

Negotiation of Property Rights: Between the Political Economy of National Elites and the Moral Economy of Local Peasantries

The chapters in this volume show how the universal principle of property manifests itself in property-related mentalities and property-based claims and social actions by political, economic and professional elites on the one hand, and denizens of rural areas on the other.[31] Ideas and images of property are rarely spread by a top-down process in which elites define a specific property concept in constitutions and laws, have it implemented by professionals in organizations available for this and finally see farmers put it into practice.[32] Both the elites' scope of action (treated above in the discussion of constraints and opportunity) and the rationale of organizations and professions essentially devoted to the pursuit of vested interests were always co-determined by peasants and rural people, whose resources and motives comprised a combination of socio-cultural conventions – that is, norms established by customary law and moral standards at the village level – experience under earlier legal and political regimes and, not least, future expectations. This mixture may be difficult to quantify, but undisguised evidence of the legal culture of landownership can ultimately be traced only at this level of analysis.

The chapters by Paweł Klint, Cornel Micu, Srđan Milošević and Jovana Diković, based on interviews with peasants in Poland, Romania and Serbia, reveal that for farmers, the symbolic value of landowning has rapidly lost meaning over the last two decades. In practice, only members of the older generation still tend to refer to land-related values and norms as defining their own personal identity, their esteem in the village community and the continuity of their family across generations. Most members of younger and middle-aged generations tend to view land as a marketable good that can be sold to anyone at any time, provided that the price is satisfactory. The 'return of the peasant', as identified by Andrew L. Cartwright in the early 1990s, has proved an ephemeral trend.[33] Instead, we see the 'death of the peasant'.[34]

The foundations of this decline were laid by socialist economic, social and educational policies. Socialist elites built on an extensive industrialization that disadvantaged the production of consumer goods. This made agriculture a residual sector with regard to the allocation of resources, leading to an increasing ageing and feminization of the agricultural workforce and rural population. Both the substantially developed education system and the high demand for industrial workers contributed decisively to migration from the country to the city. With the epochal change of 1989, which triggered not only de-collectivization and re-privatization of rural areas, but also de-industrialization in urban areas, greater importance began to be attached to rural areas and having one's own piece of land in the 1990s. However, private land's function as an area of retreat and a safety net for laid-off industrial workers is completely different from the symbolic meaning of landownership that was still widespread during the interwar period. No return to idealized pre-communist conditions is discernible in this case either.

The case of the Lemkos in Poland seems rather exceptional in this respect. Jacek Nowak shows that, even in the communist period and increasingly after 1989, the community identity of the Lemkos evoked precisely the symbolic dimension of ownership of specific estates, the very land that communist authorities had forced the Lemkos off in the 1950s, resettling them in western Poland. Here, the symbolic attribution of meaning to landownership becomes a collective resource enabling an ethnic community to act productively and effectively – just as the elites of Poland, Romania and Yugoslavia had envisaged in their interwar ethno-nationalist projects. As for practices of landownership in Vojvodina, Jovana Diković also notes that ethno-familial strategies for dealing with landholdings are far more persistent among the region's Slovaks than among their Serbian neighbours. Like the Lemkos in Poland, the Slovaks in Vojvodina strive to symbolically load the land they own, in order to keep it in the hands of their own group from generation to generation. In both cases, ethnic minorities are mounting a defensive strategy against the titular nation, in which landownership is meant to secure the existence of the group from a material and symbolic perspective and stabilize its cohesion.

For actors in rural areas, the question of which resources and options for action arise from their land has interrelated economic and political dimensions. As Dietmar Müller shows for Romania during the interwar period, the country's elites failed to muster the political will and financial means to organize the surveying, registration and administration of a functioning cadastral and land register system in which legally verifiable property rights producing security of action could offer a basis for a land market with low transaction costs. Instead, as Cornel Micu also demonstrates, farmers remained dependent on the favour of the administration and political parties, especially in the form of local networks. For their part, the political and economic elites relied not only on public administration and formal procedures, but also on ad hoc interventions and cooperation with lawyers, advocates, notaries and geodesists, who offered their professional services, implemented property rights in everyday life and pursued their own interests.[35] Bogdan Murgescu suggests that the institutional framework of Romanian agriculture – especially property rights, understood as legal instruments to efficiently market both products and land itself – was almost never designed to favour the market-oriented development of agriculture.

One of the most important institutional and organizational elements of socialist agriculture was undoubtedly the favouring of large cultivable areas organized as cooperatives or state farms. On the one hand, these led – with the significant increase in mechanization and use of fertilizers – to an unprecedented rise in East Central European agricultural output. On the other, farmers' property rights on the land they had brought into cooperatives were diluted and eventually reduced to abstract property titles, similar to shares in a joint-stock company in which they worked. Murgescu calls this 'distant property'.

The most important aspects of the role of property rights in different economic organizations, regimes and systems are summarized in Table I.3, which depicts a long-term trend of peasantization – that is, a specific institutional and organizational pattern focused on the holder of an independent economic unit and their particular social and cultural traits and attitudes – as well as the search for strategies for expanding the economic units, the rationalization and standardization of work and consumption, and the erosion of individual property rights.

A particular Habsburg-influenced culture of landowning persists in the institutions, norms, mentalities and popular historical master narratives of the regions studied in this volume. Dietmar Müller has followed this thread in

Table I.3 Economy and property: distribution of land, economic actors and organizations, and effects of property rights in twentieth-century East Central Europe

Periods	Distribution of land, economic actors and organizations, and effects of property rights
Interwar period (1918–1939)	Medium-sized and large companies barely operating in the market Peasantization, i.e. transfer of exclusive rights to land to small peasant or single farmer Disposal rights on land from agrarian reform shared between farmers/colonists and the state
Wartime and occupation regimes (1914–1918; 1939–1945)	Rights of disposal on land from agrarian reform shift to the state, army or occupation regimes
People's democracy (1945–1949)	Further peasantization Beginning of cooperatives and state farms
Stalinist regimes in the 1950s and 1960s	Forced requisitions and discriminatory taxation of private property Collective farmers' rights of disposal shared with managers and local elite Husbanding of private land dependent on state inputs
National particularities under state socialism	Low levels of collectivization in Poland and Yugoslavia Economic stagnation on private land due to ineffective allocation of resources Loss of attractiveness of agriculture: ageing, feminization of rural population
Post-Socialism after 1989	Peasantization Trend of land concentration Uncertain and expensive systèms of securing the disposal and property rights

the work of Transylvanian geodesists, cadastral officials and notaries who lobbied for the extension of the Habsburg title evidence system to the whole of Romania during the interwar period to bring about relative justice regarding land titles. Nevertheless, this specific post-Habsburg culture of property has to be seen as fading away when its sources – the corresponding institutions and professions – ran dry. Their languishing was already discernible in the interwar period, and in the years following 1945 the organizations and professions involved with real property were ultimately rejected as sources of legal culture independent of the state. Like the question of a simple opportunity to return to a pre-communist liberal-individualistic property concept, after 1989 the possibility of an integral restitution with regard to a territorially defined legal culture seems beside the point.

The recent changes in the system of property in Eastern Europe are part of a steady process that is still ongoing.[36] Although the prospect of EU accession created considerable political and economic impetus for countries such as Poland, Romania and Serbia to legally align their property systems with that of the EU, the elites of these countries, as Herbert Küpper observes in his chapter about property in East Central European legal culture, have negotiated certain terms providing for specific restrictions on, for instance, the purchase of land by foreigners. While endeavouring to relativize an accepted special East European path regarding the ownership of land, however, Küpper stresses that this exceptionalism at most consists of retaining such restrictions in constitutions.[37] These countries will thus continue, for a certain time, to adhere to a tradition that is both pre-socialist and socialist: a national-collective limitation of landowning. This does not mean, however, that a liberal-individualistic form of property will sweep into ascendancy once these limitations cease to apply. Rather, these states will develop a form of property that, like the legal systems of Western Europe, is limited by private and administrative legal guidelines with the goal of advancing, not impeding, the common good.

The property regimes in East Central Europe in the twentieth century are summarized in Table I.4, by taking together the previous three tables on the relations between property and politics, law, and economy respectively.

The chapters in this volume show that property policies imposed by the elite and the centre were frequently only partially realized and had unintended effects. It was not only political and financial constraints that limited the range of responsible decision makers; they were also often hindered by lack of knowledge about the actual ownership, property and usage situations in agriculture. This led elites to embrace voluntaristic property policies that reinforced rural and agricultural actors' reluctance to change their traditional mentalities. The state's claim – ever increasing throughout the interwar years and particularly during the communist period – to the control and planning of rural property management and ownership was never fully realized. In the long term, however, the economic measures initiated by modernizing communist

Table I.4 Property regimes in East Central Europe in the twentieth century

Period	Politics and property. Conditions, motives and strategies	Law and property. Forms and types of property rights	Economy and property. Distribution of land, economic actors and organizations, and effects of property rights
Interwar period (1918–1939)	Reconstruction and integration after war and unification Agrarian reform and nation building	Liberal-individualistic, with strong ethno-national bias in the new provinces	Large and medium-sized companies barely operating in the market Peasantization Disposal rights shared between farmers and state on land from agrarian reform and colonists
Wartime and occupation (1914–1918; 1939–1945)	Wartime economy with forced cultivation and delivery at low prices Requisitions Ethnic cleansing and expulsions	Formally liberal-individualistic, with strong ethno-national or racist bias	Disposal rights shift into the hands of the state, army and occupying regimes
People's democracy (1945–1949)	Reconstruction and integration after war Popularization of communist parties in the countryside Expulsions	Liberal-individualistic, with ethno-national and class bias	Further peasantization Beginning of cooperatives and state farms

Stalinist regimes in the 1950s and 1960s	Extensive industrialization Forced collectivization	Communist-universalist In cooperatives, residual formal property rights for individuals On large state farms, property rights for the state	Forced requisitions and tax discrimination of private property Disposal rights of collective farmers shared with managers and local elite Husbanding of private land independent of state input
National particularities under state socialism	Economic and political diversification in Comecon/Warsaw Pact Third way in Yugoslavia Uprisings in Poland National communism in Romania	Poland: persistence of individual property Yugoslavia: social property with diffuse property rights Romania: collectivist property with ethno-national bias	Low level of collectivisation in Poland and Yugoslavia Economic stagnation on private land due to ineffective allocation of resources Loss of attractiveness for agriculture: ageing, feminization of population
Post-Socialism (after 1989)	De-collectivization and re-privatization Opportunity for EU integration	Liberal-individualist regime of private property rights with dwindling remnants of ethno-national and collective bias	Peasantization Trend of land concentration Uncertain and expensive securing of rights of disposal of property

regimes finally hollowed out traditional and local concepts of ownership of agricultural land, and eroded the rural population's ideals of property rights in land. The new educational and employment possibilities in industry and cities played into this trend by encouraging rural–urban migration. Modern social security systems eventually diluted or replaced the meaning of owning land in rural people's livelihoods.

Now, more than two decades after the restoration of private ownership, the widespread reassignment of individual control and use rights, and the revival of old peasant and rural concepts of property, landownership is losing its traditional symbolic meaning. Many no longer consider land a family asset, to be kept at all costs, something that reflects values like cross-generational continuity, rootedness in the region and a claim to status; rather, they see it as a generally marketable possession. In the EU and neighbouring states (such as Serbia), East/West differences are also diminishing in this respect.

The Habsburg Institutional Path: Land Evidencing, Administration and Civil Law Codes

In his chapter about the cadastral register of Francis I, Kurt Scharr shows the decisive role of systems of land evidencing, administration and civil law codes in the rise of modern states, economies and societies in parts of East Central Europe under Habsburg rule. Over the long term, this major state project – considering its duration as well as the requisite bureaucratic and financial effort – fundamentally changed the image and function of landowning in what was then Galicia-Lodomeria and Bukovina. Initiated in the early nineteenth century with the intention of expanding the state's tax base by increasing the number of rural landholdings, and strengthening their legal status to the disadvantage of the nobility, the cadastral register of Francis I led to a dramatic change in the scope and quality of state action itself. The message the state communicated to its rural subjects via the cadastral register – that the good of the state depended also on their economic contribution, rooted in landowning – led on the one hand to farmers' consciously demanding the rule of law, and on the other to a growth in their self-consciousness as citizens.

The consequences of this combination were apparent in all East Central European regions of the Habsburg Empire, where the cadastral register of Francis I became a model for systems of land evidencing and administration – that is to say, from 1848 onwards in Transylvania and, though less consistently and over a smaller area, in Vojvodina. An early and very intensive politicization resulted everywhere, even in rural areas, and the agrarian and peasant problem rose to prominence on political parties' agendas. Whereas the Serbian and Romanian national movements included farmers in Vojvodina and Transylvania respectively, the situation was different in Galicia. Following the Austro-Hungarian Compromise of 1867, aristocratic Polish estate owners had been co-opted as members of the ruling alliance at the Viennese Imperial Court, spurring the emergence of separate Polish and Ruthenian/Ukrainian peasant parties in Galicia to compete with the traditional elites.[38]

During the interwar period, attention turned again to the question of whether the Habsburg legacy would also nourish the persistence, in Romanian Transylvania, Yugoslavian Vojvodina and Polish Galicia, of a specific property culture in the form of a cadastral and land register system together with an associated notarial system. Looking back across time, we also ask, as Kurt Scharr does in this volume, whether one result of the Habsburg inheritance in these provinces was an economic competitive advantage over other regions in the post-communist period, during which time a cadastral and land register system was developed after all in the three countries examined. The first research results indicate that in the case of Romania's restitution of expropriated land from 1989 onwards, extracts from the Transylvanian cadastral and land register of the interwar period were of great importance in establishing the old owner.[39] Furthermore, a Habsburg legacy of a multiethnic society peacefully coexisting in legal security is a primary component of regionalist master narratives, as found especially in Transylvania, the Banat and Vojvodina.

Notes

1. For an introduction with extensive literature references, see Hannes Siegrist and David Sugarman, 'Geschichte als historisch-vergleichende Eigentumswissenschaft: Rechts-, kultur- und gesellschaftsgeschichtliche Perspektiven', in Hannes Siegrist and David Sugarman (eds), *Eigentum im internationalen Vergleich*, Göttingen, 1999, pp.9–30; Hannes Siegrist, 'Die Propertisierung von Gesellschaft und Kultur: Konstruktion und Institutionalisierung des Eigentums in der Moderne', in Hannes Siegrist (ed.), 'Entgrenzung des Eigentums in modernen Gesellschaften und Rechtskulturen', *Comparativ* 16/5–6 (2006), pp.9–52; Chris M. Hann, 'Introduction: The Embeddedness of Property', in Chris M. Hann (ed.), *Property Relations: Renewing the Anthropological Tradition*, Cambridge, 1998, pp.1–47; Franz von Benda-Beckmann, Keebet von Benda-Beckmann and Melanie S. Wiber, 'The Properties of Property', in Franz von Benda-Beckmann, Keebet von Benda-Beckmann and Melanie S. Wiber (eds), *Changing Properties of Property*, New York/Oxford, 2006, pp.1–39; Arnd Bauerkämper, *Ländliche Gesellschaft in der kommunistischen Diktatur: Zwangsmodernisierung und Tradition in Brandenburg 1945–1963*, Cologne/Weimar/Vienna, 2002.
2. S.D. Zagoroff, *The Agricultural Economy of the Danubian Countries, 1935–45*, Stanford, 1955; Frederic L. Pryor, *The Rise and Fall of Collectivized Agriculture in Marxist Regimes*, Princeton, 1992; David Turnock (ed.), *Privatization in Rural Eastern Europe: The Process of Restitution and Restructuring*, Cheltenham/Northampton, MA, 1998; Dietmar Müller, 'The Governmentality of Land Ownership in South-eastern Europe – Romania and Yugoslavia: A Comparison', in Rosa Congost and Rui Santos (eds), *Contexts of Property in Europe: The Social Embeddedness of Property Rights in Land in Historical Perspective*, Brepols, 2011, pp.211–27.

3. For a comparison, and for historical approaches to transfers and relational history, see Heinz-Gerhard Haupt and Jürgen Kocka (eds), *Geschichte und Vergleich: Ansätze und Ergebnisse international vergleichender Geschichtsschreibung*, Frankfurt/New York, 1996; Hartmut Kaelble and Jürgen Schriewer (eds), *Vergleich und Transfer: Komparatistik in den Sozial-, Geschichts- und Kulturwissenschaften*, Frankfurt am Main, 2003; Hannes Siegrist, 'Comparative History of Cultures and Societies: From Cross-societal Analysis to the Study of Intercultural Interdependencies', *Comparative Education* 42/3 (2006), pp.377–404; Frank Hadler and Matthias Middell (eds), 'Verflochtene Geschichten: Ostmitteleuropa', *Comparativ* 20/1–2 (2010), special issue.
4. As the present volume is devoted to property regimes and patterns of landholding, we do not aim at a social history of the East Central European peasantry. Although different types of 'peasants' – free landowning farmers, dependent agricultural labourers, colonists with nationalist purposes, collectivized peasants and so on – do feature as agents throughout the volume, rural sociology and the history of agrarian programmes, though valuable in many aspects, are not prime avenues for an integrated analysis of property regimes. For recent, thorough analyses of one particularly interesting aspect of the social and intellectual history of the peasantry, namely agrarianism, see Helga Schultz and Angela Harre (eds), *Bauerngesellschaften auf dem Weg in die Moderne: Agrarismus in Ostmitteleuropa 1880 bis 1960*, Wiesbaden, 2010; Dietmar Müller and Angela Harre (eds), 'Transforming Rural Societies: Agrarian Property and Agrarianism in East Central Europe in the Nineteenth and Twentieth Centuries', *Jahrbuch für Geschichte des ländlichen Raumes* 7 (2010), special issue; Eduard Kubů, Torsten Lorenz, Uwe Müller and Jiří Šouša (eds), *Agrarismus und Agrareliten in Ostmitteleuropa*, Berlin/Prague, 2013.
5. Dietmar Müller, 'Vorarbeiten zu einer Begriffs- und Kulturgeschichte des Eigentums in Rumänien, 1746 bis 2009', in Vasile Dumbrava (ed.), *Geschichte politisch-sozialer Begriffe in Rumänien und Moldova*, Leipzig, 2010, pp.185–214. For the long-term history of concepts and ideas, see Dieter Schwab, 'Eigentum', in Otto Brunner, Werner Conze and Reinhart Koselleck (eds), *Geschichtliche Grundbegriffe: Historisches Lexikon zur politisch-sozialen Sprache in Deutschland*, vol. 2, Stuttgart, 1975, pp.65–115.
6. Crawford B. Macpherson, *The Political Theory of Possessive Individualism: Hobbes to Locke*, Oxford, 1962; Reinhardt Brandt, *Eigentumstheorien von Grotius bis Kant*, Stuttgart, 1974.
7. Cf. Helmut Rittstieg, *Eigentum als Verfassungsproblem: Zur Geschichte und Gegenwart des bürgerlichen Verfassungsstaates*, Darmstadt, 1975; Werner Dichmann and Gerhard Fels (eds), *Gesellschaftliche und ökonomische Funktionen des Privateigentums*, Cologne, 1993. For a historical re-evaluation of different master narratives on property, see Siegrist, 'Die Propertisierung von Gesellschaft und Kultur'. See also Dieter Grimm, *Recht und Staat der bürgerlichen Gesellschaft*, Frankfurt am Main, 1987; Jürgen Kocka, *Civil Society and Dictatorship in Modern German History*, Waltham, MA/Hanover, NH/London, 2010; Jürgen Kocka, 'Zivilgesellschaft in historischer Perspektive', in *Arbeiten an der Geschichte: Gesellschaftlicher Wandel im 19. und 20. Jahrhundert*, Göttingen, 2012, pp.191–202.
8. Only a few examples are cited from the glut of 'transition' literature of the early 1990s: Ellen Frenkel Paul, Fred D. Miller and Jeffrey Paul (eds), *Liberalism and the Economic Order*, Cambridge, 1993; Peter J. Buckley and Pervez N. Chauri (eds), *The Economics of Change in East and Central Europe: Its Impact on International Business*, London, 1994; Beverly Crawford (ed.), *Markets, States, and Democracy: The Political Economy of Post-Communist Transformation*, Boulder/San Francisco/Oxford, 1995; Marie Lavigne, *The Economics of Transition*, Houndmills/London, 1995; Mark Knell (ed.), *Economics of Transition: Structural Adjustment and Growth Prospects in Eastern Europe*, Cheltenham/Brookfield, 1996. For references to various dilemmas of transformation and a more realistic assessment of the scope of societies, see Holm Sundhaussen, 'Die "Transformation" Osteuropas in historischer Perspektive oder: Wie groß ist der

Handlungsspielraum einer Gesellschaft?' in Hellmut Wollmann, Helmut Wiesenthal and Frank Bönker (eds), 'Transformation sozialistischer Gesellschaften: Am Ende des Anfangs', *Leviathan* 15 (1995), pp.77–92; Claus Offe, *Der Tunnel am Ende des Lichts: Erkundungen der politischen Transformation im Neuen Osten*, Frankfurt/New York, 1994; Claus Offe, *Varieties of Transition*, Cambridge, 1996; David Stark and László Bruszt (eds), *Postsocialist Pathways: Transforming Politics and Property in East Central Europe*, Cambridge, 1998.

9. Cf. László Csaba (ed.), *Systemic Change and Stabilization in Eastern Europe*, Dartmouth, 1991; Roman Frydman, Andrzej Rapaczynski and John S. Earl, *The Privatization Process in Central Europe*, Budapest, 1993; Leszek Balcerowicz, *Socialism, Capitalism, Transformation*, Budapest, 1995.
10. For a general introduction to post-communist historiography, see Ulf Brunnbauer (ed.), *(Re) Writing History: Historiography in Southeastern Europe after Socialism*, Münster, 2004; Sorin Antohi, Balázs Trencsényi and Péter Apor (eds), *Narratives Unbound: Historical Studies in Post-Communist Eastern Europe*, Budapest/New York, 2007.
11. This thesis refers – on the basis of a more or less explicit comparison – to a 'Western' ideal of modernization, and to essentialist and normative Western patterns of property relations.
12. For distinct and different institutional patterns of modernity, see Shmuel Eisenstadt, 'Multiple Modernities', *Daedalus* 129/1 (2000), pp.1–29; Kaelble and Schriewer, *Vergleich und Transfer*; Siegrist, 'Comparative History of Cultures and Societies'.
13. Institutionalist research approaches are widespread in the historical, social and cultural sciences, as well as the legal and economic sciences. The institutionalist approach is the cornerstone of interdisciplinary research on the institutionalization of cultural, academic, economic and political relationships. On the concept of institutionalization, and for analysis of social, cultural, economic and historical institutions, see Douglass C. North, *Structure and Change in Economic History*, New York, 1981; John W. Meyer and W. Richard Scott (eds), *Organizational Environments: Ritual and Rationality*, Beverly Hills, 1983; Douglass C. North, *Institutions: Institutional Changes and Economic Performance*, Cambridge, 1990; Walter W. Powell and Paul J. DiMaggio (eds), *The New Institutionalism in Organizational Analysis*, Chicago, 1991; Paul Colomy, 'Neofunctionalism and Neoinstitutionalism: Human Agency and Interest in Institutional Change', *Sociological Forum* 13/2 (1998), pp.265–300; Elizabeth S. Clemens and James M. Cook, 'Politics and Institutionalism: Explaining Durability and Change', *Annual Review of Sociology* 25 (1999), pp.441–66; W. Richard Scott, *Institutions and Organizations*, London/New Delhi, 2001; Andrea Maurer and Michael Schmid (eds), *Neuer Institutionalismus: Zur soziologischen Erklärung von Organisation, Moral und Vertrauen*, Frankfurt am Main, 2002; Karl-Siegbert Rehberg, 'Institutionen, Kognitionen und Symbole: Institutionen als symbolische Verkörperungen', in Maurer and Schmid, *Neuer Institutionalismus*, pp.39–56; Marie-Laure Djelic and Sigrid Quack (eds), *Globalization and Institutions: Redefining the Rules of the Economic Game*, Cheltenham, 2003.
14. In the present volume, 'propertization' is used as a heuristic concept in the historical and comparative analysis of social, cultural and legal strategies and processes that amount to governing social relations concerning material and immaterial objects from the perspective of property. Propertization is a processual concept that aids comprehension of several concrete and abstract forms of the property-related institutionalization of cultural, scientific and economic relations See Siegrist, 'Die Propertisierung von Gesellschaft und Kultur'; Hannes Siegrist and Isabella Löhr, 'Intellectual Property Rights between Nationalization and Globalization: Introduction', in Isabella Löhr and Hannes Siegrist (eds), 'Intellectual Property Rights and Globalization', *Comparativ* 21/2 (2011), pp.7–28; Chris Hann, 'Propertization und ihre Gegentendenzen: Beispiele aus ländlichen Gebieten Europas', in Hannes Siegrist (ed.), *Entgrenzung des Eigentums*, pp.84–98; Franz von Benda-Beckmann, 'Propertization in Indonesien: Parallele und gegenläufige Entwicklungen', in Siegrist, *Entgrenzung des Eigentums*, pp.99–111.

15. See Wolfgang Schlucher, 'Interessen, Ideen und Institutionen: Schlüsselbegriffe an Max Weber orientierten Soziologie', in Steffen Sigmund et al. (eds), *Soziale Konstellationen und historische Perspektive*, Wiesbaden, 2008, pp.57–80, esp. p.57.
16. Scott, *Institutions and Organizations*, pp.33–61.
17. Bogdan Murgescu, *România şi Europa: Acumularea decalajelor economice (1500–2010)*, Iaşi, 2010; Holm Sundhaussen, *Geschichte Serbiens 19.–21. Jahrhundert*, Vienna/Cologne/Weimar, 2007.
18. On the Serbian homestead law of 1836, which was reverted to repeatedly until the interwar period, see J. Petrović, *Okuće ili zaštita zemljoradničkog minimuma*, Belgrade, 1930. On the other hand, it was standard practice in Europe to attach greater protections to personally used property than to economic property used in excess of services for the public. See Peter Häberle, 'Vielfalt der Property Rights und der verfassungsrechtliche Eigentumsbegriff', in Manfred Neumann (ed.), *Ansprüche, Eigentums- und Verfügungsrechte*, Berlin, 1984, p.90.
19. In economic history, the ethno-national reconfiguration of property rights is discussed in the framework of economic nationalism; see Leo Pasvolsky, *Economic Nationalism of the Danubian States*, New York, 1928; Frederick Hertz, *The Economic Problems of the Danubian States: A Study in Economic Nationalism*, London, 1947; Henry Szlajfer (ed.), *Economic Nationalism in East-Central Europe and South America, 1918–1939*, Geneva, 1990; Helga Schultz and Eduard Kubů (eds), *History and Culture of Economic Nationalism in East Central Europe*, Berlin, 2006; Thomas David, *Nationalisme économique et industrialization: l'expérience des pays de l'est (1789–1939)*, Geneva, 2009.
20. See Herbert Küpper, *Einführung in die Rechtsgeschichte Osteuropas*, Frankfurt am Main, 2005, pp.420f., 437ff.
21. As early as the 1917 October Revolution, much attention was paid to the Marxist property concept and to the real socialist forms of land rights and property regimes in Western Europe and the United States. Leo Zaitseff, 'Das Eigentumsrecht im Sovietstaate', *Zeitschrift für Osteuropäisches Recht* 2/4 (1926), pp.425–35; Anatole Baikalov, 'Bolshevist Agrarian Policy', *Slavonic and East European Review* 8 (1929/30), pp.533–47; Cyril Zaitsev, 'The Russian Agrarian Revolution', *Slavonic and East European Review* 9 (1930/31), pp.547–66; John N. Hazard, *Communists and Their Law: A Search for the Common Core of the Legal Systems of the Marxian Socialist States*, Chicago/London, 1969; Manfred Hoffmann, 'Bodenrecht und Bodenrechtspolitik in kommunistisch regierten Ländern unter dem Einfluß der Marx'schen Variante der Arbeitswerttheorie', *Recht in Ost und West* 33/2 (1989), pp.97–104; Gerd Bender and Ulrich Falk (eds), *Recht im Sozialismus: Analysen zur Normdurchsetzung in osteuropäischen Nachkriegsgesellschaften (1944/45–1989)*, vol. 1, Frankfurt am Main, 1999.
22. Cf. Momme Rohlack, *Kriegsgesellschaften (1914–1918): Arten, Rechtsformen und Funktionen in der Kriegswirtschaft des Ersten Weltkrieges*, Frankfurt am Main, 2001; Mark Harrison (ed.), *The Economics of The Second World War: Six Great Powers in International Comparison*, Cambridge, 1998; György Ránki, *The Economics of the Second World War*, Vienna/Cologne/Weimar, 1993; Tamara Scheer, *Zwischen Front und Heimat: Österreich-Ungarns Militärverwaltungen im Ersten Weltkrieg*, Frankfurt, 2009.
23. See Paul Latawski (ed.), *The Reconstruction of Poland, 1914–23*, Houndmills/London, 1992.
24. Z. Ludkiewicz, 'Land Reform in Poland', *Slavonic and East European Review* 8 (1929/30), pp.315–30; David Mitrany, *The Land and the Peasant in Rumania: The War and Agrarian Reform (1917–21)*, New York, 1968 [1930]; Jozo Tomasevich, *Peasants, Politics, and Economic Change in Yugoslavia*, Stanford, 1955; John B. Allcock, *Explaining Yugoslavia*, London, 2000, pp.100–44.
25. Cf. Katrin Boeckh and Natali Stegmann (eds), 'Veterans and War Victims in Eastern Europe during the Twentieth Century: A Comparison', *Comparativ* 20/5 (2010), special issue.
26. Cf. Michael G. Esch, *'Gesunde Verhältnisse': Deutsche und polnische Bevölkerungspolitik in Ostmitteleuropa 1939–1950*, Marburg, 1998. For a critique of the concept of 'agrarian over-

population', which was widespread in the interwar period, see Ian Innerhofer, '"Agrarische Überbevölkerung": Zur Konstruktion eines Problems bei Otto Frangeš und Rudolf Bićanić', in Carola Sachse (ed.), *'Mitteleuropa' und 'Südosteuropa' als Planungsraum: Wirtschafts- und kulturpolitische Expertisen im Zeitalter der Weltkriege*, Göttingen, 2010, pp.262–89.

27. See Melissa K. Bokovoy, *Peasants and Communists: Politics and Ideology in the Yugoslav Countryside, 1941–1953*, Pittsburgh, 1998.
28. For a perspective of cultural remembrance and the politics of history on the communist period, see Krzysztof Ruchniewicz, 'Die polnische Geschichtspolitik der Nach-"Wende"-Zeit am Scheideweg', in Stefan Troebst (ed.), *Postdiktatorische Geschichtskulturen im Süden und Osten Europas: Bestandsaufnahmen und Forschungsperspektiven*, Göttingen, 2010, pp.307–29, and Cristina Petrescu and Dragoş Petrescu, 'The Piteşti Syndrom: A Romanian *Vergangenheitsbewältigung*', in Troebst, *Postdiktatorische Geschichtskulturen*, pp.502–618; Todor Kuljić, *Umkämpfte Vergangenheiten: Die Kultur der Erinnerung im postjugoslawischen Raum*, Berlin, 2010.
29. Cf. *Das Eigentum im Ostblock*, Berlin, 1958; Rudolf Schlesinger, 'Diversity and Unity in the Socialist Law of Property', *Soviet Studies* 15/4 (1964), pp.474–85; Karl-Eugen Wädekin, *Agrarian Policies in Communist Europe*, The Hague/London, 1982; Pryor, *Rise and Fall of Collectivized Agriculture*.
30. Milovan Djilas, *The New Class: An Analysis of the Communist System*, New York, 1957; Ivo Lapenna, *State and Law: Soviet and Yugoslav Theory*, New Haven, 1964; György Konrád and Ivan Szelenyi, *The Intellectuals on the Road to Class Power: A Sociological Study of the Role of the Intelligentsia in Socialism*, New York, 1979.
31. The cultural anthropological method has also proved very productive in the question of land ownership, advancing to a cognitive-cultural dimension of human action. See Hann, 'Introduction: The Embeddedness of Property'; Katherine Verdery, *The Vanishing Hectare: Property and Value in Postsocialist Transylvania*, Ithaca, NY/London, 2003; Chris Hann et al., *The Postsocialist Agrarian Question: Property Relations and the Rural Condition*, Münster, 2003; Michał Buchowski, 'Property Relations and Social Identity in Rural Poland' Max Planck Institute for Social Anthropology, Working Paper 83, Halle/Saale, 2006.
32. For the classic critique of the top-down perception of peasants' potential to act, see James C. Scott, *Weapons of the Weak: Everyday Forms of Peasant Resistance*, New Haven, 1985.
33. Andrew L. Cartwright, *The Return of the Peasant: Land Reform in Post-Communist Romania*, Aldershot, 2001.
34. Verdery, *The Vanishing Hectare*, p.226
35. See Dietmar Müller and Alina Bojincă, 'Die juristische und geodätische Administration des Eigentums an Grund und Boden in Rumänien im 20. Jahrhundert', in Dietmar Müller and Angela Harre (eds), 'Transforming Rural Societies: Agrarian Property and Agrarianism in East Central Europe in the Nineteenth and Twentieth Centuries', pp.26–54; Dietmar Müller and Andrei Florin, 'Sora Notarul comunal în România: Cadrul normativ al unei instituţii moderne (1864–1940)', *Arhivele Olteniei* 25 (2011), pp.369–85; Hannes Siegrist, 'Juridicalisation, Professionalisation and the Occupational Culture of the Advocate in the Nineteenth and the Early Twentieth Centuries: A Comparison of Germany, Italy and Switzerland', in David Sugarman and Wesley Pue (eds), *Lawyers and Vampires: Cultural Histories of Legal Professions*, Oxford/Portland, 2003, pp.123–50; Hannes Siegrist, 'Die Advokaten auf dem Land', in Wolfgang Jacobeit, Josef Mooser and Bo Stråht (eds), *Idylle oder Aufbruch? Das Dorf im bürgerlichen 19. Jahrhundert: Ein europäischer Vergleich*, Berlin, 1990, pp.169–80.
36. For a legal analysis, see Georg Brunner and Dieter Pfaff (eds), *Wandlungen in der Eigentumsverfassung der sozialistischen Länder Südosteuropas*, Munich, 1990; Herwig Roggemann, 'Wandel der Eigentumsordnung in Osteuropa', *Recht in Ost und West* 37/11 (1993), pp.321–31;

Herwig Roggemann (ed.), *Eigentum in Osteuropa: Rechtspraxis in Ost-, Ostmittel- und Südosteuropa mit Einführungen und Rechtstexten*, Berlin, 1996; Ferdinand Feldbrugge (ed.), *Law in Transition*, The Hague/London/New York, 2002; R. Jerome Anderson, Igor A. Rumyantsev and Larisa G. Sudas, 'Path Dependence in Russian Land Relations: An Analysis of Recent Legislation through an Historical Perspective', *Journal of Eurasian Law* 2/2 (2009), pp.1–22.

37. For analysis of nationalist developments peculiar to Yugoslavia and Serbia in the 1990s, see Milica Zarkovic Bookmann, *Economic Decline in the Balkans*, New York, 1994.
38. See Keely Stauter-Halsted, 'The Moral Community and Peasant Nationalism in Nineteenth-century Poland', in Judith Pallot (ed.), *Transforming Peasants: Society, State and Peasantry, 1861–1930*, Houndmills, 1998, pp.73–89; Keely Stauter-Halsted, *The Nation in the Village: The Genesis of Peasant National Identity in Austrian Poland, 1848–1914*, Ithaca, NY/London, 2001; Kai Struve, *Bauern und Nation in Galizien: Über Zugehörigkeit und soziale Emanzipation im 19. Jahrhundert*, Göttingen, 2005.
39. Cartwright, *The Return of the Peasant*, pp.118, 177, 205; Verdery, *The Vanishing Hectare*, p.35; Filippo M. Zerilli, 'Sentiments and/as Property Rights: Restitution and Conflict in Postsocialist Romania', in Maruška Svašek (ed.), *Postsocialism: Politics and Emotion in Central and Eastern Europe*, Oxford/New York, 2008, pp.74–94.

PART I

ECONOMIC HISTORY

I

The Changing Landscape of Property

Landownership and Modernization in Poland in the Nineteenth and Twentieth Centuries

Jacek Kochanowicz

Introduction

Travellers traversing Poland today from north-west to south-east would observe considerable variety in the rural landscape. In Pomerania, they would drive along well-paved but rarely used side roads shaded by linden trees, looking at immense yellow fields of rapeseed.[1] From time to time, they would notice the derelict, dilapidated remains of an eighteenth-century palace – a remnant of the Pomeranian Junker class that disappeared from this land in 1945. Equally ghostly, though much less picturesque, would be abandoned buildings (usually made of ugly concrete) that relatively recently belonged to large state farms established there after 1945. The land itself, which belonged to the Junkers before the Second World War and to the state farms afterwards, has now been either rented out or sold to large-scale rural entrepreneurs who produce animal fodder, grain or pasture using modern, labour-saving technologies.

In the central parts of Poland, amidst the unattractive flatland of Mazovia, the travellers, having passed Warsaw, would drive through a zone of apple orchards stretching across the horizon. Closer to the big cities, they would notice rows of greenhouses devoted to the intensive production of vegetables and flowers (the latter now subject to fierce competition from overseas). Further south, the more densely populated Kraków region presents an almost medieval picture. They would see long, narrow stripes of land, each planted with a different crop, almost like a textbook illustration of scattered fields. The closer they get to the Tatra Mountains, the nicer the buildings would become, and the more affluent the sights. Today, of course, the livelihood of this region – notorious for its extreme poverty well into the 1950s, and for exports of redundant people as far as the United States – is based not on agriculture but tourism. Mountain slopes formerly used as sheep pastures are now traversed by ski lifts, and large houses are built with tourists in mind.

These brief glimpses aim to highlight the variety of this rural landscape. Poland has not yet produced a systematic study of these differences, as did Emilio Sereni for Italy, so mere glimpses must suffice here. But even they reflect deeper phenomena, for they show that landownership is more than just about the law. The images evoked above come from a country that was subject to the uniform policies of state socialism for about forty-five years. Since then it has been undergoing an intensive process of economic, social and cultural change that escapes easy labelling, given its various faces: post-communist transformation, building capitalism, integration within the European Union, involvement in globalization, ongoing modernization and so on. Still, the rural landscape is varied – reflecting property relations, among other things. However difficult it may be to interpret local cases, these observable differences attest to the fact that history matters. The overall forces, despite their potency, work through people and communities with different characteristics, and therefore produce somewhat different results, at least for the time being.

Told in the simplest possible way, the story of landowning in Poland is rather similar to other European cases, with its traceable trajectory from 'feudal' or 'traditional' to 'capitalist' or 'modern', with a 'collectivist' detour under state socialism. The story can be told in the language of either Marxism or liberalism, as the two traditions differ little in their appraisal of the economic superiority of individualized, modern capitalist landownership over the traditional, dispersed ownership characteristic of pre-industrial times. Obviously, however, what is most interesting is not this grand trajectory, but rather the local deviations that reflect the specificity of concrete national and local histories.

Zooming in on Poland, our focus narrows to a country that, before the advent of state socialism, was 'peripheral' (far from the centres of modern, industrial capitalism) and 'backward' (poorer, less urbanized, less educated and so on). As in most such regions, its agrarian system comprised a combination of small-scale (peasant) and large-scale landed properties, with all their attendant class, political and cultural consequences. In each case, landownership had its specific character. For the peasantry, it was a means of subsistence, a promise of physical survival. For the landowning class, it was as much a symbol of social status as it was an economic asset. This duality persisted until the Second World War. Before the war, Poland's most significant peculiarity was its very high rates of rural overpopulation. After the war, it was the settlement of the territories acquired from Germany and the abandonment of collectivization. This essay focuses on these particularities. It is organized chronologically, starting with a brief overview of the pre-industrial period, and then going into more detail moving into the twentieth century.

The Pre-industrial Legacy

The image evoked above of narrow strips of land in the south of Poland is testimony to the difficulty – indeed, nigh impossibility – of talking about the present in the twenty-first century without frequent recourse to the past and the long-term patterns that constituted agrarian relations.[2] It is tempting to start with medieval colonization and Germanic law, which brought three-field rotation with its characteristic pattern of scattered fields to the historical Polish lands (Wielkopolska, Greater Poland; Małopolska, Lesser Poland; and Mazowsze, Mazovia). Although land belonged to the nobility at the time, it was mainly used by peasants, who were free to cultivate it as long as they paid rent. The early modern period ushered in a new development – the steady rise in the importance of manorial farms, the *folwarks* – together with changes in the legal position of the peasantry – the second serfdom.[3] The manorial farms, which relied on compulsory labour, were market- and often export-oriented, their owners maximizing cash income that they then put towards luxury items and status.[4] The mechanisms that led to these developments have been a topic of long and rich historiographic debate that limitations of space keep me from recounting.[5] Regarding the question of property relations posed here, three points need be highlighted.

First, in terms of 'property' (although this concept is misleading when used in relation to the feudal epoch), the manorial *dominium directum* was gaining strength, while the peasant *dominium utile* was weakening.[6] With the gradual introduction of serfdom, peasants lost any legal protection. Land belonged to the nobility, which bought and sold (or leased) whole estates together with their serf populations. Yet a margin of freedom remained, as the small economic world of the peasantry included a land market in which small parcels of land were traded with manorial consent, according to families' needs.[7] Though peasants had no explicit property rights in land, customary rights (inheritance included) were recognized in practice, as long as labour services were duly rendered. Second, regarding the shares of land under direct manorial control and land used by the peasantry, the long-term tendency between the sixteenth and nineteenth centuries was a growth of the former and decrease of the latter from, say, a ratio of 1:10 to something closer to 1:1, accompanied by a proportional rise in labour services (corvée) due to the manor.[8] Third, the average size of the peasant farm diminished, a result of the already mentioned tendency of increasing land acquisition by the manors as well as increasing demographic pressure.

The nineteenth century brought a gradual emancipation of the peasantry in the Polish lands.[9] The process started in East (or rather East Central) Europe, particularly in the Austrian Empire. As early as the reign of Emperor Joseph II in the second half of the eighteenth century, the state curbed the lords' powers over the peasantry, mostly because the state needed taxpayers and soldiers from among the peasantry. In a legal sense, emancipation included both the abolition of serfdom and enfranchisement (granting rights to the possession of land). This reform process was largely fuelled by fears of revolutionary uprisings; in most cases legal reforms followed political unrest.

Different regulations applied in each partitioned territory of the Polish lands, usually reflecting the way the peasantry had been emancipated in each of the states that divided Poland. In the Prussian partition, serfdom was abolished in 1807, and from 1811 to 1850 peasants were enfranchised and landowners compensated in the form of land grants. What was unique was the consolidation of hitherto scattered strips of land, which greatly facilitated farmers' introduction of modern crop rotation, an important contribution to agricultural progress. In the second part of the century, the industrialization of the German Reich meant that the surplus population could move to urban centres, while agricultural producers – landowners and peasants alike – could profit from the high demand for food and other agricultural goods. Nationalist policies, though detested by the Polish educated classes, also helped in some ways, particularly by improving education and imposing protectionist tariffs. Wielkopolska, already quite developed before the partitions, became agriculturally the most advanced, modernized and capitalist of the Polish lands.[10]

In the Austrian partition, the abolition of serfdom and enfranchisement were introduced concomitantly in 1848, with landowners recompensed in money. Technologically, not much changed: dispersed fields remained in place, as did the commons (the forests, meadows and pastures to which all peasants and the manor had access). Agricultural progress was limited and poverty widespread. Meanwhile, after 1867 the relatively liberal regime of the Austrian Empire allowed the emergence of peasant political movements and parties, which later enjoyed continuity in independent Poland.

In the part of the Russian partition that came to be called the Kresy, or the Frontier Territories – parts of the Grand Duchy of Lithuania before 1795 and of Belarus, Lithuania and Ukraine today – emancipation came in 1861, as in the rest of the Russian Empire. In the rump state of Poland, the Duchy of Warsaw (which in 1815 became the Kingdom of Poland in personal union with Russia, gradually losing its autonomy after failed insurrections in 1830 and 1863), the abolition of serfdom in 1807 was part of a series of French-modelled reforms. In practice, it deprived peasants of any rights to land. Now they were treated as tenants, expected, as previously, to perform labour services. Many were evicted in the following years, when manors started to consolidate land under their direct control in the name of improvement. Enfranchisement, when at last declared in 1864, was in a way relatively advantageous to the peasantry (compared with Russia proper), as the Russian authorities had designed it with the dual intent of punishing the nobility for supporting the anti-Russian uprising of January 1863 and winning the hearts of the peasantry.[11] As in Russia, nobles were recompensed in money raised through increased taxation. And as in the Austrian partition, little changed in the agronomic sense: the system of scattered fields and communal rights to forest, meadow and pasture remained basically intact, left to individual agreements.

We can conclude this brief overview with three general observations. First, despite the reforms, the two types of landholding – large-scale and small-scale (peasant), a basic duality that itself was inherited from the pre-industrial Old Order – remained in place throughout the Polish lands. Second, although the situation of peasants obviously improved enormously as far as their rights to land were concerned, various differences remained in terms of the legal treatment of the peasant and noble ownership of land. These were least pronounced in the Austrian partition and most visible in the Kingdom of Poland, where the institution of land register, for instance, which was introduced for noble possessions in the early nineteenth century, was not extended to cover peasant properties until 1891, and even then remained optional.[12] Until the end of the kingdom's existence, various types of landownership were regulated in different ways.[13] Third, in terms of agrarian modernization, the Prussian partition was the most advanced. It was the design of the reform, as much as the overall context of economic development in Prussia and then the German Empire, that led to the 'Western' pattern of development of modern, capitalist agriculture, distancing this region from the peripheral 'east of Elbe' model.

Rural Overpopulation and Its Consequences

Throughout Southern and Central Europe, the second half of the nineteenth century and the first half of the twentieth were marked by increasing rural overpopulation, a combined result of population increase and limited urbanization (see Table 1.1). The population grew faster than before as mortality declined thanks to improved hygiene, advances in medical treatment, better living conditions and so forth.[14] The result was a demographic explosion, no longer tamed by Malthusian checks of famines or epidemics. In the years from 1820 to 1910, the population of the Kingdom of Poland, for instance, increased from 4.6 to 12 million, and the population density rose from 39 to 96 inhabitants per square kilometre.[15] In 1910, 57 persons per square kilometre had agriculture livelihoods, whereas for Germany this figure was only 33.[16] In 1914, the landless rural population numbered 1.4 million – that is, 18 per cent of the rural population.[17]

Table 1.1 Redundant population in agriculture (rural overpopulation) in East Central Europe around 1930 (as a percentage of agricultural population)

Country	%
Bulgaria	33.0
Czechoslovakia	0.8
Estonia	10.1
Hungary	9.7
Latvia	11.8
Lithuania	2.2
Poland	25.0
Rumania	30.7
Yugoslavia	36.1

Source: Wojciech Roszkowski, *Land Reforms in East Central Europe after World War One*, mimeo, 1990.

Rural overpopulation and land hunger were among the most pressing social and political issues of the interwar period, and also attracted a great deal of scholarly attention.[18]

Land hunger was particularly dire in the southern parts of interwar Poland. As early as the end of the eighteenth century, when serfdom was still well in place, lords in Małopolska stopped searching for fugitive peasants as the labour supply was abundant. The population of Austrian Poland – Galicia – increased considerably during the nineteenth century.[19] Between 1820 and 1910, it jumped from 4.5 to 8.9 million, while population density climbed from 58 to 104 inhabitants per square kilometre; meanwhile, almost a million people emigrated. This demographic trend continued in the interwar period. Between 1921 and 1939, Poland's population grew by 7.2 million. Of this, the rural population accounted for 4.5 million, whereas the urban share of the increase was only 2.7 million. Around 1.5 million peasants moved to the towns in this period, and about half a million emigrated, but this still was not enough to diffuse the demographic pressure on the land, since 70 per cent of the increase stayed in the villages. Overpopulation was most acute in the south-eastern parts of Poland.

An example worth presenting in some detail is found in an excellent micro-study done in the 1930s by the economist and historian Wincenty Styś. The study focused on Husów, a small village in a hilly landscape south of Kraków.[20] In 1789, 950 people lived there, the number growing to 1,384 in 1850 and 2,302 in 1900, reaching 2,908 in 1937. Many left: if all who were born there had stayed, there would have been 4,500 residents by 1937. Despite this increase, land fragmentation proceeded slowly until the mid-nineteenth century. In 1787, the average farm had 8.33 hectares; in 1851, 6.88 hectares. Then, however, the number nosedived: by 1883, the average farm had declined to 4.36 hectares, falling further to 2.34 hectares in 1937. A hypothetical farm was divided only once every 166 years between its original settlement and 1787, and once every 50 years between 1787 and 1850; but between 1851 and 1883 it was divided once every 3.5 years, and from 1883 to 1937, once every 1.33 years.

Fragmentation equalized the size of farms. More affluent families had more children and thus more heirs to divide property between. Under the Old Order, the dominant group of farmers was called *kmieć*, who had farms large enough to support themselves and provide labour services for the manor. The traditional unit of land measurement was the *łan*, about 30 hectares. A *kmieć* usually had either a full *łan* or half of one. Under serfdom, the size of a farm was closely related to its labour obligations. For example, larger farms that could support draft animals were required to supply not just human labour but also that of animals. In addition, a sizeable number of smallholders and cottagers supported themselves with non-agricultural pursuits, mainly weaving. The demographic pressure that lasted until the period from the 1850s to the 1870s left the number of *kmieć* intact, but the population of cottagers was growing.

The changes of the second half of the nineteenth and first thirty years of the twentieth centuries wiped out the class of *kmieć*, and smallholders with somewhere around 2 hectares of land became the dominant category. The limit to fragmentation was the area necessary for subsistence. This was not absolute, since the nineteenth and early twentieth centuries witnessed considerable agricultural progress that extended even to poor peasants. In Husów, even though the population tripled in 150 years and the area of the average farm decreased by two-thirds, production volumes increased nine-fold and famines disappeared. Nevertheless, half of Husów's farmers were still unable to produce enough food for themselves in 1937.

The process of fragmentation changed the original shape of the fields. Initially, a *łan* was a strip of land up to 2.5 kilometres long and 200 metres wide, and on the typical farm the land was all in one piece until the mid nineteenth century. When land was divided, it was cut in half lengthwise. However, when land became further fragmented in the second half of the nineteenth century and later, Husów's peasants, unwilling to allow the creation of extremely narrow, long strips of land as other villages had done, started to cut across the width of original *łans*. That led to a characteristic pattern of chequered fields that differed greatly from the original ones. In 1937, the average piece of land resulting from these divisions had an area of 0.54 hectares, being up to 136 metres long and around 40 to 50 metres wide. Peasant households now had 4.3 pieces of land on average, scattered in various places up to 1.5 kilometres from the house.

Demography was the main cause of this great change, but not the only one. Two other important factors were enfranchisement and industrialization. Both made landowning much more attractive than before. Emancipation terminated the burden of labour obligations, which previously had often exceeded a peasant family's capacity and thus bred reluctance to have a larger farm. Industrialization dealt a mortal blow to domestic industries, primarily textiles, that had allowed cottagers to survive, and land became more important to them than before. Industrialization also had the positive effect of bringing technologies (such as fertilizers and iron ploughs) that permitted subsistence on much smaller plots of land.

This demographic, legal and economic revolution also changed the patterns of inheritance. Under the Old Order, both divisible and indivisible inheritance were practised in Galicia, but the latter was more widespread, as was the case in Husów. Demographic pressure led to division of property among all heirs. After emancipation, there also developed a tendency to provide daughters with land, so that now a farm typically had two owners and consisted of parts belonging to the husband and to the wife. Legal and customary rules evolved to fit the changing conditions of the overpopulated countryside.

The process of land fragmentation, illustrated in some detail by the case of Husów, characterized the country as a whole. As mentioned above, the rural population increased by 4.5 million between 1921 and 1939, and around 70 per cent of those born in the countryside remained there. As a result, the overall number of farms increased by 14 per cent, and the number of small farms of up to 2 hectares rose by 25 per cent.[21] To a certain extent, the story of Husów is representative of all those parts of Eastern and Southern Europe where economic backwardness did not allow for the outflow of rural people from agriculture.[22]

This demographic pressure on the land ended three centuries of general increase in the share of land owned by manors and a concomitant decrease in land held by the peasantry. A reverse process started. Landowners, having lost free labour, had to convert to more modern ways of management, for which they needed capital. Many sold part of their estates to get money for improvements. Peasants, in turn, for whom acquiring land was a matter of survival, were eager to pay even very high prices, using money they borrowed or saved while working abroad. The share of land in the hands of the estates decreased from 47 to 36 per cent from 1864 to 1905 in the Kingdom of Poland (while the share of land held by peasants rose by 20 per cent), and between 1860 and 1905 it dropped in Galicia from 42 to 38 per cent and 60 to 52 per cent in Wielkopolska.[23] Still, 33 per cent of the land remained in the hands of large estates in the interwar period.[24]

Counting from a threshold of 50 hectares, there were around 15,000 landed estates at that time, and the landed class (owners and families) is estimated to have numbered around 80,000 – less than 1 per cent of Poland's population.[25] In contrast to semi-subsistence peasant farms, their estates were highly commercialized, and thus mattered as suppliers to the cities. For the same reasons, they were hit hard by the dramatic drop in prices during the Great Depression. But landed estates, as a remnant of the Old Order in which land ownership was as much a matter of material wealth as of social status, had non-economic value as well. The culture of the Polish *ziemaństwo*, landed classes, is not the topic of this chapter, but its role cannot be ignored. The landed class developed a whole ideology of self-justification, glorifying its historical role defending the country in ancient times and fighting the nineteenth-century insurrections, its share in preserving Polishness during the partitions, its willingness to help 'our people' (the peasants) in times of need and its successes in spreading agricultural progress.[26] Its lifestyle, centred on quiet life in country manors where family, friends and neighbouring landowners could be entertained, and hunting and balls organized, competed successfully with that of the relatively weak Polish bourgeoisie, who often emulated landed gentry.[27] The cultural importance of the landed class is witnessed also by Polish literary writings of the day, which portrayed it in terms either nostalgic (Jarosław Iwaszkiewicz, Maria Dąbrowska) or ironic (Witold Gombrowicz, Tadeusz Dołęga-Mostowicz).[28] The landed classes were also strong enough to make their political weight felt.[29]

The pressure on land acquired a political dimension after the First World War. Peasant parties – now political actors with some strength thanks to universal franchise – put land reform at the top of their agendas. The most radical projects were put forward during the war with Soviet Russia, when the newborn Polish state tried to win over Polish peasants in the face of the Bolsheviks, who counted on the support of the landless masses. But after Poland won the war in 1920 and a constitution protecting private property was approved in 1921, these projects were curbed, and the actual land reform (ultimately decided in 1925) was one of the least radical in Central Europe.[30] In essence, it stipulated that compulsory sale of parts of estates exceeding given limits (180 hectares, with higher limits for estates that were industrialized or located in the Kresy) could be introduced, on condition that spontaneous parcelling out in a given year did not reach a threshold of 200,000 hectares nationally. Only a small portion of the land (16 per cent) was transferred from landowners to peasants in this way, and the process practically stopped during the Great Depression. Thus, although during the interwar period the issue of land reform was hotly debated in arguments that were as much economic as political and moral in character, in practical terms the coexistence of small and large properties continued until the Second World War.[31]

The New Agrarian Order

The end of the landed class and great estates came in the period from 1939 to 1944. During the war, their fate depended upon the policies of the occupying powers. In the half of the Polish territory invaded by the Soviet Union on 17 September 1939, members of the landed class, together with the bureaucracy, intelligentsia and upper middle classes, fell victim to Soviet persecution as the Soviets began introducing collectivization and the nationalization of rural property.[32] In the parts of Poland that were directly annexed by the German Reich, the Nazis pursued even harsher policies of persecution of the Polish elite, including landowners, and the estates' farms were put under German administration. However, estates and landowners were left in relative peace in the General Government set up in central Poland, as here the occupiers wanted primarily to secure the (mandatory) delivery of agricultural products. For the same reasons, the peasant population (except in the region of Zamość, singled out for intensive German settlement) was subject to slightly less severe persecution than were their urban counterparts.[33]

With the end of the war, property relations changed even more radically. Now they were shaped as much by the new political regime as by the state's territorial shift some 300 kilometres westward. The latter resulted in Poland's loss of the Kresy, territories east of the river Bug that were incorporated into the Soviet Union and are now parts of Belarus, Lithuania and Ukraine. The agrarian relations there, which were shaped directly by Soviet policies, remain outside the scope of this chapter. The territories acquired from Germany, stretching up to the Oder and Neisse and called, in the propagandistic language of the day, 'Recovered Territories', were almost empty, abandoned by former German inhabitants who fled in 1944/45 as the Red Army approached, or were later resettled as decided by the great powers.

Further development differed substantially between the areas that had belonged to Poland before the war and those that Poland acquired from Germany. In the former, the character of the very radical land reform that had started as early as 1944[34] was shaped by the changing balance of power over the following years. The Polish Workers' Party (Polska Partia Robotnicza, PPR) dominated the scene, but until 1948 it was accompanied by the parties of social democrats, Christian democrats and peasants who managed to play some role for a time, each with its specific view as to the character of the emerging economic system.[35] The Peasant Party, like their pre-war predecessors, wanted land reform that would increase the size of already existing peasant farms to make them economically viable. Their leader was Stanisław Mikołajczyk, deputy prime minister of the provisional government formed under Soviet protection, who in 1943/44 had been prime minister of the Polish government in exile in London and thus, as a representative of the 'London Poles', lent the new regime an appearance of constitutional continuity. While some legitimacy of this sort was initially important for the PPR, it gradually came to regard the Peasant Party first as an opposition, and then as an embodiment of 'reaction' and Western interference. Fearing arrest, Mikołajczyk ultimately fled to the West in 1947. In these circumstances, the Peasant Party's views had little bearing on how land reform was actually carried out.

The Communist Party had a different vision. In the Leninist language of class warfare, they argued against the Peasant Party as a defender of 'kulaks' and landlords, meanwhile preaching the need for an alliance between workers and the landless peasantry, the 'rural proletariat'. In fact, the political aim of the reform was to neutralize, if not win over, the poor peasantry, in view of Polish society's very mixed attitudes towards the emerging, Soviet-sponsored regime. The reform that was actually introduced had a very radical character, compared with its interwar predecessor. All estates of more than 50 hectares were subject to it, and their owners, who received almost no compensation, were forced to abandon their homes. For the landed class it was indeed the 'end of the world', to quote one of their descendants, the famous Polish painter and graphic artist Franciszek Starowieyski.[36]

Land was then distributed among the landless and smallholding peasantry. Interestingly, peasants had somewhat mixed attitudes towards the reform. In the Białystok region, where residents remembered the Soviet agrarian policies of 1939 to 1941, there was general mistrust of any Communist Party policy. In Wielkopolska, agriculturally the most modernized region before the war, farm workers with no experience of individual farming were seldom willing to change over to peasant production on smallholdings. And even in the central lands, despite pre-war land hunger, a certain hesitancy was bred by some peasants' fears that easily acquired land could just as easily be retaken in the future. Land acquired through reform was of a different status than that previously held, and the former landless, now enfranchised, were treated as a lower-class category even in the next generation, to the extent that persons coming from these two social groups did not intermarry.

For the next sixty years or so, the land reform of 1944 set the basic characteristics of Poland's agrarian regime, which was based on independent peasant cultivation. However, it only partially solved one of pre-war Poland's most acute problems: rural overpopulation and land hunger. Simply, there was not enough land to distribute among the needy peasantry in central Poland.

In the western 'Recovered Territories', new settlement was the main line of development in the second half of the 1940s. The settlers came from the overpopulated central lands and from the Kresy, now incorporated into the Soviet Union. Many were demobilized soldiers who were formerly residents of the Kresy (among whom many had been gulag prisoners or exiles in Soviet Central Asia). This settlement, although supported and organized by the Polish government, was largely wild and haphazard, unsurprising in the context of the post-war situation. (Lack of effective administration even led these regions to be compared to the American Wild West.) The new settlers took over abandoned German farms and homes, sometimes informally dividing one property between multiple families. Many settlers lacked secure property titles for years, and because of this – and Germany's refusal to recognize the territorial shift until the 1970s – they feared their situation was neither permanent nor stable.

These parts of the country differed importantly from those that had belonged to pre-war Poland in the much higher share of land directly under state control in the form of large state-owned farms, called Państwowe Gospodarstwa Rolne (PGR) after 1949. In Pomerania, they became more common than in central Poland, as the former Junker estates were often nationalized rather than parcelled out. The PGRs, although their overall share of land never exceeded 20 per cent, became an important feature of the agrarian regime, as the Communist Party (as of 1948, Polska Zjednoczona Partia Robotnicza, PZPR) expected them to play a leading role in modernizing agriculture. In reality, they turned out to be a waste, a bottomless pit for resources.

Early in the communist period, the agrarian system was based primarily on small-scale peasant property and thus similar to that of the rest of Central Europe. Twenty years later, in the mid 1960s, it turned out to be quite unique, as peasant agriculture had been collectivized everywhere else in the countries under Soviet rule (excepting the otherwise communist Yugoslavia). Poland remained an exception, and peasant agriculture survived, but the PZPR never fully accepted this. Throughout the duration of state socialism, the PZPR remained locked in a fundamental dilemma. On the one hand, it recognized the need to tolerate private peasant farming in view of economic and political exigencies. On the other hand, however, it never managed to solve the riddle of reconciling this private sector with the logic of a command economy and the ideological doctrine of the need to 'socialize' agriculture.

Stalled Socialist Modernization

It is hard to say why collectivization did not succeed in Poland. Ideologically, Polish communists were committed to the idea of the 'socialization' of agriculture, not only under Stalinism but after 1956 as well. To fully unwrap the actual content of the changing ideology goes beyond the scope of this chapter, so three points must suffice. The first is the notion, often present within Marxism, that the peasantry, as an antithesis of modernity, is often plainly reactionary in economic, political and cultural terms. The second is the general idea that 'big is beautiful' – that in any industry, agriculture included, larger units of production are more modern and efficient than smaller ones. This is equally evident in the treatment of agriculture in Lenin's numerous works and in Kautsky's struggle, in *Die Agrarfrage*,[37] to explain why production in agriculture was so little concentrated compared with other branches of the economy, and why small-scale farming persisted. The third is that small-scale peasant production, partly subsistence and partly market oriented, is chaotic and thus hardly compatible with 'rational' national planning. It follows from all this that, under socialism, large-scale socialist farming, well integrated within the planned economy, should replace peasant farming.

So, with the consolidation of Stalinism after 1948, Poles, along with everybody else in the Soviet camp, started a collectivization campaign. Like other countries, methods were somewhat milder and the pace slower than was the case in the Soviet archetype of the 1930s.[38] Indeed, in the Central European countries that more or less completed collectivization, the process lasted into the 1960s and, with time, was increasingly motivated by the carrot rather than the stick. In Poland, collectivization started in 1948. Early on, the methods were far from pleasant: peasants were asked to join collectives 'voluntarily', but the unconvinced were harassed in various ways, most commonly by increasing their mandatory delivery quotas to very challenging levels. Often they were also overtly persecuted with arrests and beatings, among other measures. The peasants responded with a 'weapons of the weak' type of passive resistance that proved highly effective against the teams of PZPR activists sent from the cities to explain the benefits of collectives to the peasants – even when their persuasion efforts were backed by threats from the political police.[39] Many cooperatives were established on paper only, with peasants continuing to till their own plots.[40] The collectivization campaign dragged on for a few years, but it was pursued less and less vigorously because it provoked not only resistance but also a decrease in output. After 1956, Władysław Gomułka regained power under the banner of the 'Polish road to socialism', which retained the 'individual' ('private' being a taboo word) form of peasant farming. Gomułka, doubtless an ardent communist, was also a pragmatist. Even as a leader of the PPR in the 1940s, before his arrests he had been convinced that attempts to break various Polish specificities, including the peasantry's fierce attachment to the land, could be counter-productive. By 1956, the existing 'production cooperatives', as the collective farms were called, had mostly been disbanded, and PGRs remained the only form of 'socialized' agriculture.

But the idea of the 'socialization' of agriculture had not been abandoned, nor were peasant farmers free to run their affairs as they wished, even though the property remained in their hands. In fact, overall, the economic system precluded much freedom, for prices were set administratively, the state was the main buyer of produce and farmers were obliged to meet mandatory sales quotas; meanwhile, all the industrial inputs farmers needed (fertilizers, pesticides, machinery, construction materials and so on) were rationed. Thus, although free markets for produce were allowed, they played only a marginal role.

The PZPR meanwhile faced a dilemma: it needed to increase agricultural output, but for reasons both ideological and systemic it could hardly allow peasants to modernize in the manner of the West, that is, to allow the development of a strong commercial farming sector. Increasing output was essential, given Poland's urbanization and rising consumer expectations, which in the 1950s, 1960s and even 1970s still related heavily to food consumption, particularly the availability of meat. (Attempts to raise meat prices led several times to political unrest.) Not fully self-sufficient in grains and animal fodder, Poland had to import some from the West. Gomułka, an ascetic person himself, tried to keep the consumption and production of meat under control because greater numbers of animals required increasing imports of fodder. This view might have made some sense, but it ultimately led to his demise in 1970. Edward Gierek had no such inhibitions, and he allowed foreign credits to be used for imports, which contributed to a general crisis in the Polish economy in the mid 1970s and to his demise as well.

Increasing domestic output required investment, but – apart from the fact that resources were limited – the PZPR hesitated in allotting necessary resources to peasant farmers. Several times it bet instead on the PGRs, which turned out to be a travesty of economic efficiency. Regarding the peasantry, its tactics were that of encirclement, or more precisely, gradually including the peasants in the planned (command) economy without touching landownership or individual farming itself. For instance, in the 1960s peasants could not buy certain types of agricultural machinery but only rent it from state-controlled organizations. The idea was that, if collective ownership of land was not feasible, then the peasants should be 'socialized' (that is, brought into the planned economy) in some other way. Moreover, the state limited the size of private farms and encouraged land transfers from peasants to the state by stipulating that as, of 1968, farmers could only get pensions if they turned the land over to the state (to be used by the PGRs).

In general, a process of modernization of farming and rural life undeniably occurred, starting in the second half of the 1950s.[41] Electricity gradually reached most villages, and agricultural policies encouraged new seed varieties, the use of artificial fertilizers and the introduction of new breeds of cattle, leading to increased grain, dairy and meat production. Rural people's economic situation also improved owing to increased labour opportunities. Industrialization (in its inefficient, labour-intensive socialist form) offered various low-skilled job opportunities, thus making poorer peasants into a class of commuting peasant-workers.[42] Working on the PGRs was another possibility. No doubt the peasantry also benefited from greatly expanded educational opportunities, particularly at the elementary and vocational levels, which counted for much in a country where in the 1930s one third of the population could neither read nor write. Literacy, and later television, thus completed a process of changing 'peasants into Poles', to paraphrase Eugene Weber.[43] Rural incomes were usually lower than those in the urban sector, but farmers – who could easily sell whatever they were able to produce, and for whom inputs of production, although rationed, were available and cheap – were much more secure than they had been, say,

Table 1.2 Different categories of private (peasant) farms in Poland, 1950 to 1970 (percentages)

Year	0.5–2 hectares	2–5 hectares	5–10 hectares	Over 10 hectares
1950	20.9	33.4	32.9	12.8
1960	25.6	33.6	28.9	11.9
1970	25.4	31.9	29.2	13.5

Source: Anna Szemberg, *Przemiany struktury agrarnej w świetle narodowych spisów powszechnych 1960 i 1970*, Warszawa, 1973, p.6.

during the Great Depression of the 1930s. By the 1970s, mandatory delivery quotas had been abolished and free health care extended to farmers, already entitled to pensions. So it is unsurprising that, as the sociological research of the day revealed, the peasants supported the existing system more than other social groups did, despite the official anti-Church stance that the culturally traditional peasantry had never accepted.[44]

However, all this modernization occurred under conditions of stagnation in the structure of landowning. In 1970, there were 3.5 million farms in Poland. Small farms prevailed, the average size being less than 5 hectares, and during the 1950s the number of the smallest farms increased (see Table 1.2). True, this was attributable not to PZPR agricultural policy alone but also to demographic factors. Land reform and urbanization made rural overpopulation much less acute and dramatic than in pre-war times, but it did not eliminate it.

The PZPR's hesitant attitude towards rural capitalism had not excluded it totally. Town and city food markets (bazaars) for agricultural products – particularly vegetables and dairy products – were tolerated, even in the 1950s. Later development expanded the sectors of intensive (greenhouse) vegetable and flower production and fruit growing (particularly apples), mentioned above, for which the Soviet Union proved to be a large outlet.

Thus, not only did private landownership persist, but semi-capitalist forms of organizing production also found their niches. Institutionally and politically, they assumed a complex, often semi-formal character, as producers sometimes dressed up their activity in cooperative forms and obtained patronage through extensive local political networks. Initially, especially in the 1960s, policy makers were reluctant to allow large-scale private animal husbandry. They were under pressure to deliver more meat to consumers, but at the same time the increase depended on the availability of high-quality animal fodder, which had to be imported. But even in this regard, and particularly during the last two decades of state socialism, they gradually offered private entrepreneurs freer rein. Gierek did so to enhance his pragmatic and populist policies and thereby gain broader social support. After the serious economic crisis of the late 1970s and the subsequent Solidarity 'Polish Revolution', communist ideology was a spent force, and there lingered no illusions as to the inferiority of 'socialized' forms of agriculture. These realizations furthered the development of rural capitalism – so far as this was possible under the still existing, albeit disintegrating, command ('planned') economy.

Conclusion: Towards Capitalism

The fall of state socialism triggered a new phase in Polish agricultural and rural development. This stage has not yet attracted its historians, so here it can be sketched only very briefly and tentatively. Its two breaking points were the collapse of state socialism and accession to the European Union. After the collapse, the situation of farmers and rural people deteriorated; after the accession, it improved. It deteriorated in the 1990s because farmers were pushed into much more formidable market conditions than had existed before 1989/90. Price controls on their products were eliminated in the late 1980s, but thereafter the costs of their inputs started to rise, as did the cost of borrowing money. At the same time, opportunities for additional earnings outside agriculture or on the now-collapsed PGRs vanished. The Polish farming sector acquired a dual character, with most farms being semi-subsistence in nature and a minority fully capitalist, modern and commercial. However, neither group enjoyed an easy situation. This fact, along with the collapse of state farms and the consequent dramatic marginalization of their former workers, fuelled populist politics, one of whose effects was that farmers were perceived as a roadblock to EU accession.[45]

Contrary to many expectations, opening up to Western markets did not destroy commercial producers but allowed many of them to profit. Despite complaints that Poland was badly treated in terms of European funds for agriculture, money started to flow in, leading to boosted incomes for farmers who learned how to apply for subsidies and to infrastructure development in rural areas. (Farmers thereafter became supporters of accession.) And economic growth led to a growth in services and small businesses in the countryside, which – together with the partial opening of the Western labour market – contributed to overall better employment opportunities.

Has all this somehow radically changed property relations? Not necessarily. Whereas the Polish version of state socialism restrained farmers' economic freedom in various ways, it did not destroy the basic institution of small-scale landownership. Its survival was due to a particular constellation of factors – especially the legacy of land hunger that reinforced the peasantry's attachment to land, and the Polish communists' inability to overcome the passive resistance of various social groups – as well as a certain pragmatism exercised by Polish communists. Passive resistance was surely also influenced by the specific Polish variety of Catholicism – widespread, anti-intellectual, ritualized, populist and nationalist – and thus was very difficult to crush or uproot. Small-scale landownership also survived in another, more legalistic sense: despite political twists and turns, state socialism did not destroy the institutions of civil and land law codes and land registers. Thus, in a legal sense, no dramatic discontinuity followed the demise of state socialism, although laws protecting private property have been strengthened, and limits on trading and leasing land loosened.

Changes have occurred nonetheless. Both economic and cultural in nature, they echo the experiences of more economically advanced Western European countries. Land is obviously no longer a status symbol, as it still was for the elite before the Second World War. It is also less and less (if at all) a source of subsistence for small farmers, a marked difference from the early stages of post-communist transformation. It thus has lost the semi-spiritual value it had for the landed elite, and also for the land-hungry peasantry of the first half of the twentieth century. Instead it has become a form of investment, for rural and urban people alike. Land is an attractive investment because of its possible agricultural use, particularly given the ongoing rapid development of large-scale commercial farming.[46] It is attractive because it is scarce, as towns and cities sprawl, roads are constructed and urban people seek country retreats. It is, finally, attractive to both those seeking a secure investment and speculators going for high profits. In sum, at the end of a winding and protracted path, property relations have become capitalist.

Notes

1. According to the UN Food and Agriculture Organization, Poland is the world's seventh-largest producer of this crop, used for biodiesel.
2. This section gives only a brief account of something that has been the subject of generations of scholarly research. For a summary of this research, see Stefan Inglot (ed.), *Historia chłopów polskich*, vols. 1–3, Warsaw, 1970–80.
3. This was introduced gradually, mostly by the Sejm (lower house of parliament), but also by royal privilege, strengthening the legal position of the nobility and weakening that of the peasants. See Zdzisław Kaczmarczyk, *Historia państwa i prawa Polski*, vol. 2, Warsaw, 1971, pp.51ff., 246ff.
4. For an interpretation, see Witold Kula, *An Economic Theory of the Feudal System*, London, 1976. Kula's discussion is summarized in Jacek Kochanowicz, 'La Théorie économique . . . après vingt ans', *Acta Poloniae Historica* 56 (1987), pp.187–211.
5. For a review of this debate, see Jacek Kochanowicz, 'The Polish Economy and the Evolution of Dependency', in Daniel Chirot (ed.), *The Origins of Backwardness in Eastern Europe: Economics and Politics from the Middle Ages until the Early Twentieth Century*, Berkeley, 1989, pp.92–130; Jacek Kochanowicz, 'L'exploitation paysanne en Pologne a la charnière des XVIIIė et XIXė siècles: Théorie, historie, historiographie,' *Acta Poloniae Historica* 57 (1988), pp.203–37.
6. Kaczmarczyk, *Historia*, pp.50, 75.
7. The records of some village courts provide excellent documentation of these transactions, and several volumes of such records have been published. For one analysis, see Jacek Kochanowicz,

'The Peasant Family as an Economic Unit in the Polish Feudal Economy of the Eighteenth Century', in Richard Wall, Jean Robin and Peter Laslett (eds), *Family Forms in Historic Europe*, Cambridge, 1983, pp.153–66.

8. For an analysis of the legal means used to increase the share of land under direct control of *folwarks*, see Kaczmarczyk, *Historia*, p.46.
9. The voluminous literature on this topic is summarized in Kaczmarczyk, *Historia*, vol. 2, and Krzysztof Groniowski, *Uwłaszczenie chłopów w Polsce*, Warsaw, 1978.
10. For a very useful comparison of different modernization routes in the three partitions, see Juliusz Łukasiewicz, 'Drogi rozwojowe rolnictwa na ziemiach polskich', in Stefan Kieniewicz (ed.), *Polska XIX w. Państwo, społeczeństwo, kultura*, Warsaw, 1977, pp.13–55.
11. Konstanty Grzybowski, *Historia państwa i prawa Polski*, vol. 4, Warsaw, 1982, p.108.
12. Ibid., pp.102f.
13. Ibid., p.112.
14. Cf. Wiktor Bronikowski, *Drogi postępu chłopa polskiego*, Warsaw, 1934; Tadeusz Sobczak, *Przełom w konsumpcji spożywczej w Królestwie Polskim*, Wrocław, 1968; Michał Kopczyński, *Wielka transformacja: badania nad uwarstwieniem społecznym i standardem życia w Królestwie Polskim 1866–1913 w świetle pomiarów antropometrycznych poborowych*, Warsaw, 2006; Maria Krisań, *Chłopi wobec zmian cywilizacyjnych w Królestwie Polskim w drugiej połowie XIX – początku XX wieku*, Warsaw, 2008.
15. Irena Gieysztorowa, 'Ludność', in Antoni Mączak (ed.), *Encyklopedia historii gospodarczej Polski do 1945 r.*, vol. 1, Warsaw, 1981, p.434.
16. Stanisław A. Kempner, *Dzieje gospodarcze Polski porozbiorowej w zarysie*, Warsaw, 1922, p.80.
17. Władysław Grabski, *Rocznik statystyczny Królestwa Polskiego*, Warsaw, 1914, p.71.
18. See especially Juliusz Poniatowski, *Przeludnienie wsi i rolnictwa*, Warsaw, 1935; Ludwik Landau, Jerzy Pański and Edward Strzelecki, *Bezrobocie wśród chłopów*, Warsaw, 1939. According to Poniatowski, whose estimate was the most radical, there were over 8 million 'redundant' people in the Polish countryside. The classical Western study of this problem in Eastern Europe was Doreen Warriner, *Economics of Peasant Farming*, Oxford, 1939.
19. Gieysztorowa, 'Ludność', p.434.
20. Wincenty Styś, *Drogi postępu gospodarczego wsi*, Wrocław 1947. For his study Styś used maps, surveys and land registers dating from the eighteenth and nineteenth centuries; he also conducted a very detailed survey of each farm himself, which enabled him to draw several maps of Husów lands from the initial settlement and then for 1787, 1851 and 1937.
21. Mieczysław Mieszczankowski, *Struktura agrarna Polski międzywojennej*, Warsaw, 1962, pp.310f., 333.
22. This is shown clearly in another book by Wincenty Styś, *Wpływ uprzemysłowienia na ustrój rolny*, Lviv, 1936.
23. Marcin Kamler, 'Folwark', in Mączak, *Encyklopedia*, p.176.
24. Juliusz Łukasiewicz, 'Agrarna struktura', in Mączak, *Encyklopedia*, p.11; R. Chomać, *Struktura agrarna Królestwa Polskiego na przełomie XIX i XX w.*, Warsaw, 1970, p.98.
25. For a detailed discussion of various estimates and an analysis of landowning class structure, see Wojciech Roszkowski, *Gospodarcza rola większej prywatnej własności ziemskiej w Polsce 1918–1939*, Warsaw, 1986, pp.28–42.
26. Maria Dąbrowska, a recognized writer and herself of noble origin, presented a critique of this ideology in *Rozdroże: Studium na temat zagadnień wiejskich*, Warsaw, 1937.
27. For a depiction of country manor life in the nineteenth century, see Elżbieta Kowecka, *W salonie i w kuchni: Opowieść o kulturze materialnej pałaców i dworów polskich w XIX w.*, Warsaw, 1984; Daniel Beauvois, *Trójkąt ukraiński: Szlachta, carat i lud na Wołyniu, Podolu i Kijowszczyźnie, 1793–1914*, Lublin, 2005.

28. The main character in a satirical novel by Tadeusz Dołęga-Mostowicz, *Kariera Nikodema Dyzmy* (1932) – an upstart who makes it into high society through a combination of luck and ruthlessness – crowns his advancement with the acquisition of a landed estate.
29. Roszkowski, *Gospodarcza rola*, pp.319f.
30. Ibid. Also see Czesław Madajczyk, *Burżuazyjno-obszarnicza reforma rolna w Polsce, 1918–1939*, Warsaw, 1958.
31. For a clear argument favouring spontaneous parcelling out but opposing land reform, see Władysław Grabski, 'Parcelacja agrarna wobec struktury, koniunktury i chwili dziejowej Polski', *Ekonomista* 36/4 (1936), pp.16–52; Roszkowski, *Gospodarcza rola*, presents an overview of these polemics.
32. See the recent monograph on the fate of the Polish landed class in the East: Krzysztof Jasiewicz, *Zagłada polskich Kresów*, Warsaw, 1998.
33. Czesław Madajczyk, *Polityka III Rzeszy w okupowanej Polsce*, vol. 2, Warsaw, 1979.
34. For an extensive study of the communist land reform, see Henryk Słabek, *Polityka agrarna PPR*, Warsaw, 1967.
35. Respectively, the Polish Socialist Party (Polska Partia Socjalistyczna, PPS), the Labour Party (Stronictwo Pracy, SP), and the Polish Peasant Party (Polskie Stronnictwo Ludowe, PSL). For an analysis of the debate on the future economic system, see Tadeusz Kowalik, *Spory o ustrój gospodarczy w Polsce: lata 1944–48*, Warsaw, 2006.
36. Franciszek Starowieyski, *Franciszka Starowieyskiego opowieść o końcu świata, czyli Reforma rolna (pisała Krystyna Uniechowska)*, Warsaw, 1994.
37. Karl Kautsky, *Die Agrarfrage: Eine Übersicht über die Tendenzen der modernen Landwirtschaft und die Agrarpolitik der Sozialdemokratie*, Stuttgart, 1899.
38. Jerzy Tepicht, a leading Polish agricultural economist of the 1960s who actively promoted collectivization as a young cadre but quickly came to understand its pitfalls, produced an interesting account. He observed that Soviet experts, when asked how to proceed with collectivization, vaguely hinted that Poles should perhaps be cautious about emulating the Soviet model. Tepicht, 'A Project for Research on the Peasant Revolution of Our Time', *Journal of Peasant Studies* 2/3 (1975), pp.257–69; see also his *Marxisme et Agriculture: Le Paysan Polonais*, Paris, 1973.
39. Indeed, this type of resistance did not much differ from what we know of other times and places. See the classic analysis of peasant resistance offered by James C. Scott, *Weapons of the Weak*, New Haven, CT, 1985; see also Forrest D. Colbourn (ed.), *Everyday Forms of Peasant Resistance*, Armonk, NY, 1989.
40. For the dynamics of Polish collectivization, see the magnificent, detailed, indispensable study by Dariusz Jarosz, *Polityka władz komunistycznych w Polsce w latach 1918–1956 a chłopi*, Warsaw, 1998.
41. For more on this, see Jacek Kochanowicz, 'Stato e contadini: La politica agraria polacca negli anni 1956–1970', *Studi Storici* 3 (1988), pp.759–85.
42. Maria Dziewicka, *Chłopi-robotnicy*, Warsaw, 1968.
43. Eugene Weber, *Peasants into Frenchmen*, Stanford, CA, 1976.
44. Krystyna Naszkowska and Paweł Wroński, 'Chłopi w czasach ludowych' [an interview with Professor Dariusz Jarosz], *Gazeta Wyborcza*, 25/26 May 2002, p.10.
45. Unemployed (and often unemployable) former PGR workers with little education and few skills became, according to sociologists, a Polish version of the underclass.
46. Between 1995 and 2006, the share of farms larger than 20 hectares increased from 3.6 to 6.3 per cent, and those larger than 50 hectares grew from 0.3 to 1.1 per cent. Very small farms continue to persist, but the average farm is now close to 9 hectares. *Rocznik Statystyczny Rzeczypospolitej Polskiej* 1977, table 377.

2

Agriculture and Landownership in the Economic History of Twentieth-Century Romania

Bogdan Murgescu

The main goal of this chapter is to present some basic data on the evolution of Romanian agriculture during the interwar period and under communist rule, and to check whether these data confirm currently prevailing opinions about the country's economic performance during these periods. More precisely, the chapter will briefly examine whether there is a correlation at the macro level between different patterns of property rights (especially, but not exclusively, regarding land) and Romanian agricultural performance.

Since the demise of communism, Romanian public debates have tended to declare the communist period a failure overall, and to idealize the accomplishments of the interwar period, regarded as something of a golden age terminated by foreign aggression, war and especially the Soviet-imposed communist takeover. With few exceptions, agricultural performance plays only a marginal role in narratives praising interwar Romania,[1] likely because any historian taking even a cursory look at the sources for the period would see that peasants had faced numerous economic difficulties, despite many of them having received land in the agrarian reform of 1918 to 1921. More central to general narratives is the assessment that communist agricultural policy was a complete failure. For example, Ioan Păun Otiman, a leading Romanian agronomist as well as member and secretary general of the Romanian Academy, stated flatly:

> Romania's agricultural situation . . . which reflects the agrarian politics of the years 1945–1989, leads us evidently to a sole conclusion: the collectivist system was a

> macro-economic and macro-social experiment without precedent in the history of humankind . . . which led, without doubt, to the economic bankruptcy, the material, professional and moral degradation of the peasantry, and the transformation of agriculture from a sub-system of the market economy to a subsistence sub-system at the national level.[2]

This narrative is consistent with both the conservative-inspired glorification of the peasant farmer as a repository of the sound values of the Romanian nation, and with the liberal emphasis on private property and strong property rights as major elements fostering economic progress and performance. It is thus an entrenched view, and one that is likely to persist, even without the backing of actual historical evidence. But what are the facts? The evidential trajectory is traced below.

Statistics on the Evolution of Romanian Agriculture in the Twentieth Century

Agriculture was a major sector of the Romanian economy in the twentieth century, but it gradually declined in favour of industry and services. This evolution can be measured with the help of both macro-economic indicators and data on the composition of the labour force. Table 2.1 presents data on the structure of national revenue, which was the main macro-economic indicator used in Romania before 1989.

Table 2.1 Romanian national revenue (percentages)

	Agriculture	Industry	Construction	Material services[3]
1920/1924	38.9	30.7	7.7	22.7
1925/1929	38.3	32.5	8.7	20.5
1930/1934	41.9	31.5	8.1	18.5
1935/1939	39.4	34.5	9.1	16.9
1950	27.8	44.0	6.0	12.1
1960	33.0	44.1	9.0	8.1
1970	19.5	60.3	9.8	6.1
1980	13.8	59.5	8.5	9.8
1989	15.2	58.1	7.2	8.7

Sources: Victor Axenciuc, *Introducere în istoria economică a României. Epoca modernă*, Bucharest, 1997, p.411; *Enciclopedia de istorie a României*, vol. 2, Bucharest, 2003, p.431.

The decline in agriculture's contribution to national revenue is characteristic of most twentieth-century economies. In fact, compared with other European economies, the decline in Romania was rather belated.[4] The decline also continued after 1989. Agriculture's share of the Romanian gross domestic product (GDP) had declined to 11 per cent by 2000 and 8.9 per cent in 2005.[5]

Compared with more developed European countries, a figure of 8.9 per cent in 2005 was high, a time when agriculture made up only 2.1 per cent of the overall GDP of the EU's then twenty-five member states.[6] The relatively large agricultural sector is a symptom of the economic backwardness of Romania. This is confirmed by the fact that the decline in the agricultural sector of the labour force (Table 2.2) lagged behind its share in overall economic performance.[7] Most of this decline occurred during the massive industrialization of the country from the 1950s to the 1970s. The economic crisis of the 1980s also slowed the structural change of the Romanian economy and society, and after 1989 a severe decline in the industrial labour force led to an increase in the overall percentage of the agrarian labour force, although this also declined in absolute numbers (Table 2.3).

Table 2.2 Structure of the Romanian labour force (percentages)

	Agriculture	Industry and constructions	Services
1912	79.5	8.2	12.3
1930	78.7	7.2	14.1
1950	74.3	14.2	11.5
1960	65.5	20.0	14.4
1970	49.4	30.9	19.9
1980	29.8	43.8	26.3
1989	27.9	45.1	27.1
2006	29.7	29.3	41.0

Sources: Axenciuc, *Introducere*, p.371; Nicolae N. Constantinescu, *Istoria economică a României*, vol. 2, Bucharest, 2000, p.422; *Anuarul Statistic 2007*, p.117 (retrieved 12 February 2009 from: www.insse.ro/cms/files/pdf/ro/cap3.pdf).

Table 2.3 Number of Romanian workers employed in agriculture

Year	Number of workers (in millions)
1930	8.23
1950	6.23
1960	6.25
1970	4.87
1980	3.09
1989	3.06
2006	2.84

Sources: Constantinescu, *Istoria economică*, p.422; *Anuarul Statistic 2007*, p.122 (retrieved 12 February 2009 from: www.insse.ro/cms/files/pdf/ro/cap3.pdf).

The disappearance of 2 million people from the labour force between 1930 and 1950 is attributable more to the territorial losses of the 1940s (Bessarabia, northern Bukovina, southern Dobrudja) than to the working population's shift towards industry in the 1930s and 1940s (see the percentages in Table 2.2). The shift from agriculture to industry occurred mainly in the 1960s and 1970s. Again, this shift came late in comparison to most other European countries, and it was too modest to place Romania in the ranks of the latter in this respect. As recently as the late 1980s, the proportion of agricultural workers in the Romanian labour force (27.9 per cent) was still almost double the European average (15 per cent).[8] In the 1990s, the decline in the agricultural labour force stopped temporarily due to severe cutbacks in industry, which, along with the distribution of land after the dissolution of cooperatives, pushed many industrial workers back into agriculture. This trend peaked in 2000 and has since reversed, especially because the possibility of labour migration abroad has attracted many agricultural workers, but also owing to job opportunities in the service sector.

More profound demographic movements will have a significant impact in the 2010s, as the smaller age cohorts born after 1990 join the labour force (vastly disproportionate in urban areas) and the larger age cohorts born in the late 1940s and early 1950s gradually retire. Therefore, by approximately 2020, agriculture's share of the labour force is expected to sink to less than 10 per cent, and, as in most European countries, agricultural production will be more capital intensive than labour intensive.

One of the particularities of Romania's agriculture has been the high share of arable production as a percentage of the value of total output (Table 2.4). This contrasts with that in more developed countries, where from the 1870s to the 1930s price trends favoured livestock production, causing a partial shift from crops to livestock.[9] Romanian agriculture's lack of response to this situation is due to the fact that a high proportion of agricultural output is for subsistence,

Table 2.4 Structure of Romanian agricultural production (percentages)

Year	Arable	Livestock
1920/1924	55	45
1925/1929	59	41
1930/1934	60	40
1935/1939	63	37
1945/1947	63	37
1950	65	35
1960	66	34
1970	62	38
1980	55	45
1989	54	46

Sources: Enciclopedia de istorie, vol. 2, pp.246f.; *Anuarul Statistic 1990*, p.406.

and that policies have favoured cereal production and exports, even in times of relatively unfavourable prices. This situation changed only in the 1960s, when, as we will see below, an increase in agricultural productivity allowed subsistence to be more easily achieved and prompted a national-level decision to shift gradually to agricultural products with higher added value.

Because securing subsistence was the most important incentive for producers (as well as national-level policy makers), food-producing crops (crops intended for human alimentation) were the largest sector of agricultural production. By the beginning of the twentieth century, Romania had exhausted most of its resources of available additional land, and a very large share of its population was engaged in agricultural production. Thus the possibility of extensive increases in production was limited, and production volumes depended heavily on variations in the yields of a small number of major food-producing crops. Traditionally, these yields were low compared with those of other European countries with similar environmental conditions. To augment yields, therefore, Romania did not have to invent new agricultural techniques, for significant increases in productivity could be obtained by using methods and techniques that had already been tried elsewhere in the world.

The data presented in Table 2.5 point especially to the severe drop caused by the First World War. Often attributed to the land reform carried out between 1918 and 1921, the decline in yields was also due to the destruction and loss of labour and horsepower caused by the war. The slow pace of recovery was further hindered by a global downturn in agricultural prices after 1926, which diminished revenues and inhibited investment in agricultural machinery and fertilizers. The interwar

Table 2.5 Average yields of major crops (quintals/hectare)

Period		Wheat	Maize	Barley	Oats	Rye	Beans	Potatoes
1911–1915	Old Kingdom	11.5	13.6	10.4	9.5	8.9	8.1	81.6
	Transylvania	11.0	15.2	12.7	11.5	10.3	8.9	76.3
1919–1924		8.9	11.0	8.0	7.9	8.1	7.0	78.2
1925–1929		9.2	10.6	9.3	9.0	9.3	7.0	98.7
1930–1934		9.0	10.9	8.7	8.7	9.1	8.1	87.7
1935–1939		10.4	10.8	8.0	8.0	9.7	5.3	88.5
1945–1947		5.6	6.4	3.4	3.3	3.8	2.5	44.8
1950		8.0	7.4	6.1	5.4	8.0	2.4	69.5
1960		12.11	15.5	15.2	10.5	12.11	7.3	102.7
1970		14.36	21.2	17.8	8.9	14.36	5.9	71.1
1980		27.8	32.1	29.0	9.2	27.8	6.1	134.1
1989		33.6	24.7	44.7	15.9	33.6	6.6	123.9

Sources: Victor Axenciuc, *Evoluţia economică a României: Cercetări statistico-istorice 1859–1947*, vol. 2, Bucharest, 1996, pp.525, 526, 579, 580; *Enciclopedia de istorie*, vol. 2, pp.230, 365.

period was one of limited agricultural growth worldwide,[10] and few European countries had worse yields than Romania. For example, Romanian wheat yields fell from 115 quintals per hectare before the First World War to 8.9 in the early 1920s, and rose only to 10.3 quintals per hectare between 1934 and 1938, while in most European countries the yields were higher in the 1930s than before the First World War. For example, in France average yields were 13.2 quintals per hectare in the period 1908 to 1912, rising to 14 quintals per hectare (1920 to 1922) and 15.6 quintals per hectare (1934 to 1938); in Germany the averages were 18.5 (1908 to 1912), 17 (1920 to 1922) and 22 (1934 to 1938); and in Bulgaria, 10.3 (1908 to 1912), 12 (1920 to 1922) and 12.5 (1934 to 1938).[11]

The Second World War also caused yields to plummet, but the recovery afterwards was stronger than in the interwar period, and after 1960 yields reached levels unprecedented in Romania. This growth coincided with a significant reduction in labour input, confirming that excess labour in agriculture had been more of a hindrance than an asset to agricultural production. Diminishing labour input was compensated for by increased inputs of machinery and fertilizers. Although only a comparatively small proportion of overall investment in the Romanian economy went towards agriculture (never amounting to more than 20 per cent),[12] the volume of capital investment rose significantly from the early 1950s to the mid 1980s, boosting irrigated areas from almost nothing to more than 3 million hectares in the late 1980s, and increasing the number of agricultural machines many times over (for example, between 1950 and 1989 the number of tractors used in agriculture grew more than eleven-fold and the number of mechanical seeding machines almost seven-fold, while self-propelled combine harvesters increased from fewer than 50 in 1950 to about 62,000 in 1989).[13] Given the conditions of vast farms made possible by collectivization, this improved capital input allowed significant growth in agricultural output (Tables 2.6 and 2.7).

Until the 1980s, growth in output was significant for practically all items, especially compared to the interwar years. Yet despite this, Romanian agriculture remained less productive than that of most comparable European countries. An international comparison of agricultural yields in twenty-four European countries

Table 2.6 Total production of main crops (in thousand tons)

	Grains (totals)	Wheat[14]	Maize	Potatoes	Vegetables (totals)	Fruit (totals)	Fodder
1950	5,149	2,402	2,101	1,601	1,126	401	2,024
1960	9,826	3,553	5,531	3,009	1,831	844	3,956
1970	10,631	3,399	6,535	2,064	2,004	1,174	10,274
1980	19,366	6,340	10,563	3,942	3,369	1,328	13,353
1989	18,379	7,935	6,762	4,420	3,727	1,580	18,057

Source: Anuarul statistic 1990, pp.278–81, 344–45, 356.

Table 2.7 Total production of major animal products

	Meat (thousand tons)	Milk (thousand hl)	Wool (thousand tons)	Eggs (millions)
1950	595	18,730	15,600	1,100
1960	943	26,670	21,850	2,355
1970	1,349	30,226	29,725	3,537
1980	2,408	42,127	37,376	6,259
1989	2,186	36,294	35,386	7,040

Source: Anuarul statistic 1990, p.384.

Table 2.8 Agricultural productivity in various European countries, 1940s to 1990s (annual output of a male agricultural labourer measured in millions of calories)

	1948/52	1958/62	1968/72	1978/82	1988/92
Austria	15.2	35.0	56.2	94.7	117.9
Belgium	29.1	56.9	96.4	172.9	243.6
Bulgaria	12.5	22.3	49.2	89.5	117.3
Czechoslovakia	21.8	35.5	52.7	73.2	91.3
Denmark	58.3	90.4	146.4	225.8	346.7
France	22.3	40.8	64.8	120.2	187.3
Germany	31.8	59.7	106.7	183.9	240.6
Greece	4.5	7.0	8.6	15.0	22.3
Hungary	12.3	21.6	35.9	71.3	90.7
Italy	9.2	18.4	31.2	58.1	83.2
Ireland	20.9	31.3	38.6	64.9	94.8
Poland	19.6	28.7	35.6	40.0	45.3
Portugal	6.6	8.8	18.6	25.5	44.5
Romania	8.6	12.5	23.2	52.9	59.2
Soviet Union	21.3	38.3	55.8	58.8	63.4
United Kingdom	36.6	62.1	85.1	111.7	139.7
Yugoslavia	18.6	33.9	40.3	75.4	88.4

Source: Paul Bairoch, *L'agriculture des pays développés, 1800 à nos jours: Production – Productivité – Rendements*, Paris, 1999, p.148.

in the late 1980s ranked Romania nineteenth with respect to grains and twenty-first with respect to milk production per cow.[15] More relevant is Paul Bairoch's productivity index, which uses five-year averages of millions of calories per male agricultural labourer (Table 2.8).

This productivity index reflects not only the evolution of agricultural output, but also the magnitude of the male labour input. Therefore, and unsurprisingly, almost half of the progress of the 1960s and 1970s was due to the reduction of the agricultural labour force. Meanwhile, the significant feminization of the

Romanian agricultural labour force means that Bairoch's productivity index, which computes productivity per male agricultural labourer, tends to produce a bias in favour of the performance of Romanian agriculture. Yet even under these conditions, and notwithstanding the real progress made, Romania has consistently remained one of the least agriculturally productive countries in Europe.

Determinants of Agricultural Performance

Why did Romanian agriculture not perform better? This question is even more germane when Romania's performance is compared with that of neighbouring Bulgaria, where agricultural growth was significantly greater.[16] I would argue that Romanian agriculture paid the price of late, slow and insufficient structural change. The labour to capital ratio and the use of available land to grow surpluses of grain were basic structures that changed too little, too late.

Very little positive transformation occurred in either of these respects during the interwar period. The plunge in production that followed the First World War – measured per capita, the production of grain declined from about 720 to 730 kg yearly in the period 1911 to 1915 (890 kilogrammes in the Old Kingdom, but only 580 to 590 kilogrammes in Transylvania and 300 kilogrammes in Bukovina) to 578 kilogrammes in 1919, and about 550 kilogrammes yearly in the period 1934 to 1938[17] – diminished the marketable share of agricultural output in favour of the share dedicated to subsistence. Population growth, along with the worldwide decline in agrarian prices in the late 1920s and first part of the 1930s due to the Great Depression, maintained an input structure dominated by a huge supply of human labour and small amounts of capital. Declining cash revenues put crushing financial strain on most peasant households, which were caught in a severe debt crisis in the early 1930s. The conversion of agricultural debts saved these peasants from losing land obtained through agrarian reform, but it led to the collapse of rural credit.[18]

Under these circumstances, only a few peasants were able to invest in machines and fertilizers,[19] and state resources available for improving the labour to capital ratio of Romanian agriculture were also limited. Pressure to secure subsistence while also providing surplus grain for export determined the allocation of an ever-increasing proportion of land for grain cultivation throughout most of the interwar period, despite various plans and proposals to diminish the share of grains and to intensify agricultural production.[20]

After the Second World War, general conditions changed (Table 2.10). The late 1940s and most of the 1950s were an era of recovery from the severe drop in production caused by the war and by the turmoil of system change. At the same time, collectivization changed decision-making processes so that direct producers had less say in allocating land and resources, and the state assumed a larger role in

Table 2.9 Relative amount of land used for arable production, 1919 to 1939 (averages as percentages)

Period	Total	Grains	Other food crops	Industrial plants	Fodder	Fallow
1919–1924	100.0	79.1	2.8	1.7	4.0	12.4
1925–1929	100.0	85.3	3.4	3.1	5.0	3.2
1930–1934	100.0	84.4	3.5	2.8	5.4	3.9
1935–1939	100.0	83.3	3.6	3.6	5.5	4.0

Source: Axenciuc, *Evoluţia economică*, p.53.

Table 2.10 Relative amounts of land used for arable production, 1950 to 1989 (average as percentages)

Year	Total	Grains	Other food crops	Industrial plants	Fodder	Fallow
1950	100.0	73.9	6.4	8.8	8.1	2.8
1960	100.0	72.0	6.4	9.2	11.2	1.2
1970	100.0	60.6	7.0	11.3	14.5	6.6
1980	100.0	65.9	7.3	14.8	8.7	3.3
1989	100.0	61.2	9.7	16.2	11.7	1.2

Sources: Calculations are based on data from *Anuarul statistic 1990*, pp.265, 274–77; Ion Bold, Vasile Niţă, Petre Săbădeanu, *Revoluţia industrială în agricultura României*, Bucharest, 1980, p.165.

planning economic processes in agriculture. Under the new circumstances, a shift from grains to other, more rewarding crops was theoretically easier to enforce, but actual change in the use of land was limited and discontinuous. Areas allocated for other crops, especially industrial plants, were increased somewhat, but this can hardly qualify as a significant shift. In fact, the communist leadership did not seriously consider a radical change and continued, while paying occasional lip service to the merits of producing industrial crops and animal products, to insist on the pre-eminence of grains.[21]

This conservatism testifies not only to a lack of vision, but also to a certain intuition that grains cultivated on large areas suited the regime better. Vegetables, fruit and animal breeding, which demanded a more individual focus, might have undermined the existing leadership and organizational structures of socialist agriculture. Therefore, it is unsurprising that land allocated for vineyards and orchards, which had increased in the 1960s, decreased significantly in the 1970s and 1980s.[22] Meanwhile, allocating most of the available land for grains had side effects. Significant areas suffered processes of soil degradation, especially erosion and the accumulation of salt.[23] The situation became particularly severe in the

1980s, when soil degradation was aggravated by diminishing investment in soil conservation and inconsistent supplies of inputs (replacement parts, fuels and energy) for irrigation systems and agriculture in general.

Institutions and Property Rights: How Much Did They Matter?

The contradictory performance of Romanian socialist agriculture leads to my second major question: How did specific forms of property rights and related arrangements impact on overall production? Or, as Giovanni Federico put it, 'How much did institutional change affect agricultural performance?'[24]

Institutions are crucial in determining whether economic factors are (re) combined to allow maximization of the output expected by economic agents and/or society as a whole (whose preferences and criteria, in turn, determine the nature of the output). It follows that the nature and quality of institutions significantly impacts upon economic performance. Most theorists would argue that modern property rights and functional markets maximize performance, whereas almost all other institutional arrangements foster only suboptimal performance. How does the experience of twentieth-century Romanian agriculture fit into this picture?

The land reform of 1918 to 1921 was intended to alleviate social polarization in the Romanian countryside and, by helping to establish viable small peasant holdings, to increase output and bring prosperity to the largest part of Romanian society.[25] The outcome was far from these expectations. The property structure that resulted from land reform was structurally unfit for boosting production.

Almost three-quarters of peasant households were too small to be economically viable. Besides, the provisions of the land reform prevented the selling of land received at the time, so there were only a few opportunities to concentrate landownership. The land market was liberalized only for a short while under

Table 2.11 Landholding in interwar Romania, 1930 to 1935

Size of landholdings (ha)	percentage of landholdings	percentage of arable land
<1	18.6	1.6
1–3	33.6	11.1
3–5	22.8	15.3
5–10	17.1	20.0
10–20	5.5	12.0
20–50	1.7	7.8
50–100	0.3	4.5
>100	0.4	27.7

Source: Axenciuc, *Evoluţia economică*, p.183.

the so-called Mihalache Law of 1929, but when most peasants were in danger of losing their land due to being unable to pay their debts, the state interfered and enacted a debt conversion which practically blocked rural credit and thus the land market. These inconsistencies in enforcing modern property rights combined first with the effects of war and afterwards with those of the Great Depression and of demographic growth in the countryside in reducing both production and overall welfare.[26] Interwar Romania thus illustrates the situation postulated by Federico for 'really perverse cases': 'the reduction in output might be so great as to overcome the redistribution effect and also cause the peasants to be worse off'.[27]

After consolidating its political takeover, the communist regime began in 1949 to radically change the institutional framework of agriculture. Soviet-inspired collectivization determined a major shift in landownership, which also caused significant changes to the structure of agricultural economic enterprises and to the processes of decision making. In 1962, when collectivization was officially completed, the proportion of individual peasant holdings was reduced to about a quarter of all agricultural land, mostly in highland areas unsuited to large-scale arable production (see Tables 2.12 and 2.13). While most peasant landholdings were extremely small, generally just a plot used for gardening close to the house, the recurrent restructuring of cooperatives and state farms determined a pattern of increasing 'gigantism', stimulated by the communist regime, which reduced the number of units in order to achieve economies of scale, to ease supervision by the centre and to enhance the economic viability of cooperatives.[28]

Moreover, Romania did not join other East European states in changing the management patterns of socialist agriculture. For example, in Hungary, the logic of class struggle against the kulaks was gradually abandoned after 1956, technical competence began to prevail in the management of cooperatives, the revenues of agricultural labourers were linked less to the number of working days and more to output, prices for agricultural products were increased, and cooperatives were allowed to decide how to use the revenues they obtained. These reforms intensified in the late 1960s, making socialist agriculture in Hungary an unmitigated success; in other East European countries, like Czechoslovakia, Bulgaria and the German Democratic Republic, the reforms were less audacious, but nevertheless tried to stimulate the efficient functioning of state farms and cooperatives. In Romania, in spite of the rhetoric of introducing a 'new economic mechanism' and of implementing a 'revolution' in agriculture, the use of economic incentives was limited, official prices for agricultural products remained rather low, and the state tried to compensate for shortages by asking the peasants to sell products from their private plots at unfavourable prices. Under these circumstances, both cooperatives and state farms shared the disadvantages of 'distant ownership', and agricultural labourers cared little about the products owned by the state or by the cooperatives. To

Table 2.12 Landownership under socialism as a percentage of total agricultural land

	1962	1980	1989
State agricultural enterprises	11.8	13.6	13.9
Cooperatives	62.5	60.6	60.7
Individual landholdings	25.7	25.8	25.4

Source: Nicolae N. Constantinescu, *Istoria economică*, p.190.

Table 2.13 Average size of enterprises in the socialist sector of Romanian agriculture (in hectares)

	1962	1980	1989
State agricultural enterprises	3,072	5,003	5,000
Cooperatives	1,683	2,259	2,826

Source: Nicolae N. Constantinescu, *Istoria economică*, p.191f.

sum up, the socialist system provided some predictability in the development of farms and allowed the pooling of a certain amount of investment in machinery and in irrigation, but also fostered models of non-economic behaviour, at both the management and the labour levels.

Nevertheless, and independently of the slowdown and even the decline of the 1980s, the overall performance of Romanian agriculture under socialism was better than the levels achieved during the interwar period. Agriculture was not the most dynamic branch of the Romanian economy, but output increased and supported the processes of industrialization and urbanization, that is, the structural change of the Romanian economy and society. Thus, agricultural growth was crucial for the overall development of Romania, but the price of this development was the subordination of agriculture to the imperatives of the socialist command economy, and especially the setting of a price system and of other mechanisms which drained resources from agriculture to other segments of the economy. For a time, the shift of resources did not diminish performance – one can argue in fact that the decline in labour input was even a necessary condition for improving productivity – but at the same time the elimination of market stimuli meant that on the demand side the only factor generating growth was political command, and that demand-driven incentives emerged only at the margin of the official system. This situation is consistent with the basic pattern of the socialist economy as a supply-orientated system,[29] but at the same time it prevented the sustainable development of agriculture.

Summing up, Romanian agriculture experienced some periods of growth during the twentieth century, which alternated with periods of stagnation and even decline. The institutional framework was – excepting some short-lived attempts during the national-peasant government of 1928 to 1931 – never designed to favour the market-oriented development of agriculture. Therefore, most of the growth depended not on demand-based incentives, but on the capacity of agricultural producers to adapt to generally unfavourable economic conditions and on the more or less coordinated policies of the state to increase output.

Notes

1. On these narratives, see Bogdan Murgescu, 'The Economic Performance of Interwar Romania: Golden Age Myth and Statistical Evidence', *Jahrbücher für Geschichte und Kultur Südosteuropa* 6 (2004), pp.43–64.
2. Ion Păun Otiman, *Viaţa rurală a României în secolul al XX-lea: Un secol de iluzii, dezamăgiri şi speranţe (sau drama satului şi a ţăranului roman)*, Timişoara, 2005, p.12. Western specialists often concur with this harsh verdict on Romanian socialist agriculture. For example, Endre Antal found that, during the 1980s, Romanian agriculture was plagued by exaggerated centralism in planning and management, bureaucratization, deficient professional training, low technical levels, shortages of raw materials, fuel and replacement pieces, and especially by the lack of initiative on the part of direct producers, who were not motivated to contribute to optimizing productive processes. See Endre Antal, *Beteiligung der RGW-Länder am Weltagrarhandel in den achtziger Jahren*, Berlin, 1992, p.83.
3. This category includes transportation, communications, and domestic and foreign trade.
4. Wolfram Fischer, *Handbuch der europäischen Wirtschafts- und Sozialgeschichte*, vol. 6, Stuttgart, 1987, pp.95f.
5. Sándor Gardó, 'Rumänien: Wirtschaft in Transformation', in Thede Kahl, Michael Metzeltin and Mihai-Răzvan Ungureanu (eds), *Rumänien*, Vienna, 2006, p.659.
6. Ibid.
7. Paul Bairoch has argued that the number of *male* agricultural labourers as a percentage of the total active male labour force is a better indicator than agricultural labour as a percentage of the total active labour force because the real input of women's labour in agriculture varies greatly, and this variation is not captured by official statistics. See Paul Bairoch, *L'agriculture des pays développés, 1800 à nos jours: Production – Productivité – Rendements*, Paris, 1999, pp.29f. Although I agree with most of his arguments, the method he proposes would imply 'guesstimating' some of the data, without significantly changing the image conveyed by the statistics.
8. See Constantin Grigorescu, *Nivelul dezvoltării economico-sociale a României în context european, 1989*, Bucharest, 1993, pp.136f. Considering only the male labour force, the difference is somewhat smaller: 21 per cent in Romania versus a European average of 14.6 per cent (see Paul Bairoch, *L'agriculture*, p.32), but this situation reflects the increasing feminization of the agricultural labour force under communism, when many rural male workers commuted to industrial jobs in nearby cities while most rural women worked at both agricultural labour and household-related activities.
9. For global trends, see Giovanni Federico, *Feeding the World: An Economic History of Agriculture, 1800–2000*, Princeton/Oxford, 2005, pp.26–28.
10. Bairoch, *L'agriculture*, pp.14–19; Federico, *Feeding the World*, pp.17–19.
11. Bairoch, *L'agriculture*, p.108; Fischer, *Handbuch*, p.109.
12. *Anuarul statistic 1990*, Bucharest, 1991, p.526f.
13. Ibid., p.268f.

14. This category includes rye after 1950.
15. Grigorescu, *Nivelul*, pp.70–80. This poor performance was due largely to (still) below-average capital inputs in Romanian agriculture. Romania used only 1.5 tractors per cultivated hectare (compared to a European average of 3.5) and 117.7 kilogrammes of fertilizers per hectare (versus a European average of 157.4) (ibid., pp.82, 87f.).
16. For a comparison of Romania with Denmark, Ireland and Serbia, see Bogdan Murgescu, *România şi Europa: Acumularea decalajelor economice (1500–2010)*, Bucharest, 2010.
17. Victor Axenciuc, *Introducere în istoria economică a României. Epoca modernă*, Bucharest, 1997, p.254; the average for 1911 to 1915 and the figure for 1919 were calculated on the basis of the data in Victor Axenciuc, *Evoluţia economică a României: Cercetări statistico-istorice 1859–1947*, vol. 2, Bucharest, 1996, pp.516, 521, 645, 654.
18. Dumitru Şandru, *Creditul agricol în România (1918–1944)*, Bucharest, 1985.
19. According to Virgil Madgearu, both imports and the internal production of agricultural machines and tools declined during the Great Depression. See Madgearu, *Evoluţia economiei româneşti: După războiul mondial*, Bucharest, 1995, p.59. After 1935, when peasant revenues began to rise, high import taxes hindered imports of agricultural machinery (ibid., p.287).
20. Virgil Madgearu, *Evoluţia economiei*, p.67. For the evolution of Madgearu's concepts, see also Dietmar Müller, *Agrarpopulismus in Rumänien: Programmatik und Regierungspraxis der Bauernpartei und der Nationalbäuerlichen Partei Rumäniens in der Zwischenkriegszeit*, St Augustin, 2001; Keith Hitchins, *The Identity of Romania*, Bucharest, 2003, pp.125–44.
21. For example, the programme adopted by the Eleventh Congress of the Romanian Communist Party in 1974 stated, 'Cereals, especially wheat and maize, will continue to retain the main place in arable production' (*Programul Partidului Comunist Român de făurire a societăţii socialiste multilateral dezvoltate şi înaintare a României spre communism*, Bucharest, 1975, p.77).
22. The total area of vineyards comprised 311,000 hectares in 1960, 346,700 hectares in 1970, 309,000 hectares in 1979 and only 277,500 hectares in 1989; orchards followed a similar pattern, with 214,000 hectares in 1960, 431,800 hectares in 1970, 355,000 hectares in 1979 and only 318,000 hectares in 1989. See Ion Bold, Vasile Niţă, Petre Săbădeanu, *Revoluţia industrială în agricultura României*, Bucharest, 1980, p.165; *Anuarul statistic 1990*, p.265.
23. According to Endre Antal, soil degradation affected about 40 per cent of agricultural areas. See Antal, *Beteiligung*, p.81; different figures, though of similar magnitude, are found in Grigorescu, *Nivelul*, p.74.
24. Federico, *Feeding the World*, p.143.
25. See especially David Mitrany, *The Land and the Peasant in Rumania: The War and Agrarian Reform (1917–1921)*, New York, 1930; Dumitru Şandru, *Reforma agrară din 1921 în România*, Bucharest, 1975.
26. For the inconsistencies of Romanian policies in the interwar period, the best analysis is still Henry L. Roberts, *Rumania: Political Problems of an Agrarian State*, London/Oxford, 1951; for the impact of the Great Depression, see also Vasile Bozga, *Criza agrară în România dintre cele două războaie mondiale*, Bucharest, 1975.
27. Federico, *Feeding the World*, p.175.
28. David Turnock, *The Economy of East Central Europe, 1815–1989. Stages of Transformation in a Peripheral Region*, London/New York, 2006, p.354.
29. János Kornai, *The Socialist System: The Political Economy of Communism*, Oxford, 1992.

PART II

PROPERTY BETWEEN LAW AND POLITICS

3

Property in East Central European Legal Culture

Herbert Küpper

Property and Legal Culture

Property is not a natural phenomenon but the result of human activities, that is, a product of culture. Therefore, property can and needs to be regarded as such. In the European context, property is considered to be the legal dominance of a person (or a group of persons) over an object. This contrasts with the natural or physical dominance known as possession. In this system, the possessor is the person who 'has' the object – the driver of a rented car, for instance. On the other hand, the proprietor is the person to whom the object 'belongs', in our example the rental company that rents the car to the driver (to the possessor).

The legal difference between property and possession goes back to Roman law. Older legal systems, as far as we know, treated both phenomena as the same thing.[1] To recognize the difference between property and possession presupposes that legal culture has achieved a certain level of development. Legal thinking must be prepared to acknowledge that natural and legal dominance over a thing are not the same fact, and the law must be in a position to attach different consequences to these different facts.[2]

Property consists in the legal assignment of an object to a person, and is therefore a product of the law that can only exist in a society that has law – that is, a legal system. Where there is no law, property cannot exist; only possession can. Having decided to create the legal institution of property, a legal system needs to answer questions on several topics:

- Content of property: Which things can be owned (that is, are suitable objects for a property relationship), and which cannot? What is the content of the property relationship between a person and an object? Does the proprietor have a universal right vis-à-vis the object (full property), or only partial rights?
- Limitations of property: Which powers, rights and privileges cannot be derived from property? Do these limitations serve the interests of other persons, such as neighbours, or do they protect society at large and public interests?
- Acquisition of property: How can the individual acquire property of a given object? By sale, inheritance, donation, physical manufacturing or processing of the object,[3] acts of state[4] or natural events?[5] If the purchaser derives the property from a previous proprietor, does it suffice that the purchaser believes the vendor to have been the proprietor (bona fide acquisition), or is it necessary that the vendor indeed was the proprietor?
- Protection of property: How can the proprietor defend his property against interferences? Is the proprietor entitled to self-help, or does the state protect property, for example through the police or courts?
- Withdrawal and social duties of property: Is society (the state) entitled to take away a certain object from its proprietor, such as in the execution of some public interest? Is society (the state) entitled to use a certain object against the will of its proprietor, such as in the execution of some public interest? If so, what is the procedure, and what guarantees does the proprietor have?

A legal system engaged in creating the legal institution of property has further aspects to address, but compared to the questions enumerated above, these additional aspects are of minor importance. They concern, for instance, the risks related to the object: Who bears the risk that the object is destroyed? Who bears the risk that the object damages other persons or objects? How can adjacent objects be delimited in order to define property rights? This is especially important in the case of objects that form a natural unit with neighbouring objects, such as plots of land. What is to happen if the brook that delimits two pieces of land changes its course? What if a storm destroys the boundary posts?

All these questions lead to the basic decision a legal system has to take when accepting private property: Where is the limit between the private use and the public obligations of the objects in private property?

The rules referring to the object of property and its relationship to the proprietor and to the public interest (to the state) are called the property order. The property order regulates all questions arising from the fact that given objects are assigned to a given person as that person's property. Apart from this individual aspect of the property order, a second collective aspect refers to the distribution of potential objects of property within society: who owns what, and how much? This question of the distribution of various goods among individuals, social groups and so on may be called the assets order. In Marxist theory, the assets order is termed property relations. Law may regulate the assets order as well. There is, however, no necessity for the law to do so because society may leave the distribution of property to factors such as the market. If there is to be property as a legal institution, the legal system must have a property order. Whether the assets order, too, is to be ruled by law is a political question whose answer depends on the legal and political culture of the given society. Since the nineteenth century, many states have influenced the asset order in order to shape the social order.

Property in the Various Fields of Law

The modern legal systems of Europe or under the influence of European systems divide the mass of law into various fields. The most important fields of law are the 'classical' ones: private law, criminal law and public law. Both the delimitations between these fields and more detailed subdivisions vary from state to state and within time.

The legal rules relating to property, designed to answer the questions stated above, do not concentrate on a single field of law. Property is instead governed by rules that pertain to many different fields of law. Its most important aspects are outlined below.

Constitutional Law

Constitutions protect property as a basic right. A constitution primarily regulates the relationship between the proprietor and the state (or example, with a view to the state's powers to expropriate) and the institutional guarantees in objective law. These guarantees oblige the state to create and shape a property order through legislation. If the law is to regulate the assets order as well, its basis can generally be found in the constitution.

A constitution gives some fundamental indications as to basic decisions between the private use and the public obligations of property. In most cases, these indications are – like constitutional provisions in general – highly abstract and vague. Therefore, they both can be and need to be put into concrete legislative or administrative decisions.

Private Law

Traditionally, private law is the body of rules that governs relationships between private individuals. Its basis is the equal rank of the parties concerned. One of the core fields of private law is what has since early modern times been addressed as *ius rerum* and what today's Continental legal systems call *droit de bien*, *Sachenrecht*, *prawo rzeczowe*, *věcné právo*, *dologi jog* or *dreptul real*.[6] It deals with the legal relationship between an individual and an object (real right). The most important real right is property. Property law contains rules on the content of property as well as on the proprietor's relationship vis-à-vis other private individuals, such as the proprietor's defence against interference by a private party or the property's limitations in respect of other private individuals' rights (for example, neighbour law). The transfer of property between private parties is another part of property law. Apart from property, the *ius rerum* contains other real rights. These convey less comprehensive rights to their owner; therefore German legal science defines them as 'limited real rights' (*beschränkte dingliche Rechte*). Examples are mortgage or registered (that is, real) rights of way. Finally, rules on possession form a part of *ius rerum*.

Within the coordinates of private use and public obligations, private law deals primarily with private use and its limitations arising from the rights of other private parties.

Administrative Law

Administrative law regulates public administration and its legal relations with private individuals. Within this framework, property may be relevant in various fields, for example in the law of public property, which deals with the special features of objects of state property or in public use. Other aspects of property in administrative law are the rules on procedures for the protection of private property or possession, for instance on whether the police are to expel squatters so that the proprietor of a building can take possession, or rules on the acquisition of property by an act of state in public auctions. Public registers of real rights such as cadastres, land books and ship, plane or mortgage registries are of an administrative nature, even if in many countries the relevant rules form a part of private law by way of tradition.

However, the most important role of administrative law, with a view to property, is the delimitation of the rights of the proprietor. This delimitation against other private parties is the role of private law, whereas administrative law defines and delimits the proprietor's rights with regard to public interests and the protection of the public at large. To do this, administrative law orders, regulates or forbids numerous forms of the use of property. Road traffic law, for example, regulates the use of private vehicles operated on a public road, and no proprietor may drive on the wrong side of the road with reference to their rights as proprietors. Environmental protection law forbids or regulates numerous ways of destroying one's property. The right of shop owners to transfer property of their goods to customers is limited by the rules on opening hours. In some cases, such as narcotics or weapons designed for warfare, the relevant administrative law forbids the proprietor any transfer of title without a licence.

Another field of relevant administrative rules pertains to the use of private property in the public interest. The strongest form of this use is the taking of an object (expropriation); milder forms are the rights to use private property for certain public interests, such as public rights of way on private land. These rules are most relevant for landed property because one piece of land cannot be as easily replaced by another as a chattel can be in, say, planning location lines for traffic routes or energy pipelines. Administrative law deals primarily with the public obligations of private property by limiting the private proprietor's rights in the public interest.

Criminal Law

One of the traditional core fields of criminal law is the protection of private property. The Ten Commandments forbade interventions into other persons' property – 'Thou shalt not steal!' (Exod. 20: 15) – and today all legal systems protect property by defining crimes against property (theft, robbery, change of boundary marks and so on). Laws against other crimes such as fraud or blackmail protect private property indirectly. On the other hand, criminal law is also used to punish proprietors' use of their property outside its legal limitations (such as the conversion of seized objects, bankruptcy crimes or environmental crimes).

Property may be of relevance in still more fields of law, such as economic, labour or tax law. However, the basics of the property order are usually laid down in the fields of constitutional, private, administrative and criminal law, as mentioned above.

Property in West European Legal Culture

Before dealing with the special features of property in the legal culture of East Central Europe, a look at the West European legal culture is warranted for two reasons. First, from a historical perspective, the legal culture of East Central Europe has been part of West European legal culture since its emergence in the heyday of the Middle Ages, assuming a very basic differentiation between a Latin West European and a Greek East European culture.[7] East Central Europe on the whole always belonged to the Latin half of the continent, and therefore its legal culture is part of West European Latin legal culture. This embeddedness was disrupted – or interrupted, according to interpretation – during the decades of socialist rule, but since the fall of communism the legal cultures of East Central Europe have expressed their willingness to be part of Western (Latin) law again. The 'return to Europe' that initiated the change of systems included the legal sphere. In this sense, West European legal culture is not only the historic starting point of East Central European states and societies, but also their current target destination.

Second, legal culture – like any other part of culture – is specific to a certain area and a certain time. All statements on a given cultural phenomenon bear values and perspectives of the culture from which the statement emerges.[8] This banal insight into the limits of the objectivity of scientific statements, at least in the field of human sciences, including legal science, makes it seem appropriate to analyse one's own cultural background regarding the phenomenon at issue. This may reduce the danger that one's own cultural perspective will distort an examination of another culture.

The Origin: Roman Law

Roman law is the origin of modern European law in many respects, including those of property and possession. As the first known system in legal history to codify the difference between property and possession, advanced Roman legal culture not only developed scientifically sound, practical concepts for both legal phenomena but also created a precise terminology. Not even Greek law had unequivocal words for property and proprietor, but Roman law was in the position to differentiate precisely between *proprietarius* (or *dominus*) and *possessor*.

Roman law is moreover the source of the principle of comprehensive property. This principle means that the proprietor has full and all-embracing legal power over the object that is their property. Roman proprietors could do as they pleased with their property: possess it, use it, exclude everyone else from its possession and use, give it to others with or without remuneration (such as lease it), dispose of it (transfer the title to others or accept limited real rights on it, for example) or destroy it.[9] Thus, in Roman law the proprietor enjoyed more freedom than in the other contemporary legal systems, although the rights of neighbours and public law limited the proprietor's rights in Roman law too. Still, Roman comprehensive property indicated substantial progress over older legal systems, in which the proprietor had only an exhaustive bundle of single entitlements, limited by social commitments and embedded in an asset order that relegated certain objects solely to collective property (those of the clan, for example). The principle of comprehensive property also means that there is no proprietor of higher rank (such as the emperor, the temple or the state) above the proprietor. Unlike feudalism, Roman law contained no recognition of layered property; rather, all the proprietor's rights were united in one hand, unless the individual proprietor themselves disposed differently in a concrete case.

Individual property is another basic principle of Roman law. This principle was also a break with older legal traditions, although Egyptians and Greeks seem to have come close to some principle of this kind. Individual property means that ownership of a given object is vested in an individual person. This individualist concept of property is opposed to a property and assets order that regards certain goods – mostly land, sometimes cattle, water or even goods of higher value – as collective property, that is, property of society at large, of the family clan, of religious institutions or of other groups. The consequence of collective property is that these objects cannot be disposed of because this is either forbidden explicitly or bound to insurmountable hurdles such as the consent of all members of the clan. These objects therefore do not take part in the circulation of goods and cannot serve as security for credit because the creditor has no means of seizure in the case of non-payment. Compulsory collective ownership of important goods guarantees existence of the capital stock for the group, but forces its members into subsistence husbandry and a barter economy.

By contrast, the Roman principle of individual property makes any object a potential commodity by attributing it to one single proprietor who is given full power to dispose of it. This principle did not mean, however, that one object could not have more than one proprietor. In individual cases, joint property of more than one person, such as spouses, a community of heirs or a company, was possible. Such joint property was the result of an individual disposition and therefore a consequence of the freedom awarded by the principles of comprehensive and individual property. The concerned parties' ability to undo it at any time is the fundamental difference between joint property and the older compulsory collective property.

Thus, at the end of Roman legal history we find a very individualist property order that gave individual proprietors a wide range of freedom to deal with their property at will. Alongside this individualist property order is a liberal asset order with little influence on the distribution of property in society. However, as slaves, liberated slaves, foreigners, women and children had limited or no legal capacity, and therefore limited or no powers to become a proprietor, this individualist liberalism was reserved to quite a small part of Roman society.

Turning Away from the Origin: Medieval Feudal Law

The comprehensive individual property of Roman law presupposed a certain type of proprietor: a personally, socially and politically independent citizen such as the *pater familias*. This sociological precondition ended with the decline of the Roman Empire, and the Roman citizen system was replaced by the medieval feudal system, which was far more concerned with the various groups in which every person was embedded than with the individual person.

This new social system changed the property order, as well as the asset order. Land, as the most important good, was no longer an object of comprehensive property, but of a hierarchy of layered partial rights linked to personal legal relationships. Proprietorship of land was replaced by *seigniory*. The supreme seignior was the king. Seignior must not be confused with proprietor because the medieval seignior had (in modern terminology) both private and public rights.

To put it simply, the king concluded contracts of allegiance with his vassals. The vassal owed the king loyalty and service; the king owed the vassal protection and welfare. Allegiance was in principle an institution of the law of persons, but had a component of 'real right' as well: the fief.[10] The lord fulfilled his duty to provide for his vassals' welfare by lending the vassals certain assets – mostly land, sometimes sinecures and similar rights – for their use (fief). That is, the vassal was awarded not property but only certain rights to use the assets, and in the early days of feudalism the lord could revoke the fief at any time. A vassal's 'real right' to the fief depended on the personal relationship of allegiance: if one party terminated the allegiance, the vassal's right to use the fief ended. The king's vassals, who were neither willing nor able to cultivate the land themselves, lent the land they had received as fief to their sub-vassals. Thus, the land was handed down through the feudal hierarchy until it reached the lowest layer: the farmers. In most regions of Europe, farmers had lost their personal freedom, and therefore could neither be vassals nor receive a fief; hence, the farmer did not receive land in a relationship of allegiance but in a relationship of bondage. Thus, feudal property was not individual and comprehensive, but related to estates and layered accordingly. This was especially true for the most important good: the land.

The feudal pyramid functioned in the countryside. In other areas, different economic and social orders demanded different property and assets orders. One such area consisted of regions where farmers remained personally free, like the central Swiss valley or the Frisian lands. Free farmers had their own land, although comprehensive property was a rarity even for them. In these regions, the local community took over some functions of the seignior and assumed a certain superior propriety over the land to ensure that land use was not contrary to the public interest.[11]

Another area with a different social order was the Church. After the fall of the Roman Empire, the Roman Church had partially adopted the Empire's bureaucratic structures and, despite all its sub-organizations, considered itself a uniform institution with a uniform legal personality. It had conserved some basic knowledge of Roman law, which in part was the foundation of ecclesiastical law. Among these surviving features of Roman law were the principles of the property order. On the one hand, many clergymen were part of the feudal pyramid; in Germany, for example, many ecclesiastics were princes of the Reich, and as such vassals of the emperor or of the emperor's vassals. On the other hand, the Church was an institution both independent of the persons acting in and for it and permanent in time. Such an institution has a 'natural' interest in a property order that allows for individual and comprehensive property independent of feudal, personal or other limitations. This is why the Roman Church advocated the reintroduction of the Roman principle of freedom of testament.

In early feudal legal orders, succession was governed by fixed rules. It was in the Church's interest that any proprietor should be able to leave property to the Church, either as a donation during their lifetime or by testament. Ecclesiastical law therefore acknowledged donations and testaments in favour of the Church, and these elements of an individual comprehensive property order gradually pervaded the customary law of European peoples.

This process was aided by the reception of Roman law starting in the high Middle Ages. Central parts of the *Codex Iustinianus*, a compilation of late Roman law drawn up in Byzantium between AD 528 and 534, were unearthed in the eleventh century. This text became the starting point for the emergence of legal science in Latin Western Europe. The Church supported this process, and many law schools had their origin in ecclesiastical pedagogical institutions. The outcome was a pan-European scholarly law known to any educated lawyer from Norway to Sicily and Portugal to Poland.[12] At that time, East Central Europe was an integral part of the Latin culture of Western Europe, and its universities in Prague, Kraków and Pécs took an active part in teaching Roman law to European students.

Another alien element in the world of medieval feudal law – besides regions of free peasants, the Church and scholarly Roman law – was the cities. There, citizens did not enjoy full personal freedom but were embedded in various corporations and associations. Within cities, however, the institutions of allegiance and fiefs did not function, and an individual comprehensive property emerged *in nucleo*. In medieval towns, plots of land could be quite freely sold and bought, inherited and donated, although there were sometimes limitations on who was allowed to acquire landed property within the walls of a city. Italian cities developed their property order out of Roman legal traditions, whereas north of the Alps indigenous customs were used to develop an urban property order. This development was quite probably furthered by clergymen and municipal magistrates, who in many cases had studied Roman law at university. The law in Magdeburg, as well as South German city laws, influenced cities in large parts of East Central Europe, where local city laws thus codified a property order similar to that developed in Germany.[13]

A Return to Origins: The Bourgeois Social and Legal System

In early modern times, the feudal world of Western Europe slowly developed into a more urban society based on trade and craftsmanship instead of agriculture. The individual was rediscovered, money pervaded the rural economy, and the

Reformation so delegitimized the spiritual branch of power that the state had the chance to become the sole source of legitimate power. The process of creating a territorial state with a monopoly of power culminated in the absolutist system, which strongly influenced the development of both the law and the property order.

In the seventeenth century, all cultural and economic preconditions for a return to the individual and comprehensive property of Roman law were present. At the same time, the absolutist state 'discovered' the law and assumed responsibility for it. Until then, the legal system had consisted of multifarious local and personal laws based on custom or royal grant (privilege) and existing alongside, but hardly ever in contact with, scholarly Roman law. The absolutist state, however, assumed the task of creating the law (statute legislation) and executing it (courts of law). As a result, both the definition of the property order and its practical application became matters in the competence of the state.

The social and legal system of the absolutist state continued numerous feudal elements that limited the emergence of an individual and comprehensive property law. The breakthrough was the French Revolution, which created a bourgeois legal and property order.[14] Article 544 of the French Civil Code of 1804 (the so-called Napoleonic Code) says: 'La propriété est le droit de jouir et disposer des choses de la manière la plus absolue, pourvu qu'on n'en fasse pas un usage prohibé par les lois ou par les règlements'. This provision creates both comprehensive property ('de la manière la plus absolue') and – for want of limitations in other fields of law, such as in the law of persons – free individual property, and puts this basis of private use under the reserve of a limitation in the public interest as defined in legal norms ('prohibé par les lois ou par les règlements').[15]

This example was followed by the second central bourgeois codification after that of France, namely the Austrian Civil Code of 1811 (the Allgemeine Bürgerliche Gesetzbuch).[16] Its property order starts with 'property in the objective sense' in Section 353: 'Alles, was jemanden zugehört, alle seine körperlichen und unkörperlichen Sachen, heißen sein Eigentum'. The subsequent section defines 'property in the subjective sense': 'Als ein Recht betrachtet, ist Eigentum die Befugnis, mit der Substanz und den Nutzungen einer Sache nach Willkür zu schalten, und jeden anderen davon auszuschließen'. This rule too defines the individual and comprehensive property open to everyone (jemanden). Unlike the French code, Austrian law conserved a larger number of feudal elements in its property order. Some of these were contained in the German Allgemeine Bürgerliche Gesetzbuch (BGB), others in other statutes or in customary law. They deviated from the liberal principles in sections 353 and 354 of the Austrian code, especially with respect to landed property. Still, the Austrian code may be considered as a truly bourgeois property order.

Other West European countries followed this development by either evolution (Great Britain, the Scandinavian countries) or forced or voluntary adoption of French revolutionary legislation.[17] Still, many countries' property orders conserved various feudal elements, especially the entailed estates that create a collective property of a family or clan (including, in a way, future generations), that is, property that the members of the family may use but cannot dispose of, and whose inheritance follows predefined rules. In Germany, article 155 section 2 of the Weimar Constitution instructed the parliaments of the *Länder* to abolish entailed estates, but in many *Länder* the parliaments did not execute this order given by the constitution of the Reich.[18] As a result, entailed estates in many parts of Germany were abolished completely by National Socialist 'hereditary farm' legislation and by the later laws of the occupying powers.

Recent Developments

Since the second half of the twentieth century, the welfare state has caused certain changes in the liberal property and assets orders. Protection by the welfare state no longer concentrates on property; instead, its focus is the rights originating from dependent labour because these secure the living of the larger part of the population. As a consequence, property in a constitutional sense has encompassed more and more positions. First, it was extended to include the right of intellectual creation (author's rights, industrial and intellectual property); later, social security rights acquired through one's own contributions, such as pension insurance claims, were included in the constitutional protection of property.[19] The modern constitutional concept of property is therefore much broader than the one in private law, which continues to be limited to legal powers over corporal objects. Parallel to this development, the social state exerts a stronger influence on the assets order than its liberal predecessor did.

Below the level of constitutional law, the rules on property have remained more or less the same since the nineteenth century. The basic provisions of the French, Austrian and German civil codes, as quoted above, have been in effect without change since their enactment. A factual difference is that property no longer plays a central role in safeguarding the individual's existence. Today, one's situation in old age depends much more on the amount of one's monthly pension than on the value of the pensioner's house.

Special Features of Property in the Legal Culture of East Central Europe

Starting in early modern times, the legal culture in East Central Europe developed differently from West European legal culture. In the west of the continent, rural feudalism lost its dominance and the French Revolution finally abolished its remnants in favour of an urban, egalitarian, individualistic bourgeois social and legal order. In East Central Europe, however, the landed nobility managed to conserve their dominance (the second feudalism). When the absolutist state's claim to a territorial monopoly of power in East Central Europe was confronted with the traditional privileges of the local nobility, and thus a polycentric public power vested in associations of persons rather than in territory, the East European estates and their model prevailed, on the whole. The economic system remained agrarian, and the cities led a marginal existence.

For want of social development, the legal systems of East Central Europe stagnated at the levels achieved in the late Middle Ages. Progress was but piecemeal. The reform efforts of foreign occupying powers – Prussia, Austria and, in central Poland, Napoleonic France – only partly succeeded in introducing absolutist and later bourgeois forms of the state and the law, as did the local reform parties of the eighteenth and nineteenth centuries.[20]

Property in East Central Europe in Historical Perspective

In East Central Europe, the second feudalism prevented the emergence of the social, economic and political basis necessary for the introduction of a bourgeois individual and comprehensive property order. In this part of Europe, property rights remained layered according to feudal hierarchies within the framework of the *seigniory*.

Because feudal systems are based on agriculture, land plays a crucial role. In East Central Europe, landed property remained within feudal limitations that prevented land from becoming a 'normal' commodity. The special psychological role of the land and the proprietorship of land was undiminished in East Central Europe, even after the liberation of the peasantry and land reform (where it took place) had in principle granted farmers individual and comprehensive property rights with respect to their land.[21] Now it was no longer 'illegal' to treat agricultural land like any other commodity, though it continued to be 'improper'. Furthermore, in various regions of East Central Europe, feudal elements had survived to varying degrees, which necessitated special rules for landed property that differed from the liberal principles of an individual and comprehensive property order.

Even in the cities, individual comprehensive ownership of land emerged only as a result of industrialization. Until then, inhabitants of cities were embedded in a system of medieval corporate associations, such as the guilds. This system survived until the nineteenth century because of the weak economic and social development of cities. Although the cities of East Central Europe had adopted German city laws in the late Middle Ages, at the time these laws had not yet gone the whole way towards a liberal property order for land. Whereas city laws in Germany and Western Europe generally developed towards creating a bourgeois property order, the law in East Central European cities stagnated at the level achieved in the late Middle Ages, echoing the fate of feudal law outside the cities.

In Poland, farmers' landed property started to play a very special role after the end of Napoleonic rule, which had brought the French property order, with its individual comprehensive property in agriculture, to central Poland.[22] Faced with partition, the Polish nation considered its very existence to be at stake. A widespread contemporary belief held that the individual landed property of Polish farmers amounted to a guarantee that the nation would survive, even without a state of its own. As long as the Polish farmer was and remained the proprietor of their own plot of land, it was thought, the dwelling grounds of the Polish nation were reasonably safe from foreign infiltration.[23] Farmers' landed property became a myth sustaining the survival of the Polish nation, similar to the Polish Catholic Church. In other words, apart from the aforementioned psychological bonds of landed property, which were widespread throughout East Central Europe and responsive to the special social character of landed property, in Poland there were special 'national' bonds between landed property and the proprietors of agricultural land. For Polish farmers, selling land – especially to a person not of Polish ethnicity – became an act of 'disloyalty towards the nation'.

Property under Socialism: Triple Property of the Soviet Type

Socialism led to radical change in the property and assets orders. The ideological starting point of socialist property doctrine was the numerous relevant parts in the classics, especially by Marx and Engels, at least in the form that their Soviet reception canonized later.[24]

Socialist property doctrine broke with the uniform concept of property and introduced a threefold property (so-called triple property) pattern instead. This meant that property was differently shaped and weighed ideologically, according to its proprietor. The supreme form was state property, because the state, as the representative of the entire people, enjoyed the highest ideological esteem. Following state property was the property of various collective subjects: cooperatives, unions, social organizations and so on. These collectives represented but a part of the people, so ideologically they ranked lower than the state; their property was accordingly ranked lower than state property. The various socialist legal systems chose various terms for this form of property,[25] and there was no uniform generic term for these two forms of property either. In the Soviet Union, the term 'socialist property' was used to describe both state and other collective property, and most Soviet satellites adopted this terminology.

At the lowest level of the triple-property schema was the property of the individual, termed 'personal property', a neologism coined to differentiate it from 'private property', which was defined as the property of individuals that concerns the means of production as the basis of capitalist systems. The principles of individual comprehensive property survived in personal property, and all feudal and other limitations and inequalities were abolished in favour of the formal equality of all private proprietors. This was especially important in Hungary, the site of the largest number of feudal differentiations in property law until the communist takeover.[26] In all socialist countries, the principle of individual comprehensive property was limited by a universal reservation in favour of the common weal as defined by the regime.

Limitations on who was allowed to own what were an integral part of this property doctrine. Certain goods – mostly mineral resources, infrastructure and the key sectors of the economy – were necessarily state property. In East Central Europe, compulsory state property was limited to these goods, whereas in countries like the Soviet Union, Mongolia and Albania, the land was also exclusive state property. With very few exceptions, the individual was not allowed to own any means of production. The property order and assets order formed an indissoluble mixture.

The basis of socialist property doctrine was laid down in the first chapters of individual state's constitutions, which contained the basics of the socialist order, including questions of property. This prominent editorial position highlights the importance socialist systems attached to the property and assets orders.

Beyond the constitution, the triple property pattern could be found throughout the entire legal system. In criminal law, for example, crimes against property were layered according to the kind of property. Thus, a typical socialist criminal code contained not just one but three provisions on theft – theft of state property, theft of collective property and theft of personal property – each with its different punishment. In private law, the ideological concentration on property resulted in the replacement, in socialist civil codes, of the chapter on 'real rights' with a chapter on 'property'. This chapter dealt with property and possession, and the few, limited real rights that lived on in socialist law found their place as collateral securities to contractual claims in the chapter on the law of obligations.[27] This position was ideologically sound but dogmatically incorrect. The socialist civil codes that had stuck to the pre-socialist tradition of a chapter on 'real rights' also strongly emphasized property.[28]

East Central European states allowed some exceptions to the principle that the means of production were held solely as state or collective property to avoid exploitation and 'speculation'. In this context, the fact that the collectivization of agriculture in Poland failed bears special significance. One reason for this failure may be the special role attributed to farmers' landed property as a guarantee of the survival of the Polish nation during the period of partition.[29] This myth turned out to be stronger than ideological stipulations. Furthermore, Poland and Hungary successively diluted the principle of the means of production as exclusively socialist property in the course of their economic reforms, especially in the 1980s, creating more and more room for a private economy.[30] On the other hand, the quite generous exception in Article 11 of the Romanian Constitution of 21 August 1965 favouring private ownership of farmers' or artisans' family enterprises remained on paper only, for want of political will to realize it.

The forced adoption of the Soviet model of property thus caused a radical break in East Central Europe's legal culture. Individual comprehensive property, which had only recently been achieved after a hard-fought struggle, was replaced by an ideologically weighted, triple-layered property and assets order. Yet continuities too are evident alongside this breach, most notably the exceptional psychological position of landed property. In rejecting free trade in land and giving it to those who worked it, socialism harked back to older traditions. The illiberal traits of the overall property order also had antecedents in the feudal system, which had rejected the idea that all economically relevant goods should be tradeable commodities.

Property under Socialism: Self-administered Socialism in Yugoslavia

The property and assets order in socialist Yugoslavia differed considerably from the Soviet model.[31] Whereas the Soviet communists relied on the state as the principal instrument in creating a socialist order, and therefore ranked state property above all other property, from the 1950s onwards, Yugoslavian socialists interpreted society and not the state as the most important agent of socialist development. Therefore, the means of production were to be vested in society.

First, a form of so-called self-administration was introduced in the productive sectors and later in all workplaces. Workers' councils, and later the 'basic organizations of associated labour', were the cornerstones of economic self-administration in enterprises and at higher levels. These structures of self-administered socialism were the model for the property and assets order. The enterprise as an asset belonged to the respective bearer of self-administration. After 1953, the Yugoslavian federal constitution declared the means of production in self-administration to be 'social property'. The Federal Constitution of 21 February 1974 developed social property into 'property without a subject'. In terminology, the constitution retained the expression 'social property', but defined it in such a way that it belonged to no one – neither the state nor the employees nor the organs of the workers' self-administration. This legal absurdity was made operable in practice by defining very precisely which subject was to exercise which of the partial rights that in their totality formed the right of property. Comprehensive property was replaced by scattering the various rights contained in property across different subjects. In Yugoslavia, ideological tenets led to even greater legal contortions than in the Soviet Union; a pragmatic handling, however, guaranteed operable conditions in everyday legal and economic practice.

Social property and the allocation of proprietors' rights to workers' councils created a mentality that is still perceptible in the successor states of Yugoslavia. Here, the consensus that the means of production should, in one way or another, belong to the employees or the people at large is even stronger than in other formerly socialist countries.[32]

Property in East Central Europe Today

After the demise of communism, the legal systems of East Central Europe aimed to catch up with Western European standards as quickly as possible.[33] The Soviet-style triple property schema was abandoned immediately, as was the Yugoslavian form of social property without a subject. For some decades, socialism had emphasized the social obligations of property, but now the new systems turned towards the private use of property. This turn is reflected mainly in the new constitutions of the region's states. All the while, the mentalities that had been created or consolidated during the communist era remained active, demanding that agricultural land – or, as the case may be, all means of production – ought somehow to belong to or to be of use to the people, and should certainly not be an object of 'speculation'.

In what follows, I will analyse how these historic and psychological conditions influenced the post-socialist property orders in East Central Europe. At first glance, property orders there appear quite similar to what we are used to from Western Europe. Therefore, this chapter will deal primarily with the distinct, genuinely East Central European features.

The Property Order in Post-socialist Constitutions

All constitutions in East Central Europe contain more or less extensive rules on property.[34] Some constitutions evince a special esteem for property by including its inviolability in their catalogue of supreme constitutional values,[35] or by declaring that private property is one of the basic elements of the economic order.[36]

Property as a basic right is of special importance when viewed against the background of the socialist past. All constitutions in East Central Europe guarantee basic rights of property and of inheritance.[37] In the constitutions of Croatia and Poland, this guarantee is the first article in the sub-chapter on economic, social and cultural rights.[38] This right features more prominently in the Czech and Slovak constitutions, where property is not enumerated among economic but among basic human rights.[39] On the other hand, the Slovenian Constitution, which does not differentiate its catalogue of basic rights into sub-chapters, places the guarantee of property amid the chapter on basic rights.[40] Last, but not least, the Hungarian Constitution deals with property outside the catalogue of basic rights, that is, in its first chapter on the basics of the nation and state identity.[41] The reason is less a special emphasis on property than the fact that the Hungarian Constitution is the only basic law in Eastern Europe that is not an entirely new law but merely a large number of amendments, though very thorough ones, to the socialist constitution.[42] The legislative technique of successive piece-by-piece amendment allowed the content of various articles to be reformed, but meant that the overall structure of the text could not be changed. Property-related rules are therefore in the same place they had during socialist times: the first chapter on the basics of the identity of the constitutional order.

The core of property rights is a guarantee of unhampered private use, granting proprietors material freedom, and intended to protect them from the demands that socialism had made on their property. Still, in East Central European practice, property cannot yet play its role as 'consolidated freedom'[43] because the assets order has not yet developed to a point where larger parts of the population have sufficient property: in East Central Europe, the preponderance of social security claims over property is even greater than in Western Europe.[44] Therefore, constitutional practice in East Central Europe adopted Western European trends of including social security rights in the scope of a constitutional guarantee of property.[45]

Besides a guarantee of private use, all basic rights clauses stipulate the possibility of expropriation. At the same time, the constitutions define the limitations of expropriation: statutory authorization, prompt and full indemnification.[46] The requirement of statutory authorization is an important guarantee because it prevents the executive branch (government, public administration) from interfering with private property without involving parliament. The requirement of a statutory authorization does not mean, however, that every single expropriation needs a new parliamentary act. It suffices that a statute defines the conditions, the legal consequences and the procedure of expropriations in an abstract way. This puts an elaborate standard at the courts' disposal, enabling them to control the legality of any given expropriation measure.

The principle that property not only benefits the proprietor but imposes duties as well – as contained in Article 14.2 of the German Basic Law – is laid down in the constitutions of Croatia, the Czech Republic, Slovakia and Slovenia.[47]

In Poland and Hungary, the constitutions do not expressly mention the social obligations stemming from property, but these two countries' constitutional courts have acknowledged that the proprietor's rights may be limited in the public interest.[48]

The equality of property rights irrespective of the proprietor is emphasized in most East Central European constitutions.[49] These articles are intended to contrast with the layered socialist form of triple property, and terminate the privileges of state and other collective property vis-à-vis private property. No such clauses appear in the constitutions of Yugoslavia's successor states because, under Yugoslavian socialism, state property did not enjoy the ideologically or legally prominent position it held in the states that followed the Soviet model.

Apart from these core rules of the property order, various East Central European constitutions contain further articles with relevance to property. They include special rules on the acquisition of property by foreigners; on the property of public subjects and the obligations, short of expropriation, that can be imposed on property in the public interest; on the property and assets order of arable land; and on the protection of the environment, nature or historic monuments as a task of the state and an obligation of citizens. The latter aspect may serve as a basis to limit other rights, *inter alia* property rights.

On the whole, the constitutions of East Central Europe set out a well-balanced regulation of property's private use and social obligations. Given the experiences of the previous decades, the private interests of the proprietor and the equality of all forms of property receive special emphasis. At the same time, certain social opinions fostered during the socialist era remain palpable: that certain objects should be used only in accordance with the public weal, and that certain areas of life should not be too commercialized.

The Property Order in Private Law

The most important field of law for the property order is private law. The constitutions of the Czech Republic, Slovakia and Slovenia impose on legislators an express obligation to shape the content of property by law.[50] The other states' constitutions assume, without explicit reference, that parliament will legislate on the property order.

In the northern half of East Central Europe, the basis of the law of real rights is laid out in codes of socialist origin. The Hungarian Civil Code of 1959 is still in force,[51] the Polish Civil Code was enacted in 1964,[52] and the Czechoslovak Civil Code, which remains in force in both successor states, dates from the same year.[53] Under socialist rule, these codes were destined to regulate the parts of the economy that were based on contract and property, whereas the powers of the state to direct and control the economy (for example, by planning) were set out in legislation outside the civil codes. It was therefore possible, after the end of communism, to adapt the civil codes – though with considerable effort – to the needs of a market economy. This was done, *inter alia*, by replacing layered triple property with a uniform concept of property, by abolishing or at least reducing the special rules on state and collective property, or by abrogating the numerous reservations for the socialist public weal.

In Hungary, this situation is considered unsatisfactory because the Civil Code contains many internal contradictions and lacks modernity; for this reason, a new Civil Code is being drafted and will come into force in 2014. In the Czech Republic, Poland and Slovakia on the other hand, legislative work is concentrated on the present code, although here, too, there have been political and scientific initiatives for a new private law.[54]

A different situation prevails in the Yugoslavian successor states. In socialist times, instead of a comprehensive civil code, Yugoslavia had separate laws on the various fields of private law. Both Croatia and Slovenia enacted new real rights laws some years after the end of communism because making entirely new laws was considered easier and faster than constant adaptations to an antiquated piece of legislation.[55]

A common feature of all these laws is that the core norms establish individual comprehensive property,[56] and thus correspond to their classic 'capitalist' models in the French, Austrian and German civil codes. In these private law instruments, the proprietor's rights are limited by neighbour law and the limited real rights that the proprietor voluntarily concedes to third parties. Limitations in the public interest are contained mostly in laws of a public law nature, outside private law. The Civil Code of Poland still sets out in Article 140 the rules of social life and socio-economic purpose as limiting all property rights. In today's practice, these socialist formulas do not limit a proprietor more than is common in other, non-socialist states.[57]

Thus, private law centres on the private use of property and the coordination of private proprietors' property rights. This corresponds to the law in Western Europe, although there are many differences in detail between states.

One difference of a more substantial, though technical, nature is the survival of the typical socialist institution of the right of use, which is in principle a special limited real right that does not exist in Western European legal systems. In socialist law, its function was to give its beneficiary (the owner), in most cases a state enterprise, a comprehensive real right to use and dispose of land and of the means of production. This made the state enterprise – which legally was not identical with the state, but possessed a legal personality of its own – the quasi-proprietor of the land and the means of production in question, while also allowing the ideologically desirable state property of those objects to be retained. Private persons were also granted such a right of use to enable their proprietorship of houses or flats on land that continued to be owned by the state or some other collectivity. The aforementioned old civil codes still contain rules on the right of use,[58] although the differentiation between the formal position of a proprietor on the one hand and possession of some or all of the material rights a proprietor may have on the other is dysfunctional in a market economy. This differentiation blurs the unequivocal allocation of spheres of rights and responsibilities with regard to goods that the principle of individual comprehensive property accomplishes, and which is a pillar of the trust necessary to constitute a market economy. In East Central European practice, these rights of use still exist in favour of some of the not yet privatized successors to former state enterprises,[59] whereas new rights of use are no longer being established.

Public Property and Limitations on Property in the Public Interest

The post-socialist legal culture of East Central Europe has a contradictory attitude towards property. On the one hand, it emphasizes the freedom of property and of the private proprietor, as described above. One reason for this emphasis is that state proprietorship of the means of production was one of the cornerstones of the socialist system.

On the other hand, several decades of socialist propaganda have left their traces in the moral attitude towards the assets order and, to some degree, towards the property order. The opinion that the economic system should be 'just' – that is, that the fruits of production ought to benefit labour rather than capital – is widespread. It follows that the means of production ought to serve the people at large, or at least those who work in production. In sensitive areas, there should be some protection against 'speculation'. This public opinion generally advocates extensive social obligations of those who own the means of production. All this should be guaranteed by the state, which continues to be – in continuation of socialist attitudes – the primary agent in the realization of social expectations and morals.

Apart from these social obligations, the various post-socialist constitutions pronounce more or less extensive ecological obligations for property. However, these are quite weak in comparison to the aforementioned social obligations, both in the expectations of the East Central European public and in the relevant legislation. Ecological clauses in East Central European constitutions owe their existence mainly to what were felt to be international standards of constitutionalism.

The balance between the conflicting political expectations – to free private property from universal interventions by the state on the one hand, and to put private ownership, especially of means of production, under a comprehensive social obligation on the other – is to be drawn primarily by the public law. Constitutions and the relevant statutes have solved this dilemma in various ways, most importantly by making certain goods state property and by imposing certain obligations of a public law nature on certain objects in private property. These two ways appear to be clearly distinguishable at first sight, but in the legal realities of East Central Europe they form the end points of a scale with many possible intermediate stages. This is why these two ways are dealt with in one section in the relevant statutes.[60] Another reason to unite their analysis is that their purpose is the same: to ensure that the social obligations concerning certain goods of social relevance (mostly the means of production) are carried out. This chapter, however, does not deal with rules regarding landed property, which have strong peculiarities and therefore are analysed elsewhere.

Public property and especially state property is a method of withdrawing certain goods from private trade and thus from 'speculation'. Some East Central European states continue to resort to this method, despite widespread state property having been one of the old regime's chief instruments of power. In this context, two questions are important: Which objects (goods) *must* be and which *may* be the property of public subjects? What are the special rules, different from the property order in general, for these objects?

In Slovakia, the objects of compulsory state property are granted a special position because its scope is defined by the constitution itself: according to Article 4, mineral resources and certain tracts of water are necessarily state property. This list is short, compared to similar enumerations in socialist constitutions. Yet the sheer fact that such a rule was considered sufficiently important to be included in the constitution is itself noteworthy – even more so, since this article is not hidden somewhere in the text but features prominently in the first chapter, on the basics of the constitutional order. Other East Central European constitutions leave it to statute to determine which objects are compulsory state or other public property.[61]

These clauses do not aim to enlarge the scope of compulsory public property; on the contrary, they intend to serve the protection of private property. By stipulating that (only) statute can define compulsory public property, these clauses prevent government and public administration from employing mere administrative measures to widen the scope of the monopoly of state property to the detriment of the private sector. The statute required in the relevant constitutional norms is a guarantee for the private sector, just as references to regulation and limitation by statute are guarantees in the case of other basic rights.

Some constitutions contain a special guarantee for the property of local authorities.[62] This is quite understandable because in communist times state property always meant property of the central state; local councils could not have any property of their own.[63] The guarantee of property for local authorities, as part of the re-establishment of local autonomy, means that local authorities may have property of their own, but do not necessarily need to. No constitution in East Central Europe makes communal property of certain objects compulsory.

In practice, after communism ended, public utilities and in some countries state-owned housing facilities were given over to communal property. Since the turn of the century, East Central European states have tended, like West European ones, to privatize local public utilities in form and sometimes even in substance, leaving only control with local authorities.

Only two East Central European constitutions address the special features that differentiate state property from other forms of property. The first is the Hungarian, in which Article 10.1 stipulates that the property of the state comprises 'national wealth'. This clause has little tangible legal content, and literature on constitutional law has passed it over in silence.[64] It is a 'psychological wellness clause' designed to meet the people's expectations of a 'just' economic and asset order without strictly stipulating legal rules. Among the new EU members, Estonia is the second country which has a similar clause in its constitution.[65] Article 11 of the Hungarian Constitution guarantees a certain autonomy to state-owned enterprises, and therefore has a more tangible legal content than Article 10.1. This means that state-owned enterprises, too, are to act according to the demands of the market and are no longer agents of state politics. Everywhere in East Central Europe today, state-owned enterprises operate in the legal form of private companies; the legal person 'state enterprise' exists in only a few residual cases. Regarding its enterprises, the state no longer exercises its property rights on the basis of public law but through the channels of company law – that is, as shareholder or partner.[66] In Poland, Article 216.2 Const. stipulates that dispositions of land, holdings in companies and shares in public property require regulation by statute. This clause creates a procedural guarantee to prevent overly autonomous conduct by the executive branch of the government. The statutory regulations referred to in the constitution are partly located in the state budget law and partly in the annual budget acts.[67]

The special features of public property are shaped much more by statute than by the aforementioned, rather short constitutional clauses. The Hungarian Civil Code contains a separate chapter on state property,[68] as opposed to both the Polish Civil Code, which, upon the end of communism, ceased to mention state property,[69] and the Czechoslovak Civil Code, which declares the principle of equality between public and private property in Section 124. In the Czech Republic, Poland and Slovakia, special laws of an administrative nature deal with the special features of public property; in Hungary, numerous special administrative laws specify and modify the Civil Code's general rules on public property.[70] These administrative laws are influenced by two conflicting tendencies. The first aims to render the state a proprietor like any other proprietor, because upon the demise of communism, state ownership of the means of production was deemed to have been a pillar of the past dictatorship and a central instrument of the planned economy. The second tendency stems from the experience of the possibility of exercising power on the basis of property during socialist times: neither the post-socialist state nor its elite were inclined to cede the potential for engaging in politics and shaping society that was vested in state property. Therefore, many laws on public property are ambiguous and contradictory, apparently as a result of political compromise. Yet the aforementioned administrative laws create a 'true' public property, meaning that the property of public subjects has distinctive specific features as compared to the property of private subjects. For this reason, goods that are to be withdrawn from commerce or reserved for especially regulated commercial use are designated public property.[71] On the other hand, the commercial property of the state is – as described above – administered by means of private law, using the channels of company law and the rules on private property.

The Yugoslavian successor states have an instrument to earmark property for special purposes. Typologically it stands between public property and private property subject to public obligations. In Croatia, this is called 'property of interest for the Republic of Croatia',[72] whereas in Slovenia it is known as 'public goods'.[73] Basically, both instruments consist in attaching certain obligations to goods with certain relevance for the public interest. In Croatia, the constitution lists the sea and its coast, islands, waters, airspace, mineral resources, natural treasures and objects (including land) of special cultural, historical, economic or ecological value; statute may determine further objects. In Slovenia, the constitution leaves the enumeration of public goods entirely to statute. The real rights laws of both countries define some basic traits of the property thus specified,[74] but their legal status is in substance shaped by specialized administrative laws on various goods and their relevance for the public interest – for instance, laws on arable land. The peculiarity of the Croatian and Slovenian model lies in the fact that the status of property of interest to the Republic of Croatia with respect to public goods is independent of the person of the proprietor. The only relevant factor in determining this status is the quality of the object. It is of course easier to create this special status for an object in state or communal property. However, although a private proprietor of such an object may not object to its classification as property of interest to the Republic of Croatia as a public good, that proprietor may have a claim to indemnification for the limitations on private use that this special status invokes.

Another method of acting in the public interest is to impose obligations of a public law nature on private property. The strongest form of this obligation divesting the proprietor of the entire object (expropriation) – is a question typically addressed in constitutions and has therefore been dealt with above in the section on constitutional determinations of property orders. Some constitutions in East Central Europe contain a general social commitment clause stipulating that property imposes duties.[75] These clauses authorize a certain number of obligations on private property in the public interest. These general social commitment clauses refer to property abstractly; additional articles in the constitutions of Croatia, the Czech Republic, Poland and Slovakia allow certain public obligations to be imposed on individual objects of private property, for example, a public right of way over a private plot of land.[76] These constitutional clauses put a wide range of instruments at lawmakers' disposal. The same is true for Hungary and Slovenia, although their constitutions mention only expropriation. Constitutional practice shows that here, too, the law may oblige private proprietors to act in conformity with the public weal.

Recent years have seen a rise in mixed forms of private and public property. In this, the East Central European states follow Western European tendencies. The most popular mixed form concerns so-called public–private partnership (PPP), which has become increasingly widespread in recent years. Poland and Slovenia have already created special legal instruments for PPPs,[77] whereas in other states the general freedom of contract forms the legal basis, and the concessions, the practical model.

When it comes to constitutional and statutory regulations of public limitations of private property as a whole, the differences between East Central Europe and Western Europe are but small. The political expectations that the means of production ought not to be handed over to 'speculation' are hardly reflected in the law outside the constitutions. The property and asset orders, as well as economic and administrative law, balance private use and public obligations in ways resembling those in Western Europe, with minor differences between the various states. The instruments that pronounce the social commitment of private property sometimes continue socialist institutions, a fact that explains the difference between the Yugoslavian successor states on the one hand (special obligations with regard to the nature of the object irrespective of the proprietor) and other East Central European states on the other (public property). Yet neither group is homogeneous. In some countries the list of objects under state ownership is quite long, especially from a Western European perspective, but in no case is state property as extensive as it was under socialism. The most important special features marking distinctive differences from Western Europe concern the ownership of land.

Special Features of Landownership

All East Central European states have a distinctly special property order for land.[78] Its peculiarities continue pre-socialist and socialist stereotypes about the just use of land. Today, two issues mark clear differences between the region and Western Europe: the special regime for ownership of land and agriculture, and the limitations placed on aliens. The cadastres and land registries are a third difference, but rather than concerning structures, which are quite similar to those in Western Europe, the difference lies mainly in the fact that these documents, after decades of neglect, are highly incorrect and frequently do not cover the entire territory of a state. The following discussions concentrate on the first two aspects – agricultural land and aliens – leaving aside the more practical questions of cadastres and land registries.

Two constitutions set out a specific order for agricultural land and agriculture. The most far-reaching regulation of this kind is Article 71 of the Constitution of Slovenia. Article 71.1 provides for statutory regulation of the appropriate use of land, and Article 71.2 stipulates special legal protections for plots of arable land. These clauses allow Slovenian legislators to put landownership under an extensive special regime; in practice, special laws were enacted with regard to agriculture.[79] Regulation of land use within built-up areas lies in principle within the powers of the local authorities. Meanwhile, Article 23 of Poland's Constitution is not quite as extensive. According to this clause, the family farm is to be the basis of the agricultural system.[80] The scope of this norm is limited to agriculture, but it is nonetheless very wide because it refers not only to the property order but also to the entire structure of agriculture. This clause cannot be interpreted solely as a concession made to the Polish Peasant Party (Polskie Stronnictwo Ludowe, PSL) to 'buy' its consent to the constitution. It is rather the modern codification of the myth that it was Polish small farmers' private ownership of their plots of land that guaranteed the nation's survival in its traditional areas during the partition.[81] In Croatia, parliament used Article 52 of the Constitution to declare all agricultural land by law to be property of interest of the Republic of Croatia.[82]

In the other East Central European countries, special rules for agricultural land are set out in simple law without a special constitutional basis. These laws mix heterogeneous objects and aims: a 'just' distribution of land in agricultural communities; the creation or stabilization of sustainable economic structures in agriculture; management of the scarce resource of arable land in the interest of the greatest possible economic result, sometimes in combination with the goal of autarchy in the provision of certain agricultural goods,[83] as well as guarantees that private agriculture can carry out the necessary tasks of the management and conservation of natural treasures.

The most widespread legal instrument in East Central Europe is restriction on the acquisition of arable land. In some states, only farmers may buy or even lease arable land. If arable land is sold, in many countries the law grants the leaseholder or local farmers, local authorities and/or state-run agricultural agencies a right of pre-emption. The proprietor or possessor of arable land usually is under obligation to cultivate it appropriately.[84] This is to prevent, *inter alia*, arable land from being converted into an object of 'speculation'. Some countries try to prevent the re-emergence of large estates and to stabilize small or medium-sized farms by declaring upper limits of permissible property in arable land, sometimes adding to these upper limits the personal character of the obligation to cultivate. The strongest limitations are found in Hungary, where all the aforementioned measures have come into use cumulatively. At the other end of the spectrum, Poland is quite liberal, and the legal limitations apply only to the sale of the small portion of arable land that is state-owned and impose hardly any restrictions on the sale of arable land between private parties as long as the buyer is a Polish national.[85] In practice, Article 23 of the Polish Constitution is hardly reflected in relevant legislation. The other countries of East Central Europe fall somewhere on the spectrum between Hungarian and Polish law.

All these limitations are in breach of European Union law. They violate the free movement of capital and, according to the specifics of the limitation, other European laws as well.[86] The accession treaties granted the new members a transitional period of several years, after which the East Central European states are obliged to create free trade in arable land. So far, the new members have made only minimal use of the transitional period. Everywhere, the aforementioned limitations prevent a free market from emerging. Upon expiration of the transitional period, the free market will therefore probably hit an unprepared rural population and underdeveloped markets with full force, creating exactly the social problems that the existing limitations are meant to prevent. Yet political opposition to even discussion of possible liberalization of rules governing landownership appears to be so strong that most governments dare not put the foreseeable introduction of free trade in agricultural land on the agenda of political debate.

The other field of widespread limitations is the acquisition of land by alien nationals. After the end of communism, all Eastern European countries enacted laws forbidding or at least limiting the purchase of plots of land by foreigners, sometimes for rational purposes.[87] Because there had not been a market in land under communism, such a market had to emerge gradually after the transition to capitalism. Ridiculously low land prices and the local population's low income levels would have enabled Western Europeans to buy land on a large scale, thus squeezing local buyers out of the market. Other concerns were less rational, especially the emotional link to 'national' soil that was not to be 'sold out'. An additional element in Poland and the Czech Republic was the fear that areas formerly inhabited by German-speaking populations might become subject to 're-germanization through the instruments of private law'.[88] Thus, the rules on foreigners' acquisition of land aim to prevent German expellees and their descendants from buying their way back into their old homes. In Croatia and Slovenia, the prospect of the return of Italian expellees arouses similar fears, fuelled by the quite aggressive stance that the Italians sometimes take on this question.

All East Central European states, except for Hungary and Poland, codified limitations on alien nationals in their post-socialist constitutions. In Croatia, the law can limit foreigners' acquisition of property with regard to all objects, not only land.[89] A similar clause in the Slovenian constitution refers only to land;

purchase of land by foreigners may be determined by law or an international treaty, one relevant international treaty being the accession treaty to the EU.[90] In the Czech Republic and Slovakia, the law may limit the acquisition of property – any property, not only land – by persons residing outside the country.[91]

Unlike all other East Central European countries, the relevant constitutional clauses in the Czech Republic and Slovakia do not refer to the nationality of the purchaser, but to the place of residence. In 1992, when the constitutions were drafted, the relevant Czechoslovak restrictions on foreigners were set down in the foreign exchange law, and in this field of law residence, not nationality, is the main criterion. In view of this Czechoslovak tradition, the parliaments in Prague and Bratislava thought it natural to write the criterion of residence (instead of nationality) into the constitutions. At the level of statute law, in both countries it is still the foreign exchange law that sets out limitations on the acquisition of land by foreigners. Croatia's Property Act contains some restrictions on alien nationals,[92] whereas in Slovenia only specialized rules on agriculture, the protection of monuments and similar matters still restrict foreigners from acquiring plots of land. In Hungary, the most important limitations for aliens are contained in the Fertile Soil Act (1994), which also includes limitations referring to forms of real property (such as residential or industrial) besides agricultural land. Finally, Poland fell back on its Aliens' Land Acquisition Act (1920) – which, however, was widely amended.

All these regulations were liberalized in the course of the 1990s. First, foreign enterprises were allowed to buy land for the purpose of permanent activity in the country. Later, the private purchase of flats and houses was permitted, sometimes with the exception of especially attractive residential or leisure areas, so as to keep comparatively poor local buyers from being squeezed out of the market by richer Western Europeans. In the end, agriculture constitutes the most important case of the restricted acquisition of land. In this field, limitations apply to nationals as well. Restrictions range from requiring an official licence (Poland) to a right of pre-emption for local farmers (Slovenia), going as far as a total ban on acquisition by persons who are not farmers (for example, Croatia, Czech Republic, Hungary).

Restrictions on foreign nationals' acquisition of landed property cause even more serious problems under community law than do limitations on free trade in agricultural land. Restrictions (only) for foreigners violate not only the free movement of capital but also the principle of equal treatment. This ban on discrimination on grounds of nationality is at the heart of the single market and citizenship in the EU. This is why all candidate countries had to reduce relevant constitutional restrictions prior to accession, and to commit themselves to abolishing all legal restrictions on free trade in any kind of land after transitional periods. The longest transitional period, twelve years, was granted to Poland because Poles had the strongest reservations about foreigners' uncontrolled access to the land market, fed by the national myth of the landed property of small farmers as much as by the fears of purchases by German expellees. On the other hand, the Polish practice of granting acquisition licences is quite generous, and EU citizens can probably buy agricultural land more easily in Poland than in any other East Central European country.[93]

Not only in Poland but throughout East Central Europe, public opinion generally opposes foreigners having total freedom to acquire land, especially agricultural land. Western European buyers, with their – by East Central European standards – well-stuffed wallets, are blamed for pushing up land prices in major cities and attractive leisure areas to levels far beyond the purchasing power of the local population. This is why political initiatives to prepare local populations and national law for the imminent expiry of the transitional period are just as rare as initiatives to liberalize the property order of agricultural land. The two problems are interdependent because the strongest restrictions on alien nationals concern agricultural land, and are part of an overall property order that places considerable limitations on national buyers as well.

Political life in all East Central European states reveals the potential the issue of rural landownership has to heighten emotions. Poland even has a political party, the PSL, established to defend exactly these interests. In Hungary, a considerable proportion of people's initiatives, which are presented to the National Elections Committee for the obligatory preliminary control of legality, aim to preserve or even expand restrictions on the ownership of agricultural land. The committee has rejected most of these initiatives because they violate the law, but in some cases it has allowed such initiatives to proceed, as it is obliged to do when there are no legal objections. In July 2007, the National Elections Committee accepted three initiatives intended to introduce another right of pre-emption of arable land and of farms in favour of other farmers. Acceptance of these initiatives allowed the initiators – in these cases, mostly on the political Right – to start collecting the signatures that, if assembled in sufficient quantity before the legal deadline, enable a referendum to be held.

Final Remarks

On the whole, East Central Europe managed to return to a liberal individual comprehensive property order after the end of communism. Conflicting expectations about both property-related freedoms and the social obligations of proprietorship, especially in the case of the means of production, are reflected mainly in the region's constitutions. Below the level of the constitution, however, private law and public law strike a balance between private use and public obligations that is very similar to that in Western Europe, even though some of the instruments date back to socialist times. On the other hand, a certain delay precedes imitation of Western European trends such as formal or substantial privatization in the field of public utilities or public-private mixed constructions.

A marked difference between Western and East Central Europe is observable in the field of agriculture. In East Central Europe, a widespread consensus dictates that arable land is to remain under a restricted property and assets order to stabilize the economic and social structures of farming. Restrictions are advocated especially with regard to foreigners, who face even more impediments to 'speculation' in agricultural land than nationals do. These opinions are partly based in irrational ideas, dating back to pre-socialist times, about arable land and the farming community, but they partly stem from a very real background of underdeveloped land markets and the low purchasing power of local populations compared to Western European buyers.

The expiry of transitional periods may lead to conflicts between the EU, which insists that community law be observed, and East Central European member states, where the free movement of capital in agriculture can only be introduced against the will of the majority of the population. Should the EU fail to develop an understanding of these facts – if not the psychological situation – with regard to its new members, and the East Central European peoples fail to bid farewell to partially pre-modern myths about arable land and small farming as the essence of agricultural justice, defusing this conflict may prove difficult. In any case, a clash is imminent between the 'liberal' old EU, where the free movement of capital makes everything a tradable commodity, and the 'traditional' new member states of East Central Europe, where pre-socialist and socialist traditions oppose an overgenerous form of liberalism in the property and assets order.

Notes

1. On pre-Roman Sumerian, Babylonian, Egyptian, Hebrew and Greek law, see Uwe Wesel, *Geschichte des Rechts: Von den Frühformen bis zum Vertrag von Maastricht*, Munich, 1997, pp.108, 132–34.
2. Ancient Greek law was vaguely aware of the fact that the person physically holding a thing need not necessarily be its proprietor. However, it ignored possession quite completely and pronounced rules only on property: Wesel, *Geschichte des Rechts*, pp.132–33.
3. This question arises when, for example, someone carves a statue from a piece of wood: Who acquires the property of the statue? Its carver? The proprietor of the piece of wood? The proprietor of the knife that was used? Or the owner of the factory where the statue was carved?
4. A common example of the acquisition of property by an act of the state is a public auction.
5. Natural processes leading to the creation of new things that then may become objects of property rights are, *inter alia*, the reproduction of animals, the growth of plants, the dropping of fruit from trees, or the emergence of land where there had been water.
6. In English, there is no proper word for this because the common law systems do not combine the rules on property and on the other real rights in one single field of law.

7. Since the law in Europe centres on the state as its source, legal culture may be defined by states and according to their boundaries. This means that the East Central European legal culture is composed by Poland, the Czech Republic, Slovakia, Hungary, Slovenia and Croatia. Lithuania is moving towards north-east European legal culture, and thus belongs to it. Other regions are moving towards the legal culture of East Slavonic Eastern Europe (western Ukraine) and of south-eastern Europe (Transylvania, Vojvodina and, in a certain sense, Croatia). Although western Ukraine, Transylvania and Vojvodina belong to states that are not part of East Central European legal culture, their societies share certain features with East Central European legal culture. Similarly, the eastern hereditary provinces of Austria and Germany east of the river Elbe formed transitional regions between West European and East Central European legal cultures. On this, see Georg Brunner, 'Rechtskultur in Osteuropa: Das Problem der Kulturgrenzen', in Georg Brunner (ed.), *Politische und ökonomische Transformation in Osteuropa*, 3rd edn, Berlin, 2000, pp.111–32; Herbert Küpper, 'Rechtskultur(en) in Ostmitteleuropa: Hemmschuh oder Quelle der Hoffnung auf dem Weg ins 21. Jahrhundert?', in *Berichte und Beiträge des Geisteswissenschaftlichen Zentrums Geschichte und Kultur Ostmitteleuropas e.V. 1999, Öffentliche Vorträge 1998/99*, Leipzig, 1999, pp.331–77; Herbert Küpper, *Einführung in die Rechtsgeschichte Osteuropas*, Frankfurt am Main, 2005, pp.15–42.
8. Since the person who makes the statement necessarily belongs to some culture, there are no 'non-cultural' or 'objective' statements on cultural phenomena but only statements influenced by the cultural background of their author.
9. A normative example for the principle of comprehensive property is art. 903 phrase 1 of the German Civil Code, formulated in the late nineteenth century on the basis of Roman law: 'The proprietor of an object may, unless the law or the rights of a third party object, deal with the object at will and exclude others from all interference'.
10. The difference between the law of persons and real rights is based on modern legal thinking, and therefore anachronistic for medieval phenomena. Although medieval law considered allegiance a uniform legal relationship, here modern terms are used to make orientation easier for today's readers.
11. A similar system emerged in Russia after the liberation of the peasants in 1861. The peasant community – the so called *mir* or *obshchina* – replaced the seignior in governing the peasants, who were free only on paper. On this, see Heike Kathrin Litzinger, *Juristen und die Bauernfrage: Die Diskussion um das bäuerliche Grundeigentum in Russland von 1880 bis 1914*, Frankfurt am Main, 2007.
12. Only in Britain did the reception of Roman law take a different course. At that time, West European legal culture split into the two central legal families of the common law, in Britain, and the *ius commune*, on the Continent. The *ius commune* is the origin of the later Romano-Germanic family of law: Küpper, 'Rechtskultur(en) in Ostmitteleuropa', pp.334–42.
13. On this, see Katalin Gönczi, *Ungarisches Stadtrecht aus europäischer Sicht: Die Stadtrechtsentwicklung im spätmittelalterlichen Ungarn am Beispiel Ofen*, Frankfurt am Main, 1997; Herbert Küpper: *Autonomie im Einheitsstaat: Geschichte und Gegenwart der Selbstverwaltung in Ungarn*, Berlin, 2002, pp.30–40; Ilpo Tapani Piirainen, *Das Stadt- und Bergrecht von Kremnica/Kremnitz*, Heidelberg, 1983; Julius Weiske, 'Bemerkungen über das Brünner Schöffenbuch', *Zeitschrift für deutsches Recht und deutsche Rechtswissenschaft* (1853), pp.113–54.
14. Stefan Korioth, 'Der Eigentumsschutz in den europäischen Verfassungsordnungen in historischer Sicht', in Gerrit Manssen and Boguslaw Banaszak (eds), *Wandel der Eigentumsordnung in Mittel- und Osteuropa*, Berlin, 1998, pp.9–27.
15. An example of such a prohibitive law is the following art. 545 of the Civil Code, which contains the possibility of expropriation.
16. This Austrian code had a sort of 'test run' even before the French Code Civil was enacted: the West Galician Code of Law of 1797 was an experiment to see how the rules of the future all-

Austrian code would work in practice. On the West Galician Code, see Wilhelm Brauneder, 'Europas erste Privatrechtskodifikation: Das Galizische Bürgerliche Gesetzbuch', in Heinz Barta, Rudolf Palme and Wolfgang Ingenhaeff (eds), *Naturrecht und Privatrechtskodifikation*, Vienna, 1999, pp.303–20.

17. On this, see Korioth, 'Eigentumsschutz in den europäischen Verfassungsordnungen', pp.15–25.
18. Otto Meissner, *Die Rechtsverfassung*, Berlin, 1919, pp.221f.
19. The dynamics of this development is highlighted by a decision of the German Constitutional Court published in *Neue Juristische Wochenschrift* (2005), p.589, which states that the constitutional concept of property protects the right to a given internet domain.
20. Küpper, *Einführung in die Rechtsgeschichte Osteuropas*, pp.221–37.
21. The situation was different elsewhere – for example, in South East Europe – where forms of collective property such as the *zadruga* and similar constructions remained, especially with regard to landed property; see ibid., pp.377–78, 402.
22. Similar processes took place in the Austrian and Prussian parts of Poland, but not in eastern Poland, where at first old Lithuanian law remained in force and later Russian law was enacted.
23. Therefore, after independence, in the Polish Constitution of 17 March 1921, art. 99.2 defined the land as 'one of the most important factors in the existence of the nation and of the state'. This phrase may be interpreted as a positive incorporation of that myth into the normative text of the constitution. On this myth, see Jan Wiktor Tkaczyński, *Polen im Umbruch: Skizzen aus Geschichte, Wirtschaft und Politik*, Berlin, 1997, pp.53–57.
24. On property under socialism, see the essays in Gerd Bender and Ulrich Falk (eds), *Recht im Sozialismus: Analysen zur Normdurchsetzung in osteuropäischen Nachkriegsgesellschaften (1944/45–1989), Enteignung*, vol. 1, Frankfurt am Main 1999; *Das Eigentum im Ostblock*, Studien des Instituts für Ostrecht München, vol. 5, Berlin, 1958.
25. Article 10 of the Soviet Constitution of 1977 used the expression 'property of collective economy and of cooperatives'.
26. The standard work by Károly Szladits, *Magyar Magánjog*, 6 vols, Budapest, 1939–1942, names these differentiations in numerous parts, especially in law of persons, of family and of inheritance, but also in property law proper. A similarly strong survival of feudal elements can be found in the nineteenth and early twentieth centuries only – beyond the region we analyse here – in the Baltic Private Law of 1864 and in pre-revolutionary Russian law; see Küpper, *Einführung in die Rechtsgeschichte Osteuropas*, pp.160–65, 194–95.
27. This was the case in the Hungarian Civil Code of 11 August 1959, as well as in Bulgaria, where private law was laid down not in a code, but in several acts. In this context, the Law on Property of 2 November 1951 is relevant.
28. These were the Polish Civil Code of 23 April 1964 and the Czechoslovakian Civil Code of 26 February 1964.
29. Hubert Izdebski, 'Ownership in "People's Poland": Shaping, Growth, and Decomposition of the Theory of Socialist Ownership in the Years 1944–1990', in Bender and Falk, *Recht im Sozialismus*, vol. 1, pp.57–72.
30. On this, see Klaus Westen, Georg Brunner and Friedrich-Christian Schroeder, *Sozialistisches Wirtschaftsrecht zwischen Wandel und Beharrung*, Berlin, 1988.
31. On this, see Küpper, *Einführung in die Rechtsgeschichte Osteuropas*, pp.605–14; Ivo Lapenna, 'Die Rechtsnatur des gesellschaftlichen Eigentums in Jugoslawien', *Osteuropa-Recht* 8 (1962), pp.216–35; Radomir Lukić, 'Notions de la propriété dans l'Europe socialiste et dans les états capitalistes', *Rabels Zeitschrift für ausländisches und internationales Privatrecht* 26/2 (1961), pp.238–54.
32. This mentality is expressed, for example, in art. 75 of the Slovenian Constitution, which declares the co-determination of employees in enterprises to be a principle of constitutional rank.

33. This article includes legal developments until mid-2007.
34. Comprehensive accounts of the post-socialist property order in Eastern Europe are given by Joachim Lippott, 'Das Eigentum in den osteuropäischen Verfassungen der Gegenwart', *Zeitschrift für Vergleichende Rechtswissenschaft* 95 (1996), pp.227–60; Herwig Roggemann (ed.), *Eigentum in Osteuropa: Rechtspraxis in Ost-, Ostmittel- und Südosteuropa mit Einführungen und Rechtstexten*, Berlin, 1996; Christian Tomuschat, *Eigentum im Umbruch: Restitution, Privatisierung und Nutzungskonflikte im Europa der Gegenwart*, Berlin, 1996.
35. Constitution of Croatia, art. 3: 'Apart from the respect for human dignity, property is the only basic right enumerated among these supreme values'. At the same time, art. 3 lists values such as the conservation of nature and the environment, which may lead to limitation of property rights.
36. Constitution of Poland, art. 20. On this, see Bogusław Banaszak, *Prawo konstytucyjne*, 2nd edn, Warsaw, 2001, pp.240–47.
37. On this, see Georg Brunner, 'Verfassungsrechtlicher Eigentumsschutz und Restitution enteigneten Vermögens in Osteuropa', in Manssen and Banaszak, *Wandel der Eigentumsordnung*, pp.29–68; Wolfram Gärtner, 'Die Eigentumsgarantien in den Verfassungen Polens, Ungarns, der Tschechischen und der Slowakischen Republik – Verfassungsrechtliche Grundlagen und Verfassungspraxis', in Roggemann, *Eigentum in Osteuropa*, pp.219–31.
38. Constitution of Croatia, art. 48; Constitution of Poland, art. 64.
39. Constitution of the Czech Republic, art. 11, 'Charter of Basic Rights and Freedoms', which is an integral part of the constitutional order (art. 3); Constitution of Slovakia, art. 20.
40. Constitution of Slovenia, art. 33.
41. Constitution of Hungary, art. 13. In this context, Poland requires mention as well because its constitution contains, apart from the guarantee of property as a basic right in art. 64, a parallel guarantee in the first chapter (art. 21). The doubling of regulations at various places in the constitution is a common feature of the Polish Constitution, and contributes to the considerable length of its text.
42. Therefore, the Hungarian Constitution is formally still Act 1949: XX of 20 August 1949. On this phenomenon, see Herbert Küpper, *Die ungarische Verfassung nach zwei Jahrzehnten des Übergangs: Einführung mit Textübersetzung*, Frankfurt am Main, 2007, pp.36–41, 57, 111–15.
43. On this, see the German Federal Constitutional Court (Bundesverfassungsgericht), decision of 18 December 1968, official collection of decisions *BVerfGE*, vol. 24, pp.367, 389.
44. From this fact, Lippott, 'Eigentum in den osteuropäischen Verfassungen', p.235, derives his criticism that, when creating their constitutions, post-socialist Eastern European parliaments committed a major mistake by adopting Western European constitutional clauses without taking into account the aspects of modern redistribution policy.
45. Brunner, 'Verfassungsrechtlicher Eigentumsschutz', pp.36–38; Tina de Vries, 'Die Eigentumsgarantie in Polen', *WGO-Monatshefte für Osteuropäisches Recht* 42 (2000), pp.173–81.
46. See the constitution of Croatia (art. 50.1), the Czech Republic (art. 11.4), Hungary (art. 13.3), Poland (art. 21.2), Slovakia (art. 20.4) and Slovenia (art. 69); the latter is regarding immovable property.
47. See the constitutions of Croatia (art. 48.2), the Czech Republic (art. 11.3), Slovakia (art. 20.3) and Slovenia (art. 69); the latter obliges legislators to create a property order corresponding to the economic, social and ecological functions of property.
48. Regarding Poland, see Decision of the Constitutional Court of 5 December 1995, K 6/95, Orzecnictwo Trybunału Konstytucyjnego, *Collection of Decisions of the Constitutional Court OTK* 1995, no. 2, pos. 38, 191; de Vries, 'Die Eigentumsgarantie in Polen', p.174; Tanja Diemer-Benedict, 'Die Grundrechte in der neuen polnischen Verfassung', *Zeitschrift für ausländisches öffentliches Recht und Völkerrecht* 58 (1998), pp.205–38; Gärtner, 'Eigentumsgarantien in den Verfassungen', pp.224–26; Marc Liebscher and Fryderyk Zoll, *Einführung in das polnische Recht*,

Munich, 2005, p.167. Regarding Hungary, see Decision of the Constitutional Court 64/1993 (XII. 22.) AB, Az Alkotmánybíróság határozatai [Collected Decisions of the Constitutional Court] 1993, p.373; Gärtner, 'Eigentumsgarantien in den Verfassungen'; József Petrétei, *Magyar alkotmányjog*, vol. 3, Pécs/Budapest, 2004, pp.495–96.

49. See the constitutions of the Czech Republic (art. 11.1), Hungary (art. 9.1), Poland (art. 64.2) and Slovakia (art. 20.1).
50. See the constitutions of the Czech Republic (art. 11.2), Slovakia (art. 20.1) and Slovenia (art. 67.1).
51. Act no. 1959: IV of the Civil Code of 11 August 1959.
52. Civil Code of 23 April 1964.
53. Act no. 40/1964 Sb. Civil Code of 26 February 1964 remains in force in both the Czech Republic and Slovakia. However, since the end of the federation and the independence of its successor states on 1 January 1993, amendments in one country are not valid in the other, which means that the Civil Code has different wordings in each state. Meanwhile, since the end of the 1990s, Czech and Slovak legislators have begun to harmonize their amending of old Czechoslovak law, not only as regards civil law but in many fields, with the result of a certain rapprochement of Czech and Slovak law.
54. On Poland, see Dorota Kempter, *Der Einfluss des europäischen Rechts auf das polnische Zivilgesetzbuch*, Baden-Baden, 2007, pp.314–17.
55. For Croatia, see the Act on Property and Other Real Rights of 2 October 1996; for Slovenia, see the Real Rights Code of 27 September 2002.
56. See Croatia's Property Act (1996), § 30; Czechoslovakian Civil Code §§ 123–28 (for Czech Republic and Slovakia); Hungary's Civil Code, §§ 98–101, 112–16; Poland's Civil Code, art. 140; and Slovenia's Real Rights Code, art. 37.
57. Peter Diedrich, in Stephan Breidenbach (ed.), *Handbuch Wirtschaft und Recht in Osteuropa*, Munich, 1997, vol. 2; Elżbieta Skowrońska-Bocian, in Krzysztof Pietrzykowski (ed.), *Kodeks cywilny: Komentarz do artykułów 1–449*, Warsaw, 2005, art. 140, nos. 4–13. The modern function of Civil Code art. 140 is highlighted by a comparison to the socialist doctrine on this article as expressed e.g. in Zbigniew Resich, 'Kodeks cywilny: Komentarzs', *Wydawnictwo Prawnicze*, vol. 1, Warsaw, 1972, art. 140, no. 4.
58. For the problems of transforming these instruments in the law of the German Democratic Republic into the system of real rights of the German Civil Code after reunification, see Beate Grün, 'Transformation spezifischer DDR-Sachenrechtsinstitute in das Recht des BGB durch die Sachenrechtsbereinigung', in Manssen and Banaszak, *Wandel der Eigentumsordnung*, pp.85–106.
59. For Poland, where these old structures are most widespread, see Izdebski, 'Ownership in "People's Poland"', pp.71–72.
60. Brunner, 'Verfassungsrechtlicher Eigentumsschutz', pp.38–42, also unites both aspects under the heading 'social obligations and public goods' (Sozialgebundenheit und öffentliche Sachen).
61. See the constitutions of the Czech Republic (art. 11.2), Hungary (art. 10 abs. 2) and Slovakia (art. 20.2, for objects beyond the list in art. 4).
62. See the constitutions of the Czech Republic (art. 101.3), Hungary (art. 12.2, § 44/A sect. 1 lit. b), Poland (art. 165.1) and Slovakia (art. 65.1). On Poland, see de Vries, 'Die Eigentumsgarantie in Polen', p.174; on the Czech Republic, see Petr Havlan, 'Das Eigentum der kommunalen und regionalen Selbstverwaltungen im tschechischen Recht', *Jahrbuch für Ostrecht* 2 (2004), pp.351–61; on Hungary, see Herbert Küpper, *Autonomie im Einheitsstaat*, pp.271–75, 318–26.
63. In Yugoslavia, the situation differed in that local councils too were entitled to have property. This is why the present constitutions of Croatia and Slovenia do not have a guarantee of communal property: it is a matter of course that does not need to be stressed or protected in contrast to the socialist past.

64. Tímea Drinóczi, *Gazdasági alkotmány és gazdasági alapjogok*, Budapest/Pécs, 2007, p.179, dedicates one phrase to art. 10.1 of the Constitution in the framework of her analysis of the constitutional property order. According to her, that clause indicates that the state as proprietor cannot rely upon the guarantee of property as a basic right the way a private proprietor can, because the state cannot be the subject of basic rights. However, this idea arises from the general principles of basic rights anyway – as Drinóczi herself acknowledges. Therefore, this interpretation of art. 10.1 would render that clause superfluous at best. A somewhat different interpretation is given by János Zlinszky, 'Superflua lex? Non loquitur?' *Magyar Jog* (2007), pp.724–28. He interprets art. 10.1 as a partly material, partly formal ban on privatization, the formal ban meaning that only a parliamentary statute may dispose of state property through privatization. This interpretation is based on the proceedings at the round table between the Communist Party and the opposition in summer 1989, and therefore bears no compulsory, but at best persuasive authority – and now, twenty-plus years after the round table, probably not even that.
65. On this, see Herbert Küpper, 'Sozialistische Überreste in den Verfassungen der neuen EU-Mitgliedstaaten im Lichte des gemeinschaftsrechtlichen Homogenitätsgebots', *Jahrbuch für Ostrecht* 2 (2007), pp.203–61.
66. From a technical perspective, the state may choose among various options. Until 2006, the Hungarian state secured its say in its companies through 'golden shares' that grant its proprietor special votes. Then the law was amended – partly under pressure from Brussels – and the institution of the 'golden share' was rescinded. Since then, the state has sent special representatives into the decision-making bodies of these companies. On this, see Michael Pießkalla, *Goldene Aktien aus EG-rechtlicher Sicht*, Hamburg, 2006, pp.275–92; Michael Pießkalla, '"Goldene Aktien": Ungarisches Privatisierungsgesetz geändert', *Wirtschaft und Recht in Osteuropa* 16/7 (2007), pp.193–97.
67. The most important regulations are contained in specialized statutes pertaining to state budget law. On this, see Liebscher and Zoll, *Polnisches Recht*, p.169.
68. Hungarian Civil Code, art. 172–81.
69. The relevant norms in the Polish Civil Code, especially in art. 126–29, were rescinded in 1990.
70. The most important of these laws is Act 2007: CVI on state property of 17 September 2007. This law also terminates the privatization process.
71. Goods outside commercial use are, for example, public roads that are open to everybody without toll, pavements and parks. Goods in special commercial use include mineral resources and tracts of water. The most common instrument to admit controlled private use of these commodities is the concession.
72. Constitution of Croatia, art. 52.
73. Constitution of Slovenia, art. 70.
74. Constitution of Croatia, arts. 4, 32.2 and 35, and the Property Act (1996); Slovenia's Real Rights Code (2002), art. 19, 44.
75. See the constitutions of Croatia (art. 48.2), the Czech Republic (art. 11.3) and Slovakia (art. 20, abs. 3).
76. See the constitutions of Croatia (art. 50.2), which concerns rights to property and entrepreneurial freedom; the Czech Republic (art. 11.4), under the same conditions as expropriation; Poland (art. 64.3), under strict condition that actions proceed under the authority of a statute, and with respect to proportionality and to the essence of the property right; and Slovakia (art. 20.4), under the same conditions as expropriation.
77. Regarding Poland, see Act on the Co-Operation between Public and Private Partners of 28 July 2005; regarding Slovenia, see Act on the Private-Public Partnership of 23 November 2006.

78. An up-to-date, practical overview is provided by the various country reports in Susanne Frank and Thomas Wachter (eds), *Handbuch Immobilienrecht in Europa: Zivil- und steuerrechtliche Aspekte des Erwerbs, der Veräußerung und der Vererbung von Immobilien*, Heidelberg, 2004.
79. The most important of these laws is the Act on Farmland of 23 October 1996.
80. On the situation before the enactment of the 1997 Constitution, see Pawel Czechowski, 'Die Sonderrolle landwirtschaftlich genutzten Bodens am Beispiel Polens', in Tomuschat, *Eigentum im Umbruch*, pp.165–78.
81. Lech Garlicki, *Polskie prawo konstytucyjne*, Warsaw, 2002, p.82, interprets art. 23 as a constituent part of the canon of values enshrined in the Polish Constitution; see also Piotr Winczorek, 'Die neue Verfassung der Republik Polen – ein Streit um Werte', in *Forschungsstelle Osteuropa an der Universität Bremen: Recht und Kultur in Ostmitteleuropa*, Bremen, 1999, pp.279–95.
82. Act on Agricultural Land of 16 July 2001, § 1.1.
83. This attempt at autarchy does not necessarily target the food supply, but may have other aims, such as a higher degree of energy independence. In some countries of East Central Europe, the conversion of plants into fuel is progressing well.
84. This legal obligation is set out with special emphasis in the Czech Republic and Hungary.
85. See Act on the Administration of Agricultural Land of the State of 12 May 1995. On this, see de Vries, 'Die Eigentumsgarantie in Polen', pp.176–77; Erhardt Gralla, 'Immobilienerwerb und -nutzung in Polen', *Jahrbuch für Ostrecht* 2 (1996), pp.303–34; Aneta Suchon and Jan Schürmann, 'Grundstücksverkehr mit landwirtschaftlichen Grundstücken in der Republik Polen', *Agrar- und Umweltrecht* 34/6 (2004), pp.169–74.
86. On the free movement of capital, see Treaty on the Functioning of the European Union (Lisbon, 2009), article 63, para. 1.
87. A comprehensive description of more or less all formerly communist countries in Eastern Europe – though somewhat dated – is given by Brunner, 'Verfassungsrechtlicher Eigentumsschutz', pp.43–51, and by Herwig Roggemann, 'Eigentum in Ost und West – Zur Entwicklung eines Rechtsinstituts aus rechtsvergleichender Sicht', in Roggemann, *Eigentum in Osteuropa*, pp.17–58.
88. In Poland, these fears are the counterpart of the imagined conservation of the nation via the private property of farmers during the era of partition. Just as the landed property of Polish farmers is believed to have protected the dwelling grounds of the Polish nation, the landed property of Germans is believed capable of threatening or even terminating the existence of the Polish nation in the affected territories. On this, see Roland Freudenstein and Hennig Tewes, 'Stimmungstief zwischen Deutschland und Polen: Für eine Rückkehr zur Interessengemeinschaft', *Internationale Politik* 2 (2000), pp.49–56.
89. Constitution of Croatia, art. 48.3.
90. Constitution of Slovenia, art. 68; this clause was liberalized in 2003 in preparation for accession to the EU.
91. Charter of the Czech Republic, art. 11.2; Constitution of Slovakia, art. 20.2.
92. Property Act (1996), art. 355–57.
93. Suchon and Schürmann, *Grundstücksverkehr mit landwirtschaftlichen Grundstücken*, pp.170–172.

4

The Habsburg Cadastral Registration System in the Context of Modernization

Kurt Scharr

Introduction. The Land Register of Francis I: An Object of Political Communication?

The land register of Emperor Francis I of Austria (reigned 1804 to 1835) and its socio-political significance, hitherto neglected by historical science, have mainly been the object of (cause-related) considerations frequently reduced to technical aspects.[1] Such considerations are of great value in dealing with the land register as a source, but they only barely attempt to place Francis I's undertaking in a larger context, balanced in its depth by the modernization of the state at a macro-political level.[2] At the opposite level, however, these considerations leave regional or local access untouched (except for the numerous accounts of local history that content themselves with, for example, visually representing a place), or generally refer to the land register's importance for cultural landscape research.[3] They only occasionally refer to the value of the land register as a source of social and economic history.[4]

It is precisely this land register's role as a medium and object – as it is seen by modern cultural history[5] – that allows researchers to ask, 'under which communication structures are the social, economic, religious, cultural and moral transformed into the political, and how are the limits of transformability determined?'[6] This land register should thus be re-analysed over its long duration as an 'institution' from the perspective of a cultural history understood as a history of the political.[7] Social efficacy, as applied to Francis I's land register, should meanwhile be checked not only in terms of legal traditions and legal understanding, but also in terms of territoriality. The land register is intrinsically tied to the territory as a social construct. Is Francis I's land register consequently also a means of spatial construction? With regard to the scope of the present volume, I consider Francis I's land register to be a significant component ('agent') of the process of 'propertization' addressed in the Introduction.

The Land Register of Francis I: A Means of Spatial Construction?

The modern state needs a spatially comprehensible, statistically manageable and precisely defined – both externally and internally – territory, within which its norms, equally applicable to all citizens, become legally effective, so that its political area can be constituted to lasting effect. This is an abridged paraphrasing of the territorial ligation of the political system that has developed in the modern period. Francis I's land register, introduced into the Habsburg territories as the basis of a direct and equal tax system, thus constituted a medium of political communication aimed, among other things, at excluding and weakening individual corporate interests in favour of a newly standardized direct relationship between the citizen and an abstract state. This state became comprehensible, both objectively and as a judicial body, by means of its omnipresent administrative centre – the imperial capital – and legal measures (for example, tax regulation). Thus the available spatial organization of social relations and power relations assumes a new quality, beyond formally determining geographical location.[8]

As will be shown in the case of Bukovina, an institutionalized concept of standardization that has existed long enough (Francis I's land register was crucial to this) lends momentum to these ascriptions and suggestions to the cadastre, so that, deterministic statements aside, one may presume that space will have repercussions on society.[9] The reform plans of Maria Theresa and Joseph II, as discussed below, appear to have been short-lived from a fiscal point of view, perhaps because the emperor's social position was too weak and the resistance of the estates was at first too strong, or because the early death of Joseph II prevented many of these attempts at innovation from developing to sufficient stability, or because the state had been in a latent and permanent existential crisis ever since Maria Theresa's accession to power. However, if the various undertakings are evaluated together, in terms of the process of rebuilding the state and with reference to land tax (and the land register as their basis), then these steps in the process of reform exhibit a continuity of effect spanning the whole nineteenth century and they (esp. the land register) were reinvigorated by the latter on installed land exoneration, land tax adjustments and so on.

Bukovina, as the youngest Crown land, was especially affected by this process. Previously a part of Upper Moldova, occupied by imperial troops in 1774 and incorporated into the Habsburg Empire in 1775, Bukovina was, more than other provinces, shaped by a bundle of measures in the course of state reforms that indeed gave it its form as well as a (supranational) regional identity that developed throughout the second half of the nineteenth century. To be sure, Francis I's land register was hardly the sole cause of this. However, it is the land register and its efficacy beyond its physical (legal) relevance (until the years between 1945 and 1948, and since 1989) that reveal this area as a medium of social system relations[10] and a conveyor of these over time, and which permit its examination as such. Work with the land register of Francis I is therefore an attempt to analyse the ideas and effects of the territorial state on a macro-political level, and thereby differentiate and evaluate the spatial-organizational and, in reaction (in combination with other measures and developments), the space-forming character of a region.

The cadastre and later land register, as modern organizational instruments of Habsburg rule and its massive Western influence on Moldova from the late eighteenth century, strengthened the existing geopolitical segments (in terms of imperial presence and rule) on the basis of Eastern and Western Europe's differing rates of development,[11] which immediately affected each other in this relatively small area (Upper Moldova, Bukovina and the rest of Moldova). Bukovina especially exemplified a spatially non-homogeneous rate of development and structure in an originally uniform political area (the Principality of Moldova). By the end of the eighteenth century, Bukovina, together with Galicia-Lodomeria, presented a special case of non-synchronized development within the Habsburg Empire. Large but often utterly inefficiently managed manorial systems stood next to completely poor smallholders.[12] The widespread nineteenth-century process of social modernization did not help Bukovina attain equal status with the other lands of the Empire, but it did produce a decisive, structural head start in comparison to the rest of Moldova, which either became part of the Russian Empire (Bessarabia, from 1812) or belonged to the Kingdom of Romania. After 1918, the new centre (Bucharest) often looked on Bukovina as an exemplary reflection of its own arrears, which it had to clear in connection with 'Europe'.[13] Modernization processes (including agrarian reform) initiated during the interwar period largely failed. Right up to the present day, therefore, the former Romanian region (Moldova and Walachia as the first Romanian kingdom from 1881 to 1922) lacks an area-wide cadastre, whereas Western-influenced regions such as Banat, Bukovina and Transylvania have a significant and continuing structural advantage in ongoing transformation processes in Romanian (and to some extent Ukrainian) society.

Can Francis I's land register ultimately be regarded as a 'spacing', now gaining momentum, that made and is making a significant contribution to the dynamically processual constitution of areas (regions)? Is the cadastre more than just a means of recording and organizing an area? Does it undergird an interstice in which a cultural landscape can come into being? These questions are part of a continuing research project on the land register of Francis I at the Universities of Klagenfurt and Innsbruck.[14] This brief theoretical sketch of the subject is followed by an attempt to show the development and the 'state-political' objectives surrounding the land register of Francis I. The aim addressed at the regional level of Bukovina itself – although it cannot, at this early stage of the project, go far beyond suggestions – will enter the formulation of further questions in contexts to be disclosed.

A Beneficial Christmas Present to Subjects?

> In consideration of the incongruities arising from allocating land tax in accordance with the existing measure of distribution for entire provinces, circles, districts and communities, as well as for individual contributors, we have decided, after careful consideration of this grievance and how best to redress it, to establish in all our German and Italian provinces a fundamentally cheap and in its application fixed system of land tax. Our guiding principles in this generally useful undertaking have been: to apply the strictest form of equality, to encourage the culture of the land by applying the correct measure of land tax, and where possible to promote its beneficial advances. (Emperor Francis I, Preamble, supreme patent of 23 December 1817)

When Emperor Francis I decreed this patent on the eve of 24 December 1817, the modern, self-constituting territorial state was preparing to deal with the financial and state crisis that had culminated in the state bankruptcy of 1811. The state had been in a sustained phase of rebuilding since at least the reign of Maria Theresa (1740–1780) and throughout the tenures of her successors, Joseph II (1765–1790) and Leopold II (1790–1792). The focus was on development and reinforcement, in part through territorial and manorial standardization, of the increasingly hierarchical state power at the expense of the estates and lands – more succinctly, the *Unum Totum* (All in Entirety). With Francis's acceptance of an Austrian Empire in 1804 and the unlawful abdication of the Imperial Crown of the Holy Roman Empire in 1806, the Habsburg state had cleverly managed to overcome its identity crisis and the question of its own legitimacy, but modernization itself was by no means concluded. On the contrary, the Napoleonic Wars had painfully laid bare the state's deficits and, by increasing the need for capital, inflamed the smouldering crisis that left the credit standing of the state 'as good as destroyed' for years to come.[15]

As other studies of cadastres in Europe have shown, the tax surpluses expected immediately upon implementation of the land register of Francis I were initially low in comparison to the expense of creating and maintaining it.[16] One reason for this discrepancy was that the land register, as a basis for measuring the land tax, raised a net amount that was far lower than the regularly and actually obtained amounts.[17] This was particularly so in Bukovina, and was attributable above all to the relevant applicable temporary tax solutions, whose calculation, and the inconstancy of their basis, had been influenced by the long period needed to create the land register itself.[18] Here, the specific intention to exclude any corporate co-determination of estates as a serious intermediary body in raising taxes appears – at least at first – to have been of considerable importance, promising more long-term benefit for the modern state.[19] Exact parcelling of land, spatially traceable placements, the survey of an entire region and the way of estimating returns – in which this land register differed substantially from its eighteenth-century predecessors – ultimately created a basis for new structures that allowed the land register of Francis I to assume new attributes of shifting emphasis throughout its long existence.

This situation had three important outcomes: the conclusive limiting of corporate power to a politically irrelevant level; the progressive and increasingly irreversible organization of a centralized, territorially rounded national territory; and its sustenance and indirect financing (independent of the will of the estates) via the new tax basis of the basic returns tax.

With the introduction of the Austrian Civil Code (the Allgemeine Bürgerliche Gesetzbuch, ABGB) in 1811, the founding of the Austrian National Bank in 1816 and the previously mentioned Supreme Patent concerning Basic Tax of 1817, the political foundations of a new financing system had been created. The beginning of a systematic, state-led – albeit still strongly military – mapping in the land survey of Francis I launched in 1806 (followed by a second topographical land survey between 1806 and 1869) paved the way for the first standard cartographic survey of the entire national territory (at a scale of 1:28,800). Its result was the indispensable (technical) basis for the later addition of a spatially represented land tax register of the Empire.

From contemporaries' point of view, the tax revenue reflected the fitness of the state: 'The true strength of the state can be judged most reliably on the basis of this . . . because without taxes there are no weapons, and without weapons no state'. On the other hand, a system of this kind was also associated with a desire to smooth out the numerous spatial and social differences in tax liability into a political system obliged to an *Unum Totum*: 'It is generally acknowledged in the state economy that one of its first and most important tasks is to introduce a land tax which is equal and fair in all possible relations . . . but it is also the most difficult of all to solve'.[20]

As early as the second half of the eighteenth century, the Habsburgs in Vienna had begun using a land taxation system as a means of 'adjusting screws'[21] to effectively change the idea of sovereignty from the principle of an association of people to that of a territory. The taxation system in general, and its concrete implementation – in this case, the land register of a community based in an agricultural area and governed by the Austrian Empire in the late eighteenth and early nineteenth centuries – are indisputably an expression of political communication. The aspiration to tax equity and the equality of all citizens in this respect was a significant driving force behind the *Unum Totum*, whose sincerity, whether the state's or the emperor's, cannot be denied. From this perspective, Francis I's conscious staging of this legal act on the eve of the Christmas festivities of 1817 may rightly be viewed as a 'present to his subjects'. However, the raising of inland revenue and the corporate mediatization (i.e. the ongoing political exclusion of diets) or 'de-regionalization' of the state (in the sense of the state's power) proceeding step by step in parallel to this were equally important aspects.

The legal standardizing aspect of Francis I's land register should not be overlooked, especially considering its lasting effects on the makeup of society in general. At the level of individual tracts of land, the instrument of the land register, drawn up in the form of tract boundaries, not only assumed a function of error control, but also exactly and verifiably established property boundaries, which were necessarily set with the agreement of all parties involved (owners and state).[22] In this light, therefore, we are presented with a detailed survey of property by means of a standardized and (in its scale) far-reaching communication process in the society itself.

From 'Ideological Myth' to Complete Fiscal Control of a Territory

The attempted reforms to improve basic taxation under Maria Theresa and Joseph II clearly indicate that estates reacted most vehemently to the threat of losing power.[23] Neither landlord and farmer nor lordliness and rusticity were inseparably related. A determined tendency to standardize jurisdiction as part of territorial consolidation had been evident since the thirteenth century (the early land settlement in Tyrol under Meinhard III is a classic Central European example of this). By the eighteenth century at the latest, the territorial principle had risen to the status of a national-political maxim. This essentially left the estates (that is to say, the landlords) with only fiscal jurisdiction, to which the sovereign had previously had little if any direct access.

The first comprehensive attempt to equalize relations between liege or landlord and farmer at a level controlled uniformly by the sovereign, undertaken by Leopold I (1657–1705) in Austria ob der Enns (present-day Upper Austria) in 1679 (*Tractatus de ruribus incorporabilis*), failed due to massive rejection by the estates, whose political support the emperor at this time depended on. In the end, the Habsburg Empire's precarious financial situation, which it had slid into as a result of the politically controversial succession of Maria Theresa, forced a renewed attempt. Maria Theresa's patent of 16 September 1748 established legal regulations separating lordly and rustic land,[24] and included them permanently in taxation for the first time.[25] This standardizing legal act for Austrian and Bohemian hereditary lands attempted to suppress the exchanges taking place in areas with strong manorial structures, frequently to the disadvantage of farmers (from rustic to lordly land). This legislation had little effect on states such as Tyrol, where a special situation had brought about a considerably earlier transition to hereditary lease, but it fell heavily on the more eastern states of the Habsburgs (for example, Galicia-Lodomeria). Nearly a quarter of a century later, the monarch launched a renewed, more successful attempt, in which the general taxation obligation affecting both landlords and farmers was enshrined as a legal principle for the first time.[26] In reality, these steps triggered improvements only in the land tax constitution of different hereditary lands over the following decades; comprehensive standardization beyond their borders remained out of reach for the time being.[27] The tax assessment base was created using assessments based on the average market value of the relevant property, as stated by property owners.[28] A by-product of the *Fassion* (of Maria Theresa) introduced by this,[29] which set up local district offices for tax regulation, was the district councils that emerged in the nineteenth century and exist to this day.

Through tax regulation, Joseph II made a renewed attempt to equalize relations between landlord and farmer in 1785, although this time the emperor aimed to tax the (gross) profit per tract of profitable land (that is, not including unproductive land), regardless of the social position of the owner or proprietor.[30] This form of general and equal taxation of land was completely groundbreaking in Europe at the time – not until 1790 did the French National Assembly decide to abolish all tax privileges.[31] With the exception of Bukovina and Tyrol-Vorarlberg, this regulation included all hereditary lands,[32] except the lands under the crown of Stephen and the Prince Archbishopric of Salzburg, which was still sovereign at that time. The national-political significance of the emperor's radical cadastral survey can be gauged simply from the facts that, in only four years, over 200,000 square kilometres were surveyed, and that Vienna arranged a provisional abeyance of an ongoing military mapping in Inner Austria and Tyrol in order to have sufficient specialist staff at its disposal.[33] The estates, which saw this system as depriving them of a significant proportion of their income and political power, renewed their opposition to this measure with such vehemence that ultimately its implementation had to wait until 1790, during the reign of Leopold II (though this delay was probably also due to Joseph II's premature death and technical problems).

All these reform plans, especially those of Maria Theresa and Joseph II, should rightly be regarded as forerunners of the Francis I land register,[34] and were undoubtedly in line with the ideological trajectory of the state in its newly defined self-image.[35]

The Land Register of Francis I: An Undertaking of European Scale

Francis I's 'present to his subjects', developed within fifty years, was divided into three main components of existing sources: writings (especially land and building records concerning tracts of land), files (land-register documents) and assessments (profit assessments for individual tracts of land, economic cadastral municipality descriptions). Centralized, tight specifications, uniform methods of collecting data and rigorous checks[36] enabled a remarkable achievement: the recording of 30,556 cadastral municipalities consisting of 49,138,140 properties in 164,375 file documents for a total surveyed area of 30,008,200 hectares.[37] Hungary's inclusion would follow in the course of the 1848 revolution.[38] The land-register survey (conducted from 1817 to 1861) thus comprised a significant portion of Central Europe, from Bregenz (Vorarlberg) in the far west to Czernowitz (Bukovina) in the easternmost Crown territory.

The protracted duration of the levy unearthed the disadvantages of a permanent land register, so that even during the work certain re-measurements and situation updates became necessary. In 1869, two years after the settlement with Hungary, the Imperial Diet had to pass a property tax law incorporating revised land-register documents.[39] Once all subsequent entries were agreed on, this would allow everything to be kept on file, enabling standardization.[40] The undertaking nevertheless took thirteen years to complete. Flanking these measures were the land register's introduction in 1871 and passage of a file-keeping law in 1883,[41] together with a law revising the land tax register.[42] They were meant to remove any errors and violations in property assessment, as well as any permanent changes to measures concerning the attached cultural categories or the realignment of boundaries. These legal measures, as the examples of Tyrol-Vorarlberg and Bukovina demonstrate, were not successfully implemented immediately or in their entire scope in every Austrian territory.

Implementation of the Land Register of Francis I in Bukovina

In 1775, Bukovina, a relatively small (barely 10,000 square kilometres), economically weak area of Upper Moldova on the eastern slopes of the Carpathian Mountains, entered into Habsburg possession by means of skilled negotiations and military pressure on the Sublime Porte. From 1775 to 1786, Bukovina stood under the direct administration of Vienna; after this, it belonged to the Kingdom of Galicia-Lodomeria (nineteenth district) until 1849, when it became a Crown territory, the 'Duchy of Bukovina'.[43] The aim of the 'Austrian' administration in this young province of the Habsburg Empire was above all land organization, which was to spread from this area to the remaining areas of the Empire as quickly and efficiently as possible. Making agricultural culture and its income the most important element of the physiocratic state conception was an urgent task whose importance is expressed in its direct administration, until 1786, by the Court War Council in Vienna.[44]

Although the resident manorial system in Bukovina was structurally speaking relatively weakly developed in comparison to other provinces, the relationship between landlord and farmer still proved largely unregulated. This opened the floodgates to the arbitrariness of the authorities.[45] Standardizing the organization of these legal relationships was thus crucial to any enduring land organization in the interest of the state. The Court War Council, as a responsible agent of the central authorities in Vienna, pointed openly to these land proprietorship-related grievances against the emperor, and recommended a comprehensive land-register survey.[46]

Thus a (land register) survey was conducted between 1782 and 1784 for the economically important region of Bukovina between the Prut and Dniester rivers.[47] However, this first attempt to economically map Bukovina was discontinued in 1784 on the highest orders, since neither state nor sovereign (the emperor) possessed much property in this province.[48] The situation did not change decisively until a Greek-Oriental Bukovina religious fund was set up (from previous Church property), making the state de facto the largest landowner in the territory. This political-economic undertaking of the survey was concluded in at least one respect in 1789, insofar as the village settlements of Bukovina received legally binding and registered boundaries for the first time.[49] Another reason for discontinuing the survey surely also lay in the difficulty of implementing it in practice, since Joseph II's land register had allowed for individually calculating the gross profit from one parcel of land to another but did not assume – as the later Permanent Land Register did – degrees of creditworthiness.[50] This incompleteness alone made it impossible to achieve any significant improvement in the situation, which is why, as early as the beginning of the nineteenth century, another untenable tax burden had to be declared in Bukovina.[51]

In 1818, Emperor Francis I ordered a provisional land tax solution for Bukovina, to apply until the end of the actual land-register work begun there in 1819.[52] This temporary regulation taxed the property listed in older registers oriented to profits from goods. But at the same time, tributary communities had to determine and pay their tax debt according to an individual form of contribution ability (*Tschisla*), which the authorities had no direct influence over.[53] For the time being, the individual community remained taxable as a collective, assessing the tax debt itself according to its own system based on the individual possibilities of its members. Although the surveying authorities had begun to draw up files for their land register and divide land-register communities relatively early in Bukovina, by 1823 these tasks were only partially completed.[54] Unsurprisingly, the provisional land tax solution had to be updated in 1835, as the full extent of the tax debts could hardly be gauged.[55] Overall, however, the (first) clear division between manorial and tenants' land took prominence in work on the land register in Bukovina, even from a contemporary point of view.[56]

The land-register survey work in Bukovina remained incomplete until the years 1854 to 1856 (with subsequent entries until 1862). The delays were undoubtedly due to the political upheavals during the revolution of 1848. In addition, one should not forget that the survey of Galicia-Lodomeria met with considerable resistance among the estates, and Bukovina's district of Czernowitz was in fact a marginal area of Galicia. It thus seems logical that when the emperor visited Czernowitz in 1823, the survey work that had begun very early ground immediately to a halt. In other Galician districts, work on the land register was taken up again in 1824. The surveying was also hindered by a raging cholera epidemic in 1830/31, which, as demonstrated by comparison with the land-register data of the other Crown territories, produced a lengthy setback. Undoubtedly, the Polish uprising in neighbouring Russia affected Galicia similarly. Starting in 1844, consistent steps were taken to complete the Galician districts, and their survey was finished in 1854. After this, it was Bukovina's turn once again. An exoneration, introduced in 1848 but which could nonetheless only be implemented by the land register, led to delays for the latter at the same time. The full extent of the land register never came into force for Bukovina.[57] Until the land regulation of 1880, further provisional solutions had to suffice here.[58] Nonetheless, after a total of eight years of work, Bukovina's balance sheet had 319 surveyed, registered and admitted land-register communities amounting to 1,045,000 hectares and 798,707 parcels of land.[59]

For now, we can go no further into questions of the detailed progress of the land-register survey, the interplay between various authorities (especially in Bukovina) and the population concerned, the selection of the officials acting locally, their 'communication' with the union representatives appointed by the communities, or finally the concrete implementation and acceptance of this new regulation system. These are all topics for subsequent research.

Summary

In a state structured along predominantly agrarian lines, such as that represented by the mid-nineteenth-century Habsburg Empire, land use, property distribution, exploitation rights and the tax jurisdiction demanded by the central state were of fundamental importance as a complex system in the development of the whole organization of the 'state'. The foregoing has clearly demonstrated that the state's tax reform plans in the context of state modernization were ultimately of a secondary nature in the long term. The reform endeavours of Maria Theresa and Joseph II in this sector clearly emphasize the greater problems facing this reform process across the whole state. During an externally controlled period of crisis, the state doubled down on its project of internal consolidation. But the power of the estates and territories hampered this project – an undertaking that, given the physically limited administrative capacities of the centre and the defended power of the periphery (territories), could hardly have been implemented in the medium term anyway.

Within this whole process, the land register of Francis I was thus a decisive milestone on the path towards the modern centralized state. Its contribution to the development of a new legal system appears to have been of key importance in connection with nineteenth-century legal actions arising as a consequence of or prior to its completion (such as the successive land register and the Austrian Civil Code), especially because it established or precisely defined property and legal boundaries for the first time, both at the level of the relevant cadastral community and between the individual owners and/or users at the level of the smallest unit, the tract of land. It thereby laid the cornerstone of the legal understanding of property and property laws, which was still largely a novelty, especially in Bukovina at that time. Moreover – with regard to the original intention of the land register in the imperial patent of 1817 – the longevity of the institution of the land register itself, especially in its connection to the land register set up in the late nineteenth century, has played a remarkable role in the organization and understanding of property in society. The vast cost of drawing up the land-register files and records, and the ultimate lack (due to the prolongation of the levy) of the comparability of basic income (and thus also of actual land value) between territories – already known to contemporaries[60] – also point to the importance of Francis I's land register above and beyond pure land taxation.

Introduction of the land register established a legal basis for a new understanding of property, which resulted, especially in Bukovina, in an enduring separation of manorial and farmers' land, and thus ultimately a legal, albeit in reality quite slow, betterment of farmers' progress in this province. Indeed, not every state regulation on landowning restricts power of disposal over it from the outset, or inhibits economic development. When the situation under the nineteenth-century Habsburg Empire is compared to the further development in Romania in the twentieth century, the contrary effect of these processes of building a modern state (depending on one's socio-political starting position) becomes particularly striking, the more so as development can be gauged from the example of Bukovina becoming part of Romania after 1918. Taking the thought to its logical conclusion prompts one to ask to what extent the presence or absence of a land register might be a structural advantage or disadvantage of serious consequence right up to the present time, in a society undergoing transformation (such as Romania or Ukraine since the fall of communism). Do former (agrarian) peripheral areas like Bukovina presently profit from it? If yes, to what extent? These questions naturally also concern the spatial identity of the area's inhabitants and cannot simply be reduced to economic advantages.

From the perspective of regional identity in Bukovina, the land register of Francis I is a strong motif in an overall mosaic. The Austrian Constitution of 1861, by approving 'autonomous' parliaments, supported the development of provincial identities (especially after 1867), particularly those that leant, as Bukovina did, on the central *Unum Totum*, which had in the meantime developed into a *Viribus Unitis* (With United Forces) However, this constitution specifically granted the parliaments co-determination and decision-making rights in the development of the provinces via associations.[61] The standardizing and shaping land register was consequently a co-factor in the development of socially perceived and constructed cultural landscapes like that of Bukovina, which matured into the essence of regional identification.

Notes

Research for this chapter was conducted with the aid of the Austrian Science Fund (FWF), which generously financed the research project 'Der "Franziszeische Kataster" (1817) Kärnten/Bukowina, 2008–2011' (P20219).

1. Ingrid Kretschmer, '150 Jahre Österreichischer Grundsteuerkataster', *Mitteilungen der Österreichischen Geographischen Gesellschaft* 110/1 (1968), pp.63–71; Ingrid Kretschmer, 'Die Entwicklung der österreichischen Katastralmappen und ihre Bedeutung für die Geographie', *Mitteilungen der Österreichischen Geographischen Gesellschaft* 116 (1974), pp.206–18; Karl Lego, *Geschichte des Österreichischen Grundkatasters*, Vienna, 1968; Robert Messner, 'Der Franziszeische Grundsteuerkataster: Ein Überblick über seinen Werdegang und sein Wirken', *Jahrbuch des Vereins für Geschichte der Stadt Wien* 28 (1972), pp.62–105, and 29 (1973), pp.88–141; Robert Messner, *150 Jahre österreichische Grundkataster*, Vienna, 1967.
2. Luca Mannori presents a newer approach to cadastral research. He describes the cadastre as 'one of the emblems of state modernization, whose acceptance represents the separating line between state harmonization and the continued existence of a traditional conglomerate of obsolete imperial structures unwilling to renounce their own sovereignty in favor of a greater whole': Luca Mannori (ed.), *Kataster und moderner Staat in Italien: Spanien und Frankreich (18. Jh.)*, Baden Baden, 2001, Editorial, retrievable from: http://www.rsf.uni-greifswald.de/heyen/jev/jev-13/editorial.html.
3. For instance, Andreas Moritsch, 'Der franziszeische Kataster und die dazugehörigen Steuerschätzungsoperate als wirtschafts- und sozialhistorische Quellen', *East European Quarterly* 3 (1970), pp.447f.; Hanns Bachmann, *Das Buch von Kramsach*, Innsbruck and Munich, 1972, attempts to apply the land register of Francis I to regional questions of farmland and settlement development. Bachmann applies the method of writing back, developed by A. Krenzlin, to Tyrol. See Anneliese Krenzlin and Ludwig Reusch, *Die Entstehung der Gewannflur nach Untersuchungen im nördlichen Unterfranken*', Frankfurt am Main, 1961. Austrian economic history discovered this source at a relatively early stage. See Johann Peisker, 'Die österreichische Wirtschaftsgeschichte und ihr wichtigster Behelf', lecture held at the monthly assembly of the Anthropological Society of Vienna, 12 January 1897, pp.1–7.
4. Roman Sandgruber, 'Der Franziszeische Kataster als Quelle für die Wirtschaftsgeschichte und historische Volkskunde', *Mitteilungen des Niederösterreichischen Landesarchivs* 3 (1979), pp.16–28; Roman Sandgruber, 'Österreichische Agrarstatistik 1750–1918', in Alfred Hoffmann, Herbert Matis and Michael Mitterauer (eds), *Materialien zur Wirtschafts- und Sozialgeschichte*, vol. 2,

Vienna, 1978, pp.29–34. By contrast, the same author finds no suitable place for the land register of Francis I as a central mechanism in implementing the modern state in his survey of Austrian economic history. See Roman Sandgruber, *Ökonomie und Politik: Österreichische Wirtschaftsgeschichte vom Mittelalter bis zur Gegenwart*, Vienna, 1995, pp.216, 224. Helmut Rumpler's monograph on the development of the Habsburg state sees the land register of Francis I as far more than a mere means of tax regulation, and assigns it primary importance during this reform period. See Helmut Rumpler, *Eine Chance für Mitteleuropa: Bürgerliche Emanzipation und Staatsverfall in der Habsburgermonarchie*, Vienna, 1997, pp.150–53.

5. The new cultural history rejects attempts at definition based on specific objects and tries instead to open up a specific perspective on all possible objects. See Ute Daniel, *Kompendium Kulturgeschichte: Theorien, Praxis, Schlüsselworte*, Frankfurt am Main, 2001, p.8.
6. Ute Frevert, 'Neue Politikgeschichte: Konzepte und Herausforderungen', in Ute Frevert and Heinz-Gerhard Haupt (eds), *Neue Politikgeschichte: Perspektiven einer historischen Politikforschung*, Frankfurt/New York, 2005, p.24.
7. For theoretical discussion, see Barbara Stolberg-Rilinger, 'Was heißt Kulturgeschichte des Politischen: Einleitung', in Barbara Stolberg-Rilinger (ed.), 'Was heißt Kulturgeschichte des Politischen?' *Zeitschrift für Historische Forschung, Vierteljahresschrift zur Erforschung des Spätmittelalter und der frühen Neuzeit* 35 (2005), pp.9–24.
8. Peter Meusburger, 'Subjekt – Organisation – Region: Fragen an die subjektzentrierte Handlungstheorie', in Peter Meusburger (ed.), *Handlungsorientierte Sozialgeographie: Benno Werlens Entwurf in kritischer Diskussion*, Stuttgart, 1999, pp.95–132.
9. In other words, the strength of areas' social development and their real reaction to it depend on both the social power of the actors creating the area and on the durability of institutionalization of the areas themselves, once constituted. Christof Parnreiter, *Historische Geographie: Verräumlichte Geschichte. Mexico-City und das mexikanische Städtenetz von der Industrialisierung bis zur Globalisierung*, Stuttgart, 2007, p.76.
10. Peter Weichhart, 'Vom "Räumeln" in der Geographie und anderen Disziplinen: Einige Thesen zum Raumaspekt sozialer Phänomene', in Jörg Mayer (ed.), *Die aufgeräumte Welt: Raumbilder und Raumkonzepte im Zeitalter globaler Marktwirtschaft*, Rehburg-Loccum, 1993, p.228.
11. Vasile Surd, 'Ein Teil von Europa wird ausgegrenzt', *Tübinger Geographische Studien* 128 (2000), p.140.
12. Alfred Hoffmann, 'Grundlagen der Agrarstruktur der Donaumonarchie', in Alfred Hoffmann and Roman Sandgruber (eds), *Österreich-Ungarn als Agrarstaat: Wirtschaftswachstum und Agrarverhältnisse im 19. Jahrhundert*, Vienna, 1978, p.16.
13. Mariana Hausleitner, *Die Rumänisierung der Bukowina: Die Durchsetzung des nationalstaatlichen Anspruchs Großrumäniens 1918–1944*, Munich, 2001. See also the discussion of failed modernization in Holm Sundhaussen, 'Wandel ohne Modernisierung: Theorien nachholender Entwicklung unter besonderer Berücksichtigung Südosteuropas', in Krista Zach and Cornelius R. Zach (eds), *Modernisierung auf Raten in Rumänien: Anspruch, Umsetzung, Wirkung*, Munich, 2004, pp.27–32.
14. 'Der "Franziszeische Kataster" (1817–61)', retrievable from: www.fwf.ac.at/de/abstracts/abstract.asp?L=D&file=d:\site\fwf.ac.at\de\abstracts\p20219d.html, a research project by the universities of Klagenfurt and Innsbruck, supported by the FWF-Österreich.
15. Rumpler, *Chance für Mitteleuropa*, p.124; Sandgruber, *Ökonomie und Politik*, pp.221–24. This situation was by no means new. During the reign of Maria Theresa, the susceptibility to crisis of the tax systems in the Habsburg lands had revealed itself on many occasions and set reforms in motion.
16. See Mannori, *Kataster und moderner Staat*, Editorial, retrievable from: http://www.rsf.uni-greifswald.de/heyen/jev/jev-13/editorial.html.
17. Hermann von Schullern zu Schrattenhoven, *Geschichtliche Darstellung der Besteuerung der land- und Forstwirtschaft*, Vienna, 1899, p.966. Contemporaries were also aware of this fact:

see Josef Wessely, 'Österreichischer Grundsteuerkataster', *Österreichische Revue* 2. Band (1865), pp.147f.; *Zur Grundsteuerregulierung in der Bukowina: Denkschrift der Vertreter der Bukowinaer Grunndsteuerträger*, Vienna, 1880.

18. The costs of the cadastral work carried out in Bukovina in 1846 alone totalled 210,455 guilders: *Tafeln zur Statistik der österreichischen Monarchie 1855–57*, vol. 3, Vienna, 1857, Table 29a/b. Chlupp reveals that the costs of drawing up a stable cadastre on the monarchy's state region (bearing in mind that cadastral work in Hungary began only in 1849) reached 22 million guilders by 1853, and a further 8 million guilders were projected for the years 1862 to 1869 in the budget proposals. In total, Chlupp claims, over 45 million guilders were spent on introducing the land tax register over the whole period. See Chlonau Johann Moritz von Chlupp, *Systematisches Handbuch der direkten Steuern im Kaisertum Österreich*, Prague, 1874, p.56.
19. For an equally exemplary study of Lower Austria, see Berhard Hackl, *1853 Die Theresianische Dominikal- und Rustikalfassion in Niederösterreich 1748–1756, ein fiskalischer Reformprozess im Spannungsfeld zwischen Landständen und Zentralstaat*, Frankfurt am Main/Vienna, 1997.
20. Johann R. Carli, *Maylands Steuerverfassung*, Vienna, 1818, Vorwort.
21. Hannes Siegrist, Dietmar Müller, Bogdan Murgescu and Stefan Troebst, 'Bodenrecht, Kataster und Grundbuchwesen im östlichen Europa 1918–1945–1989', research project, Leipzig University, retrievable from: http://hsozkult.geschichte.hu-berlin.de/projekte/id=14.
22. These far-sighted considerations had already been voiced by Johann Jakob Marinoni (1676–1755) when he was appointed to the Milan land register. Kretschmer, 'Die Entwicklungen der Österreichischen Katastralmappen', p.207.
23. Cf. Hackl, *Die Theresianische Dominikal- und Rustikalfassion.*
24. The *Theresianische Steuerrektifikation* (Theresian tax certification) is also more generally known as the *Theresianische Kataster* (Theresian land register).
25. Chlupp, *Systematisches Handbuch*, p.22. Hungary and Galicia were not affected by this. The estates temporarily succeeded, however, in thwarting Maria Theresa's land tax reform. The court decree of 12 November 1756 returned most of their tax power to them; Hackl, *Die Theresianische Dominikal- und Rustikalfassion*, p.183.
26. The patent of 1771 opened with the assertion that the patent enacted on 22 September 1746 'had in no wise been achieved to introduce God-given equality into tax law'. Karl von Eyberg, *Chronologisches systematisches Compilationswerk über das Steuer- und Peräquationswesen Tyrols*, Innsbruck, 1793, appendix.
27. However, these improvements also included Maria Theresa's *robot* regulations (1774, 1775, 1778), which sought to use the state to bring the relationship between landlords and farmers to a preferable, more neutral level.
28. Messner, 'Der Franziszeische Grundsteuerkataster', p.85.
29. It seems inaccurate to describe this chronicle of property relations as a land register, since significant characteristics of the land register (completely new measurement and classification, in addition to a standardized taxation norm) were missing from the Maria-Theresian form.
30. Schullern zu Schrattenhoven, *Geschichtliche Darstellung der Besteuerung*, p.944. The owners themselves determined the area (mostly using measuring ropes and fathom poles). The gross proceeds were also based on the owners' own figures. Both measurements were subject to considerable error due to time pressure. Chlupp, *Systematisches Handbuch*, pp.42, 26ff.
31. See Lego, *Geschichte des Österreichischen Grundkatasters*, pp.15–22.
32. Bohemia, Moravia, Silesia, Galicia-Lodomeria, Austria above and below the Enns, Styria, Carinthia, Carniola, Görz and Gradiska. However, in Messner, 'Der Franziszeische Grundsteuerkataster', p.104, the assumption that no Josephine tax regulation was carried out in Bukovina must be relativized.

33. During the cadastral survey carried out under Francis I, military staff were also preferred for cost reasons. Oskar Regele, *Beitrag zur Geschichte der staatlichen Landesaufnahme und Kartographie in Österreich bis zum Jahre 1918*, Vienna, 1955, pp.19, 21.
34. Messner, *150 Jahre*, p.85.
35. Mannori, *Kataster und moderner Staat*, Editorial, retrievable from: http://www.rsf.uni-greifswald.de/heyen/jev/jev-13/editorial.html.
36. *Instruction zur Ausführung der zum Behufe des allgemeinen Catasters in Folge des 8ten und 9ten Paragraphen des Allerhöchsten Patentes vom 23. December 1817 angeordneten Landes-Vermessung*, Vienna, 1824. New versions of these instructions were constantly published throughout the course of the survey, as were partly separate instructions for individual lands. See *Anleitung zur Aufnahme, Untersuchung und Entscheidung der Einsprüche und Beschwerden gegen die Ansätze des Flächenmaßes u. d. Grundertragsausmittlung zum Behufe des allgemeinen Catasters*, Laibach 1835; *Staly Kataster w Galicyi (der ständige Kataster in Galizien)*, Lemberg, 1866; K.K. Generaldirektion der direkten Steuern (ed.), *Instruction zur Ausführung der in Folge der allerhöchsten Patente vom 23. XII. 1817 und 20. X. 1849 angeordneten Katastralvermessung*, Vienna, 1865.
37. Messner, *150 Jahre*, p.187. The scale of the individual pages is mostly 1:2,880, in the mountains 1:5,760 and in the cities partly 1:440 or 1:720. At the same time, a standard measurement came to be set for the cadastral survey (Lower Austrian fathoms). As early as 1785, Joseph II had decreed that 1 span should be implemented with 1,600 Viennese (Lower Austrian) square fathoms for all Austrian lands (1 fathom equals 1,896 metres; 1 Lower Austrian span equals 5,744,642 square metres). These units of measurement remained valid until the legal introduction of the metric system in Austria in 1871. Cf. Wilhelm Johann Rottleuthner, *Die alten Localmasse und Gewichte nebst den Aichungsvorschriften bis zur Einführung des metrischen Mass- und Gewichtssystems und der Staatsaichämter in Tirol und Vorarlberg*, Innsbruck, 1883.
38. *Reichsgesetzblatt* [hereafter *RGBl.*] Nr. 422/1849, ksl. Patent v. 20. X. on the introduction of the land tax register in Hungary and the setting of an interim land tax solution until the stable land register had been completed. The actual cadastral survey began in 1853, and until the end an interim land tax solution applied to it also. *RGBl.* Nr. 423/1849, ibid., for Transylvania. Tax exemption in Hungary was not lifted until 1848 (§ 4). *RGBl.* Nr. 80/1850, ksl. Patent v. 4. III., when an interim land tax solution (based on the net proceeds) was introduced in Hungary, Croatia and Slavonia together with the coastal region, Transylvania, the Serbian voivodeship and the Banat of Temesvar. Alignment with Hungary in 1867 brought a renewed adjustment. Areas on the military border were excluded from the cadastral survey until 1867, whereupon they gradually disintegrated and were legally incorporated into Hungary.
39. *RGBl.* Nr. 88/1869, v. 24. IV. on the land tax regulation.
40. *RGBL.* Nr. 88/1869, v. 24. IV. § 20: 'the cadastral operations required in order to determine the net yield of the properties will be carried out at the same time in all lands'.
41. Ultimately, it is thanks to this law (and the continuous intersection/actualization between land register and cadastre) that cadastral documents have been preserved as such. Nonetheless, the evidence-retaining law had no effect in Hungary. Continuous actualization did not take place in the kingdom, so the operating factors rapidly became obsolescent and ultimately unusable. This in turn led partly to costly new measurements, such as those carried out in 'Burgenland', which at the time belonged to Hungary and later to Austria. Kretschmer, 'Die Entwicklung der österreichischen Katastralmappen', p.210.
42. *RGBl.* Nr. 95/1871, v. 25. VII. on the introduction of a general land register law. *RGBl.* Nr. 83/1883, v. 23. V. on the evidence retaining of the land tax register (here esp.§ 11, congruence between the land register and the cadastre); *RGBl.* Nr. 121/1896, v. 12. VII. regarding the revision of the land tax register. Evidence retention was nonetheless associated with implementing a revision and was not carried out continuously. Cf. Sandgruber, 'Österreichische Agrarstatistik', p.34.

43. Kurt Scharr, 'Die innere Verwaltungsentwicklung der Bukowina 1775–1918: Beharrlichkeit alter und Heranwachsen neuer politischer Strukturen', *Jahrbücher für Geschichte Osteuropas* 55/2 (2007), pp.178–209.
44. Kurt Scharr, 'Erfolg oder Misserfolg? Die Durchsetzung des modernen Territorialstaates am Beispiel des Ansiedlungswesens in der Bukowina von 1774–1826', in Hans-Christian Maner (ed.), *Grenzregionen der Habsburgermonarchie im 18. und 19. Jahrhundert: Ihre Bedeutung und Funktion aus der Perspektive Wiens*, Münster, 2005, pp.51–87.
45. Raimund Friedrich Kaindl, *Das Unterthanswesen in der Bukowina: Ein Beitrag zur Geschichte des Bauernstandes und seiner Befreiung*, Vienna, 1899. In addition, numerous processes developing from these unclear relations hindered the administrative process. For instance, the imperial audience on the occasion of the sovereign's presence in Czernowitz in 1817 is described in the travel programme as follows: 'Fourth day, afternoon. Audiences for the occupants of Bukovina, who are swarming together from all sides, completely addicted to complaining'. State Archives Chernivci (Ukraine) 1/1/3280, fol. 114. On the arrangement of the stay in Czernowitz.
46. 'Regarding the new facilities to improve the district (Bukovina), our imperial will was not aimed at a border militia, but at useful political means of helping Bukovina to the new form demanded of a well-led province. Our economic survey is therefore not merely meant to measure and describe the content of land area, but also to gain knowledge of its character . . . and more generally of everything which belongs to a basic division, to introducing a fair tax base, to determining the relationship between lords and subjects and otherwise to agriculture and a well-ordered cadastral registration'. Allerhöchster Vortrag 4. II. 1782, Court War Counsellor to the Emperor, Austrian State Archives (ÖSTA) Kriegsarchiv, quoted in J. Paldus, 'Die Einverleibung Galiziens und der Bukowina in die österreichische Monarchie im Jahre 1772 und die Landesaufnahme durch den k.k. Generalquartiermeisterstab 1775–1783', *Mitteilungen der Geographischen Gesellschaft Wien* 59 (1916), p.449.
47. Ibid., pp.446, 449.
48. Emperor Joseph II harboured this attitude because, in his opinion, 'the economic survey in Thesi begun one year ago may be well grounded; in theory, however, such in a land in which the aerario [i.e. the state] is not entitled to the property of any of the land, or whose land is not determined by a military border, where every customs official is remunerated, is a useless and very costly affair'. Ksl. Handschreiben, Czernowitz 19 June 1783; see also Johann Polek, 'Joseph's II. Reisen nach Galizien und der Bukowina und ihre Bedeutung für letztere Provinz', *Jahrbuch des Bukowiner Landesmuseums* 3 (1895), p.61.
49. Cf. Johann Polek, 'Die Bukowina zu Anfang des Jahres 1801', *Jahrbuch des Bukowiner Landesmuseums* 15 (1907), pp.22f., *Arhivele Naţionale Bucureşti, Consiliul Aulic de Război* (ANB-CAR) I/85, Galizisches Gubernium an Hofkriegsrath, Lemberg, 15 March 1777 und ANB-CAR I/91, detto, 9 April 1777. The survey could not be continued until Joseph II renewed his decision regarding the tax regulation necessitated by the union with Galicia-Lodomeria. ÖSTA *Allgemeines Verwaltungsarchiv*, Hofkanzlei Karton 233, ksl. Handbillet an Graf Kollowrat, Lemberg, 6 August 1786.
50. Schullern zu Schrattenhoven, *Geschichtliche Darstellung der Besteuerung*, p.944.
51. '[T]he untenability of the different taxes which the landowners in Bukovina had to pay had made itself clearly felt . . . [T]hey were just as great a burden for the subjects as they were insecure and inadequate for the state's requirements, which meant being able to look to a relative, previously determined tax amount even from this country': Joseph Linden, *Die Grundsteuerverfassung in den deutschen und italienischen Provinzen der österreichischen Monarchie, mit vorzüglicher Berücksichtung des stabilen Katasters*, Vienna, 1840, pp.242f.
52. Similar interim solutions – regionally adapted in each case, right up until the prospect of completing a stable cadastre even in other lands appeared as a transitional solution – assumed

a kind of valve function for the growing tax inequality in such places as Bohemia, Tyrol-Vorarlberg, Illyria (without Carinthia), in the Venetian provinces, Dalmatia and the lands under the Hungarian Crown.

53. Ibid. The spelling of the Slavic word Числа (approximately 'figure') varies between German (*Tschisla*) and Polish (*Czisla*) transcriptions. See A. Joseph Lippert, 'Die Entwicklung des Grundsteuerwesens im Herzogthume Bukowina unter österreichischer Herrschaft', *Czernowitzer Zeitung* 1 (6 January 1868) 1, 1 (28 January 1868) 13, 1 (22 April 1868) 61.
54. Emperor Francis I stayed in Czernowitz in 1823, where he was presented with the cadastral work completed so far. 'After Mass I looked at some parts of the cadastral surveys of Bukovina and appertaining records. The district captain and the survey director were present. The survey is almost completely ready. It is even already beginning in the Kolomyia district. The woodlands are on the documents to a lesser extent than the other objects'. See Rudolf Wagner, *Die Reisetagebücher des österreichischen Kaisers Franz I. in die Bukowina (1817 und 1823)*, Munich, 1979, p.90. The depiction, like the one mentioned above, does not seem to ring exactly true but rather to correspond to the impression it wished to consciously (?) convey to the emperor. Cf. also the survey plan from 1826, where hitherto only the city of Czernowitz and a small number of communities between the Prut and Dniester rivers had been surveyed. State Archives Chernivci (Ukraine) 1/5/408; Linden, *Grundsteuerverfassung*, p.552.
55. 'have informed His Majesty . . . that the distribution of the land tax must be carried out among the individual dominical contributors according to income from urbarial [i.e. tax register] and tithe sums and basic proceeds, and among the rural tax communities according to the proceeds of their concrete property, and that the levies necessary for this purpose must be made unstopped at the expense of the state treasury'. The cadastral data gathered between 1819 and 1823 could thus be referred to as a basis for estimation. Linden, *Grundsteuerverfassung*, pp.243–44.
56. State Archives Chernivci (Ukraine) 1/2/268, fol. 2–4, Gubernium Lemberg an Kreisamt Czernowitz 29. VII. 1803: 'some suggestions regarding a better set up of the Bukovina district', separating the dominical from the rural grounds, 'assigning them to the subjects for their constant use'.
57. K.K. Finanzministerium, *Instruktion zur Ausführung von Vermessung mit Anwendung des Messtisches behufs Herstellung neuer Pläne für die Zwecke des Grundsteuerkatasters (sog. Grüne Instruktion)*, Vienna, 1907, p.11, quoted from Messner, 'Der Franziszeische Grundsteuerkataster', p.97. The profit estimates for Galicia-Lodomeria, Bukovina and Tyrol-Vorarlberg were still missing in 1859, and were apparently not carried out at the current level of knowledge for the stable cadastre. Cf. Sandgruber, '*Österreichische Agrarstatistik*', p.32. The relatively late completion of the stable cadastre in Bukovina (as well as in Tyrol-Vorarlberg) may have contributed to the fact that it was no longer referred to when surveying land tax. As flexible taxation of income slowly began to establish itself, the land tax increasingly lost its importance.
58. Messner, 'Der Franziszeische Grundsteuerkataster', p.139.
59. K.K. Finanzministerium, *Instruktion zur Ausführung von Vermessung*, quoted following Walter Kamenik, 'Katastralvermessung, historische Kontinuität und zeitgenössische Aspekte', in Robert Messner (ed.), 'Der Franziszeische Grundsteuerkataster', *Jahrbuch der des Vereins für Geschichte der Stadt Wien* (1972), p.83. Most of Bukovina appears to have been divided into cadastral communities by 1823. Communities founded later appear in the allocation of the stable cadastre as part of the original cadastral community.
60. Adolph Ficker, 'Die Statistik der Bodenpreise und der bisherigen Methoden ihrer Ermittlung', *Mitteilungen aus dem Gebiete der Statistik* 15 (1869), pp.31–33.
61. See Hoffmann and Sandgruber, *Österreich-Ungarn als Agrarstaat*, p.15.

5

Property between Delimitation and Nationalization

The Notion, Institutions and Practices of Land Proprietorship in Romania, Yugoslavia and Poland, 1918–1948

Dietmar Müller

Introduction

From Tallinn to Belgrade, the historical master narrative of the countries of East Central Europe regards the time between the two world wars as a 'golden age' in which the nation was once again united as a nation-state, and thus connected to modern Europe. The reforms introduced throughout the political, scientific and social spheres after the First World War were to have taken place in the context of a parliamentary democracy and a liberal market society, and extensive agrarian reforms in particular were to have created a solid basis for this liberal-democratic polity in the form of a broad tier of proprietors.[1]

This reading of the interwar period has enjoyed great popularity, especially since 1989, as both private property and the institutions for administering it, like cadastres and land registries, have simultaneously undergone a spectacular ideological rehabilitation in the post-communist transformation of the societies of East Central and South-East Europe. The de-collectivization of agriculture and the redistribution of land in particular are described as a return to liberal European norms and values, as well as indigenous, pre-communist institutions and legal forms.[2] The idea implicit in this bold assertion is that communism produced a radical break in agrarian and property history after 1945, whereas the interwar period was a golden age of liberal and democratic values and institutions, ones that have been restored since 1989. However, using the notion and institution of landownership as *tertium comparationis* to compare these two periods will reveal striking continuities in the governance and administration of land in Romania, Yugoslavia and Poland from the agrarian reforms after the First World War to those after the Second World War.[3]

In what follows, I will discuss this thesis from three angles.[4] At the level of the discourse on property, I will first discuss the reshaping of the liberal-individualistic concept of property, which was increasingly reorganized along collectivist-nationalistic lines over the course of the interwar period. Politically and legally, property increasingly tended to be framed and defined not so much as an individual right but as something serving the nation and the state. The second perspective, set against this nationalization and state control of the legal concept of property, is the distinctive impotence of state institutions to influence real events in agriculture, which could approach sheer blindness in the mere registering of land transactions in rural areas. The winding history of cadastres and land registers illustrates this well. Finally, at the level of practices in landownership, the results of this nationalizing trend in conditions of constant institutional poverty are analysed as a form of increasing statist intervention in agriculture, which passed over into agrarian politics after 1945 without significant breaches in continuity.

Ownership of Land: Liberal Promises and National Realities

In the constitutions of the countries analysed – ratified in Poland in 1921, in Yugoslavia in 1921 and in Romania in 1923 – the notion of property was at once extended and restricted.[5] Some articles basically guaranteed property of any kind, whereas expropriation was limited to public need, with such cases being defined by law and amounts of compensation determined by courts.

Legislators thus found themselves embedded in a history of Western ideas and institutions in which the right to property and the inviolability thereof, protected by the state, had attained the status of a human right ever since the American and French revolutions in the late eighteenth century. Prior to this, and following Scottish, English, French and German philosophers and economists, individual property had to fulfil the function of a moral and material basis for a civil society. Property in this sense is conceived as the basis for a society of property owners, that is, a system of general and formally equal property rights in which key social resources, long-term property rights and rights of disposal are decoupled from traditional conditions such as social estate, ancestry, regional and national background, religious denomination, ethnicity and so on. The promise of this liberal-individualist property regime is two-fold. First, the goods – land, in this case – would go to the ablest peasants, assuring an economically effective allocation of property rights. Politically this would then create a stratum of citizens, including peasants, capable of independent, self-confident participation in public and political space.

In comparison to the hitherto valid constitutions of Serbia and Old Romania, which had been sovereign states since the 1830s and 1860s respectively, property in Greater Romania and in the Kingdom of Serbs, Croats and Slovenes (SCS) – known since 1929 as Yugoslavia – was no longer conceived as unrestricted, in liberal-individualist terms. Property had still been defined as 'sacred and inviolable' in the Romanian constitution of 1866,[6] whereas in 1923 it was 'guaranteed' but also attributed a 'social function'.[7] Similarly, the SCS constitution stated, immediately after guaranteeing property in Article 37, that simple laws would regulate its contents, scope and limitation. The Yugoslavian public understood this generally as an invitation to restrict individual property and adapt it to social aims.[8] In the Polish constitution, Article 99 made clearer reference to the liberal property tradition of the nineteenth century: 'The Polish Republic recognizes all property, whether it be the personal property of individual citizens, or the common property of citizens, institutions . . . as one of the most important foundations for building up a society and for legal order, and guarantees all inhabitants, institutions or collectivities the protection of their property'.[9]

Yet legislators were significantly less willing to enact a liberal-individualist property regime when it came to landownership. The 'transitional regulations' chapter of the Romanian constitution, under Article 131, included central regulations on agrarian reforms in Old Romania and the new provinces of Transylvania, Bessarabia and Bukovina, which constitutionally sanctioned considerable intrusions on the liberal-individualist property regime.[10] In the case of Yugoslavia, the Serbian conception of a suitable property structure was dominant, so the SCS constitution clearly favoured a 'land-to-the-tiller' form of social organization, and thus announced and sanctioned intrusions on the property rights of large and medium-sized farmsteads, especially those belonging to members of ethnic minorities. Polish legislators also announced their clear intention, in Article 99, to treat ownership of land in a protectionist manner for reasons of social and ethno-national politics:

> Land, being one of the most important factors in the people's and state's life, must not be the object of unrestricted trade. Laws regulate the right, to which the state is entitled, to purchase land by force and to trade with land, taking into account the principle that the agrarian constitution of the Polish Republic should be based on a form of agriculture capable of rational production and constituting personal property.[11]

Regardless of whether the definition of property in the constitution now had a restrictive meaning, in political reality the Polish, Romanian and Yugoslavian elites, like those of most East Central European states, faced enormous challenges that made pursuit of a liberal laissez-faire economic policy a formidable task.[12]

As successors to collapsed multi-ethnic states, Poland, Romania and Yugoslavia – together with Galicia, Transylvania, Bukovina, Vojvodina, Croatia and Slovenia – had to incorporate areas that in many ways differed in structure from the core areas around Warsaw, Bucharest and Belgrade. 'Minorities' not belonging to the titular nation made up relatively high proportions of their populations, totalling 41.8 per cent in Transylvania,[13] 46 per cent in Vojvodina[14] and 45 per cent in Galicia.[15] In Transylvania and Vojvodina, the minority problem largely correlated with the property structure of land, as over 80 per cent of large estates (often hedged as estate in fee tail) and the corporately regulated property of the Church and trusts were in the hands of Hungarians and Germans. In Galicia, the situation was almost the exact opposite in this regard; here, the ruling class consisted of Polish large landowners and nobility, who, following the Austro-Hungarian Compromise of 1867, had supported the conservative ruling alliances in the Viennese Imperial Council, whereas most Ruthenian/Ukrainian farmers owned only as much land as was needed for subsistence.[16] All three countries shared similar economic structures: 70 to 80 per cent of the population was active in agriculture, agrarian products were the only significant source of exports and the rural population was the only possible source from which to extract capital for a strategy of modernization in other economic sectors, such as industry.[17] The new political elites perceived these conditions as alarmingly backward in comparison to Western Europe. In addition, all East Central European elites feared that Bolshevik ideas would spread in the countryside, especially through the experiences of farmer-soldiers returning home from the war, and lead to unregulated distribution of land.

Much of the research in national historiographies concerning post-First World War agrarian reforms considers only two of the cited plethora of arguments, namely the fear of Bolshevism and the legitimate levelling of social inequalities. However, it only substantiates the elites' reactive dealings with the concept of property in agrarian reform, meanwhile failing to research this conception of landowning in terms of its being turned towards the future. The Romanian and Yugoslavian constitutions legislated restrictions on the concept of property that essentially represented a legalization of the expropriation provided for, and largely already carried out, by the agrarian reforms. And the fact that Poland did not restrict the concept of property in its constitution does not mean that a liberal-individualistic property regime was operative. The future-oriented character of the agrarian reforms and property regime in the interwar period is analysed below, first as socially and economically motivated and then as ethno-nationally motivated and protectionist.[18]

The Interwar Agrarian Reforms

The most salient characteristic of post-1918 agrarian reform in East Central and South-East Europe was the state's significantly increased role in allocating assets, property rights and social rights derived from land property. Legislators and executive bodies of the state determined which groups were to be expropriated, who would receive land and how much, and the legal status of the land. In a clear break with the state's earlier pattern of self-restraint outside the role of guaranteeing property rights, as practised in the age of liberalism in nineteenth-century Western Europe, the state now assumed the additional role of active agent. Yet agrarian reforms in Romania, Yugoslavia and to a lesser extent Poland were just the beginning of a process in which the state increased its sway in economic matters. This process would continue throughout the 1930s, increasingly taking on the form of dirigisme and corporatism.[19]

To be clear, intrusions on property rights – essentially understood as economic handling rights and political civil rights and liberties – were hardly confined to Eastern Europe in the first half of the twentieth century in Europe, a period framed by the two World Wars. Modern warfare, with its need to mobilize all economic and military resources, had required intensified state intervention in the economy, which continued after the First World War in the form of state dirigisme. The tendency was reflected not only in fascist Italy and Nazi Germany, but also in the liberal-democratic United States, with Franklin D. Roosevelt's New Deal.[20] After the Bolshevik assault on private property, further possibilities surfaced for undermining the bourgeois-liberal property regime by collectivist means.

But for Romania, Yugoslavia, Poland and other Eastern European states after the First World War, these trends are not quite sufficient to explain the massive encroachment on property rights that occurred between 1918 and 1948. It is also necessary to analyse the role of property and its protection with respect to the envisioned political systems, social and economic conditions and ethnic population mixes.

Social and Economic Protectionism

For the reasons mentioned above, post-First World War agrarian reform in East Central and South East Europe had a different impact from country to country. The reforms can be assessed as more or less radical according to the extent and type of redistributed land, and the allotted compensation.[21] However, all the agrarian reforms were similar in that they consisted of three phases, analytically speaking – the expropriation, allocation and administration of land – and the role of the state clearly increased significantly with each phase.

In June 1917, Romania's Constituent Constitutional Convention, assembled in Iaşi, modified Article 19 of the Constitution to allow privately owned land to be expropriated not only for 'public' but also for 'national needs'.[22] Specifically, land owned by several state institutions, foreign citizens and absentee landlords was to be expropriated entirely, along with all but 100 hectares of all other landowners' property. Overall, the measure was to make 2 million hectares of land available for redistribution. In formal terms, it amounted to expropriation, not confiscation, since the principle of law was served by the promise of compensation. Under the premises of the actual constitutional order, parliament was justified in undertaking such an expansive encroachment on property rights. What is more significant, however, is that parliamentarians based their decision on 'national needs'. Further, by citing the amounts of land to be expropriated, the first steps were taken towards a state-authored economic plan.

In Yugoslavia, the amount of land to be expropriated was not announced, but a total of about 2.5 million hectares – a small portion of this from state reserves – was distributed in the course of agrarian reform. More than 2 million hectares became available through expropriation of all Habsburg family estates, all entailed estates and all land owned by absentees who rented it out or did not cultivate it, in addition to latifundia (large estates) in general. Not even the first Transitional Provisions for the Preparation of Agrarian Reform of February 1919 contained a general definition of large-scale land holdings. They specified only that areas of 100 to 500 cadastral yokes (roughly 58 to 288 hectares) were to be considered as such, and were to be expropriated 'according to the land-tenure and economic conditions of the given location'.[23] Thus, the deciding factor in flexibly determining the maximum allowable size of landholdings was not the productivity of a given estate, but the demand for land.

The growing role of the state was even more evident in the allocation of land. Thus, a number of Romanian laws and regulations after 1918 entrusted various public institutions, depending on the historical province, with the task of distribution. In Yugoslavia, it was the district agricultural offices and agriculture directorates that were responsible – in other words, state institutions. Their decisions could be appealed against only in the Ministry of Agrarian Reform, that is, an additional executive body. The central institutions or their subordinate agencies at the district or local level allocated land or legalized its appropriation in line with a general principle: every farmer ought to have as much land as they could work with their hands. In effect, legislators presumed to have a monopoly on defining how much land it was necessary, useful and legitimate to own. All peasants were to receive the minimum of farmland and pasture necessary for their survival, regardless of their previous performance, their present capacity or their future performance potential. All previously owned property was more or less openly suspected of having been acquired through exploitation and other illegitimate means, an attitude that consequently extended to the meritocratic principle in the allocation of opportunities in life.

The same social and political logic that applied to expropriating and allocating land – a logic that was anything but economic – was also apparent in the legal status the state's agrarian reform legislation accorded to this land. In the provisions on agrarian reform, the state retained a voice in several respects regarding the sale, mortgage, inheritance and even cultivation of land distributed under agrarian reform. In Romania, Article 120 of the Agrarian Reform Law contained a regulation from the Old Kingdom stipulating that the land could be sold, traded or inherited only after it had been occupied five years, occupation being legally valid after the whole of the transfer fee for the land had been paid to the state.[24] In Article 122, however, the state retained a right of first purchase on all land distributed in this and all preceding agrarian reforms. Moreover, during these five years only state or state-authorized institutions could mortgage land. A minimum of 1 hectare, along with a yard and house, was to be protected entirely from the effects of the money market as well as from inheritance practices.[25] Articles 137 and 139 even gave the land-reform agency (Casa Centrală a Împroprietăririi) the right to prescribe which crops the peasants receiving land were to plant and how they were to be cultivated. If they were unable to do so to the satisfaction of the authorities, the land could be taken away from them.[26]

In Yugoslavia, war volunteers were prioritized recipients of land in the colonization process following agrarian reform – colonization being defined as distribution of land to non-locals who had moved to the area, sometimes from other historic regions, to receive land – so the majority of protectionist measures applied to this group.[27] But besides enjoying extensive privileges, such as the free allocation of land and three years of tax exemption, colonists had to endure considerable restrictions on their freedom of action once they received land. As compulsory members of the state cooperatives from which they leased their land, they were subject to the cooperatives' rules and regulations for ten years before the land became their own. This of course involved payment of rent, as well as the obligation to cultivate the land in a certain way and observe the ban on relations with perceived enemies of the state, such as Kosovar Albanians. It went without saying that the land they received could not be rented out or sold during this period.[28]

All these regulations were intended to prevent various forces from undoing the results of land redistribution in the near future. Apart from this intent, however, the regulations had the primary effect of significantly restricting property rights. The actual benefits peasants could derive from their land were often close to nil, because it could not be used as collateral for a bank loan. And because cooperative banks and other agrarian credit lines could not be established in time to keep up with demand in Yugoslavia and Romania, small family farms had access only to bank capital with high-risk interest rates, leading to a high level of debt in a short period of time.[29]

Interwar Polish agrarian reform is considered one of the least radical in East Central Europe, considering the quantity of redistributed land, speed of redistribution and question of compensation payments. The immediate reasons for this relate closely to the political history of Poland in the interwar period. In a longer historical perspective, however, the reasons lie in the different political and economic market constellations in Polish lands that had been divided among three neighbouring empires in the 'long nineteenth century'. The Polish elites faced the same challenge confronting elites in countries throughout East Central Europe, namely, more intensive integration of farmers mobilized by the experiences of the First World War. Also in Poland, improving social and economic relations on the land through an agrarian reform that redistributed land in the centre, thereby making farmers landowners, was also deemed an appropriate measure against the threat of Bolshevik influence from the Soviet Union. On an event-related level, it appears that the perceived Soviet threat was not effective enough to inspire the Polish elites to enact an agrarian reform as radical as those carried out in Romania and Yugoslavia.[30] In the 1919 parliamentary sessions dedicated to agrarian reform, the parties that viewed themselves as interest groups for Polish owners of large estates managed to formulate conditions in such a way that the agrarian reform would scarcely have looked any different from a free land market under extremely unequal property relations. However, the serious threat of Bolshevism in the form of the Red Army before the gates of Warsaw, combined with farmers' unwillingness to fight in the summer of 1920, led to swift, unanimous passage of a more generous agrarian reform law on 15 July 1920.

Nonetheless, as soon as the immediate danger was over, the major landowners and the interest groups and parties representing them became unwilling to implement this law. Thus the actual beginning of Polish agrarian reform is only traceable to the law of 28 December 1925. The major landowners' ability to initially treat the agrarian question in a dilatory manner, and then to pass an agrarian reform law that was relatively conservative – in the East Central European context – was due primarily to the existence of a coalition partner in the camp of the farmer parties. The Polish Peasant Party (Polskie Stronnictwo Ludowe-Piast), predominant in west Galicia, saw itself as representing the interests of medium-sized landowners who would have been disadvantaged by radical agrarian reform.[31] In the longer term, the notion that the Polish nation's survival in times of Polish statelessness was attributable to the courts and goods of numerous nobles and medium-sized landowners, both great and small, also appears to have played a role. Once statehood had been regained, this perception became permanent.

The agrarian reform law of 1925 aimed to nurture a viable class of medium-sized landowners by creating new farmsteads and providing the very smallest farms with extra land[32] that would come predominantly from the great landowners. Unlike the law of 1920, the 1925 reform made great landowners responsible for piecing out allotments from their property themselves.[33] At the same time, the state retained a central role, announcing at the beginning of the calendar year what quantity of land was to be allotted in any district. If this norm was not met by the end of the year, the state authorities were to determine which great landowner was to provide what land, and enforce the decision.[34] This situation led to great uncertainty, a resultant general decline in land prices and a drastic deceleration of improvement work. The allotted land was first transferred to a land fund administered by the state and then distributed to those farmers with greatly restricted property rights. The delivered land could be divided, sold, leased or lent only after the release price had been fully paid to the state or the state agrarian bank.[35] Regardless of falling land prices, this process and its basic financial regulations meant considerable encroachment on the financial options of all parties involved: state compensation payments to great landowners were insufficient to modernize their remaining manors; meanwhile, the state had already used up most of its provisions for agriculture.[36] Thus very little was left over to support the new farming businesses that, for their part, had paid dearly for the land. A visible consequence of this shortage of capital was the fact that the stipulated annual countrywide allotment of 200,000 hectares of land was rarely accomplished.

The reasons behind the many stipulations and practices of agrarian reform in Poland, Romania and Yugoslavia cannot be understood without taking dimensions of ethno-politics into account alongside socio-political and economic considerations, and it is to this that we next turn.

Ethno-political Protectionism

Particularly in newly acquired provinces, such as post-Habsburg Galicia, Transylvania and Vojvodina, the formerly Russian Kresy and Bessarabia, and formerly Ottoman Kosovo, the institution of landownership was developed as an instrument of ethnically conceived nation-building, thereby undermining the promise of a society of property owners. Although land reform, as a buffer against the spread of communist ideas, seems to have reflected rather immediate fears, the three countries' elites also shared a long-term perspective of their national historical mission. According to their rationale, various foreign ethnic groups had infiltrated their hereditary territories and the nation in general during the periods under Prussian, Habsburg, tsarist and Ottoman rule. This 'historical injustice', they argued, had to be rectified through various measures, ranging from the physical occupation of territories by ethnic co-nationals to mental re-nationalization.[37]

The political representatives of ethnic minorities from the new provinces criticized agrarian reform as a widely applied shifting of honestly obtained property to their disadvantage – in short, as Polonization, Romanization or Serbianization/Slavization. Even if some of their arguments can be regarded as excessive attempts to represent their own interests, the legislators had nonetheless provided sufficient grounds for diagnosing ethno-political bias in the practice of agrarian reform. The minority representatives, as well as Polish, Romanian and Yugoslavian journalists and politicians from the new provinces, critiqued agrarian reform in three ways.[38]

First, they all shared a perception that discrimination existed, favouring titular nations over ethnic minorities, and the central provinces of Poland, Romania and Yugoslavia over the new provinces. This was probably due partly to ignorance of local relations, but it was also the result of ethno-political intent. The redistribution of land in Galicia, Transylvania and Vojvodina clearly revealed a preference for colonizers and war veterans, to the detriment of the local population. Because the German and Hungarian populations in Romania and Yugoslavia, like the Ukrainians in Galicia, were roughly defined as representatives of the former foreign rulers, their rural poor were only peripherally involved in the redistribution of land.[39]

In Romania's new provinces, both the maximum remaining area a landowner was permitted to own and the compensation they were due were significantly lower than in the Old Kingdom. The maximum farm size was only 100 hectares in Bessarabia and 250 hectares in Transylvania, whereas in the Old Kingdom it was 500 hectares.[40] The extent of unequal treatment was further increased by expropriation procedures, which in the new provinces counted all an owner's property as a whole that was then expropriated up to the maximum legal limit, whereas in the Old Kingdom each separate piece of a landowner's land was examined and expropriated up to the maximum permissible limit.[41] Moreover, compensation in the Old Kingdom was calculated in relation to the commercial price, but calculations in the new provinces used the often significantly lower average price of the last years prior to the war. The definition of a large landed estate in the new provinces included the land owned by German and Hungarian religious denominations, which had served to support the private school system. A comparable case of shared property in Bessarabia was the *proprietatea embaticară*, formerly jointly owned by farmers on the one hand and banks, the Russian state and communes on the other, but now transferred to become the exclusive property of the Romanian state. A considerable amount of this and other land now at the state's disposal was given, much to farmers' indignation, to non-local and non-farmer war participants and civil servants, who in turn generally leased it again to farmers.[42] Similarly conspicuous is the fact that only 7.7 per cent of the expropriated land in the Old Kingdom remained in the state reserve, whereas this figure was 18.5 per cent in Transylvania, 26.4 per cent in Bessarabia and 30.1 per cent in Bukovina.[43] Further, only in Bessarabia and Transylvania was all forest ownership nationalized.[44]

Yugoslavian legislators' timing of acts and laws on colonization, which were generally decreed earlier than general agrarian stipulations,[45] indicates that the ethno-national moment was of great importance. The colonization of Kosovo, Macedonia and Vojvodina was not a mere sideshow to Yugoslavian agrarian reform; it was central to it.[46] If we compare the colonization of Kosovo with that of Vojvodina, we can see a common goal implemented in completely different ways.[47] In Kosovo after the First World War, the authorities pursued their project of a Slavic-Serbian population majority more ruthlessly than they did in Vojvodina because they perceived Germany and Hungary as greater threats, diplomatically and militarily, than Albania. In both Kosovo and Vojvodina, however, it was possible for colonists to settle on expropriated land now under state control in communities and villages. After 1912, free state land in Kosovo was mainly the former property of pious Albanian Muslim foundations (*vakıf*); in Vojvodina, it had previously been church parish property of predominantly Hungarian and German religious denominations supporting the (private) school system.[48] In Vojvodina, already considerably urbanized, the problem of communal land for agrarian reform became acute when land formerly owned by mainly Hungarian and German cities, which hitherto had used income from leasing the land to subsidize communal services, fell into colonists' hands.[49]

The whole of Kosovo was seen as a potential area of settlement, since land occupied by Southern Slavs did not have to be returned to its previous Albanian owners if they could not prove legal entitlement to it. This especially concerned land declared fallow because its owners had fled in the turmoil of war or were considered to be insurgents (*Kačak*). In Kosovo, estates amounting to 50 hectares were defined as large. Even though most Albanians owned little land, they were still defined as major landowners and expropriated to a minimum of 5 to 15 hectares. This practice was radicalized in the mid 1930s, when a wave of expropriations – especially in border areas and places where Albanians comprised a particularly large share of the population – reduced the minimum amount of land left to the Albanians to 0.4 hectares per person.

Also in the mid 1930s, Yugoslavian legislators also wanted to 'Serbianize' the province of Vojvodina, where medium-sized holdings of most individual German and Hungarian landowners had not been harmed significantly.[50] Across the board, the Germans and Hungarians in the province were seen as representatives of former foreign rulers, which meant they had neither voting nor co-determination rights on the agrarian committees. Minority village paupers' participation in land allocation was consequently minimal.[51] Nonetheless, for around a decade after agrarian reform began, the Yugoslavian authorities seemed alarmed that German and Hungarian farmers who succeeded on the market were managing to enlarge their landholdings again. A law of February 1938 obstructed these tendencies by providing for a 50 kilometre wide strip along the state border in which practically all sales of land were blocked.[52] Until then, land surrendered to colonists had been traded in both Vojvodina and Kosovo. Belgrade had chiefly focused on settling as many Serbs and south Slavs as possible in the two provinces, so the colonists' suitability or will to settle there permanently and farm the land was often beside the point. Many of them only made use of the numerous benefits, immediately illegally leasing the land they had received to local Albanians, Germans or Hungarians, or even selling it later.[53] Politically, the policy of land reform aimed not only to 'Serbianize' the province from an ethnic perspective, as in the case of Romania and Transylvania, but also to 'Šumadize' it, that is, to transfer from the heartland of Serbia a client-structured political system based on a little-differentiated society in which political parties mobilized and integrated a homogeneous class of small farmers, generally through a populist approach.

As in Romania, the Habsburg legacy of a functioning cadastral and land register system was rejected in Yugoslavia: despite a decision taken as early as 1931 to extend the land evidence systems from Vojvodina to the entire country, very little of this was actually carried out.[54] Both agrarian reform and subsequent land transactions made it impossible to realize in practice the economically desirable logic of land going to the best farmers. On the contrary, farmers found themselves forced into illegal practices, or at the very least into transactions leading to insecure property rights in their land, to increase production. This resort to illegal actions meant that there was a high and constant risk of being discovered by state authorities, especially in Vojvodina.

In Poland, the character of the agrarian reforms and colonization in eastern Galicia and Kresy was mainly determined on the one hand[55] by the fact that the larger landed estates were predominantly Polish-owned, and on the other by the state's striving to hold and consolidate Polish dominance.[56] This resulted in numerous special stipulations for these areas that also affected overall agrarian reform. First, the target size of farm businesses in Kresy and Pomerania was 35 hectares, whereas this figure was 15 hectares in the rest of Poland. Second, the maximum expropriation from a large estate was 300 hectares in Kresy and 400 hectares in Galicia, but only 180 hectares in the rest of Poland.[57] Leaseholders from the voivodeships of Kresy were essentially entitled to buy the leased land, unless they 'had expressed . . . hostile ideas against the Polish state' and had not worked on the land at a specific point in time or for longer than a year.[58]

Contemporary Ukrainian and German portrayals of ethnic minority positions regarding agrarian reform in east and south-east of Poland allude to two further points.[59] Observers of the situation, clearly arguing in their own interests, particularly stressed that the local authorities in general, as well as the offices specially concerned with agrarian reform, had great leeway regarding the measurements involved in implementing it. Thus the council of ministers could arbitrarily determine how much land great landowners had to provide and in which local government districts, and it could just as easily decide which individual great landowner was to be expropriated upon failing to meet the requirements of the annual allocation plan. Moreover, such decisions could not be appealed to the relevant authorities but only pursued by legal means, which in most cases were in turn strictly limited to the highest level of jurisdiction, the Supreme Administrative Court.[60] The principle of equal rights for all citizens proclaimed in the Constitution was thus unable to prevent a coalition of the authorities and the upper social class of the Polish great landowners from systematically discriminating against Belarusian and Ukrainian minorities.

Although only clues rather than explicit evidence point to a state programme of Polonizing the regions at this point, such a programme is very clear in the case of military veterans who settled in Kresy.[61] As in Kosovo, the measures for settlement of eastern Poland were justified in terms of strategy and civilization. Not only were front-line soldiers and officers to be rewarded for their services to the fatherland; they were also to provide military protection for the threatened eastern regions and raise them to a higher level of civilization.[62] In reality, however, the settlement programme shrank constantly over the course of the interwar period due to lack of funds and declining interest from potential settlers, so that in total a mere 10,000 persons were settled. A considerable number of them, meanwhile, wound up re-leasing their land to neighbouring Belarusian and Ukrainian farmers because they lacked the capital, expertise or, as still-active soldiers, time to run a farm. The shortcomings of the veteran settlement – in terms of an antagonized White Russian and Ukrainian population – thus appear to have been significantly greater than the gains from a Polish ethno-political perspective.

Cadastre and Land Register: The Institutional Gap

The property and agrarian history of large parts of twentieth-century Eastern Europe is characterized by a peculiar paradox regarding the state's relationship to its citizens in terms of landownership and the institutions governing it. On the one hand, the state's role in allocating landownership rights and defining the legal status of land was growing in the interwar period. On the other hand, attempts to build up institutions of land recording, such as cadastres and land registers, were plagued by a series of setbacks and aborted projects. Hence, the state's claim of increased control, regulation and planning was matched by its – at best – perpetual blindness to real-estate transactions between actors in the countryside.

The Habsburg Empire successor states of the interwar period inherited not only territory and inhabitants, but also institutions and their actors, with attendant patterns of behaviour. When it came to agriculture, cadastral maps and land-register entries for rural property had been part of daily life in rural areas of Transylvania, Vojvodina and, to a lesser degree, Galicia for generations. Literature cites the resulting legal security as the most likely reason for the low number of legal disputes involving land law, as well as the relatively easy access peasants had to affordable bank loans. Politically, the upward economic and social mobility of peasants, among others, lent the Romanian, Serbian and, again to a lesser degree, Polish national movements in Transylvania, Vojvodina and Galicia a quality that can best be described as integrative and emancipatory.[63] For various reasons, the situation differed considerably for peasants in the Old Kingdom of Romania, Poland's Russian Partition and Serbia. Until 1918, Romanian peasants had been a politically irrelevant group, even though their labour power formed the economic basis for Romania's agricultural exports. Their precarious living conditions, which contrasted grossly with the luxurious lives of latifundia owners, had never been recorded in public, transparent cadastres and land registers, not least out of a desire to hide this neo-feudal state of affairs in the countryside from the public eye.[64] Land that had been allocated to peasants in smaller agrarian reforms (in 1864) was merely recorded in non-standardized local registers. Thus, bank loans were available only to latifundia owners, whereas peasants had to resort to loans with usurious interest rates. In Poland's Russian Partition, the Russian authorities preferred farmers at the expense of the Polish nobility, but this did not lead to radical agrarian reform, let alone the establishment of a cadastre and land register.[65] Lastly, in Serbia, where as early as the first half of the nineteenth century most of the agrarian land had gone to farmers after the withdrawal of the Ottoman latifundia owner class, the long-reigning Radical Party's glorification of the *zadruga* on the one hand and its sweeping hostility to modern institutions on the other had prevented farmers' property from being understood on an individual basis and measured and registered as individual parcels.[66]

The post-First World War agrarian reforms aimed to put an end to such practices. In Romania, the allocated land was to become the full property of peasants only after each parcel was geodetically surveyed and entered into the land register. In other words, a cadastre and land register were to be created alongside the carrying out of agrarian reform. The upshot of this ambitious plan, however, was to prolong the unclear legal situation for peasants in the Old Kingdom while simultaneously importing it into the new provinces. Geodesists and land-office officials could not be trained in sufficient numbers to keep pace with the allocation of land in the Old Kingdom, and the new central authorities lacked significant willingness to continue and respect the regional traditions and particularities of the new provinces.[67]

As early as 1919, a Cadastre Directorate (Direcţia Cadastrului) was established at the Romanian Ministry of Agriculture, and a training programme for geodesists (*Şcoală de topometrie*) was also initiated. The cadastral registration of parcelled land – that is, until it stopped altogether in 1924 due to lack of funds – was largely carried out by students of geodesy under the guidance of their instructors, who tended to be trained geographers rather than geodesists.[68] In addition to these professional shortcomings, evidence of large-scale fraud in the survey's land accounting appeared, and by the late 1920s there was talk of having to re-do the survey work that had already been completed.[69] As far as the land register was concerned, the standard practice – common in the Old Kingdom since 1864 and based on the French-Belgian model – was retained, despite being considered insufficient in a number of respects: the organizing principle was the individual and not the parcel of land, a land transaction was considered legally valid even without being entered into the register, and neither testamentary nor non-testamentary inheritance or other forms of transferring land rights were registered.[70] In general, this system of land accounting overburdened the land market with extremely high transaction costs, with the net effect of the market having a very low volume. Furthermore, a multitude of legal disputes over land were initiated, mostly among peasants. Legal proceedings usually lasted several years, if not decades, because the hearing of evidence depended on the statements of witnesses.

In early 1928, the professional Association of Romanian Geodesists (Asociaţia Generală a Topometrilor din România) began to lobby extensively in its newly founded periodical (*Revista Cadastrală*) for the resumption of paid cadastral work.[71] In numerous articles, the journal's contributors called attention to the overall importance of their work, pointed out that the state had not paid its bills for several years, drafted a law for establishing a new cadastre office, and were active in other ways. Despite their efforts, the training programme for geodesists was wound up as early as 1928, and legislators passed a new cadastre law in 1933 without consulting this professional body. Among other things, the law allowed survey work to be undertaken by staff of the Military Geographic Institute, who had no geodetic training. What one critic had called 'the Great Panama in the Cadastre Office',[72] referring to large-scale fraud and embezzlement, would now continue unabated. Only in 1938 did the royal dictatorship pass a law on the land register, in essence decreeing the adoption of the system used in Transylvania[73] after sporadic scholarly essays from the Old Kingdom,[74] and the frequent intervention of politicians[75] and practitioners from Transylvania advocating the Habsburg land register system had failed to win over parliamentarians.

Yet all these efforts for a land register ultimately had little effect on the efficiency of the land-recording system in practice, for a functioning land register is dependent on reliable cadastral work, which never materialized. The impending world war and lack of funds were certainly not the only reasons for the logjam in the Romanian institutions responsible for land recording. A likelier explanation is as follows: Romania's political class, consistent with its general neglect, even contempt, of rural areas and their inhabitants, simply ignored the legal insecurity that was rampant in the countryside, contenting itself instead with legislative window dressing. This neatly corresponded with both the political parties' paternalistic style of governing and the increasingly state-oriented economic policies of the governments in power, which had no room to foster the initiative of peasants by granting them the legal security and security of action provided by property rights. Meanwhile, a look at other professions important to the administration of landed property, such as notaries and lawyers, reveals that lawyers from the Old Kingdom successfully blocked the introduction of Habsburg-Transylvanian institutions.[76] Thanks to their strong representation in both chambers of the Romanian parliament (42 per cent in the Assembly of Deputies and 26 per cent in the Senate in the interwar period), they managed to defend their monopoly of the administration of property rights in land by rejecting proposed laws, such as the one drafted by Minister of Justice Gheorghe Mârzescu in 1924, in the parliamentary commissions.[77]

Space does not permit as detailed an analysis of the administration of property rights in land in Yugoslavia and Poland as is given for Romania.[78] In Yugoslavia, legislators passed a cadastral law and a land-registry law as early as 1928 and 1931, providing on the one hand for a geodetically demanding procedure and on the other hand for adjustment to the German-Austrian system of land ownership registration.[79] This shift abolished the Ottoman *Tapu* system in Old Serbia, which had generally been an unsystematic collection of documents and, like the French system, had as its organizing element the landowner rather than the parcel of land.[80] However, according to the Yugoslavian geodesists' journal's assessment of the progress in measuring the individual parcels of land, results during the interwar period appear to have been insubstantial.

After the First World War, the Polish elites faced the daunting task of standardizing three legal traditions, which extended also to cadastral and land register law. However, whereas no institutions existing in the Russian Partition had earned these titles, cadastres and land registers had been designed for the Prussian and Habsburg partitions in the second half of the nineteenth century.[81] Unlike the Prussian land statistics, however, entries concerning farmland in the Galician land registers reflected real property relations only very incompletely. In Galicia, prevailing inheritance customs subjected farmland to permanent splitting, and subsistence farmers had very few opportunities for employment in other economic sectors or countries.[82] Consequently, the fees for re-measuring strips of land and registering them in the land register were so high in relation to the value of the land that farmers generally carried out land transactions independent of these systems. In the interwar period, Polish legislators established provisions for introducing the Prussian land measurement system across the country, but even in western and southern Poland, the number of cadastral offices and functionaries employed in them declined by up to 50 per cent.[83] The number of certified geodesists available to measure land in Kresy was more inadequate than ever, to the extent that most of the work there, as in Romania, was performed by auxiliary staff.[84]

In summary, the elites in Poland, Romania and Yugoslavia during the brief interwar period evidently lacked the ability to integrate the farming population as citizens or as legal and economic subjects of their nation-states. It is clear in hindsight that the time available to them was as brief as it was replete with great challenges, such as bringing different areas of land together and, of course, the Great Depression. From an economic perspective, the mediocre results of agrarian reform were due not least to the state's difficulties in prioritizing its actions, as has been shown by exploring the reform's dirigiste and ethno-political bias. The development of land-measuring systems also lagged far behind the requirement to provide legal security and a certainty of expectations that were crucial to investment decisions made by peasants and other actors in agriculture. On the other hand, the horizon of the farming population's expectations had shifted to a frame of state action in the wake of state interventions in property structures and economic policies, which during the interwar period had departed significantly from a liberal-individualistic political attitude to the economy. Taken together, these elements rendered the bourgeois elites ill equipped to defend themselves against the socialist transformation of their countries after the Second World War.

Post-1944 Agrarian Reform

Lastly, an analysis of post-1944 agrarian reform will serve to show, by way of comparison, that the twentieth-century agrarian and property history of Romania, Yugoslavia and Poland was more of a continuum than a development marked by profound breaks.

Though the agrarian reforms of 1944/45 and 1918 certainly differed in some respects, their similarities in other, essential aspects are so striking that 1944/45 can be viewed as a logical outcome of 1918. The most salient difference was the much greater speed with which respective resolutions and laws were passed and implemented after 1944. Discussions lasted only a few weeks, and implementation took but a few years, whereas parts of post-1918 agrarian reform were still incomplete at the end of the Second World War. This, of course, points to the political determination underlying the agrarian reforms of 1944/45, which ascribed secondary importance to economic considerations, almost entirely sidelined as they were by egalitarian-populist and ethno-political motives. Furthermore, the infringement of property rights was no longer unusual anymore in 1944/45. On the contrary, since the post-1918 reform, such infringements had proven a reliable means of pushing the state's idea of order and good political conduct through in the countryside, as well as bringing about a desirable ethnic mix by means of colonization.

In no way can post-1944 agrarian reform in Eastern Europe be interpreted as a mere prelude to communist collectivization. In Romania, for instance, renewed encroachment on property rights enjoyed the backing of a broad consensus of political parties.[85] In Romania, it was not the communist-dominated National Democratic Front (Frontul Naţional Democrat) that suggested the most radical measures. The call to establish large-scale collective farms (kolkhozy) came from institutions aligned with latifundia owners,[86] whereas the National Peasant Party (Partidul Naţional Ţărănesc) envisioned the inclusion of the greatest possible number of farmers in cooperatives.[87] The Communist Party, by contrast, presented itself as a guarantor of private property.[88] In any case, the reform itself, instead of proceeding in a lawful manner, ultimately allowed available land to be 'snapped up' in a frenzied process of appropriation, which was then given the stamp of legality by a bill passed on 23 March 1945.

The new law prescribed four categories of landowners targeted for expropriation. Three were clearly punitive in character, aiming to dispossess individuals who had saddled themselves with a burden of guilt in the Second World War as collaborators, war volunteers and war criminals. The category of collaborator was directed at Germans in Romania, the mere fact of belonging to the 'German ethnic group' (*Grupul Etnic German*) being proof positive of collaboration. The land of a fourth category, landowners who were absent or who let arable land without involving themselves in agriculture, was likewise expropriated, along with all agriculturally productive land over 50 hectares per person. As in the first agrarian reform, preference in distributing land was to be given to war veterans and invalids, to their widows and orphaned children, and only thereafter to farm workers and peasants. The following statistics from January 1947 sum up the results of the agrarian reform. Around 1.4 million hectares of land had been expropriated from approximately 143,000 landowners, only 11,600 of whom were latifundia owners. And of the 1.4 million hectares, only about 1 million had been distributed among around 1 million people.[89]

These figures reveal both the populist and the ethno-political thrust of the reform. Once again, a large portion of land – about 400,000 hectares – had been kept in state reserves. The amount of land distributed was thus so small that there could be no talk of a significant increase in the amount of land available to farmers. Without any consideration of the productivity of expropriated latifundias or individual Germans' involvement in Nazi crimes, their respective lands were expropriated without compensation – in the case of the Germans, in its entirety.

In Yugoslavia, the source of expropriations, besides land from Germans, war criminals and collaborators, was above all the large estates (maximum 45 hectares), the property of major landowning farmers (maximum 20 to 35 hectares), and the land of banks and other corporations, churches, monasteries and foundations.[90] Accordingly, about 1.5 million hectares of land was expropriated from around 162,000 owners, 40 per cent of it from Germans alone, who themselves accounted for 60 per cent of the dispossessed. A mere 800,000 hectares, representing 51 per cent of the land, was allocated to those for whom the land reform had allegedly been intended: 'Farmers owning no land or only an inadequate amount of land', as the very first article of the Agrarian Reform Law postulated.[91]

In Poland, the Polish Committee of National Liberation (Polski Komitet Wyzwolenia Narodowego) passed the Decree on the Implementation of the Land Reform as early as 6 September 1944.[92] This law provided for the development of a national land fund from which landless farmers or agricultural labourers would be able to receive up to 5 hectares of land. This fund would include not only the land of farming estates that exceeded 50 hectares in useable area or 100 hectares in total, but also the land owned by citizens of the Third Reich – ethnic Germans and so-called persons of German origin – who were the first to be expropriated of all their land and without compensation. Land released in this way in the so-called 'Recovered Territories', as well as in central Poland, was settled by homeless refugees from all over the country but especially from Kresy, which had been incorporated by the Soviet Union.

It is safe to say that National Socialist and Soviet practices, particularly those of the occupying regime during the Second World War, had introduced a new dimension of population policies regarding forced settlement and ethnic expulsion associated with serious infringements of property rights. This was very clear in the cases of Poland and Yugoslavia, though less so in Romania, which had allied itself with the German Reich to fight against the Soviet Union in the war. Very shortly after the occupation and territorial division of Poland and Yugoslavia, National Socialist territorial and population policies prompted radical discussions about the post-war order among the Polish exile government in London and the Yugoslavian partisans.[93] When envisaging expulsion of the German population from both countries, they explicitly had recourse to the National Socialist actions as a convenient precedent for a 'structural readjustment' of an agricultural state suffering from 'overpopulation'.[94] The high degree of congruence between the ways the old and new elites in Poland and Yugoslavia connected these two complexes is evident in the continuity of specialists and politicians involved in questions of the design, planning and implementation of expulsion, expropriation and colonization. In the Second Yugoslavia, Vasa Čubrilović and Sreten Vukosavljević, the ministers responsible for post-Second World War agrarian reform and colonization, had emerged in the interwar period, advancing ethno-national ideas and concepts while also glorifying a specific – namely, collective – south Slavic property regime.[95] In Poland, large sections of the underground state's technocrat class made themselves available to the new authorities on their own territory, the Government Delegation for Poland (Delegatura Rządu Rzeczypospolitej Polskiej na Kraj), and were readily accommodated by, for example, the Ministry for the Recovered Territories (Ministerstwo Ziem Odzyskanych).[96]

In both 1918 and 1944/45, political elites in Romania, Poland and Yugoslavia attacked property rights for the same three reasons, albeit in different measure: out of populism turned paternalist, out of state dirigisme aspiring to an economic plan, and out of a drive to exclude minorities and ensure one ethnic group's predominance within the state. Nominally, private property was maintained between 1918 and 1944/45. Its promise of freedom was blocked, however, because the grasp of dirigisme virtually precluded rights of action ensuing from property. Moreover, freedom – if it is to mean more than 'might makes right' – requires legal security above all. This condition was likewise not created, since land-recording systems, developed only cautiously in the period between the wars, were left to collapse after 1944/45. If property rights to land are taken as the measure of comparison, then it was not the agrarian reform of 1944/45 and subsequent collectivization that were the crucial events in Romanian, Yugoslavian and Polish agrarian and property history, but the agrarian reform that followed the First World War. It was the latter that introduced the practices, investigated here, of politically motivated encroachments on property rights, practices that now, more than twenty years after 1989, have still not completely ended in Romania, Poland or the successor states of Yugoslavia.

Notes

1. For an overview of post-communist historiography, see Smaranda Vultur, 'New Topics, New Tendencies and New Generations of Historians in Romanian Historiography', in Ulf Brunnbauer (ed.), *(Re)Writing History: Historiography in Southeastern Europe after Socialism*, Münster, 2004, pp.236–76; Predrag Marković, Miloš Ković and Nataša Miličević, 'Developments in Serbian Historiography since 1989', in Brunnbauer, *(Re)Writing History*, pp.277–316; Maciej Górny, 'From the Splendid Past into the Unknown Future: Historical Studies in Poland after 1989', in Sorin Antohi, Balázs Trencsényi and Péter Apor (eds), *Narratives Unbound: Historical Studies in Post-communist Eastern Europe*, Budapest/New York, 2007, pp.101–72; Christina Petrescu and Dragoş Petrescu, 'Mastering vs. Coming to Terms with the Past: A Critical Analysis of Post-communist Romanian Historiography', in Antohi, Trencsényi and Apor, *Narratives Unbound*, pp.311–408.
2. Abundant literature with an underlying optimism concerns the restoration of a liberal-individualistic property regime in post-communist Eastern Europe. To name but one: Jozef M. Brabant, *Privatizing Eastern Europe: The Role of Markets and Ownership in the Transition*, Dordrecht/Boston/London, 1992. The most outspoken critique of this perspective is voiced in social anthropology; see Chris M. Hann, 'Introduction: The Embeddedness of Property', in Chris M. Hann (ed.), *Property Relations: Renewing the Anthropological Tradition*, Cambridge, 1998, pp.1–47.

3. See also Dietmar Müller, 'The Governmentality of Land Ownership in South-Eastern Europe: Romania and Yugoslavia, a Comparison', in Rosa Congost and Rui Santos (eds), *Contexts of Property in Europe: The Social Embeddedness of Property Rights in Land in Historical Perspective*, Brepols, 2011, pp.211–27; Dietmar Müller, 'Landreformen, *Property rights* und ethnische Minderheiten: Ideen- und Institutionengeschichte nachholender Modernisierung und Staatsbildung in Rumänien und Jugoslawien 1918–1948', in Karl-Peter Krauss (ed.), *Agrarreformen und ethnodemographische Veränderungen: Südosteuropa vom ausgehenden 18. Jahrhundert bis in die Gegenwart*, Stuttgart, 2009, pp.207–34.
4. Ulrich Herbert, Dan Diner and Tony Judt also argue against the conventional conceptualization and periodization of twentieth-century European history, and orientate themselves primarily towards political history. See Ulrich Herbert, 'Europe in High Modernity: Reflections on a Theory of the Twentieth Century', *Journal of Modern European History* 5/1 (2007), pp.5–21; Dan Diner, *Das Jahrhundert verstehen: Eine universalhistorische Deutung*, Munich, 1999. Pointing to the high degree of state intervention in the economy of Eastern Europe in the 1930s, Tony Judt insists that 'state-direction of the economy in eastern Europe did not begin in 1945'; Judt, *Postwar: A History of Europe since 1945*, London, 2005, p.38.
5. For a comparison across East Central Europe, see V. Alton Moody, 'Agrarian Reform before Post-war European Constituent Assemblies', *Agricultural History* 7/2 (1933), pp.81–95.
6. For the Romanian constitution of 1866, see Cristian Ionescu, *Dezvoltarea constituţională a României: Acte şi documente 1741–1991*, Bucharest, 2000, pp.414–28.
7. Romanian Constitution (1923), Article 17. On the constitution of 1923, see Ionescu, *Dezvoltarea constituţională*, pp.559–74, here p.560; Alexandru Costin, 'Concepţiile actuale ale proprietăţii şi constituţia', in *Noua Constituţia din 1923 în dezbaterea contemporanilor*, Bucharest, 1990 [1923], pp.356–80.
8. The Yugoslav constitution of 1921 is found in *Srpski ustavi od 1835. do 1990. godine sa ustavima Kraljevine SHS i Kraljevine Jugoslavije*, Belgrade, 2004, pp.189–224, here p.198. For the Yugoslav discussion of property, see Mihajlo Konstantinović, 'Pitanje svojine: Od svojine individualnog prava ka svojini socialnoj funkciji', in *Generacija pred stvaranjem. Almanah jedne grupe*, Belgrade, 1925, pp.7–16; Živojin M. Paunović, 'Svojina i njena ograničenja u srpskom zakonodavstvu', *Arhiv za pravne i društvene nauke* 12/1 (1926), pp.40–52; 12/2 (1926), pp.112–32; 12/3 (1926), pp.209–21.
9. Vereinigung des deutschen Volkstums in Polen and the Deutschtumsbund Polen e.V. (ed.), *Die Verfassung der Polnischen Republik vom 17. März 1921*, Bromberg/Posen, 1921, p.16.
10. Ionescu, *Dezvoltarea constituţională*, p.573.
11. *Verfassung der Polnischen Republik 1921*, p.16. Article 99 of the constitution of 1921 remained valid in the constitution of 1935, as did art. 109–120 (minority protection clauses). *Die neue Verfassung der Republik Polen. Nach dem amtlichen Text vom Sejmabgeordneten Eugen Franz*, Katowice, 1935, p.21f.
12. For an overview, see Max Sering (ed.), *Die agrarischen Umwälzungen im ausserrussischen Osteuropa: Ein Sammelwerk*, Berlin, 1930; Wilfried Schlau, 'Die Agrarreformen und ihre Auswirkungen', in Hans Lemberg (ed.), *Ostmitteleuropa zwischen den beiden Weltkriegen: Stärke und Schwäche der neuen Staaten, nationale Minderheiten*, Marburg, 1997, pp.145–59; Uwe Müller, 'Landreformen und Wirtschaftsnationalismus in Ostmitteleuropa', in Dagmara Jajeśniak-Quast et al. (eds), *Soziale Konflikte und nationale Grenzen in Ostmitteleuropa*, Berlin, 2006, pp.171–87.
13. According to the Romanian census of 1930, the countrywide proportion of minorities totalled 28.1 per cent. In Transylvania, minorities totalled 41.8 per cent of the population; Hungarians (at 26.7 per cent) and Germans (at 9.8 per cent) made up the two largest groups. Béla Köpeczi, *Kurze Geschichte Siebenbürgens*, Budapest, 1990, p.669.

14. According to the Yugoslav census of 1931, the proportion of minorities countrywide totalled 14.9 per cent. In Vojvodina, minorities accounted for 46 per cent of the population, Hungarians (at 22 per cent) and Germans (at 21 per cent) being the two largest groups. Michael Portmann, *Die kommunistische Revolution in der Vojvodina 1944–1955: Politik, Gesellschaft, Wirtschaft, Kultur*, Vienna, 2008, p.73.
15. According to the Polish census of 1931, the proportion of minorities across the country was 31.9 per cent. Significantly higher than this was the proportion of minorities in eastern areas (Kresy) and in the three east Galician voivodeships: Lvov 42.3 per cent, Tarnopol 50.7 per cent, Stanisławów 87.6 per cent. In east Galicia, the Ukrainians were the greatest minority, followed by Jews and Germans. Bogdan Zaborski, *Les nationalités et les confessions en Pologne d'après le recensement de 1931: Remarques générales*, Warsaw, 1937.
16. Christoph Freiherr Marschall von Bieberstein, *Freiheit in der Unfreiheit: Die nationale Autonomie der Polen in Galizien nach dem österreichisch-ungarischen Ausgleich 1867. Ein konservativer Aufbruch im mitteleuropäischen Vergleich*, Wiesbaden, 1993.
17. For analysis of the economic policies of the major Romanian parties in the interwar period, see Dietmar Müller, *Agrarpopulismus in Rumänien: Programmatik und Regierungspraxis der Bauernpartei und der Nationalbäuerlichen Partei Rumäniens in der Zwischenkriegszeit*, St Augustin, 2001. More generally, see Alice Teichova, *Kleinstaaten im Spannungsfeld der Großmächte: Wirtschaft und Politik in Mittel- und Südosteuropa in der Zwischenkriegszeit*, Munich, 1988. Exemplary among contemporary works is Leo Pasvolsky, *Economic Nationalism of the Danubian States*, New York, 1928; see also Walter Hoffmann, *Südost-Europa: Bulgarien – Jugoslawien – Rumänien. Ein Querschnitt durch Politik, Kultur und Wirtschaft*, Leipzig, 1932; Frederick Hertz, *The Economic Problems of the Danubian States: A Study in Economic Nationalism*, London, 1947.
18. Drawing on James C. Scott, the policy of accelerated, catch-up modernization can be called 'high modernism'. Scott, *Seeing Like a State: How Certain Schemes to Improve the Human Condition Have Failed*, New Haven, 1998.
19. For the three countries analysed, see David Mitrany, *The Land and the Peasant in Rumania: The War and Agrarian Reform (1917–21)*, New York, 1968 [1930]; Josef Matl, *Die Agrarreform in Jugoslavien*, Berlin/Breslau, 1927; Jozo Tomasevich, *Peasants, Politics, and Economic Change in Yugoslavia*, Stanford, 1955; Friedrich Hellwege, 'Agrarverfassung und Agrarreform in Polen', in Sering, *Die agrarischen Umwälzungen*, pp.154–204; Aleksander Matwiejew, *Die Agrarreformen Polens im XX. Jahrhundert*, Kiel, 1958.
20. See Wolfgang Schivelbusch, *Entfernte Verwandtschaft: Faschismus, Nationalsozialismus, New Deal, 1933–1939*, Munich/Vienna, 2005.
21. It is not within the scope of this chapter, however, to provide a general study and assessment covering all legal, financial, agronomic and general economic dimensions of the agrarian reforms.
22. See Eleodor Focşeneanu, *Istoria constituţională a României (1859–1991)*, Bucharest, 1998, p.55ff.; Ion Agrigoroaiei, 'Problema reformelor agrară şi electorală din România între anii 1916 şi 1918', *Cercetări Istorice* 1 (1975), pp.179–94.
23. Article 10 of the *Predhodne odredbe za pripremu agrarne reforme*, in Bogdan Lekić, *Agrarna reforma i kolonizacija u Jugoslaviji 1918–1941*, Belgrade, 2002, p.223.
24. Identical stipulations are found in the agrarian reform laws for the new provinces of Transylvania, Bessarabia, Bukovina and, even more restrictive in trend, Dobrogea. For the relevant laws, together with stipulations on the agrarian reform, see *Codul General al României*, vol. 9/10, 1919–1922, Bucharest, n.d.: for Bessarabia pp.265–71 and pp.864–908, the Old Empire pp.653–732, and Transylvania pp.733–803. For an analysis of agrarian reforms and colonization in Dobrogea, see Dietmar Müller, *Staatsbürger auf Widerruf: Juden und Muslime als Alteritätspartner im rumänischen und serbischen Nationscode. Ethnonationale Staatsbürgerschaftskonzeptionen, 1878–1941*, Wiesbaden, 2005, pp.362–74.

25. Octav I. Goruneanu, *Regimul circulaţiunii pământurilor rurale: Studiu economico-juridic. Legislaţie – doctrină – jurisprudenţă*, Constanţa, 1932, p.110ff., 75.
26. Valeriu Bulgaru, *Către o nouă reformă agrară?* Iaşi, 1936, p.12.
27. Not all war volunteers were rewarded with land in other parts of the country, and not all colonists had been war volunteers, but the overlap between the two groups is considerable. Furthermore, the cultural image of the colonist appears to have been that of a romanticized farmer-soldier: 'They lay down to sleep with rifles in their hands, stood up with rifles in their hands and with rifles in their hands tilled the land'. Đorđe Krstić, *Kolonizacija u Južnoj Srbiji*, Sarajevo, 1928, p.74.
28. See Matl, *Die Agrarreformen in Jugoslavien*, pp.111f.; Ludwig Fritscher, 'Die südslawische Agrarverfassung und die Agrarverordnungen von 1919/21', PhD diss., Berlin, 1922/23, pp.322ff.
29. According to Lucreţiu Pătrăşcanu, this phenomenon was termed 'Balkan interest' (*dobânzi balcanice*) in the financial world. Pătrăşcanu, *Probleme de bază ale Romîniei*, Bucharest, 1946 [1944], p.111.
30. Cf. Isaj Lifszyc, *Die Agrarfrage in Polen*, Lodz, 1928, pp.54–69; Gerhard Doliesen, *Die polnische Bauernpartei "Wyzwolenie" in den Jahren 1918–1926*, Marburg, 1996, pp.162ff. For the political context of the agrarian reform, see Antony Polonsky, *Politics in Independent Poland 1921–1939: The Crisis of Constitutional Government*, Oxford, 1972.
31. On the history of the Polish peasant parties, see Stanislawa Leblang, 'Polnische Bauernparteien', in Heinz Gollwitzer (ed.), *Europäische Bauernparteien im 20. Jahrhundert*, Stuttgart/New York, 1977, pp.271–322b; Peter Brock, 'The Politics of the Polish Peasant', *International Politics of Social History* 1/2 (1956), pp.210–22. On Wincenty Witos, the longtime leader of Piast, see W.J. Rose, 'Wincenty Witos', *Slavonic and East European Review* 25 (1946/47), pp.39–54.
32. For a translation of the law of 28 December 1925, see Matwiejew, *Die Agrarreform Polens*, pp.73–94.
33. For an officious portrayal of the Polish agrarian reform, see Z. Ludkiewicz, 'Land Reform in Poland', *Slavonic and East European Review* 8 (1929/1930), pp.315–30; Witold Staniewicz, 'The Agrarian Problem in Poland between the Two World Wars', *Slavonic and East European Review* 43 (1964), pp.23–33 – Staniewicz was minister for agrarian reform, 1926 to 1930.
34. For a strong critique of the statism of the Polish agrarian reform and agrarian politics, see Matwiejew, *Die Agrarreform Polens*, pp.70ff.; Georg Primas, 'Die Staatsintervention auf dem polnischen Agrarmarkt', *Berichte über Landwirtschaft* 22/1 (1937), pp.41–82.
35. Article 54.1 of the agrarian reform law of 1925. Matwiejew, *Die Agrarreform Polens*, p.86.
36. Cf. Rudolf Freund, 'Die polnische Agrarreform', *Weltwirtschaftliches Archiv* 24/2 (1926), pp.315ff.
37. For an analysis of Romanian and Serbian national codes and their effects on the minority and citizenship policies of these states, see Müller, *Staatsbürger auf Widerruf*. For Poland, see Dieter Gosewinkel and Stefan Meyer, 'Citizenship, Property Rights and Dispossession in Post-war Poland (1918 and 1945)', *European Review of History* 16/4 (2009), pp.575–95.
38. For examples of critiques by ethnic minorities, see, for Germans and Hungarians from Siebenbürgen, Gustav Adolf Klein, *Soziale und nationale Probleme der Agrarreform in Siebenbürgen*, Hermannstadt, 1927; Wilhelm Klein, 'Die Liquidierung des siebenbürgisch-sächsischen Nationalvermögens', *Nation und Staat* 10 (1936/37), pp.721–30; Eugen Darkó, 'Die rumänische Agrarreform und die ungarischen Kirchen', in Emerich Lukinich (ed.), *Die Siebenbürgische Frage: Studien aus der Vergangenheit und Gegenwart Siebenbürgens*, Budapest, 1940, pp.366–80. For Russophones in Bessarabia, P.V. Synadino, *Însemnătatea reformei agrare în Basarabia*, n.p., 1926; P.V. Synadino, *Memoriul agricultorilor având peste 25 hectare pământ din Basarabia*, Chişinău, 1921; *Confiscarea pădurilor particulare din Basarabia*, n.p., 1922. For Germans from Vojvodina, *Die Agrarreformen im Königreich der Serben, Kroaten und Slowenen und ihre Folgen*, Novi Sad, 1924. For Germans from Poland, Alexander Spickermann, *Agrarfrage und neustaatliche*

Bodenreformbestrebungen in Polen, Lodz, 1928; Willy Wiese, *Die polnische Bodenbesitzpolitik: Untersuchungen auf dem Gebiete der Agrarreform und der landwirtschaftlichen Organisationen in Polen während der Jahre 1919 und 1926*, Berlin, 1928; Alexander von Harnier, *Entwicklung und Ergebnisse der Agrarreform in Polen*, Danzig, 1931.

39. See Zoran Janjetović, 'Die Konflikte zwischen Serben und Donauschwaben', *Südost-Forschungen* 58 (1999), pp.119–68, esp. p.142; Nikola Gaćeša, 'Nemci u agrarnoj reformi i vlastništvu obradivog zemljišta u Vojvodini 1919–1941', in Nikola Gaćeša (ed.), *Radovi iz agrarne istorije i demografije*, Novi Sad, 1995, pp.286–308, esp. p.290; Edouard Conte, 'Land und "ethnische Reinheit" im polnisch-ukrainischen Grenzgebiet', in Edouard Conte and Christian Giordano (eds), *Es war einmal die Wende . . . Sozialer Umbruch der ländlichen Gesellschaften Mittel- und Südosteuropas*, Berlin, 1999, pp.35–82.
40. Cf. Mitrany, *The Land and the Peasant in Rumania*, pp.122ff.
41. Cf. Ifor E. Evans, *The Agrarian Revolution in Roumania*, Cambridge, 1924, p.108.
42. Cf. Ion Ţurcanu, *Relaţii agrare din Basarabia în anii 1918–1940*, Bucharest, 1991, p.28ff., 36.
43. Cf. Mircea Georgescu, *Principii şi metode în legiuirile Române pentru reforma agrară*, Bucharest, 1943, p.132ff.
44. Cf. *Confiscarea pădurilor*.
45. For the central laws and regulations of the agrarian reform and colonization in Kosovo, see Jusuf Osmani, 'Zakonski propisi o agrarnoj reformi i kolonizacija na Kosovo između dva svetska rata', *Vjetar i arkivit të Kosovës* 20 (1985), pp.169–89.
46. Cf. Christian Giordano, 'Agrarreformen als Potential ethnischer Spannungen in Osteuropa: Das Beispiel Jugoslawiens. Das Prinzip der Staatsnation und der Mythos der ethnischen Reinheit', in Catherine Bosshart-Pfluger (ed.), *Nation und Nationalismus in Europa: Kulturelle Konstruktion von Identitäten*, Frankfurt am Main, 2002, pp.463–80. In contrast, Jozo Tomasevich hides the ethnonational bias of colonization ('the political strengthening of the Christian sector in Bosnia-Herzegovina and Macedonia') and does not take the economic consequences into account. Tomasevich, *Peasants*, pp.358ff.
47. On colonization in Kosovo, see Milovan Obradović, *Agrarna reforma i kolonizacija na Kosovo (1918–1944)*, Priština, 1981; Vladan Jovanović, *Jugoslovenska država i Južna Srbija 1918–1929: Makedonija, Sandžak, Kosovo i Metohija u Kraljevini SHS*, Belgrade, 2002, pp.208–23; Michel Roux, *Les Albanais en Yougoslavie: Minorité nationale et développment*, Paris, 1992, pp.191–203; Noel Malcolm, *Kosovo: A Short History*, London/New York, 1998, pp.265–88; Müller, *Staatsbürger auf Widerruf*, pp.436–53.
48. *Das Schicksal der Deutschen in Jugoslawien*, Munich, 2004 [1961], p.20E.
49. Cf. the Novi Sad city officials' claims in *Predlog slobodne i kraljevske varoši Novog Sada u predmetu sprovađanja agrarne reforme*, Novi Sad, 1920.
50. Cf. Zoran Janjetović, 'Die Konflikte zwischen Serben und Donauschwaben', pp.141ff.; Zoran Janjetović, *Between Hitler and Tito: The Disappearance of the Vojvodina Germans*, Belgrade, 2005, pp.35ff.
51. Cf. Matl, *Die Agrarreformen in Jugoslavien*, p.101.
52. Cf. Gaćeša, 'Nemci u agrarnoj reformi', pp.294ff.
53. This is maintained not only by possibly biased German contemporaries such as Matl, *Die Agrarreformen in Jugoslavien*, p.127, and Fritscher, *Die südslawische Agrarverfassung*, pp.322ff., but also in the writings by direct representatives of German interests: *Die Agrarreformen im Königreich*, p.17. Very negative evaluations of the colonists' agronomic ability and national sense of duty, and of the competence of the politicians and civil servants involved in agrarian reform, often appear also among contemporary south Slav authors. For Kosovo, see esp. Krstić, *Kolonizacija u Južnoj Srbiji*.

54. *Zakon o izdavanju tapija na području Kasacionog Suda u Beogradu i Velikog Suda u Podgorici*, Belgrade, 1931. For the admittedly embellished history of the Yugoslav cadastral and land register system, see *Le cadastre, le livre foncier et la reforme agraire en Yugoslavie*, Belgrade, 1936.
55. In the interwar period, the voivodeships of Vilno, Novogródek, Polesie and Wołýn were merged into Kresy, while Lvov, Tarnopol and Stanisławów were considered to form east Galicia. For Kresy, see Werner Benecke, *Die Ostgebiete der Polnischen Republik: Staatsmacht und öffentliche Ordnung in einer Minderheitenregion 1918–1939*, Cologne, 1999; for east Galicia, see Conte, 'Land und "ethnische Reinheit"'.
56. For Poland's minority politics, see Stephan Horak, *Poland and Her National Minorities, 1919–39: A Case Study*, New York, 1961; Peter D. Stachura, 'National Identity and the Ethnic Minorities in Early Inter-war Poland', in P.D. Stachura (ed.), *Poland between the Wars, 1918–1939*, London/New York, 1998, pp.60–86. For cases that came before the League of Nations, see Martin Scheuermann, *Minderheitenschutz contra Konfliktverhütung? Die Minderheitenpolitik des Völkerbundes in den zwanziger Jahren*, Marburg, 2000, pp.88–148.
57. Cf. Freund, 'Die polnische Agrarreform', p.315; Anton Heinrich Hollmann, 'Die polnische Agrarreform', *Berichte über Landwirtschaft* 5/1 (1926), pp.128ff.; Conte, 'Land und "ethnische Reinheit"', p.56.
58. Hellwege, 'Agrarverfassung und Agrarreform', p.180.
59. Cf. Freund, 'Die polnische Agrarreform', pp.314f.; Hollmann, 'Die polnische Agrarreform', pp.127ff.; Hellwege, 'Agrarverfassung und Agrarreform', pp.179ff.; *Ausrottung der Ukrainer in Polen*, Prague, 1930, pp.22ff.; Basil Paneyko, 'Galicia and the Polish-Ukrainian Problem', *Slavonic and East European Review* 9 (1930/1931), pp.567–87; L'Association de l'Ukraine Occidentale pour la Societé des Nations, *La situation de la population ukrainienne en Pologne*, Lyon, 1924, republished as *Irredentist and Nationalist Questions in Central Europe, 1913–1939, Poland*, vol. 2, Nendeln, 1973.
60. Cf. Hellwege, 'Agrarverfassung und Agrarreform', p.186; Freund, 'Die polnische Agrarreform', p.129.
61. Cf. Benecke, *Die Ostgebiete*, pp.123–33, and Christhardt Henschel (this volume).
62. For this perspective, see Stanislaw Srokowski, 'The Ukrainian Problem in Poland: A Polish View', *Slavonic and East European Studies* 9 (1930/1931), pp.588–97; A.G. Macdonnell, 'East Poland after Ten Years', *Fortnightly Review* 33 (1933), pp.492–502; M.B. Winsch, 'Scenes in Eastern Poland', *Contemporary Review* 146 (1934), pp.472–79.
63. For a comparison of the Romanian and Serbian national movements in Austro-Hungary and the national states, see John Breuilly, *Nationalism and the State*, Chicago, 1994, pp.135–39; John Breuilly, 'Approaches to Nationalism', in Gopal Balakrishnan (ed.), *Mapping the Nation*, London/New York, 1996, pp.146–74. For a case study of Transylvania, see Dietmar Müller, 'Wirtschaftsprogrammatik und -politik für den ländlichen Raum Rumäniens: Zwischen Agrarpopulismus und bäuerlichem Mittelstandsdenken', *Zeitschrift für Siebenbürgische Landeskunde* 23/1 (2000), pp.6–23. For Galicia, see Keely Stauter-Halsted, *The Nation in the Village: The Genesis of Peasant National Identity in Austrian Poland, 1848–1914*, Ithaca/London, 2001; Kai Struve, *Bauern und Nation in Galizien: Über Zugehörigkeit und soziale Emanzipation im 19. Jahrhundert*, Göttingen, 2005.
64. Constantin Dobrogeanu-Gherea, *Neoiobăgia: Studiu economico-sociologic al problemei noastre agrare*, Bucharest, 1910.
65. Stefan Kieniewicz, *The Emancipation of the Polish Peasantry*, Chicago/London, 1969.
66. Holm Sundhaussen, *Geschichte Serbiens. 19.–21. Jahrhundert*, Vienna/Cologne/Weimer, 2007, p.151; Gale Stokes, *Politics as Development: The Emergence of Political Parties in Nineteenth-century Serbia*, Durham, NC/London, 1990; for the *zadruga*, see Srđan Milošević (this volume).

67. For a history of the cadastre and land register in Transylvania, see Alexandru Herlea, *Cărţile de proprietate în Transilvania*, Braşov, 1945. For a Romanian translation of the Austro-Hungarian cadastral stipulations, see Ioan Papp and Paul Balaşiu, *Cartea funduară: Colecţie de legi, regulamente, ordonanţe şi formulare, referitoare la cărţile funduare*, Cluj, 1922.
68. Cf. Constantin Tudor, 'Aspecte din activitatea de măsurări terestre şi cadastru', in *Geodezie, cadastru şi organizarea teritoriului* 15/4 (1971), pp.4–14; Orest I. Cozloschi, *O interpelare: Fraudele dela cadastru*, Roman, 1933, pp.25ff.
69. For a debate on the working methods and results of the cadastral survey, see Cozloschi, *O interpelare*; *Restabilirea Adevărului asupra situaţiunei dela Direcţiunea Cadastrului*, n.p., n.d., written by a group of cadastral technicians.
70. For a comparative study of the Habsburg and French-Belgian systems, see Alexandru Herlea, 'Organizarea şi principiile publicităţii imobiliare reale în România după Unirea din 1918', in A. Herlea, *Studii de istorie a dreptului*, vol. 2: *Dreptul de proprietate*, Cluj-Napoca, 1985, pp.160–96; Nicolae Boş, *Cartea funciară şi expertiza tehnică topo-cadastrală*, Bucharest, 2003.
71. Cf. *Revista Cadastrală: Organ al Asociaţiunei Generale a Topometrilor din România*, whose publication ran over three volumes from 1928 to 1930.
72. Cozloschi, *O interpelare*, pp.24ff.
73. *Expunerea de motive şi proectul de lege pentru Cartea Funciară alcătuite de Consiliul Legislativ*, Iaşi, 1938; Salvator A. Brădeanu, *Către o nouă legislaţiune funciară*, Bucharest, 1938.
74. In particular, see the early lecture of Andrei Rădulescu, *Publicitatea drepturilor reale imobiliare şi registrele de proprietate*, Bucharest, 1923 – Rădulescu was a member of the Romanian Academy.
75. Cf. writings by the prefect of Satu-Mare county, I.C. Puşcaşiu, *Agricultura, reforma agrară, colonizările, cadastrul şi cartea funduară*, Satu-Mare, 1931.
76. As in the case of the geodesists, several journals with printing locations in Transylvania published appeals for the countrywide introduction of the notarial system; see *Administraţia Română* (edited in Lugoj), *Ardealul Juridic* (Cluj) and *Notariatul Public* (Cluj).
77. I.T. Cosma, 'Problema notariatul public', *Notariatul Public* 2/8 (1938), pp.141–44.
78. For a history of the Polish legal professions in the interwar period, see Claudia Kraft, *Europa im Blick der polnischen Juristen: Rechtsordnung und juristische Professionen in Polen im Spannungsfeld zwischen Nation und Europa 1918–1930*, Frankfurt am Main, 2002. However, an added difficulty in reconstructing the functioning of the cadastre, the land register and the professional groups involved with them in Yugoslavia and Poland is the fact that, during the Second World War, far more of this work was destroyed in those countries than in Romania.
79. Cf. Ferdo Čulinović, 'O upisima u zemljišne knjige', *Arhiv za pravne i društvene nauke* 39/5 (1931), pp.360–72, and 39/6 (1931), pp.447–61; Adam Lazarević, 'Stari i novi zakon o izdavanje tapija', *Arhiv za pravne i društvene nauke* 41/4 (1932), pp.296–307; *Le cadastre, le livre foncier et la reforme agraire en Yougoslavie*, Belgrade, 1936.
80. Sergij Vilfan, 'Jugoslawien', in Helmut Coing (ed.), *Handbuch der Quellen und Literatur der neueren europäischen Privatrechtsgeschichte 3. Bd.: Das 19. Jahrhundert, 5. Teilband: Südosteuropa*, Munich, 1988, p.440.
81. Cf. Jakub Glass, Alfred Kraus and Fryderyk Zoll, *Instityсja ksiąg gruntowych na ziemiach polskich*, 3 vols, Warsawa/Kraków, 1921.
82. Kurt Ballerstedt, *Erbrecht, Erbsitten und Grundbesitzzersplitterung in Polen*, Stuttgart/Berlin, 1939, pp.148ff.
83. *Kataster gruntowy w świetle cyfr i rzeczywistości*, Lvov, 1933, p.30.
84. Benecke, *Die Ostgebiete*, pp.109ff.
85. Dumitru Şandru, *Reforma agrară din 1945 în România*, Bucharest, 2000.
86. See the exposé published by the Uniunea Centrale a Sindicatelor Agricole din România (Romanian Union of Agrarian Syndicates) in 1945: *Memoriu prezentat Comisiei de Studii pentru*

Reforma Agrară. The Academia de Agricultură din România (Romanian Academy of Agriculture), *Reforma Agrară*, Bucharest, 1945, also pleaded for maintaining what remained of large estates.

87. *Proect de lege pentru Expropriere şi Împroprietărire: Lupta Partidului Naţional-Ţărănesc pentru reformele agrare*, Bucharest, 1945. See also a speech by one of the economic experts of the Partidul Naţional Ţărănesc, Gheorghe Taşcă, which he delivered before the Asociaţia Economiştilor (Association of Economists) on 22 February 1945: Gheorghe Taşcă, *Reforma Agrară*, n.p., 1945.
88. *Reformele agrare din 1920 şi 1945*, Bucharest, 1945.
89. Şandru, *Reforma agrară din 1945*, pp.120ff., 190ff.
90. The Law on Agrarian Reform and Colonisation is printed in *Das Schicksal der Deutschen in Jugoslawien*, pp.223–33E; here art. 3, 5 and 10.
91. Cf. John B. Allcock, *Explaining Yugoslavia*, London, 2000, pp.126f.
92. For a political history of the upheavals in Poland in the wake of the Second World War, see Krystyna Kersten, *The Establishment of Communist Rule in Poland, 1943–1948*, Berkeley/Los Angeles/Oxford, 1991 [1984].
93. On Poland, see Detlef Brandes, *Der Weg der Vertreibung 1938–1945: Pläne und Entscheidungen zum, Transfer der Deutschen aus der Tschechoslowakei und aus Polen*, Munich, 2001. On Yugoslavia, Zoran Janjetović, *Between Hitler and Tito*.
94. On terms and concepts used in the case of Poland, see Michael G. Esch, *'Gesunde Verhältnisse': Deutsche und polnische Bevölkerungspolitik in Ostmitteleuropa 1939–1950*, Marburg, 1998.
95. On Vasa Čubrilović, see Müller, *Staatsbürger auf Widerruf*, pp.452f., 469. On Sreten Vukosavljević's work as minister for colonization (March 1945 to February 1946), see Nikola Gaćeša, 'Delatnost Sretena Vukosavljevića kao ministra kolonizaciju od marta 1945. do februara 1946. g'., in Gaćeša, *Radovi iz agrarne istorije i demografije*, pp.413–23. On Vukosavljević's ethnological research on land property, see Ivan Kovačević, *Istorija srpske etnologije II. Pravci i odlomci*, Belgrade, 2001, pp.208–38; on his collectivistic notions regarding property in the Serbian past, which were also trend-setting, see Sreten Vukosavljević, 'Postanak privatne zemljišne svojine u nas', *Arhiv za pravne i društvene nauke* 30/1 (1940), pp.91–100. On his term as colonization minister, see Sreten Vukosavljević, 'Zajednički radovi na selu', *Arhiv za pravne i društvene nauke* 1/1–2 (1945) pp.30–35; Sreten Vukosavljević, 'Zajednička zemljišna svojina', *Pravna Misao* 11/1–4 (1945), pp.17–29.
96. Esch, *'Gesunde Verhältnisse'*, p.72.

6

Front-line Soldiers into Farmers

Military Colonization in Poland after the First and Second World Wars

Christhardt Henschel

Twice in the twentieth century, in 1918 and in 1945, Poland had to rebuild its statehood after a destructive world war. Each new republic legitimized its existence with reference to the narrative of the suffering of the Polish nation and the merits of Polish soldiers on the front of each world war. Thus the so-called Second Republic (1918–1939) emphasized the armed struggle of Polish soldiers in the First World War (1914–1918), and military conflicts with Germany, Ukraine, Lithuania and Soviet Russia between 1918 and 1921, whereas communist Poland after 1944 focused on the heroic fight together with the Red Army against the German occupiers, and the new society that emerged thereafter. Both the Second Republic and communist Poland rewarded a number of their front-line soldiers with land on the eastern or western borderland areas (Kresy Wschodnie; Kresy Zachodnie/Ziemie Odzyskane), where the national bond to the Polish heartland was seen as needing reinforcement. This chapter will discuss and compare both of these settlement programmes, known as *Osadnictwo wojskowe* or military colonization, in the context of the property discourses in Poland in the first half of the twentieth century.

Military Colonization and Agrarian Reform in Poland's Eastern Provinces after 1920

As a pivotal site in the war between the tsar's empire and the Central Powers (Germany, Austria-Hungary), Poland was particularly affected by the consequences of the First World War. Since the beginning of the war in 1914, the possible establishment of Polish statehood under Russian, German or Austrian domination had been a subject of negotiations in the framework of these countries' political calculations. Meanwhile, the Polish political scene was preparing itself for the founding of a new state. In short, two political camps could be distinguished, called 'activist' and 'passivist' according to the strategies they followed to achieve the 'rebirth' of Poland as a state. The passivists and their leader, Roman Dmowski, placed their hopes in loyalty to Russia and negotiating Polish independence with Britain and France. The 'activists', led by the socialist Józef Piłsudski, followed the idea of military intervention on the Eastern front, on the side of the Central Powers, that would push Poland back onto the European fold. Piłsudski and his supporters consequently stylized the struggle of the Polish Legions (Legiony Polskie) as the 'armed deed' (*czyn zbrojny*) of a small, patriotic elite representing the whole Polish nation. After Piłsudski became head of state (*Naczelnik Państwa*) in November 1918, the dramatic defeat of Bolshevik troops near Warsaw in August 1920 became one of the founding myths of the Second Republic, and gave rise to the celebration of Piłsudski as a national hero.[1]

Even during the fighting, certain political circles had brought up the question of how to reward the heroic courage of soldiers and volunteers after their demobilization.[2] On 15 July 1920, four weeks before the decisive Battle of Warsaw in the Polish–Soviet War (1919–1921), the Sejm Ustawodawczy (Constituent Assembly) unanimously accepted the Act on the Realization of Agrarian Reform, establishing preferential treatment of soldiers in the parcelling out of land (deserters were excluded from this regulation).[3] The parties in the Sejm hoped for an uprising of peasant volunteer soldiers during national mobilization against the Soviet invasion. Faced with a dramatic situation at the front, the Polish prime minister and chairman of the Polish Peasant Party (Polskie Stronnictwo Ludowe-Piast), Wincenty Witos, substantiated the regulations of agrarian reform for meritorious soldiers in a press appeal 'To the National Army'.[4]

The politicians' promises, which were not based on fully elaborated plans, put the government authorities under pressure to act. Two million war refugees and returnees who had fled or been removed from the combat zone flocked into the country now that the war was over.[5] Distributing land in the ethnically mixed Kresy Wschodnie seemed an appropriate way to meet the expectations of demobilized soldiers. On 15 October 1920, three days before the armistice between Poland and Soviet Russia, PSL-Piast accelerated the course of events in the Sejm by proposing that land be allocated to outstanding soldiers.[6] Finally, on 18 October 1920, Piłsudski promised soldiers a generous reward:

> Any soldier who has made so much effort for Poland will not go unrewarded. The grateful Fatherland will not forget him. We conquered huge territories which became depopulated and ravaged by the World War and nearly changed into a desert.

> I proposed to the government that part of this land should become the property of those who made it Polish by washing it with Polish blood. This land, exhausted by the bloody war, is waiting for peace and for those who are willing to exchange their swords for ploughshares. I wish you to gain as many peaceful victories during this future work as you did during the work of fighting.[7]

Piłsudski's support accelerated the legislative procedure, leading to two acts on 17 December 1920. First, the Act on the Transfer of Land into Public Ownership created a land fund in the eastern (mainly Volhynian) voivodeships consisting of former Russian properties of the state, the tsar and the Russian Orthodox Church, in addition to deserted private manors and expropriated private property.[8] Afterwards, the Act on the Conferment of Land to the Soldiers of the Polish Army enabled distribution of the property among deserving soldiers, volunteers who had fought on the front lines and war invalids. The remaining soldiers could buy land from the fund. Each land parcel could amount to a maximum of 45 hectares in size. The beneficiaries of the fund received material support from the army's demobilization of movables, as well as financial aid from a credit fund of two million Polish marka, a sum that was no more than symbolic after hyperinflation hit Poland in the early 1920s.[9]

The conveyance of title to land as a reward for fighting for the independence of one's own nation was not a specifically Polish phenomenon; integrating war returnees and invalids, and appreciating their patriotic achievements were discussion topics in nearly every European country after the First World War.[10] Which soldiers should be recognized as combatants and financially supported was a difficult and major question in the Polish debate. On the one hand, millions of Poles had served under the German, Russian or Habsburg flag. On the other hand, combatants such as the Polish Legionnaires established a specific group identity and regarded themselves as a patriotic elite whose deeds should be highly rated by Polish society.[11] In the end, a wider definition of war combatants was accepted. It included Polish soldiers who served in non-Polish armies,[12] which was only possible because many of them had later fought in the Polish–Soviet War and thereby became patriotic defenders of Polish soil. Front-line soldiers extended their claims for adequate compensation to all fighters for independence, particularly because it was assumed that they would also follow their national ideals in future: 'The Polish soldier from the period of struggle for independence was not a militarist, but a citizen who fought for freedom when it was necessary, but who wanted to work when the second stage of rebuilding the Fatherland had come'.[13] Soldiers were also rewarded with privileges apart from allocation of land, for example, the granting of retail trade licences in tobacco and spirits, which were state-owned monopolies. Another possibility was to favour combatants by employing them in the local and public sector, or in larger workshops and factories.[14]

The initial colonization plans intended 40,000 settlements for demobilized soldiers. This number was limited to 8,000 after numerous discussions in the Sejm.[15] By 1923, the Polish state had taken over 366,738 hectares of agrarian land, but given only 258,030 hectares to combatants. Then, during that year, only 5,557 out of 8,732 allocated plots of land were permanently settled.[16] At the same time, 22,503 out of a total of 99,513 candidates' applications were accepted. Another 1,300 were rejected, and the remaining requests were left unanswered.[17] Yet until the mid 1930s, only 9,082 colonists benefited from the Act on the Conferment of Land to the Soldiers of the Polish Army,[18] most likely because of enormous organizational problems and complicated bureaucratic procedures on the one hand, and rapidly dwindling support for the colonization programme from political parties and the public on the other. Piłsudski's temporary retreat from active politics in 1922 brought the political pro-colonization initiatives to a standstill, and after much criticism of colonization in the press and the Sejm, land redistribution was shelved.[19] The next year, the new minister of military affairs, Władysław Sikorski, cut the programme's budget by 50 per cent, and also shrank its administrative apparatus.[20]

In 1925, the recent Act on the Execution of Agrarian Reform abandoned military colonization as an independent programme. 'Soldiers of outstanding merits and invalids of the Polish army, and Polish volunteer organizations' became one of various groups given priority in the process of land allocation.[21] However, Piłsudski's return to power in May 1926 changed this situation, and in 1930 the military colonization programme was renewed. In March 1932, despite international announced protests from the Belarusian and Ukrainian deputies to the Sejm, a new law opened up the possibility to affiliate more land to the state land fund and to change less fertile plots for land of superior quality.[22] Nevertheless, lack of land brought colonization to a halt again in 1935.[23]

Implementation of the Act on the Conferment of Land to Soldiers of the Polish Army of 17 December 1920 started in spring 1921. The typical farm carried debt of around 5,350 zloty. The average farm size ranged from 10 to 20 hectares, depending on soil quality, though so-called model farms owned by experienced, well-educated farmers could be as large as 45 hectares.[24] As for the social structure of the colonists, over 42.3 per cent were non-commissioned officers, 40.7 per cent were enlisted soldiers, 15.8 per cent were officers and 1.2 per cent were generals. More than two thirds of the beneficiaries originally came from Congress Poland, and around a quarter from Małopolska. Only 6.5 per cent of the settlers had benefited from higher education; the majority of them had elementary or secondary education.[25] To prepare for the mass settlement of military colonists, so-called work columns (*kolumny robocze*) were formed to prepare the land for incoming settlers.[26] Because the supervising Agency for Demobilization Matters of the Ministry of Military Affairs was unable to control the whole process, numerous settlers took possession of much more land than they were supposed to; about 25 per cent of the land occupation was later quashed by courts of appeal.[27] Such behaviour, together with the temporary accommodation of the work columns in local peasants' homes and the requisition of portions of the harvest, increasingly aggravated the local Ukrainian population, who were still suffering the consequences of seven years of war, hunger and lack of farmland, and insisted on solving their own economic problems.

Osadnictwo wojskowe shared the structural problems of eastern Polish agriculture. Most peasants in Kresy Wschodnie were subsistence farmers; only a small number of large estates produced on a larger scale. A rural middle class did not exist. In addition, a number of traditional conditions burdened agriculture in eastern Poland, for example, the common law-based regulation of landownership, and the system of equitable servitudes. The Kresy inhabitants pinned their hopes on the agrarian reform that Polish politicians had discussed since 1920 and hesitantly put into practice. The main aim of Polish agrarian reform, however, was not to redistribute the land but to improve on inefficient agricultural structures.[28] New colonists faced great difficulties caused by weak local infrastructure and insufficient support from the army and authorities.[29] They had to take large investment loans to buy seeds, buildings and livestock. Though the farms were unaffected by the traditional succession of the estate, fields were often located away from each other, which made farming more difficult.[30] The small size of their farms led many of colonists to cooperate with each other. However, even the temporary stabilization of the economic situation in the mid 1920s could not countervail the settlers' lack of capital and insufficient agricultural expertise. Moreover, the subsequent world economic crisis and drop in prices did not spare the colonists' farms.[31]

Delays in resolving property rights issues also hindered the development of farms. Although state land distribution was seen as a form of compensation for the historical injustice committed by the tsarist policy of de-Polonization, it was not automatically affiliated with the assignment of full property rights to colonists. It took years to resolve the legal situation of title and the question of outstanding mortgages on many farms. Up to 1927, only 20 per cent of the colonists could consider themselves the rightful owners of their farms.[32]

In the beginning, the distribution of land to soldiers of outstanding merit took a patriotic tone. Gradually, however, ethno-national arguments increasingly gained importance in discussions about the legitimization of *Osadnictwo wojskowe*. One of the most important arguments for temporarily discontinuing land distribution in 1925 was the rising antipathy of the Belarusian and Ukrainian rural populations, which felt the colonists discriminated against them. They demanded a more general form of agrarian reform that would also consider the interests of local people.[33] They had trouble accepting that more than 98 per cent of the colonists were Catholics, meaning that they belonged to the Polish titular nation.[34] The military colonization programme exacerbated lingering issues regarding agrarian reform and national minority rights. Combining military settlements with the distribution of formerly state-owned land invited criticism from minority politicians, especially Ukrainians. The land hunger of Ukrainian peasants, whose loyalty to the Polish state after 1918 proved very fragile, and disputes over the Ukrainian-speaking school system burdened Polish–Ukrainian relations, sparking anti-colonist resentment in some places.[35] Moreover, a number of peasants living near the Soviet border were very attracted by the Soviets' New Economic Policy and the policy of indigenization (*korenizatsiya*), which was an attempt to integrate non-Russian nationalities into the Soviet Union.[36]

The importance of military installations in safeguarding Kresy as an area of Polish settlement was frequently emphasized. From Warsaw's perspective, it was unfortunate that the 'Polish element' in Kresy seemed to have been the subject of 'de-nationalization' (*wynarodowienie*). Most Polish politicians perceived Kresy as a virulent national security problem, which meant that they viewed widespread settlement of loyal soldiers as a 'factor of military politics and a corrective of national minority policy'.[37] In this situation, distribution land grants among meritorious soldiers seemed a good way of strengthening Polishness in ethnically mixed Kresy, influenced as it was by Ukrainian irredentism, and of punctuating the Polish claim to power. Poles themselves had had a similar experience with Prussian settlement and the Prussian national policy towards the Polish minority living in Prussia before 1914.[38] To date, no study has shown whether Polish politicians attempted to transplant these settlement ideas into policy concerning Kresy after 1918.

The tradition of the Kresy mythology in the Polish romanticism of the nineteenth and twentieth centuries loomed over the army's and politicians' engagement with settlement policy. Polish romantic literature represented the Polish *dwór* (manor house) as a symbol of the Polishness of Kresy. The motif of the *Polak-rycerz* (chivalric Pole) that underpinned Polish claims to Kresy was derived from that idea.[39] In a way, military colonists were seen as heirs of this tradition, reactivating the traditional ethos of the *Polak-rycerz* as a pioneer and moral authority. In the same way, the *dwór* was treated as the ideal model of a Polish settlement in the uncivilized eastern provinces. Scarred by the devastation of the wars between 1914 and 1921, and more than 120 years under tsarist rule, and then incorporated into the new Polish state, Kresy needed this new creative spirit of protecting the Polish state and forming 'strong eyries of resistance against the eastern danger'.[40]

The voivode of Volhynia and Piłsudski's follower, Henryk Józewski (1892–1982), wrote in his memoirs that the colonists, characterized by a certain 'ideology and military shape', styled themselves as 'liberators of the fatherland' with the mission of the 'defence of the Polishness' of Kresy Wschodnie. Józewski – simultaneously an advocate of a Polish–Ukrainian agreement and a supporter of the *Osadnictwo wojskowe* – noted that this dimension of the colonizing mission disappeared as time went by, and the colonists came closer to local reality: 'Volhynia became accustomed to them and they became accustomed to Volhynia'.[41] Several contemporaries judged the success of military colonization in that respect. For them, it would be a success 'when the ownership of a piece of land tied him [the colonist] here and smelted a passionate Volhynian from a "Posener", or a "Galician from Congress Poland" (*Galicyjak z Kongresówy*)'.[42]

Considering the settlers' relatively small numbers, low disposable liquid assets and lack of agricultural knowledge, it may be assumed that the settlement of former soldiers did not leave lasting economic or demographic traces in Kresy. The idea of settling devastated, sparsely populated areas turned out to be incorrect; colonization was concentrated in the relatively populous Volhynia.[43] The extent of the settlements never reached the figure projected in 1920. Despite the attractions, many colonizing projects were of extremely limited durability.

Nevertheless, military colonization was 'one of the most emotionalized elements of the Polish Kresy policy',[44] this because the ethno-national legitimization of distributing property rights to a group of soldiers brought Ukrainian and Belarusian politicians to the scene. Moreover, right-wing National Democrats accused the settlers of losing their Polish identity (de-nationalization) in Ukrainian-dominated areas, which meant that they were unable to strengthen the Polish character of the territory. Other criticisms targeted the insufficient realization of land distribution, the poor agronomic qualifications of the colonists and the programme's high costs.

Within the context of tense inter-ethnic relations in Kresy during the 1920s and 1930s, the colonization programme was not well thought out politically.[45] However, it should be pointed out that the soldiers never played the role of soldier peasants or merciless 'Polonizers', even though Polish military tradition was very important in their social life.[46] The beginning of the Second World War brought an end to the *Osadnictwo wojskowe* in eastern Poland. The colonists, seen as symbolic representatives of Poland's oppressive attitude towards Kresy, became a subject of Soviet occupation politics.[47] In February 1940, the Soviets deported most of them to the far interior of the Soviet state.[48]

Military Colonization and the Anti-German Rampart in the 'Recovered Territories' after 1945

A new chapter of military colonization in Poland began with the westward displacement of the country's borders after the Second World War. The parallel progress of the Red Army and the Polish communist government's accession to power led to new internal and external political constellations. First of all, the Polish Workers' Party (Polska Partia Robotnicza, PPR; after 1948 Polska Zjednoczona Partia Robotnicza, PZPR), whose power derived from the presence of Soviet troops, had to stabilize the supply situation for the people, restore basic infrastructure and reinforce its power in a Poland shaped by anti-Soviet and anti-communist sentiment.[49] The loss of Kresy Wschodnie to the Soviet Union caused a new wave of migration to Poland, even as hundreds of thousands of liberated forced labourers, concentration camp survivors and former partisans flowed into the country.

Even before the Potsdam conference, the new Polish authorities tried to consolidate their power by pursuing a policy directed against the German population remaining on new Polish territory. Only at this level could they be sure of the people's support, and thus gain legitimization of their existence and power.[50] The communist authorities dissociated themselves from the eastern-oriented Polish territorial policy connected with the political tradition of the early modern, Jagiellonian-era state, as well as with interwar Poland. They aimed instead to return to the conception of 'Piast Poland', which included the former German eastern provinces that had belonged to the medieval Polish state under the Piast dynasty. The Ziemie Odzyskane ('Recovered Territories') were to be incorporated into the Polish state and the German population resettled. Incoming Polish 'repatriates' – that is, Polish nationals who had been forced to leave their homes in Kresy Wschodnie, but also settlers from other parts of Poland and people returning from the war – were to populate Ziemie Odzyskane.[51]

The Polish army (formed in the Soviet Union in 1943) played a special role in the 're-Polonization' of Ziemie Odzyskane. These armed forces, unofficially known as the Polish People's Army (Ludowe Wojsko Polskie), were used to safeguard agricultural infrastructure, crops and livestock, and to establish the first administrative structures. Furthermore, the Polish People's Army organized the resettlement of the remaining German population and was responsible for protecting the new German–Polish border, which had not yet been officially acknowledged. These facts, apart from their psychological effect on Poles, became a fait accompli that strengthened Poland's position during the Potsdam negotiations.[52] At the same time, the pro-Soviet political leadership tried to discredit all other Polish military formations that had fought against the German occupation. The Home Army (Armia Krajowa), the largest armed organization under the command of the Polish government in exile in London, and which did not accept communist domination of Poland, was especially affected by the propaganda. As in the case of former combatants in the Second Republic, Second World War veterans were divided into several groups whose contributions to the triumph over Germany were interpreted unequally. After 1918, Polish Legionnaires had tried to monopolize their status as patriotic heroes within the framework of parliamentary democracy, and, later, the authoritarian *Sanacja* regime. Now, three decades later, the PPR/PZPR tried to establish a similar myth about the soldiers of the Polish People's Army. Unlike their predecessors in the interwar period, they used political, physical and psychological violence to implement their vision of Polish history in the twentieth century.

As early as May 1945, the new Polish authorities took the decision to have the army remove Germans from a 'border cordon' and settle families of Polish soldiers in the area.[53] The counties of Kamień Pomorski-Wolin (Cammin-Wollin), Gryfino (Greifenhagen), Sulęcin (Zielenzig), Rzepin (Reppen), Krosno Odrzańskie (Crossen an der Oder), Gubin (Guben), Żary (Sorau), Żagań (Sagan), Zgorzelec (Görlitz), Lubań (Lauban) and Lwówek Śląski (Löwenberg in Silesia) were earmarked for the new *Osadnictwo wojskowe* (military colonization).[54] The goal was to Polonize and secure the immediate border zone. The distribution of land to soldiers was seen as a reward for their struggle against the Germans. As defined in the Molotov–Ribbentrop Pact, the Kresy Wschodnie territories occupied by the Soviet Union, home to about 44 per cent of the soldiers in the Polish People's Army, did not return to the Polish state. Facing a foreseeable shift of the borders and affected by anti-Polish ethnic cleansing in Volhynia, they were very interested in removing their families to the Polish heartland.[55]

Establishment of a region settled by soldier-peasants had first been considered in 1944. In September of that year, the new Soviet-supported governmental body, the Polish Committee of National Liberation (Polski Komitet Wyzwolenia Narodowego, PKWN), signed agreements with the bordering Soviet republics concerning the exchange of populations.[56] In November 1944, the PKWN and the Soviet government agreed in Lvov to evacuate Polish soldiers from the territories of the Soviet Socialist Republic of Ukraine to central Poland, where they would be sent on to the new western provinces.[57] As practised after 1920 and confirmed in the annex to the PKWN Decree on the Execution of Agrarian Reform,[58] veterans of the Polish People's Army, war invalids and 'fighters for a democratic Poland' were favoured in the land redistribution.[59]

The colonization plans were realized in two phases: from June to September 1945, under the auspices of the army, and between October 1945 and July 1948, as part of the army-assisted civil colonization of the new western provinces.[60] The basis of the organized colonization was Order No. 111 of the Supreme Command of the Polish Army (3 June 1945), which announced a rapid settlement of soldiers but did not address the problem of property rights over the redistributed land. Order No. 111 entitled front-line soldiers, non-commissioned officers and officers, partisans, resistance fighters and their families to benefit from the colonization programme. Persons who had fought against the new regime were excluded from this rule.[61] In 1946, disabled functionaries of the security services also qualified for land grants under the colonization programme.[62] On 14 January 1948, the Ministry of the Recovered Territories declared all settlers in western Poland who had taken part one way or another in the struggle against Germany, including war invalids, demobilized soldiers, partisans and resistance fighters, to be military settlers. This meant that, theoretically, even fighters from the underground Home Army, defamed by propaganda as reactionary and quasi-fascist, could benefit from the programme.[63] However, one can assume that in practice, the allocating institutions ignored members of the non-communist resistance and the authorities often blocked approval of their disability pensions.[64]

Even though more than two thirds of the Polish People's Army were peasants, only 15,000 soldiers registered as interested settlers during the first phase (during August 1945). The High Command had reckoned on a figure of 100,000 candidates. Not even among the 49,000 soldiers registered as repatriates from Kresy was *Osadnictwo wojskowe* popular.[65] There were several reasons for this: firstly, demobilization of the army did not keep up with the need for colonists; secondly, soldiers were not allowed to choose their plots of land themselves; thirdly, property rights were restricted to the colonists themselves, so their children could not inherit the land; and fourthly, relatively poor soil, a high degree of destruction and despoliation, and an unstable security situation made large areas of the borderland unattractive for colonization. In addition, it turned out in many cases that civilian settlers had already taken over the best plots of lands. Furthermore, the transporting of families from Kresy to the west was not guaranteed, because favouring them during the 'repatriation' was not realizable.[66]

After preparations in June, the first farms were established in July 1945. Different detachments had to take responsibility for each county. The First Army took charge of an especially huge territory, in keeping with its status as the custodian of national tradition. No systematic procedure was applied in parcelling out the land, so the settlements lacked a close-knit structure.[67] The military authorities offered material support to settlers who had received a parcel of land: the privileged allotment of jobs, assistance with building projects and transport, and help obtaining financial support, loans, education, health care or concessions.[68] The task of organizing the settlement process fell to the Commission for Military Colonization (Komisja Osadnictwa Wojskowego), directed by the army. Contact with the public administration was maintained by the Inspectorate of Military Colonization (Inspektorat Osadnictwa Wojskowego) within the Ministry of Public Administration. Local commanders oversaw the colonization and coordination of the resettlement of Germans. Their cooperation with government agencies proved inadequate; instead, they tended to broaden the competences of the military administration to the disadvantage of the civil administration.[69]

The arguments for military colonization were both pragmatic and ideological. Filling the demographic gap following the removal of the German population of this area was regarded as the settlers' most important role. In addition, the army leadership had promised thousands of soldiers and their families who had had to leave Kresy a new home in Ziemie Odzyskane. The army looked for people who 'were able to combine [the] defence [of borders] with social, economic and political tasks'.[70] Soldiers of the Polish People's Army were able to cope with this responsibility, as they were psychologically and morally prepared, and had already proven their patriotic and ideological convictions. Moreover, it was suspected that they would have a special emotional relationship to the land on which their fathers, brothers and relatives had been killed in the war: 'One can safely say that the tomb of the Polish soldier became the most resistant rampart of the reborn Fatherland'.[71]

According to PPR ideology, war veterans were supposed to fortify the deserted borderland – their material existence was of much lesser importance. Counting all 'participants of the armed struggle against the occupier' and their families, one could calculate a total of some hundred thousand soldier families that might find settling in western Poland attractive. The regime's aim was to establish settlement centres radiating 'strength and a strong national spirit'.[72] By integrating their settlement policy into the national ideology of struggle against Germany, the communist authorities tried to bind front-line soldiers into close-knit communities, and to enhance their potential during the process of integrating the population of the new territories into the state and society.

Nonetheless, PPR propaganda strongly emphasized the fact that the government was compensating military colonists for their efforts on the front lines of the war. At the same time, the colonists were presented as guarantors of a lasting Polonization of western Poland, as formulated in the above-mentioned Order No. 111 of the Supreme Command of the Polish Army:

> Understanding and appreciating the input of bravery and exertion of the Polish soldier in his effort for freedom and the greatness of Poland, the Polish government, fulfilling its promises, gives the priority right to soldiers and their families to take possession in the western territories.
>
> Each family of a soldier from the Polish Army is guaranteed a five hectare parcel of land. Amongst the millions of Polish families which in the next month will settle the western territories, the first ones would be the families of Polish soldiers.[73]

PPR propaganda was not dominated by the rhetoric of class struggle but by national overtones and threats of renewed German aggression. The colonists' presence and activities were depicted as a continuation of the military's fight against the external enemy. The settlers were to build a 'wall of Polishness' against the German threat. Polish armed forces, in cooperation with their Soviet allies, were presented as guaranteeing the territorial and national integrity of the new Poland: 'Poland – be calm. Work and build your power. The one who obtained your freedom for the effort of his blood keeps watch over your magnitude. On the Oder River the Polish soldiers keep watch'.[74] Land grants to soldiers were, in the aforementioned context, 'the best recompense for their efforts and fighting, and faithfulness to the nation'.[75] Seen as established representatives of the Polish nation, the soldiers' objective was to facilitate the integration of new settlers from all parts of Poland and play a prominent role in the administration and economy of Ziemie Odzyskane.[76]

When the first phase of military colonization had not brought about any satisfactory results, the second stage began in October 1945, lasting until July 1948. It was initiated by an order of 24 September 1945 that also put civilian authorities at the voivodeship, county and communal levels in charge of military settlement. The demobilization of the First and Second armies began at the same time.[77] Additionally, in February 1946, landed properties in the military's charge were dissolved and handed over to the civil administration, which was to distribute the land among soldiers. The fundamental concept of colonization – creating a coherent milieu along the border, grounded in the experience of common struggle during the Second World War and benefiting from certain privileges not extended to civilian settlements – was increasingly neglected. This development exacerbated the sense of discrimination that had embittered combatants since the start of land redistribution.[78] As *Osadnictwo wojskowe* was transferred to civil control, it lost its character as a stand-alone category of 'military' colonization.[79] In January 1948 the designated area of settlement was expanded to the entirety of the Recovered Territories.[80]

By 1948, approximately 60,000 families (170,000 to 180,000 persons) had settled as military colonists in the Polish western borderland, most highly concentrated in Lower Silesia.[81] The land allocated to them comprised 44,000 farms, taking up about 60 per cent of the farmland in the region.[82] However, only one third of eligible soldiers settled in the framework of the *Osadnictwo wojskowe* programme – the majority took over farms as civil colonists. In January 1948, all farm members who had served in the army received the status of military colonists. Hence, the circle of people participating in the colonizing programme grew to a total of 175,000 families (500,000 persons), corresponding to 12 per cent of all Polish settlers in the Ziemie Odzyskane.[83]

One of the unsolved problems of *Osadnictwo wojskowe* was the question of the colonists' limited property rights. The land parcels had been bestowed on the settlers, and therefore could not be passed on to their descendants. Then, in the course of the collectivization process of Polish agriculture during the Stalinization of Poland, military colonists were no longer treated as a special group. The introduction of socialist forms of property and production – such as, for example, cooperatives and collective farming – aroused little interest among the settlers.[84] Furthermore, the extension of full property rights to colonists was interrupted and would resume only during the Gomułka Thaw after 1956.[85]

In review, it seems that the ambitious plan for military colonization of Ziemie Odzyskane was doomed to failure from the very beginning.[86] The aforementioned organizational and operational difficulties support this thesis. After a short phase of activism up to September 1945, the colonization programme lost its extraordinary status as a military and population-policy project. *Osadnictwo wojskowe*, uniting 'repatriates' from eastern Poland, people resettled from Central Poland and returnees from the war, was part of the general settlement process in the new western provinces of Poland.[87] After the first few years, the main aim of the project became to exploit *Osadnictwo wojskowe* for purposes of official communist propaganda, which suggested that only the 'guard on the Oder' kept by Polish soldiers together with the Soviet Army could protect the thousand-year-old Piast national territory of Poland and guarantee peace.

Conclusion

In both cases of government-supported colonization programmes for demobilized soldiers in endangered borderlands, the ruling elites tried to mould a centralized state from disparate territories extensively devastated by war. The *Osadnictwo wojskowe* projects after both world wars used similar national rhetoric. Protection of national territory against external and, in the case of the Second Republic, the internal danger of 'de-Polonization' and loss of territory was meant to justify the allocation of land to reliable peasant-soldiers. The 'guard on the Oder' was compatible with the 'strong eyries of resistance against the eastern danger' in eastern Poland, even though the enemies were Germans in one case and Ukrainians and Russians in the other. After 1945, anti-German rhetoric had a state-doctrinaire character legitimizing the westward shift of Poland's borders, whereas argument during the interwar period was directed against both the internal threat from Ukrainians and the danger of the establishment of Bolshevik ideas in eastern Poland. *Osadnictwo wojskowe* was often questioned, so one cannot speak of a consensus on colonization before 1939. The programme in interwar Poland itself was much milder than the one after 1945, as its only aim was to establish and maintain Polish settlement in ethnically mixed territories. In the end, the military colonization programme of 1920 lost its Polonizing aspiration due to a lack of political support. Military farms were not established in especially endangered areas or in Ukrainian strongholds where there was a low percentage of Poles in the population. It seems that soil quality was of major importance.[88] Meanwhile, rapidly diminishing parliamentary and governmental support spoke against Polonization. State support for Polish farms proved insufficient to overcome the structural problems of Kresy agriculture.

The national impact of interwar *Osadnictwo wojskowe* was perhaps greatest at the propaganda level. In the post-war reality of 1945, this aspect was all the more important. Military colonists were seen as determined Polonizers, border guards protecting the Polish nation against Germany's return. Polish soldiers were coming into a land where only a few Germans were left. The settlers were to re-establish the tradition of the Slavic settlement discontinued hundreds of years ago. *Osadnictwo wojskowe* after 1945 was only one part of the Polish state's intensive effort to fully 're-Polonize' territories that had not been under Polish rule for several hundred years. The PPR was firmly engaged in restoring Polish culture, architecture and history in Ziemie Odzyskane. In this understanding, military colonists were genuine pioneers of Polishness.

To the architects of both concepts, the war veterans seemed to represent an especially well-suited pool of potential colonists. They had proven their patriotic disposition on the front, and usually were somehow tied to the conquered territories. They were supposed to engage actively in colonization, and thereby justify the property rights granted them. Thus, the element of patriotic struggle, alongside the ethnic origin of the settlers, became the most important criterion for owning land.

Nevertheless, neither programme achieved the desired effect. The number of military colonists during the interwar period proved too small to change the ethnic situation in Kresy. Even if the colonization process had been better organized, the Polonization of Kresy would have been an unrealistic goal. After 1945, larger numbers of settlers took part in the *Osadnictwo wojskowe* project. In some regions, the percentage of military colonists was clearly noticeable. But in fact, the Polish People's Army made little effort to support the settlers after it lost direct control over the organization of *Osadnictwo wojskowe*. Gradually they became simple combatants, whose organization, Związek Osadników, became part of the communist Society of Fighters for Freedom and Democracy. There is no evidence that colonists made better progress in acculturation in their new homeland, or became more engaged in rebuilding Ziemie Odzyskane. In time, the military colonists differed from the other settlers only in that they wore army uniforms on public holidays.

It bears repeating that the authors of both colonizing projects paid significant attention to their 'own' politically close combatant milieus. Satisfying the needs of disillusioned war veterans was a way of guaranteeing their support in political questions. In 1920, the army command, legitimated by a broad political consensus, for a brief historical moment acted as an almost autonomous state authority. Full parliamentary and governmental control over the military – and in consequence the *Osadnictwo wojskowe* project – was established only after the entry into force of the democratic constitution of 17 March 1921.[89] In 1945, however, Poland was ruled by a different constellation of power characterized by the direct influence of the Soviet military, the Communist Party authorities, developing Polish administration and the vacuum left after the Germans' withdrawal at the local level. In this situation, party and state institutions officially entrusted the army with the colonization of the borderland.

However, the initiators of both programmes had not thought through the question of organizing property rights regarding the parcelled land. Neither the Second nor the People's Republic abandoned the liberal-individual definition of property.[90] Beyond all ideological differences, both states tried to transform individual property rights into a nation-based, collective definition of property rights. Not individual subjects but the national collective was underlined as central to the question of property.

Notes

1. Janusz Szczepański, *Społeczeństwo Polski w walce z najazdem bolszewickim 1920 roku*, Warsaw, 2000; Norman Davies, *White Eagle, Red Star: The Polish–Soviet War 1919–1920 and 'The Miracle on the Vistula'*, London, 1972. On the cult of Piłsudski, see Heidi Hein, *Der Piłsudski-Kult und seine Bedeutung für den polnischen Staat 1926–1939*, Marburg, 2002.
2. Janina Stobniak-Smogorzewska, *Kresowe osadnictwo wojskowe 1920–1945*, Warsaw, 2003, pp.17–18.
3. 'Ustawa z dnia 15 lipca 1920 r. o wykonaniu reformy rolnej', *Dziennik Ustaw Rzeczypospolitej Polskiej* [hereafter *Dz. U.*] 70 (1920), position 462. See Lidia Głowacka and Andrzej Czesław Żak, 'Osadnictwo Wojskowe na Wołyniu w latach 1921–1939 w świetle dokumentów Centralnego Archiwum Wojskowego', *Biuletyn Wojskowej Służby Archiwalnej* 28 (2006), pp.140–64; Werner Benecke, *Die Ostgebiete der Zweiten Polnischen Republik: Staatsmacht und öffentliche Ordnung in einer Minderheitenregion 1918–1939*, Cologne/Weimar, 1999, pp.89–96.
4. Stobniak-Smogorzewska, *Kresowe osadnictwo*, p.19.
5. Benecke, *Die Ostgebiete*, p.124; Stobniak-Smogorzewska, *Kresowe osadnictwo*, pp.20–21.
6. Stobniak-Smogorzewska, *Kresowe osadnictwo*, p.17. In another motion, PSL-Piast requested that 11,000 of the 22,000 demobilized officers be employed in civilian service to replace non-Polish nationals: see Tadeusz Antoni Kowalski, *Mniejszości narodowe w siłach zbrojnych Drugiej Rzeczypospolitej Polskiej (1918–1939)*, Toruń, 1998, p.64.
7. Józef Piłsudski, *Pisma zbiorowe: Wydanie prac dotychzas drukiem ogłoszonych*, 10 vols, Warsaw, 1937, vol. 5, p.176.
8. 'Ustawa z dnia 17 grudnia 1920 r. o przejęciu na własność Państwa ziemi w niektórych powiatach Rzeczypospolitej Polskiej', *Dz. U.* 4 (1921), pos. 17.
9. 'Ustawa z dnia 17 grudnia 1920 r. o nadaniu ziemi żołnierzom Wojska Polskiego', *Dz. U.* 4 (1921), pos. 18; Stobniak-Smogorzewska, *Kresowe osadnictwo*, pp.17–34.
10. Regarding the distribution of land to combatants in Europe, see Czesław Brzozowski, 'Akcja osadnictwa wojskowego na Kresach Wschodnich 1920–1931', PhD diss., Warsaw, 1938, pp.3–10; cf. Dietmar Müller, 'Die Gouvernementalität des Bodeneigentums im östlichen Europa', *Comparativ* 16/5–6 (2006), pp.112–29.
11. Piotr Wróbel, '"Kombatanci kontra politycy": Narodziny i początki działania Związku Legionistów Polskich 1918–1925', *Przegląd Historyczny* 76/1 (1985), pp.77–111; Elżbieta Kossewska, *Związek Legionistów Polskich 1922–1939*, Warsaw, 2003; Marek Jabłonowski, *Sen o potędze Polski . . . Z dziejów ruchu byłych wojskowych w II Rzeczypospolitej (1918–1939)*, Olsztyn, 1998.
12. Christhardt Henschel, 'Der Erste Weltkrieg zwischen Erinnerungskultur und Politik in Polen am Beispiel der Stadt Lublin (1918–1939)', *Nordost-Archiv* 17 (2008), pp.201–11; Julia Eichenberg, *Kämpfen für Frieden und Fürsorge: Polnische Veteranen des Ersten Weltkriegs und ihre internationalen Kontakte, 1918–1939*, Munich, 2011.
13. Jerzy Bonkowicz-Sittauer, *Osadnictwo wojskowe*, Równe, 1933, p.16, reprinted in Leon Popek (ed.), *Osadnictwo wojskowe na Wołyniu*, Lublin, 1998.
14. Julia Eichenberg, 'Stiefsöhne des Vaterlands: Die polnischen Veteranen des Ersten Weltkriegs und die Debatte um ihre Versorgung 1918–1939', *Nordost-Archiv* 17 (2008), pp.176–94; Henschel, 'Der Erste Weltkrieg'.

15. Bonkowicz-Sittauer, *Osadnictwo wojskowe*, p.17.
16. Andrzej Gawryszewski, *Ludność Polski w XX wieku*, Warsaw, 2005 p.182. Bonkowicz-Sittauer estimated the success rate of permanent settled farms at 80 to 85 per cent; see Bonkowicz-Sittauer, *Osadnictwo wojskowe*, p.12.
17. Gawryszewski, *Ludność Polski*, p.182; Benecke, *Die Ostgebiete*, p.127.
18. Stobniak-Smogorzewska, *Kresowe osadnictwo*, p.103, table 4. The 9,082 military colonists include 817 civilian colonists who acquired the status of military colonists owing to a law from 1932: *Dz. U* 32 (1932), pos. 335. There are different data on the total number of military colonists. The figure of 44,000, including the families of the colonists, seems to be realistic. Cf. Stobniak-Smogorzewska, *Kresowe osadnictwo*, pp.287–288; Bonkowicz-Sittauer, *Osadnictwo wojskowe*, p.17; Głowacka and Żak, 'Osadnictwo Wojskowe', p.143.
19. Głowacka and Żak, 'Osadnictwo Wojskowe', p.144.
20. Stobniak-Smogorzewska, *Kresowe osadnictwo*, pp.83–98; Głowacka and Żak, 'Osadnictwo Wojskowe', pp.144–45.
21. 'Ustawa z dnia 28 grudnia 1925 o wykonaniu reformy rolnej', *Dz. U*. 1 (1926), pos. 1; Stobniak-Smogorzewska, *Kresowe osadnictwo*, pp.92–93.
22. 'Ustawa z dnia 14 marca 1932 r. uzupełniająca przepisy o nadaniu ziemi żołnierzom Wojska Polskiego', *Dz. U*. 32 (1932), pos. 335; Głowacka and Żak, 'Osadnictwo Wojskowe', p.147.
23. Kowalski, *Mniejszości narodowe*, pp.64–65.
24. Gawryszewski, *Ludność Polski*, p.382; Głowacka and Żak, 'Osadnictwo Wojskowe', p.144.
25. Gawryszewski, *Ludność Polski*, pp.382f.; Bonkowicz-Sittauer, *Osadnictwo wojskowe*, p.17.
26. Głowacka and Żak, 'Osadnictwo Wojskowe', pp.142–43; Stobniak-Smogorzewska, *Kresowe osadnictwo*, pp.35–42.
27. Bonkowicz-Sittauer, *Osadnictwo wojskowe*, p.17; Benecke, *Die Ostgebiete*, pp.126f.
28. Benecke, *Die Ostgebiete*, pp.82–88.
29. Benecke, *Die Ostgebiete*, p.128. The promised material support from the army's stocks was difficult to obtain and had to be transported over very long distances, and state financial assistance dissolved upon the enormous decrease in the Polish marka's purchasing power. Stobniak-Smogorzewska, *Kresowe osadnictwo*, pp.43–47, 64–82.
30. Benecke, *Die Ostgebiete*, p.127.
31. Bonkowicz-Sittauer, *Osadnictwo wojskowe*, pp.14f.; Głowacka and Żak, 'Osadnictwo Wojskowe', p.146.
32. Głowacka and Żak, 'Osadnictwo Wojskowe', p.146; Stobniak-Smogorzewska, *Kresowe osadnictwo*, pp.130–44.
33. Their critique took aim at the distribution of Polish land to colonists, the farms' high costs and low revenues, the settlers' lack of agricultural qualifications and their poor relationship with the locals. See Głowacka and Żak, 'Osadnictwo Wojskowe', pp.31–33, and Stobniak-Smogorzewska, *Kresowe osadnictwo*, pp.83–97.
34. Stobniak-Smogorzewska, *Kresowe osadnictwo*, pp.126–29.
35. Głowacka and Żak, 'Osadnictwo Wojskowe', p.145. The conflicts were mainly with Slavic peasantry; with the Jews, however, relations appeared quite good because Jews were typically engaged in handicrafts and trade, and thus did not compete with Polish farmers: Janina Stobniak-Smogorzewska, 'Osadnicy wojskowi a ludność żydowska na Kresach Wschodnich 1920–1940', in Krzysztof Jasiewicz (ed.), *Świat niepożegnany: Żydzi na dawnych ziemiach wschodnich Rzeczypospolitej w XVIII–XX wieku*, Warsaw, 2004, pp.559–69.
36. Jörg Baberowski, 'Stalinismus und Nation: Die Sowjetunion als Vielvölkerreich 1917–1953', *Zeitschrift für Geschichtswissenschaft* 54/3 (2006), pp.199–213; Bernhard Chiari, '"Nationale Renaissance", Belorussifizierung und Sowjetisierung. Erziehungs- und Bildungspolitik in Weißrußland 1922–1944', *Jahrbücher für Geschichte Osteuropas* 42/4 (1994), pp.521–40; Yuri

Slezkine, 'The USSR as a Communal Apartment, or How a Socialist State Promoted Ethnic Particularism', *Slavic Review* 53/2 (1994), pp.414–52.

37. Benecke, *Die Ostgebiete*, p.125; Kowalski, *Mniejszości narodowe*, p.65.
38. Uwe Müller, 'Modernisierung oder Diskriminierung? Siedlungspolitik in den preußischen Ostprovinzen zwischen nationalitäten- und agrarpolitischen Zielen', in Uwe Müller (ed.), *Ausgebeutet oder alimentiert? Regionale Wirtschaftspolitik und nationale Minderheiten in Ostmitteleuropa (1867–1918)*, Berlin, 2006, pp.147–65.
39. Dorota Sapa, *Między polską wyspą a ukraińskim morzem: Kresy południowo-wschodnie w polskiej prozie 1918–1988*, Kraków, 1998; Bolesław Hadaczek, *Kresy w literaturze polskiej: Studia i szkice*, Gorzów Wielkopolski, 1999.
40. Bonkowicz-Sittauer, *Osadnictwo wojskowe*, pp.33, 16. On the image of Poland as the 'bulwark' of Europe, see Małgorzata Morawiec, 'Antemurale christianitatis: Polen als Vormauer des christlichen Europa', *Jahrbuch für europäische Geschichte* 2 (2001), pp.249–60; Stefanie Zloch, 'Nationsbildung und Feinderklärung: "Jüdischer Bolschewismus" und der polnisch-sowjetische Krieg 1919–1920', *Jahrbuch des Simon-Dubnow-Instituts* 4 (2005), pp.279–302.
41. Henryk Józewski, 'Zamiast pamiętnika (2)', *Zeszyty Historyczne* 60 (1982), p.141. In the same vein, see Głowacka and Żak, 'Osadnictwo Wojskowe', p.141, and Stobniak-Smogorzewska, *Kresowe osadnictwo*, pp.217–30. For Józewski's biography, see Timothy Snyder, *Sketches from a Secret War: A Polish Artist's Mission to Liberate Soviet Ukraine*, New Haven, 2005; Jan Kęsik, *Zaufany komendanta: Biografia polityczna Jana Henryka Józewskiego 1892–1981*, Wrocław, 1995.
42. Bonkowicz-Sittauer, *Osadnictwo wojskowe*, p.12.
43. Ibid., p.125.
44. Benecke, *Die Ostgebiete*, p.123.
45. For the anti-Orthodox Church policy of the Polish authorities and the so-called 'pacification', see Snyder, *Sketches from a Secret War*, 147–67; Cornelia Schenke, *Nationalstaat und nationale Frage. Polen und die Ukrainer in Wolhynien (1921–1939)*, Hamburg, 2004, pp.397–452.
46. Stobniak-Smogorzewska, *Kresowe osadnictwo*.
47. Jan Jerzy Milewski, 'Osadnicy wojskowi na Kresach', *Biuletyn Instytutu Pamięci Narodowej* 12 (2004), pp.44–50.
48. Stobniak-Smogorzewska, *Kresowe osadnictwo*, p.287. Around 10 per cent of the settlers proceeded to the General Government. The narrative of deportation and Polish–Ukrainian antagonism dominates the memory of the *Osadnictwo wojskowe* to the present day; see e.g. the collection of testimonies in Henryka Łappo, Danuta Gradosielska and Bronisława Kacperek (eds), *Z kresów wschodnich Rzeczpospolitej: Wspomnienia z osad wojskowych 1921–1940*, London, 1998; Renata Jurecka-Krzyżanowska, *Mój ojciec: Wspomnienia rodziny wojskowej z Brzeżan od roku 1923 do 1945 roku*, Kraków, 1997.
49. Krystyna Kersten, *The Establishment of Communist Rule in Poland, 1943–1948*, Berkeley, 1991.
50. For the important role of the nationalist legitimization of communism in Poland, see Marcin Zaremba, *Komunizm, legitymacja, nacjonalizm*, Warsaw, 2001; Kryzsztof Tyszka, *Nacjonalizm w komunizmie: Ideologia narodowa w Związku Radzieckim i Polsce Ludowej*, Warsaw, 2004.
51. On the 'repatriation' of Poles from the Kresy Wschodnie, see Stanislaw Ciesielski, *Umsiedlung der Polen aus den ehemaligen polnischen Ostgebieten nach Polen in den Jahren 1944–1947*, Marburg, 2006; Witold Sienkiewicz, *Wysiedlenia, wypędzenia i ucieczki 1939–1959. Atlas ziem Polski: Polacy, Żydzi, Niemcy, Ukraińcy*, Warsaw, 2008.
52. Arakadiusz Ogrodowczyk, *Nad Odrą i Bałtykiem: Osadnictwo wojskowe na zachodnich i północnych ziemiach Polski po II wojnie światowej*, Warsaw, 1979, pp.17–38; Patrycy Dziurżyński, 'Udział Wojska Polskiego w zasiedlaniu i zagospodarowaniu Ziem Odzyskanych', *Przegląd Zachodni* 23/1 (1967), p.74; Bronisław Gralak, 'Miejsce osadnictwa wojskowego w planach zasiedlania i zagosp-

odarowania ziem zachodnich w latach 1945–1947', *Śląski Kwartalnik Historyczny Sobótka* 29/2 (1974), pp.220–25.

53. Krzystyna Kersten, 'Osadnictwo wojskowe w 1945 roku. Próba charakterystyki', *Przegląd Historyczny* 55/4 (1964), p.644. On the resettlement of the German population, see Bernadetta Nitschke, *Vertreibung und Aussiedlung der deutschen Bevölkerung aus Polen 1945–1949*, Munich, 2003, and Włodzimierz Borodziej and Hans Lemberg, *'Unsere Heimat ist uns ein fremdes Land geworden . . .' Die Deutschen östlich von Oder und Neiße 1945–1950. Dokumente aus polnischen Archiven*, 4 vols, Marburg, 2000–2004.
54. Kersten, 'Osadnictwo wojskowe', p.645. Later on, the counties of Nowogard (Naugard), Szczecin powiat (Stettin) and Jelenia Góra (Hirschberg) were also colonized, for sailors along the coast of the Baltic Sea.
55. Kersten, 'Osadnictwo wojskowe', pp.641f.; Ciesielski, *Umsiedlung der Polen*, pp.314–20.
56. Kersten, 'Osadnictwo wojskowe', p.641. For the text of the agreements, see Ciesielski, *Umsiedlung der Polen*, pp.96–107; Eugeniusz Misiło, *Repatriacja czy deportacja: Przesiedlenie Ukraińców polskich do USRR*, Warsaw, 1996, pp.30–34.
57. Gralak, 'Miejsce osadnictwa wojskowego', p.219.
58. Dekret Polskiego Komitetu Wyzwolenia Narodowego z dnia 6 września 1944 r. o przeprowadzeniu reformy rolnej, *Dz. U.* 4 (1944), pos. 17.
59. Dekret z dnia 17 stycznia 1945 r. w sprawie zmiany dekretu Polskiego Komitetu Wyzwolenia Narodowego z dnia 6 września 1944 r. o przeprowadzeniu reformy rolnej, *Dz. U.* 3 (1945), pos. 9. see also Gralak, *Miejsce osadnictwa wojskowego*, pp.219–21; Ogrodowczyk, *Nad Odrą i Bałtykiem*, p.58.
60. Ogrodowczyk, *Nad Odrą i Bałtykiem*, pp.57, 79–108; Dziurżyński, 'Udział Wojska Polskiego', pp.75–81; Jerzy Konieczny, 'Osadnictwo wojskowe na Pomorzu Zachodnim: Ogólna ocena stanu badań i postulaty badawcze', in Bogusław Polak (ed.), *Dwa powroty Polski nad Bałtyk: 1920 i 1945. Materiały z konferencji odbytej dnia 28 i 29 marca 1985 roku w Koszalinie i Kołobrzegu*, Koszalin, 1985, pp.430–40; Tadeusz Langner, 'Organizacja i przebieg osadnictwa wojskowego w powiatach słubickim i sulęcińskim w latach 1945–1946', *Przegląd Zachodni* 23/1 (1967), pp.89–107.
61. Ogrodowczyk, *Nad Odrą i Bałtykiem*, p.58; Gralak, 'Miejsce osadnictwa wojskowego', p.222; Kersten, 'Osadnictwo wojskowe', p.646.
62. Dziurżyński, 'Udział Wojska Polskiego', pp.87–88.
63. Ogrodowczyk, *Nad Odrą i Bałtykiem*, pp.58–60. During the 1960s, the term *osadnik wojskowy* was broadened to include members of the security services and Voluntary Reserve of the Civic Militia, invalid fighters against the anti-communist underground and combatants of the September campaign of 1939 who had been held in captivity: Ogrodowczyk, *Nad Odrą i Bałtykiem*, pp.237–38, and Kazimierz Mamak, *Osadnictwo wojskowe na Ziemi Lubuskiej*, Poznań, 1979, pp.26–29.
64. There is no information about this thesis in the secondary literature. For the relationship between the communist government and the combatants, see Joanna Wawrzyniak, *ZBoWiD i pamięć drugiej wojny światowej 1949–1969*, Warsaw, 2009, pp.57–104.
65. Ogrodowczyk, *Nad Odrą i Bałtykiem*, pp.55, 76–78, 108.
66. Kersten, 'Osadnictwo wojskowe', pp.651–55; Ogrodowczyk, *Nad Odrą i Bałtykiem*, pp.76–78.
67. Kersten, 'Osadnictwo wojskowe', pp.651–55.
68. Dziurżyński, 'Udział Wojska Polskiego', p.86; Mamak, *Osadnictwo wojskowe*, p.24.
69. Kersten, 'Osadnictwo wojskowe', pp.647f.
70. Mamak, *Osadnictwo wojskowe*, p.5.
71. Ibid., p.6.
72. Kersten, 'Osadnictwo wojskowe', p.645.
73. *Polska Zbrojna*, No. 111, 8 June 1945.
74. *Orzeł Biały*, No. 75, 28 May 1945, cited by Ogrodowczyk, *Nad Odrą i Bałtykiem*, p.30.

75. Ogrodowczyk, *Nad Odrą i Bałtykiem*, pp.54f.
76. Mamak, *Osadnictwo wojskowe*, p.17–19; I. Blum, *Z dziejów Wojska Polskiego w latach 1945–1948*, Warsaw, 1960, p.148.
77. Ogrodowczyk, *Nad Odrą i Bałtykiem*, p.118.
78. Gralak, 'Miejsce osadnictwa wojskowego', pp.226f.
79. Kersten, 'Osadnictwo wojskowe', pp.656f.
80. Mamak, *Osadnictwo wojskowe*, pp.23f.
81. Ogrodowczyk, *Nad Odrą i Bałtykiem*, p.160; Gralak, 'Miejsce osadnictwa wojskowego', p.228.
82. Ogrodowczyk, *Nad Odrą i Bałtykiem*, pp.140, 153–63. A few colonists settled in towns, where they worked as craftsmen or in local administration. The largest urban community of military colonists was in Szczecin/Stettin (about 3,000 persons), ibid., pp.148–52, 164; cf. Dziurżyński, 'Udział Wojska Polskiego', p.84.
83. Ogrodowczyk, *Nad Odrą i Bałtykiem*, pp.168f.
84. Gralak, 'Miejsce osadnictwa wojskowego', p.228.
85. Konieczny, 'Osadnictwo wojskowe', p.432.
86. Kersten, 'Osadnictwo wojskowe', p.643.
87. Ibid., p.640; Ogrodowczyk, *Nad Odrą i Bałtykiem*, p.53; Gralak, 'Miejsce osadnictwa wojskowego', p.219.
88. Benecke, *Die Ostgebiete*, p.130.
89. Ibid., p.236
90. Müller, 'Die Gouvernementalität', pp.121–23.

7

The Country Road to Revolution

Transforming Individual Peasant Property into Socialist Property in Yugoslavia, 1945–1953

Jovica Luković

Introduction

Since the collapse of socialism, the 'history' of property has indeed entered a new stage. The developments we are witnessing seem in themselves to be rather paradoxical. On the one hand, the classic liberal paradigm is experiencing a comeback in formerly socialist countries that hope to master transitional processes primarily by reorganizing property structures in spheres such as land or real-estate ownership.[1] The policy of 'restitution overrides compensation' has been assumed to not only make up for the historical injustices of the communist regime, but also to connect explicitly with these post-socialist countries' own nascent civic legal traditions. The term 'property' is, again, associated with private property. Generally, as post-socialist countries endeavour to successfully promote development, the spreading process of globalization in particular seems to enforce a 'capitalist property system'.[2]

On the other hand, we have been witnessing a 'new revolution of property'. The term property, in its classic liberal form, has been extended to cover intellectual production. Body parts and even a person's image have become objects of branding, and genetic material too has been gripped by what has been called 'propertization'. Furthermore, Jeremy Rifkin has envisioned capitalism as verging with high-tech science wherein property structures dissolve into access.[3] In general, a tendency to 'delimit (*Verflüssigung*) and dematerialize property' has been observed.[4]

Revolutions in property orders are a familiar phenomenon in the countries of South-Eastern Europe. In their frequency, scope and radicalness, they showcase the extreme character of the twentieth century. The contradictory nature of these revolutions has been perhaps most evident in agriculture, particularly agricultural reform. Here as elsewhere, agrarian reforms launched the reformation of property structures that were considered the basic condition for the elimination of material poverty in society in general, and the emancipation of the peasant class in particular. However, the expropriation of privately owned land sometimes went hand in hand with complete denial of the liberal principle of the sanctity of life, limb and property. It was not uncommon for expropriations to be accompanied by robbery and vandalism, which was only the first step in destroying the proprietors themselves.

This chapter concentrates on the socialist variety of propertization in agriculture after the communists seized power in 1944 – that is, on the practice of establishing a new property order and embedding it in the socialist political-economy. It is well known that communism radically transformed and even eliminated private property in favour of collective property, endeavouring to usher in a new age in the history of mankind. Initially, Yugoslavia followed the Soviet path of eliminating peasant-proprietors through nationalization and collectivization in agriculture, dogmatically and strictly in line with Soviet party politics. The political breach with the USSR in 1948 was also emphasized economically, by basing the economic system as of 1950 on so-called 'societal property'. But whereas this 'Yugoslavian way' was hailed as an ideological and economic alternative to the socialism of the Soviet bloc, philosophers and legal experts racked their brains over the new form of property.

I will not, however, analyse the clarity of property-related terminology in socialism; neither will I dwell on the foundation of property rights in socialist law.[5] Rather, I will follow the argument that established property rights – namely, the exclusive, legally founded disposal of a thing towards a third party – are a necessary, though not sufficient, condition for understanding a system of property ownership. Hence, my focus extends from the codification of property rights to the formation of property relations.[6] I will thus concentrate on the systemic conditions that mark limits to the use of property – that is, leasing, mortgaging, selling or bequeathing it.

Limits to the free disposal of property are scarcely taboo under capitalism. However, their ubiquity and extent in socialism highlight the communist leadership's endeavour to socialize private property. Awareness of this aim helps to understand the specific characteristics of the socialist property order, which result from a field of tension: whereas individual farmers in fact held private property rights, the communist government's ideological ambition was to enforce collective property in agriculture. In Yugoslavian agriculture, private property was not transformed into collective property in one stroke, by revolution, as it was in other sectors. The process, I will argue here, rather resembled an assimilation of private to collective property. This also sustains the idea of the plurality of property relations under socialism.

As Ernst-Wolfgang Bockenförde affirms, there is an immediate correlation between society and the property order.[7] Moreover, the property order can be a source of abstract values such as freedom, but also a basis for the development of each individual. Under socialism, both the general economic, social and political order, and the opportunity for individual development are defined through collective ownership of the means of production.

The property order also defines a framework under socialism in which farmers try to assert their social status. In terms of socialist ideology regarding workers, 'active producers' working with the socialized means of production, peasants were considered the agricultural part of the working class. But the question remains whether this realignment in discourse was able to reconcile the discrepancy between the dogmatic image of the individual farmer – the private owner – as a class enemy, and the actual economic and social importance of farming. In fact, the factual importance of farming seemed to be the main criterion for the development of socialist conditions – and not only when measured by the leadership's own doctrinal principles.[8]

In terms of doctrine, the Yugoslavian communists avoided facing a dilemma regarding the property order – a feat that in practice was not so easy to achieve. In this chapter, I will concentrate on the first decade after the communists' rise to power – that is, the era of socialist propertization and the establishment of socialist property structures in the countryside. For a better understanding, however, I will expand the focus onto the years of the Second World War, during which the communists acquired the experience and strategies needed to deal with problems of property. Such a focus illuminates how peasants, having participated actively in the war, acquired social capital that proved helpful to them during the transformation of private into collective property.

The War as Laboratory

The victorious partisan struggle gave the communists the legitimacy they needed for a revolutionary change of power, given that the war delegitimized broad sections of the bourgeois classes and thus any economic system based on private property. Crucially, institutions that showed traces of the socialist property order to come were established under the conditions of the wartime economy. As early as February 1942, the communist leadership decreed the so-called Foča precepts (*Fočanski propisi*), the first legal basis for the new regime. The central task of these economic activities was to supply food to the army, the local population and refugees.[9]

Throughout the war – for example, in autumn 1941, when the so-called Republic of Užice was established in western Serbia – partisans brought territories of varying size under their control. Wrested from the rule of the occupying forces, these places found their whole lives reorganized on a new foundation. The so-called People's Liberation Councils (Narodnooslobodilački odbori) were established as a central authority in the new power structure. One of the eight council divisions, known as the People's Liberation Fund, dealt especially with economic affairs.[10] Funds were used to activate production in local industry and agriculture, to set up a local financial system and above all to organize the distribution of scarce resources.

The funds were amassed by drawing on several sources: war loot from granaries and arsenals or shipments of the occupying forces; the holdings of state institutions or churches and monasteries; and private property, preferably that of rich farmers. The funds were not only responsible for the food supply; they also procured means of production, such as work equipment and means of transport, livestock, storage buildings and, most importantly, cultivable land. Economic life, as organized under partisan command, was therefore made possible largely by expropriation.

Expropriation was an important means in the fight against the occupying forces, yet its execution followed a detailed set of legal criteria. The partisans resorted to diverse practices of expropriation. Among them was confiscation, the uncompensated and sometimes complete seizure of property from farmers classified as enemies – called 'kulaks' in accordance with the Soviet model – sometimes involving violence. Whereas confiscation suspended every protection of property, as well as the protection of life and physical condition, requisitions involved something quite different. In this case, although the partisans' needs may have been deemed more important than the individual needs of farmer-producers, the lives of the latter were usually not seriously threatened, and they were also entitled to replacement or payment, though these could be claimed only after the war. The relationship between partisans and farmers was by no means only antagonistic – as demonstrated, for instance, by the donations and gifts that constituted an additional source of funding for the People's Liberation Fund.

It was not only the extraction of food that sustained the partisan economy. Another, equally important pillar was food production under the partisans' own auspices. The region of Srem – part of Vojvodina, the granary of the country, between the Danube and the Sava – is a particularly representative example of this. From an administrative perspective, Srem belonged to the Axis-allied Croatian Ustaša state from 1941, but its rural areas were predominantly under the control of the partisans. Srem was a strategically important region for the partisan movement because it enabled them to supply other liberated regions in the country with grain. Consequently, the fight for grain was declared a second battlefront. Lots were listed in funds and subsequently leased to local peasants in need of land, or tilled by the local youth and women's brigades in a collective campaign. That is, the partisans used the land, but its property status remained unchanged. For the time being, the lots were declared sequestered property whose definite status would be determined only after the war. Seizures of this kind were of a temporary nature. Given the rapidly changing front lines at the time, people did not always reap the harvest they had sown themselves, and one might also reap the harvest that others had sown and cultivated. What could not be seized was burnt under the slogan 'No grain for the enemy'. This destruction of property was in fact one of the most important ways of waging war against the occupiers and their local collaborators.

Meanwhile, the communist leadership generally regarded the principle of private property as irrevocable. In their conflicts with Stalin over whether the partisan struggle was an anti-fascist struggle of liberation or a straightforward social revolution, Yugoslavian communist leaders revealed that they were striving to realize social equality in rural areas. This implied a well-balanced distribution of land – without, however, questioning private property itself. Any course of action to the contrary – in particular forced expropriation and collectivization along the lines of the Soviet model, which occurred again and again within the partisan movement – was declared to be an extreme left-wing deviation and firmly combated.[11]

From a doctrinal point of view, the communists focused less on the inalienable right to property than on its fair distribution. In fact, the communist principle of distributive justice corresponded to the egalitarian, hermetic world-view of peasants, in which no one could own more than others, except by taking it away from them. The relationship between plenty and poverty provided criteria for a taxonomy of the peasant class. This differentiated view of peasants made a relatively late entrance into communist dogma. Friedrich Engels, in one of his final essays, was the first to liberate landowning peasants from the stigma of belonging to the bourgeois class.[12] Later, pressured by revolutionary circumstances and searching for allies, Lenin ennobled parts of the peasant class as proletarians.[13]

Thus the Yugoslavian communists, too, developed a differentiated view of peasants. Owners of large estates, who either employed hired labourers and obtained profit without working themselves or obtained rent from leasing out land, were considered exploiters and classified as a class enemy. However, only 3 per cent of farmers in Yugoslavia owned estates of more than 35 to 40 hectares. By contrast, owners of medium-sized properties, despite being neither short of land nor able to do without foreign labour, were regarded as the real victims of capitalist circumstances, even though they did enjoy a certain petit-bourgeois status. Communists tended to veer between affection and rejection, but generally considered medium-sized farmers to be on their side.[14] Above all, they saw the peasant class, and in particular the landless, as their actual allies.

At the same time, the communist leadership knew how to convert class-ideological affiliation into the political currency of patriotism, and integrate it into the People's Front structures of the struggle for liberation. In keeping with the friend/enemy dichotomy conditioned by the war, it was difficult for the communists to let go of their image of farmers as part of the bourgeoisie who bore political guilt for the economic decline and military defeat of the country – even more so as a significant number of farmers had fought against them in the units of the numerous home-grown national armies, and thus made themselves guilty of collaboration. However, their sights were set most firmly on the farmer-dominated German minority in Yugoslavia, who were collectively labelled as enemies on account of their ethnicity. Under the terms of war, these ascriptions were not mere semantic distinctions; rather, they legitimated unrestricted access to the property of these groups.

The war made clear that communists did not regard private property rights as inviolable, but they were not made entirely negotiable either. The communist leadership's frequent interventions against excesses of violence towards farmers and their property testify to the tension between communist claims regarding class struggle and the concrete reality of war. On the one hand, the Yugoslavian communists enjoyed great popularity precisely among the peasant class; on the other, farmers, as landowners, were ideologically considered supporters of rural capitalism who were to be combated as a class. This is supported by a statement by Tito himself that farmers run after whoever offers more.[15]

The Early Post-war Years

Immediately after the war was over, Doreen Warriner travelled through Yugoslavia and compiled a report on the country's economic situation for the United Nations Relief and Rehabilitation Administration (UNRRA). Her observations of the daily life of the population illustrate the extent of the destruction. On almost impassable roads she reached Bosnia, where agriculture seemed to have hit rock bottom: 'Two men were pulling a plough'. In particular, Warriner provided a clear analysis of a society that had broken down, but which was still determined to build the country up again. The highest priority was given to restoring agriculture.[16]

A communist party fixated on the revolution of the industrial proletariat seemed ill equipped for this, however. As the history of party conferences shows, hardly any ideological discussions concerned farming, and the peasant question played only a secondary role.[17] Furthermore, despite all the theoretical analyses of capitalist economy and programmatic drafts for a classless society of free producers, Yugoslavian communists had in fact not worked out a concept for the development of the country, and there was no economic programme ready for implementation in 1945. Instead, party functionaries disclosed the course of agricultural policy in individual statements in the relevant media, indicating that they were designing an agricultural policy ad hoc. Yet their goal remained immovably fixed: as part of the country's general development, agriculture was to be led out of its backwardness, and socialist conditions would be established in rural areas.

By citing a general backwardness as the justification for their agricultural policy, the communists in fact resumed interwar debates conducted among bourgeois politicians and publicists.[18] Furthermore, their diagnoses were much the same: they noted the poor material equipment and over-indebtedness of farms, the lack of competitive products and general overpopulation. The Yugoslavian communists focused on another factor, however: the unequal distribution of land. In 1931, 67 per cent of small landowners (about 1.2 million farms), held on average less than 5 hectares, and 700,000 of them owned less than 2 hectares.[19] This was not really an unknown fact,[20] but the communists drew a concrete conclusion from it: the unequal distribution of land meant that capitalism still prevailed in rural areas. However, capitalism was deemed incapable of remedying backwardness in agriculture, and held to lead to greater pauperization among peasants, resulting in a host of exploited peasants in need of land. According to the communists, improving agriculture without initially remedying social inequality – that is, without solving the peasant question – was a contradiction in terms. The quintessence of socialist policy in rural areas was a close link between the social and economic question.

The Yugoslavian communists may not have had a well-designed concept for development, but their actions were far from lacking in orientation. While they were able to draw on the rich experience of the wartime economy, they were also, and above all, able to follow the practical experiences of the Soviet agricultural model, which guided all communists in two respects. First, as in the Soviet Union, in Yugoslavia the revolutionary change of power had been preceded by war. The new rulers faced the task of attenuating the acute consequences of war, particularly by organizing provisions for the population and averting the threat of famine.[21] Then, in the medium term, they had to cope with the transition from a wartime to a peacetime economy. Second, in both cases, revolutionary upheaval had not occurred in developed but in backward countries clearly dominated by agriculture. Economic development was to fortify the social revolution only subsequently. Individual farms were particularly important during the war's immediate aftermath, since they alone were able to be productive and avert famine with little material cost and without delay. In the longer term, agriculture was to be modernized to an extent that would enable it to catalyse the development of the entire economy.

Thus the Yugoslavian communists followed the Soviet model. Its significant features were the nationalization of farm land, especially large estates, the collectivization of farmers' land, the industrial production model and centralized planning according to five-year plans. Major agricultural holdings were held up as showpieces of Soviet agricultural policy. They had emerged from nationalization and collectivization, and thus were born of immediate, radical interventions in the property system of individual farmers. The significance of agriculture in the USSR was defined by the primacy of industrialization, more precisely by the development of heavy industry. Agriculture was chiefly intended to serve the accumulation of capital in the industrialization process. Agricultural collectives, invested with large areas of land, equipped with heavy machines and supplied with a strong concentration of labour, took up the performance-oriented industrial paradigm of mass production based on a complex division of labour.[22] Collective farming constituted the main pillar of Soviet agricultural policy. Moreover, it was the first link in a causal chain at whose end private property was to be transformed into collective property, which in the USSR was perceived de facto as state property. Hence, collective farming was viewed as a necessary precondition of the socialist economy.

International communism pursued the thesis of a uniform path towards socialism – a kind of latecomer, as socialist models went – and the comrades in Yugoslavia initially followed this path. Even though the Yugoslavian constitution of 1946 was modelled on the Soviet one, it in fact avoided calling the state 'socialist', which caused some irritation; just as vague were references in the legal texts to a socialist social order, or to the socialist revolution.[23] It is hardly surprising, therefore, that the matter of property was not subject to codification. In economic practice, the Soviet path to socialism had all the more impact because its policy of nationalization had already been implemented in industrial firms, mines, the financial sector, transport and trade in 1945. In agriculture, by contrast, total expropriation was initially avoided.

There were several reasons for this, some of which concerned the economic situation and natural resources of the country. Firstly, Yugoslavia's total area of cropland was relatively small, which limited production capabilities in the first place. In 1948, only half of the total 14.6 million hectares of agricultural land were used as cropland, whereas woodland and pasture prevailed.[24] Secondly, some important cultural conditions held sway. In contrast to the Russian peasants' tabula rasa, Yugoslavian peasants had a very distinctive connection with the land,[25] although peasants' private property in Yugoslavian rural areas dated back only a few generations.[26] Thirdly and most importantly, peasants had obtained huge political and social capital from actively participating in the partisan struggle. Eighty per cent of partisan fighters came from this class, and at the end of the war, over 40 per cent of Communist Party members were peasants. Their situation thus differed considerably from that of the Russian peasantry in 1917. The Russian Revolution had occurred in an urban setting, and was yet to implement socialist ideas in the rural areas, but in Yugoslavia, large sections of the peasantry had already become a class ally. Nationalization was not urgently necessary, not least because there had been enough land to distribute to farmers in 1944 – in part from the first series of expropriations from large estate holders and institutions, but mostly from the expelled German minority. Their holdings alone amounted to over 700,000 hectares of land, along with substantial quantities of buildings and modern equipment in 'gains' for the land fund. Instead of nationalization, and in line with their declarations during the war, the communists resorted to more conventional practices of agrarian reform.

Agrarian Reform: Revolution through Propertization

Agrarian reforms are usually marked by strong social and economic components, and although frequently charged with ideology they are nonetheless endorsed by political consensus. All parts of the provisional Yugoslavian 'national government', which represented both the agrarian left and the bourgeois parties, reached consensus on this measure. Any resistance that might still have existed was swept away by the general sense of a new era, promoted by the communists themselves. The country was overrun by slogans such as 'land to the farmers' (*zemlja seljacima*), which, combined with the slogan 'factories for workers' (*fabrike radnicima*), made agrarian reform unavoidable, and clearly showed that private property had lost its aura of sanctity.

But even before the passage of the law on agrarian reform in August 1945, the seizure of property had been partially legalized. In 1944, the still provisional parliament had denied members of the royal family, collaborators and 'traitors to the people', access to their property.[27] The group that was most affected was the German minority, collectively declared to be part of the occupying forces and followers of fascism. More than half a million Yugoslavian Germans suffered a particularly drastic form of expropriation. Not only were they legally disentitled to their private property, but in this case the expropriation also involved physical expulsion. The practice of expelling Germans made it clear that total expropriation opened the floodgates to actual threats to life. During the interwar period, German peasants had earned positive stereotypes for themselves in public consciousness on account of their progressive economic strategy, modern cooperative systems and first-class yields. Now they were declared enemies of the people by the communists because of their ethnicity, and removed to the lawless area of detention camps until their final expulsion from the country.

At the outset, the criteria for expropriation were primarily political: the former ruling class, or those belonging to it, were voted out, and disposal over their property was adapted to the new legal situation. Then the political criteria were extended to the social and economic spheres. Now expropriations turned to church property, legal entities and institutions, those 'alien to agriculture', the property of persons missing in action and so on, totalling thirteen such sources.[28] All major landed estates over 45 hectares, or 25 to 35 hectares of pure arable land, were affected by expropriation.[29]

The law of 1944 had been primarily restricted to expropriation, but the Law on Agrarian Reform and Colonization of 23 August 1944 went farther, establishing criteria for land allocation and naming the target groups.[30] In accordance with Section 16 of the law, the agrarian reforms favoured war veterans, invalids, orphans and members of partisan families, clearly paralleling the criteria of the 1918 'bourgeois' agrarian reform. Underlying the set phrase 'need for land' was the principle of gratification for wartime merits rather than the actual productive capacity of entitled persons. The size of the lots – up to 40 hectares – amounted to the area of a medium-sized farm. In fact, the communists seemed to have met the demands of critics of the agrarian reform of 1918, which had envisaged allocations of a maximum of 4.57 hectares but only allotted 2.28 hectares on average.

The post-war agrarian reform is interpretable in part as the completion of goals already formulated during the war, but partly also as the extension of the state-regulatory regime beyond the war. But although the Yugoslavian agrarian reform was one of the most radical in the communist countries of Eastern Europe, it nevertheless bore no totalitarian marks. Rather, the reform programme broadly strengthened and consolidated private property in agriculture.[31] In the first regular session of the new Yugoslavian parliament in February 1946, its president, Moša Pijade, affirmed: 'We want the peasant to receive the land as private property'.[32] Peasants may have owned over 70 per cent of the private property in the entire land fund, but land from expelled Germans made up two thirds of their holdings; about 8.7 per cent of peasants, or 8,600 farms in Yugoslavia, were affected by expropriation (122,000 hectares out of a total of 1.5 million hectares).[33]

A shift occurred within the peasantry. In practice, the Yugoslavian agrarian reform was actually closer to a partial expropriation because exceptions were arranged for nearly all expropriated groups. Thus each church, for example, was allowed to retain up to 10 hectares of land. Not even the Germans were expropriated without exception: partisan fighters and all people in mixed marriages with Germans were nominally exempt. Yet this had little effect on the collective stigmatization of these sections of society. In any case, 98 per cent of agricultural land was still in private hands in 1948; by comparison, over 95 per cent of industrial plants had been nationalized over the same period.

With agrarian reform, the communists vindicated their claim that producers ought to be the owners of the means of production, which strengthened private property. It was the private sector that profited most from agrarian reform. Over half of the land fund passed into private ownership: 150,000 families were allocated 800,000 hectares of land.[34] The fact that private property dominated the property structure of the early post-war years revealed certain paradoxes inherent in socialist agriculture. There was an ideological paradox, in that private property strengthened the economic basis of a class commonly perceived as supporting capitalism in rural areas. The vocabulary that accompanied the agrarian reform left little doubt that social revolution would be accomplished in the countryside. It warned in particular of rich farmers, a relict of the old classes, who would constantly endeavour to make other peasants materially dependent on themselves and obtain political influence over local institutions and organizations.[35] As in the Soviet model, the socialist transformation of agriculture in Yugoslavia was accompanied by the harsh rhetoric of collectivization and the removal of peasant-proprietors.

Agrarian reform also revealed an economic paradox in agriculture: it strove to create equitable property relations in rural areas, but ways of organizing an efficient socialist form of agriculture still had to be found. Socializing the rest of the expropriated land from the land fund – over 700,000 hectares – strengthened the socialist sector in the countryside. Agrarian reform thus assumed the character of nationalization. But set against this was the disadvantageous property structure of small and medium-sized peasant farms, whose fragmented, scattered landholdings did not provide suitable conditions for modernizing agriculture. Agricultural production would have been completely impossible without individual peasants, who owned the bulk of productive property such as livestock and farming equipment.

Significantly shaped by agrarian reform, socialist agricultural policy in the early post-war years allowed the plurality of property forms to continue to exist – or, at least, little could be changed concerning the extent of private property. In the early post-war era, as we have seen, the framework of agricultural production was limited by new ideological constellations and the effects of the wartime economy. The enhancement of private property did not mean that the socialist leadership disavowed their aim of socializing property. Socialist agricultural politicians took up the cause of economic efficiency and successful modernization themselves. The question now was the extent to which farmers could make use of their property rights. I will cover four aspects of the actual use of property rights as well as the reasons they were restricted.

Restrictions in Property Relations

The first aspect was the macro-political order of the economy, or more precisely its centrist organization, which was designed to regulate production according to planned-economy specifications – at first annually and then, after 1947, by way of five-year plans. In agriculture among individual peasants, the centrist thrust was reflected in a series of compulsory measures such as the compulsory cultivation of specific crops on defined lots of land, the compulsory fattening of animals and so on. But because the peasants had already had to experience this during the war, it was initially hard to recognize anything socialist in the policy; rather, they would have perceived it as regimentation imposed by an agrarian bureaucracy and state coercion.

This centrist form of forced husbandry also meant control in financial affairs. Complete debt relief meant great improvement in the lot of peasants. High levels of debt remained from the disordered agricultural policies of the interwar period, when peasant farms had not enjoyed any sort of protection against economic fluctuations or any support in the event of crop failure.[36] Free procurement of credit on the disordered capital market had boosted a flood of speculation, and driven peasants into the hands of private moneylenders. As it was not unusual to find local, well-to-do farmers among these, the debt write-off also affected such farmers, who in a certain sense were expropriated a second time. But although the peasants were now able to resume production without the financial restriction of old debts, the debt relief measures did restrict individual peasants' access to new loans. Trade in real estate was now forbidden by law, so the last potential source of capital for peasants effectively dried up.

Progressive taxation of real estate was another part of this bundle of measures. The better the performance, the higher the rate of taxation: this must have had a negative effect on peasants. Meanwhile, the progressive tax system shifted the main burden to richer farmers.[37] The macro-economic scope of the socialist financial and market politics affected Yugoslavian farmers to the extent that they had no possibility of bringing their property into economic circulation by mortgaging or leasing it. The land was supposed to serve elementary productive purposes by being cultivated exclusively by its owners.

A second type of restriction resulted from the abolishing of the market and the introduction of *otkup*, a compulsory sale of products to state agencies to fixed and lower than market prices. In 1945, laws were decreed for compulsory sale of grain, cattle, wool, hides, cotton, vegetables, milk and so forth. Such measures were nothing new to most peasants, but rather were perceived as a continuance of the practice of requisition from the wartime economy. The quotas were reset every year. These laws enabled the state to lay claim to peasants' yields before the latter were able to satisfy their needs. The peasants were also hit substantially in terms of efficiency, as the quotas were fixed according to the quantity of arable land rather than the actual yield. This led to a huge crisis in the countryside, especially during the drought years of the early 1950s that threatened seeds and nutrition, and thus 'simple reproduction'. Besides, there was no financial compensation for the levy. The policies constrained farming output, not least because farmers were deprived of any possibility of reinvesting their returns. In brief, the levies were clear proof to the peasants that, under communism, and despite all guarantees and avowals to the contrary, private property by no means enjoyed absolute protection.

The centrally controlled policy of redistributing scarce food was a pragmatic act that ultimately prevented famine in the land, to the extent that Yugoslavia was spared the Soviet experience after collectivization.[38] Nonetheless, this practice shook the very foundations of communist ideology. Only large estate holders and affluent farmers were affected by agrarian reform, but the obligatory levies applied to all peasants. By unduly burdening farmers, the communist ideologues had arrived at the same situation they had blamed the bourgeoisie for – in other words, they had usurped the surplus of the labour of producers. And as the effect on farms was often substantial, the communists were essentially exploiting the majority of society. From an agricultural perspective, history seems to have actually, farcically, repeated itself. In any case, it was the levies that would have the most enduring impact on the collective memory of peasants in socialist Yugoslavia.

A third type of restriction concerned the labour force's availability for public works (*radne akcije*). This initially involved rebuilding destroyed infrastructure – streets, train lines, telecommunications – or building up new settlements such as Novi Beograd. Although these measures, organized by the Communist Party, were received with collective enthusiasm, it should not be forgotten that peasant labour for their implementation often had to be forcibly mobilized. In any case, the workforce was absorbed from agriculture and invested in other sectors. Unpaid work of several weeks' duration was credited to the peasants as a contribution to the country's reconstruction by the people's community (*opštenarodna obnova*), and registered in the ideological account of 'fraternity and unity'. This was the only way of explaining how the practice could be introduced at a time when the century-old economic institution of compulsory labour (*kuluk*) was forbidden by law. In other words, expropriated economic capital was rededicated as symbolic capital.

The fourth restriction was due to the state's concern for the socialist market. Its essential function – ensuring admittedly scarce but at least regular provisions for the population – could be performed only with great effort. The essential administrative measures included the regulation of quantities of goods on the market, price control and the monitoring of the distribution network. The state tried to achieve this by founding consumer cooperatives. These cooperatives developed into hubs for the economic activity of productive peasants. More precisely, peasants became dependent on cooperatives in many ways. The cooperatives guaranteed that their products would be purchased, which met one of the most important demands farmers had had in the pre-war period, when they were completely exposed to the financial fluctuations of markets and rarely able to cover the costs of production. With the security of quota, the cooperatives became the peasants' most important means of access to the market. Under conditions of a price monopoly and fixed prices, this still amounted to a repetition of the criticized practices of the pre-war period. However, the cooperatives' primary function was to regulate farmers' access to different means of production, such as machines, fertilizers, seeds and stud animals, or to specialist knowledge; in these key areas, cooperative members were given preference over individual farmers.

Limits on the use of property are not characteristic of the socialist property order only. Whereas liberal property theory elevates the inviolability of property – as private property – to the status of a principle, there are in fact many limitations to it. These tend to derive from objective conditions such as scarce resources and states' strategic interests, but they can also stem, if temporarily, from certain situations such as wars or economic crises. Moreover, they can be founded in morally inspired arguments such as obligations towards the community or, as in recent times, holistic arguments about a sustainable economy. It is often overlooked that even classical forms of public-law administration via taxes and duties do not allow an unlimited disposal of property.[39] Unlike the socialist understanding of property, however, these forms always respect private property and never treat it as a source of stigmatization. Whenever property is expropriated, compensation is paid. Introduction of collective property, when it occurs, does not negate but rather adds to private property. Furthermore, private property does not enjoy a privileged status, as collective property did under socialism.

In brief, a socialist production paradigm based on plural property relations made it clear that free disposal over private property was subject to considerable restrictions. In the Constitution of 1946, property was defined generally as the people's property. This legitimized the socialist form of the delimitation of property, which stood opposed to the liberal concept. Ideologically speaking, property was derived from the common welfare of the community and placed above any formal, legal considerations. Thus, it was primarily administrative mechanisms that substantially regulated, or more precisely restricted, free disposal over private property. Or, to put it another way, private property was codified and peasants enjoyed certain possibilities of free disposal, but, as it depended on allocation by state authorities, property was by no means legally guaranteed but rather permitted. Under conditions of administrative, socialist production relations, private property acquired a materially earmarked, rather than a formal, individual character. In this respect, socialist institutions have a peculiar corporate feature.

Thus the question remained of how to convert private peasant property into socialist property. Systemic restrictions on the free utilization of private property were basically attempts to drive peasants towards the socialist sector. However, the clearly doctrinaire prescriptions provided no straightforward guidance on how to implement socialist relations in the countryside. As both domestic and foreign policy suffered from tensions, agrarian cooperatives acquired more and more importance as a genuinely socialist production method and as transmitters of property relations. Within only a few years, Yugoslavian agricultural politics had experienced a double reversal: from 1948, collective property was strengthened by establishing agricultural cooperatives; then, from 1953 onwards, the means of production became self-governed social property.

The Enhancement of the Socialist Sector: The Cooperative System

In the years that preceded the confrontation with Stalin in 1948, the socialist sector in Yugoslavia occupied itself chiefly with establishing the cooperative system. Yugoslavian agrarian politicians were well aware of the general trend towards the concentration of property in large estates, which had been under way in the West and East since the 1920s. They knew of the American farming system, but for ideological reasons they were oriented towards collectivization as it was practised in the USSR. In the first ordinary meeting of the new parliament in 1946, the Law on Cooperatives (Zakon o zadrugama) was passed,[40] admitting all 'classic' forms of cooperatives – consumer, production, credit and other. By the year's end, the number of members had already reached 80 per cent of the level in 1939, though out of approximately 900,000 members, only 740,000 were active in consumer cooperatives and a mere 53,000 in peasant work cooperatives.[41] Until 1948, agriculture struggled to match the achievements of the pre-war years. Whereas industrial production had exceeded the 1939 level by 67 per cent in 1947, agricultural production was only at 88 per cent of its pre-war level.[42] Not only were yields below expectation, but the substance had eroded. Livestock numbers were declining, and fallow land increased by 3.5 per cent.[43]

Hope was placed in the cooperatives because they promised an increase in productivity. Cooperatives were designed to mobilize the resources of individual farmers, bundle them into a standard production form and manage them, with the centrist measures of agricultural politics, according to the guidelines of the five-year plan. But the cooperatives' role was not to be limited to economic performance. As institutions that promoted knowledge transfer by the use of machines, agro-technical means and modern work methods, they became gateways to modernization in rural areas. This was due to their function of promoting agriculture as well as introducing farmers to socialist production relations – or, from a different angle, the cooperatives were the socio-political means of consolidating socialist conditions in rural areas. In the countryside, in immediate contact with farmers, cooperatives took on the crucial role of implementing socialist agricultural policy: 'The social economic development of the village is achieved today exclusively by the development of the new type of cooperatives'.[44]

Cooperatives were ultimately supposed to absorb private property. Their development revolved primarily around ways of realizing this aim, or around means of transferring the private property of cooperative farmers. The title holder in the socialist sector was clearly designated: when the minister of economy Boris Kidrič spoke of 'popular property', he specifically meant 'popular property under state administration' (*pod državnom upravom*), which essentially corresponded to the Soviet property model: the state acts as a trustee of collective property. 'Cooperative property and state property represent two forms of socialist property growing ever closer to each other. The long-term development of the cooperatives only leads to the development of a general form of property, owned by the people, by way of the means of production'.[45] To Kidrič, 'socialist' meant 'bringing together [connecting, coordinating] all general [public] interests in a single union by means of the initiative and interest of individuals'.[46]

Over the following years, the Basic Law on Agricultural Cooperatives (Osnovni zakon o zadrugama) of 1949 clearly charted a path towards the socialist form of property.[47] This course correction was made necessary by the alarmingly poor performance of agriculture, particularly in the socialist sector. However, ideological disconnection from the Soviet economic model was needed before a major reversal in Yugoslavia's economic policy was at all possible. The Cominform resolution of 28 June 1948 accused Yugoslavian communists of reluctance in implementing socialist agricultural policy, and thus of protecting the kulaks (peasant-proprietors), among other things. The subsequent general conversion of the Yugoslavian economy to an autonomous system was proclaimed in 1950,[48] and speedily implemented in industrial companies; not until 1953, however, did agriculture too begin to depart from the Soviet model. In agriculture, paradoxically, rejection of the Soviet model of socialism was countered by promotion of Soviet-style cooperatives in a Bolshevik manner. In July 1948, the Fifth Party Congress, which rejected Cominform's accusations, still expressed high esteem for the achievements of Soviet agriculture. Thus, in 1949 the party organ *Komunist* virtually invoked the Stalinist example. In the country's hour of isolation, there seemed to be only a single way of securing production: concentration of all forces of production in agrarian cooperatives.

The Basic Law on Agricultural Cooperatives regulated two forms of cooperatives – 'general agricultural cooperatives' and 'peasant work cooperatives'.[49] The cooperatives were defined in Article 61 as production units organized by the peasants themselves, who were to procure means of production – land, equipment, livestock and so on – to carry out collective work. Article 62 defined three types of general agricultural cooperatives: trade cooperatives (*otkupno-prodajne zadruge*), credit cooperatives and general processing cooperatives. In the first two types, the farmers remained private owners who were compensated for the land and means of production they invested, by way of either a type of pension or interest on the estimated value of the land. Wages were calculated according to performance, in units of workdays (*trudodani*), as in the Soviet model. In the third type of cooperative, farmers retained legal title to their estates but were not compensated.[50]

Private property was formally guaranteed, and depending on the intensity of the fusion of private and cooperative property, there were gradations among the different types of general cooperative. Cooperative members acted as sovereign parties who voluntarily entered into a contractual relationship limited to three years, but still retained property rights over the land and equipment they earned returns on. If they withdrew from the cooperative, they were able to keep their property or receive compensation. While the 'general agricultural cooperatives' (*Opšta zemljoradnička zadruga*, OZZ) still showed characteristics of traditional cooperative forms, 'peasant work cooperatives' (*Seljačka radna zadruga*, SRZ) were declared genuinely socialist cooperatives.

The Yugoslavian communists' concept of developing socialist agriculture was expressed clearly by the party leader, Josip Broz Tito:

> The peasant remains the proprietor, but essentially, if we look at reality, he tills the land that is common property – which is the existential basis for the whole society. We have not broken the individual rights of peasants but it is our endeavour that the peasant finds a way towards socialist agriculture because he realizes that it is more rewarding for him. One day, as he is actually a symbolic owner, he will say: Why should I make a contract with a cooperative? I want to become a member of the cooperative![51]

What was defined as evolutionary gradualism – 'bottom-up' development 'from the least to the most highly developed' – amounted to 'transferring the production form from small-scale farming to collective cooperative production'.[52] Owing to their politically and economically privileged position, the peasant work cooperatives became oases of socialist relations in the countryside, and had strong appeal to individual peasants. And as they introduced socialist production conditions – collective disposal over the means of production, division of labour, performance standards, performance-based pay, use of technologies in production – they were considered the cutting edge of socialist agricultural development. The inclusion of individual farmers in agricultural development that thus took place via cooperatives was compared to a climb up 'flights of stairs on which farmers find their path towards collective production and practise the organization and method of collective work in the cooperative'.[53]

For collective farming to actually become a source of prosperity, it was necessary to spread the socialist cooperative system whilst making allowance for local economic and geographical relations, that is, the 'conditions, traditions, level of consciousness and cooperative experience of the farmers'.[54] But even upon entering an SRZ, when a landholder's property title was assigned entirely to the cooperative, private property was not eradicated. The right to one hectare of land with house and livestock was granted – a relict of the nineteenth-century Serbian *okućnica* concept of private lots.[55] This type of individual property, which Marx and Engels had envisaged for their classless society, was already common practice in the USSR.[56]

In reality, the socialist cooperatives' demonstration of efficiency influenced peasants, as did exposure to comprehensive ideological agitation by the Communist Party. From 1949 onwards, the growth curve climbed steeply: the number of peasant work cooperatives quintupled, while the number of cooperative peasants quadrupled. There was scant indication of any compulsory measures: as Edvard Kardelj, the chief ideologist of the Yugoslavian communists, stated, the programme was conducted 'exclusively on a voluntary basis and based on the conscious decision of peasants themselves. Any artificial forcing or administrative pressure would only destroy and slow down this process'.[57] Nonetheless, the ideologues of the socialist transformation of agriculture well understood that neither agrarian reform nor collectivization could take place without provoking resistance. Kardelj located its source in 'smallholders' (*sitnosopstveničke*) habits and mentality'.[58]

This practice became imprinted on farmers' collective memory as 'exaction': a mass form of compulsory collectivization accompanied by great excesses. In principle, however, it tells us more about the general perception of communist agricultural policy or about the mental state of rural people than about the actual extent of the escalation of violence. The thesis that farmers engaged in open resistance to this oppressive, arbitrary exaction has been disproved.[59] Anyway, it was not nearly as brutal as the Soviet measures. When the party functionaries deplored the 'opportunism' of peasants, they meant the 'passive resistance' with which they ignored the appeals of the government. More characteristic of the countryside was the mood of uncertainty and fear that led peasants to destroy their own mobile productive property, sell their equipment and pre-emptively slaughter their livestock.[60]

Scrutiny of the composition of cooperatives in Yugoslavia leaves no doubt that the economic dynamic of cooperative development was remarkably weak. Reasonably high concentrations of cooperatives were achieved only in Vojvodina, east Slavonia and Macedonia. And the primary support for the communist government's campaign came from the colonists there, clearly reflecting their loyalty towards the communist leadership. For the colonists – the winners in the agrarian reform – property meant a source of prosperity.

How did 'hunger for land' turn into 'weariness of land'? An explanation can be found in the actual circumstances of colonization. The state had tried to arrange an orderly transfer of colonists without separating families; in general, entire clans and village communities were set up in the same place, noticeably changing the social structure of Vojvodina as a result.[61] But at the same time, colonists were under various types of structural pressure to conform as they sought their place in a new socio-cultural and ethno-confessional environment. Above all, they faced growing economic pressure as the moral economy of what were mainly transhumant herders, or landless and small-scale peasants from mountainous regions of the country, encountered the specific ecological and agro-technical requirements of the Pannonian Plain. Moreover, the established business structures of German farms that were now to be run by colonists posed considerable challenges.[62] In this situation, cooperatives offered the convenient opportunity of handing the land over to collective agriculture and thus avoiding individual liability. Entering the SRZs essentially amounted to voluntary self-expropriation.

The socialist cooperatives ultimately failed to boost the economy. Instead of becoming a source of foreign exchange, they led to a worsening of Yugoslavia's trade balance. In 1954, the country had to acquiesce to a 92 per cent increase in food imports. Collectivization only lasted about three years, so it was a measure of relatively short duration, and its highest intensity was confined to only a few specific regions of the country. In late 1951, Tito had still been emphasizing that 'we haven't created cooperatives for just three years',[63] but in 1952, Mijalko Todorović, minister of agriculture, finally closed the door on state SRZs by describing them as 'a strange mixture of patriarchal family cooperatives, forced labour camps for peasants who are half compulsory labourers and half wage workers, and collective small estates'.[64]

In essence, the cooperatives lacked capital, technical equipment, qualified labour and the organizational structures required to set up modern agriculture.[65] Retrospectively, Edvard Kardelj said it had been necessary to take pressure off farmers – and to pay more attention to their interests. 'It is absurd to measure socialism in the countryside by the degree of collectivization of the land'.[66] His statement marked the end of this period in Yugoslavian agriculture. And though there had been attempts to force collectivization in Yugoslavia by way of Stalinist brutality, Soviet-style measures were hardly required to pragmatically give it up. The system experienced a collapse on Yugoslavian soil, and in 1953 the SRZs were dismantled.[67] This initiated the second turnaround in agriculture. Paving the way conceptually, and remaining the great enigma of property theory ever after, was the new form of property that had been defined in 1951: social property with the means of production self-governed by the producers. And as in the case of the first turnaround, its implementation in rural areas was anything but easy.

Self-government in the Countryside

The system of self-government was conceived when the Yugoslavian leadership broke with the idea of taking the big, well-trodden Bolshevik road towards socialism. The starting point of a critique of the Soviet model was its bureaucratic and state-centrist character. According to Tito, 'the workers nowadays still don't have any shares in the administration of factories but this is done by the factory directors or by employees appointed by the state'.[68] In the minds of Yugoslavian communists, there should no longer be an intermediary between producers and the means of production that could control the production process.

They also believed that, by removing state bureaucracy from the production process, they would advance the general abolishment of the state, whereupon the state would no longer be either an instrument of the Communist Party's power or the owner of the means of production. In this latter role, the communists believed, the state had come to totally dominate the entirety of production relations, thereby perpetuating the alienation of producers from the results of their work. Nationalizing private property would not, according to Yugoslavian communists, lead to an overthrow of capitalist relations of exploitation, but only disguise them. However necessary the abolition of private property might be to the development of a classless society, municipalizing it, as in the USSR, presented no real alternative.

The dogma hitherto prevailing in Yugoslavia – of 'property of the people in the hands of the state' (Kidrič) – was abandoned in favour of producers' immediate control of the means of production. 'By making the workers responsible for the management of companies, state property, the lowest and most primitive form of socialist property, is transformed into general popular property as the highest form of socialist property'.[69]

Thus the postulate of socializing the means of production acquired a different meaning by shifting its basis to a new property form. With their system of self-government, the Yugoslavian communists developed an alternative model of so-called social property: 'Cooperative and state property are two forms of socialist property which are converging more and more. The long-term development of cooperatives leads to the formation of only one general form of popular property of the means of production'.[70] This difference was also made visible semantically, since now, instead of the people (*narod*), it was society (*društvo*), or more precisely workers (*radni ljudi*), that became the subject of all property.[71]

Property under the self-government system suffered the same fate as anywhere else under socialism: the removal of private property by way of its transformation into collective property. However, two specific characteristics warrant emphasis here. Private property was by no means meant to be condemned; rather, it was supposed to continue to exist as individual property, at least during the transitional period of socialism.[72] Yet at the same time, the socialist form of collective property differed from its counterpart in capitalism in that a cooperative was not based on a group of individual proprietors or on employees holding shares in a company, but on an immediate collective command of the means of production by the producers.

If property is defined as a right to a thing that excludes the claims of others, then general social property lacks the constitutive other vis-à-vis whom any claims of exclusive property can be made. And although the organization of property under the Yugoslavian self-government system was clearly defined, in legal terms, as having society as a subject, the property relations were anything but clear. This was mainly because social property had no clearly defined proprietor. Everyone was, as a producer – even in the service sector – at the same time a co-proprietor of the means of production, and was, as a worker, included in the socialist property order. Academic discussion among legal experts, which centred mainly on the question of entitlement, failed to resolve the matter.[73] Even leading officials remained obviously undecided. Thus Milovan Djilas commented, 'Property is not property, but just management'.[74] This uncertainty, expressed right at the beginning, clearly shows that even among communists, the understanding of property was deeply rooted in the liberal model based on private property. Peasants, for their part, had no truck with the semantic and legal details of social property. They were facing a different sort of challenge.

Social Property in Agriculture

During the first decade of the socialist economic order up to 1953, there was a discrepancy in the growth of the private sector and the socialist agrarian sector, with the latter expanding but then experiencing a sustained slowdown. The tense relationship between the two had to be put in order again. A turnaround in agricultural politics seemed necessary. The Yugoslavian communists attempted to dissipate the emerging tension between the two sectors with a change of method in agricultural policy. Eliminating private property would not be a condition of socialist agriculture; rather, promoting agricultural development would actually accelerate the conversion of the private into the socialist agrarian sector. Instead of private property being abolished via collectivization, it would die out by being integrated into social property.

The Law on the Creation of a National Land Fund and Regulation of Its Distribution of 27 May 1953 heralded agriculture's shift away from the Soviet model.[75] 'The process of development must proceed gradually and in line with the development of the whole economy and with the possibility of replacing individual production with social production'.[76] This model, henceforth referred to as 'the Yugoslavian model', could only succeed if it managed to resolve an intrinsic paradox: the private sector of smallholders, which was supposed to be absorbed into the socialist sector, still had to be promoted; otherwise it risked missing out on overall development, or even handicapping it.

As in the past, the shift in agricultural policy was introduced through agrarian reform, and it involved a wave of expropriation. Despite striving to realize the principle that no one should exploit another and that everyone should have sufficient means of production, the reform reduced the private property holdings of individual peasants with 25 to 30 hectares of land to a new maximum of 10 hectares; those who were not full-time farmers could, depending on the situation, own between 3 hectares (of arable land) and 5 hectares (of woodland). The reduction affected 66,000 estates, from which 275,000 hectares were expropriated – on average, about 4 hectares per farm. The land was allocated to manors, cooperatives and other organizations, or transformed into social property, so this time there was no shift within the peasant community. Thus social property was expanded and the private sector, although reduced, nonetheless had its legitimacy consolidated. By the end of the 1960s, over 50 per cent of farmland was still in private hands.[77]

Self-government nominally meant complete control over the means of production, but it involved hardly any changes for the peasants. Free disposal of property was still subject to the same systemic limitations, which would remain in effect until the 1960s. There was hardly any possibility of taking out private loans, that is, to mortgage estates, let alone to trade estates privately. Nonetheless, a certain market for estates developed – with the socialist sector appearing as purchaser and leaseholder. This real-estate market gained ground, partly because of socio-economic development in rural areas. The advance of industrialization spurred labour migration to the cities, and the consequent shortage of labour power in agriculture, together with the ageing of the peasant population, resulted in uncultivated areas of land. This led in turn to a leasing market, in which private owners, particularly of medium-sized or small estates, leased land to the socialist sector. But since not all peasants were in fact able to lease their land – due to small and scattered lots, unsuitable territory, poor access routes, unsuitability for heavy farm machinery, high transaction costs and so on – the expansion of the socialist sector faced limits.

Meanwhile, taxes on privately owned land ceased to be a burden, as taxation according to yield was abolished in favour of a flat tax based on soil quality. The tax rate was then adjusted from time to time, depending on improvements to the quality of the soil, but it consistently remained below the real yield. Hiring agricultural labour was no longer taboo,[78] although farmers were obliged to pay social security benefits for their workers. The fact that wage relations beyond the socialist sector were now encouraged – or, strictly speaking, that a socialist agrarian proletariat was being generated – was ignored. While government price control remained effective, the introduction of local produce and livestock markets from 1950 onwards meant relief for farmers.

Free disposal of land was further restricted by regulations on ecology and the cultural landscape. In particular, the Law on the Cultivation of Untilled Areas of 25 February 1957 stipulated a mandatory minimum of cultivated land, with the quantity defined by local standards. Violation of this regulation resulted in temporary expropriation for up to three years. On 19 October 1959, passage of the Law on the Exploitation of Agrarian Land put the general interests of society above that of individual landowners' freedom of disposal. Changes to the original function of areas under cultivation, for example with the aim of residential building, were not solely the concern of the owner. Similarly, it was possible to forbid or require different forms of cultivation, such as converting grassland into fields, or switching from annual plants to perennials or woodland.[79] The 'most rational use of agricultural land' was always considered. This ecological framework for dealing with private property hints at a concept of natural law: the land may be in private hands, but in fact it is a general good like any other natural resource.

Given these systemic stipulations, disposal of private property remained subject to considerable limitations. The micro-economic dynamics that private property usually begets – by mortgaging property, hiring wage labourers, being present on the market under a legally protected name, protecting innovation and so on – were suppressed, or became a function of peasants' cooperation with the socialist sector. Thus, instead of exaction, the communists resorted to cooperation in a fresh attempt to attract individual peasants to socialist production conditions.

The socialist sector itself was reorganized in the process. It rested essentially on two institutions: the self-governed cooperatives and, augmenting them, so-called agro-industrial combines that were established from the 1960s onwards. The communists invented the combines primarily to realize their integral approach to the economy, from the production of food, fodder and raw materials to industrial processing, the manufacture of consumer goods and distribution via their own transport and trade networks: 'The goal of the combines is a higher specialization of production, more rational labour exploitation, an economic determination of the cost of goods sold, reduction of loss due to spoilage, storage etc.'[80] They were now declared to be the yardstick of socialist progress in agriculture.

The cooperatives, especially their genuinely socialist type, the SRZ, were obviously unattractive to Yugoslavian farmers – having rapidly lost their appeal when the three-year term of collectivization expired – and had to be realigned. Their reorganization initially consisted of establishing the self-government system in agricultural holdings, although hardly anything changed in the gradation of the types of cooperative. Instead of the SRZ, the General Agricultural Cooperative emerged, boasting a wide range of specialized activities from arable crop or livestock farming and fruit growing to the purchasing, storage and processing of proprietary products; in addition, the cooperatives were responsible for landscape conservation (*agro-minimum*).[81] It seemed that the scope of the social sector's 'services' to peasants was to some extent unlimited. Over thirty different types of contract were used in Serbia alone, covering, for instance, the use of machinery for ploughing, sowing, threshing and harvesting grain, or in transportation; indeed, cooperation was most common in arable farming. Cooperatives also provided loans linked to specific cooperation projects and limited to one production cycle.[82]

Although social property increased in terms of surface area, its development was, however, shaken by crises, and doubts regarding social property persisted until the end. Heated debates during the crisis that ignited in Yugoslavia in the 1980s repeatedly deplored the 'complete loss of socialist cooperation in the cooperative system'.[83] As for individual peasants, the OZZ continued to be regarded as a higher form of cooperative and the ultimate target of socialist agricultural development.

Conclusion

The agricultural sector remained the main obstacle in the way to establishing the socialist paradigm of collective property. Private property, despite many attempts to transform it into the socialist form of property, survived and even temporarily became the central pillar of the whole economy. Whereas the Yugoslavian agricultural reform of 1946 introduced forms of collective property, it also made the ideological paradox of socialist agricultural politics obvious: agricultural reform expropriated, or rather cut down, the property of the small class of owners of large estates, but it also turned the landless into landowners, strengthened the large class of smallholders and thus legitimized private property in rural areas. Propertization had its own peculiar dynamics, yet it was, at least in Yugoslavia, always codetermined by exogenous factors. Hence the social capital peasants had acquired in the popular war of liberation, along with the factual economic relevance of the agricultural sector during the country's reconstruction phase, made private property the economic and political security of the peasantry.

The tension between the actual historical necessities that affirmed private property and the ideological norms that aimed at its dissolution in collectivist forms of property – be they state or so-called social property – proved irresolvable. What was passed off as a temporary agreement between the private and the social sector turned out to be a symbiosis of two partners that, though unalike, remained indispensable to each other. Their cooperation established a new principle in Yugoslavian agricultural politics: balance between the interests of the private and socialist sectors. The cooperatives' interests lay in expanding their production opportunities into the private sector and increasing accumulation. Meanwhile, peasants – who hoped for higher incomes and a general modernization of agriculture – increasingly assumed the role of service providers. But the Yugoslavian communists never lost sight of their ambition to introduce socialist conditions in the countryside. They assumed that the experience of material prosperity would in itself enhance 'socialist consciousness' among the peasantry. Yugoslavia's support of both the socialist and private sectors renders it an example of plurality in socialist forms of property. The interaction of these two sectors shows the diversity of property orders.

The defining distinction of the socialist property order was that private property could not be freely disposed of. The nature of the system meant that property could not be mortgaged; thus it became a burden to certain parts of the peasantry – for instance, colonists. Yet it would be wrong to question the liberal theory of people's natural drive towards acquiring property. Rather, one might qualify the assumption that farmers are by nature bound to their earth: people strive for the kind of property that facilitates material prosperity, social recognition and individual happiness, or which helps them avoid stigmatization. Nevertheless, the example of agricultural cooperatives, especially when they originated in forced collectivization, shows an immediate correlation between economic efficiency and the property status of the means of production.

The example of Yugoslavian agricultural politics obviously puts the assumed validity of collective property under socialism into perspective. However, the legal situation of the so-called social form of property remained ambiguous. A focus on its regulation by public law would advance our understanding of it. Was there – despite radical breaches in 1950 and 1953 – a line of continuity between property as 'people's property under state administration' (*pod državnom upravom*), as Boris Kidrič put it in 1946,[84] where the state acted only as a trustee, and social property as common land, as in Elinor Ostrom's definition? In Yugoslavia many different paths were taken towards socialist conditions in rural areas, but the transformation of private into socialist property always relied on the same strategy: making property relations seem less and less based on classical property rights while keeping peasants from regarding this as a loss.

Notes

1. Chris Hann (ed.), *Postsozialismus: Transformationsprozesse in Europa und Asien aus ethnologischer Perspektive*, Frankfurt am Main, 2002; Katherine Verdery, *What Was Socialism, and What Comes Next?* Princeton, 1996; David Stark and Laszlo Bruszt, *Postsocialist Pathways: Transforming Politics and Property in East Central Europe*, Cambridge, 1998.
2. Hernando de Soto, *Freiheit für das Kapital! Warum der Kapitalismus nicht weltweit funktioniert*, Berlin, 2002.
3. Jeremy Rifkin, *The Age of Access: How the Shift from Ownership to Access Is Transforming Capitalism*, Harmondsworth, 2000.
4. Hannes Siegrist and David Sugarman, 'Geschichte als historisch-vergleichende Eigentumswissenschaft: Rechts-, kultur- und gesellschaftsgeschichtliche Perspektiven', in Hannes Siegrist and David Sugarman (eds), *Eigentum im internationalen Vergleich (18.–20. Jahrhundert)*, Göttingen, 1999, p.10.
5. Jovica Trkulja, 'Der Realsozialismus und der Rechtsstaat', *Rechtstheorie* 24 (1993), pp.33–53.
6. Rosa Congost, 'Property Rights and Historical Analysis: What Rights? What History?' *Past and Present* 181 (2003), pp.74–106.

7. Ernst-Wolfgang Bockenförde, 'Eigentum, Sozialbindung des Eigentums, Enteignung', in E.-W. Bockenförde, *Staat, Gesellschaft, Freiheit. Studien zu Staatstheorie und Verfassungsrecht*, Frankfurt am Main, 1976, p.318.
8. Melissa K. Bokovoy, *Peasants and Communists: Politics and Ideology in the Yugoslav Countryside, 1941–1953*, Pittsburgh, 1998.
9. See Moša Pijade, the author of these precepts – which became the law 'O narodnim odborima' on 25 May 1946 (Službeni list FNRJ, No. 43/1946) – in Moša Pijade, 'O predlogu Opšteg zakona o narodnim odborima', in M. Pijade, *Izabrani spisi*, vol. 1, book 4, Belgrade, 1966, pp.182–210; Djordje Kosanović, 'Uloga fondova narodnooslobodilačkih odbora u materijalnom obezbedjenju odluka od 1941do početka 1944', *Vojno-istorijski glasnik* 5 (1957), pp.30–49.
10. Leon Gersković, *Dokumenti o razvoju narodne vlasti*, Belgrade, 1948, p.36.
11. Nikola Gaćeša, 'Koncepcija Komunističke partije Jugoslavije o agrarnom pitanju i seljaštvu tokom narodnooslobodilačkog rata i socijalističke revolucije', *Zbornik za istoriju Matice Srpske* 19 (1979), pp.9–48.
12. Friedrich Engels, 'Über die Bauernfrage in Frankreich und Deutschland' [1894], in Karl Marx and Friedrich Engels, *Werke*, vol. 22, Berlin 1969, pp.483–505; Peter Gay, *Der Begriff des Eigentums bei Karl Marx: Zur Kritik des klassischen Eigentumsparadigmas von Locke, Smith und Hegel*, Frankfurt am Main, 1981.
13. Lenin (Vladimir Iljitsch Uljanov), *Über das Bündnis der Arbeiterklasse mit der werktätigen Bauernschaft: Eine Sammlung ausgewählter Aufsätze und Reden*, East Berlin, 1961.
14. This seems to have been a recurrent problem in communist thinking. See Alec Nove, *An Economic History of the USSR*, Harmondsworth, 1986, p.166.
15. Milovan Djilas, *Der Krieg der Partisanen: Memoiren 1941–1945*, Vienna, 1978, p.127.
16. Doreen Warriner, *Jugoslavia Rebuilds*, Neudeln/Lichtenstein, 1979. On the UNRAA relief to Yugoslavia, see Jozo Tomasević, 'Postwar Foreign Economic Relations', in Robert J. Kerner (ed.), *Yugoslavia*, Berkeley/Los Angeles, 1949, pp.402ff.
17. Nikola Gaćeša, *Agrarna reforma i kolonizacija u Jugoslaviji 1945–1948*, Novi Sad, 1984, pp.20ff.; Žarko Jovanović, *KPJ prema seljaštvu 1919–1941*, Belgrade, 1984.
18. Otto von Frangeš, *Die sozialökonomische Struktur der jugoslawischen Landwirtschaft*, Berlin, 1937; Mijo Mirković, *Agrarna politika*, Belgrade, 1940.
19. Mijo Mirković, *Ekonomska historija Jugoslavije*, Zagreb, 1958, p.350. 'In 1931 there were more farms in Yugoslavia than in all countries of Latin America', ibid., p.351.
20. Also not to the bourgeois public of the land. Early on, contemporaries indicated the failure of the agrarian reform of 1918, and the farms' size, which barely guaranteed subsistence. Slavko Šećerov, *Iz naše agrarne politike*· Belgrade, 1930.
21. Nove, *Economic History*, pp.86ff.; Robert Conquest, *The Harvest of Sorrow: Soviet Collectivisation and the Terror-Famine*, New York/Oxford, 1986, pp.43ff.
22. Deborah Fitzgerald, *Every Farm a Factory: The Industrial Ideal in American Agriculture*, New Haven/London, 2003, pp.157ff.; Robert W. Davies, *The Soviet Collective Farm, 1929–1930*, Basingstoke, 1989 [1980].
23. Dušan Bilandžić, *Historija Socijalističke Federativne Republike Jugoslavije: Glavni procesi 1918–1985*, Zagreb, 1985, pp.106ff.
24. Svetolik Popović, *Die Agrarpolitik in Jugoslawien*, Belgrade, 1964, p.7.
25. Richard Pipes, *Die Russische Revolution*, vol. 1: *Der Zerfall des Zarenreiches*, Berlin, 1992, p.195; Stephan Merl, 'Einstellungen zum Privateigentum in Rußland und in der Sowjetunion', in Hannes Siegrist and David Sugarman (eds), *Eigentum im internationalen Vergleich*, p.150.
26. Thus, although the Habsburg settlement had already established independent farmers in Vojvodina, most of them could not call a parcel of land their own until the land was released, in 1848 at the latest. In Serbia, farmers had been unable to found family farms until the 1830s,

under the liberation of the Ottoman rulers in the course of the wave of containment (*zahvatanje*); Ružica Guzina, 'Regulisanje svojinskih odnosa u Srbiji XIX veka na bazi običajnog prava', in Srpska Akademija nauka i Umetnosti (ed.), *Obicajno pravo i samouprave na Balkanu i u susednim zemljama*, Belgrade, 1974, pp.455–66. In Bosnia, by contrast, a broad peasant class did not arise until 1918. See Milivoje Erić, *Agrarna reforma u Jugoslaviji 1918–1941*, Sarajevo, 1958.
27. Decree No. 25 of 25 November 1944.
28. Ranko M. Brashich, *Land Reform and Ownership in Yugoslavia, 1919–1953*, New York, 1953, p.49.
29. Discussion in parliament, see Gaćeša, *Agrarna reforma*, pp.106–12.
30. Vlajko Begović, 'Naša poljoprivreda i pitanje njenog preobražaja', *Komunist* 4/3 (1949), pp.83–111. Begovič headed the Federal Planning Commission.
31. On the huge increase in small landed estates in Serbia, see Begović, 'Naša poljoprivreda', p.93.
32. Moša Pijade, 'O seljačkim radnim zadrugama' (1946), in *Izabrani spisi*, vol. 1, book 4, Belgrade, 1966, p.176.
33. Popovič, *Die Agrarpolitik*, p.8.
34. Ibid., p.9.
35. Boris Kidrič, 'O nekim principijelnim pitanjima naše privrede', *Komunist* 2/2 (1947), pp.47–58.
36. Mijo Mirković, 'Regulisanje seljačkih dugova', *Arhiv za političke i društvene nauke* 33 (1936), pp.347–52; Milan J. Komadinić, *Problem seljačkih dugova*, Belgrade, 1934.
37. All those with an income of 50,000 and tax of 18,000 dinar per annum: Begović, 'Naša poljoprivreda', p.92.
38. Conquest, *Harvest of Sorrow*, pp.217ff.
39. Bockenförde, 'Eigentum'.
40. Službeni list FNRJ, No. 49, 23 July 1946.
41. Mihajlo Vučković, *Zadrugarstvo*, Belgrade, 1947, p.139.
42. Begović, 'Naša poljoprivreda', p.94.
43. Velimir Vasić, *Putevi razvitka socijalizma u poljoprivredi Jugoslavije*, Belgrade, 1960, p.55.
44. Begović, 'Naša poljoprivreda', p.101.
45. Ibid.
46. Kidrič, 'O nekim principijelnim pitanjima', p.52.
47. Službeni list FNRJ, No. 49, 9 June 1949.
48. *Zakon o upravljanju državnim privrednim preduzećima i višim privrednim udruženjima od strane radnih kolektiva* of 2 July 1950.
49. Službeni list FNRJ, No. 49, 9 June 1949.
50. Popović, *Die Agrarpolitik*, pp.27ff.
51. J. Broz Tito's speech in Rankovičevo (Kraljevo) on 7 September 1951: 'Mi nismo stvarali zadruge samo za tri godine', *Socijalistička poljoprivreda* 2/11 (1951), pp.1–6.
52. Begović, 'Naša poljoprivreda', p.100.
53. Ibid., p.101.
54. Ibid., pp.103f.
55. Jelenko Petrović, *Okućje i zaštita zemljoradničkog minimuma*, Belgrade, 1930.
56. Merl, 'Einstellungen zum Privateigentum', pp.152f.
57. Edvard Kardelj, *Problemi socijalističke politike na selu*, Belgrade, 1959, p.100.
58. Ibid.
59. John B. Allcock, *The Collectivisation of Yugoslav Agriculture and the Myth of Peasant Resistance*, Bradford, 1981; Bokovoy, *Peasants and Communists*, pp.134–40.
60. Ljubomir Veljković, 'O uzrocima i borbi protiv kolebanja u seljačkim radnim zadrugama', *Socijalistička poljoprivreda* 2/11 (1951), pp.7–15.
61. Gačeša, *Agrarna reforma*, p.346, asserts that about 225,000 people were already settled there by 1947, which amounted to 13 per cent of the new population: 70 per cent were Serbs and 18 per

cent were Montenegrins. By comparison, the first agrarian reform of 1918 had brought Vojvodina only 95,000 new inhabitants. About 150,000 people moved in the greatest resettlement campaign in history to date – the Habsburg population resettlement – which, however, extended over a whole century. This can be understood as part of the *metanastasic* movements in the Balkans, as formulated by Jovan Cvijić.

62. Darinka Kostić, *Promene u društvenom životu kolonista*, Belgrade, 1963, p.176, n.17; Žarko Gavrilović, *Osnovne odlike telesnog razvoja prve generacije doseljenika iz Hercegovine u Vojvodinu*, Novi Sad, 1970.
63. Tito, 'Mi nismo stvarali', p.16.
64. Mijalko Todorovic, *Komunist* 7/1–2 (1952), p.77.
65. In 1949, there were only 4,530 tractors in Yugoslavia. In 1951, the ratio of mechanical to animal power was 1:19. See Bilandžić, *Historija Socijalističke Federativne Republike Jugoslavije*, pp.131, 232.
66. Kardelj, *Problemi*, pp.14ff.
67. Uredba o imovinskim odnosima i reorganizaciji SZZ, Službeni list FNRJ, No. 14, 1953.
68. Tito, 'Mi nismo stvarali', p.16.
69. Ibid.
70. Branko Horvat, *Die jugoslawische Gesellschaft: Ein Essay*, Frankfurt am Main, 1971 [1969], pp.24f.
71. Tito, 'Mi nismo stvarali', p.16.
72. For Marx's critique of the planned programme, see 'Kritik des Gothaer Programms', in Marx and Engels, *Werke*, vol. 19, pp.11–31.
73. The academic law magazine *Anali pravnog fakulteta u Beogradu* covered the controversial debate on that issue during the 1950s. The legal character of social property, though undoubted, required great interpretative skills. See the summary in Ivo Lapenna, 'Die Rechtsnatur des gesellschaftlichen Eigentums in Jugoslawien', *Osteuropa-Recht* 8 (1962), pp.216–36.
74. Ibid., p.227.
75. Službeni list FNRJ, No. 26, 31 May 1953.
76. Popović, *Die Agrarpolitik*, p.13. Here it should be emphasized that the authors – both the immediate creators of this policy and the architects of the shift in agriculture – were unwilling, in retrospect, to go into detail regarding this period. The writings of Kardelj and Popović transform the collectivization phase, making violence but a small stain on the agrarian mental map of Yugoslavian society.
77. In other areas, private property under socialism looked, or was meant to look, different in this regard; see Horvat, *Die jugoslawische Gesellschaft*, pp.81–86, who uses the example of a tradesman.
78. Popović, *Die Agrarpolitik*, p.23.
79. Dragoljub Stojanović, 'Pozitivno-pravna ograničenja privatne svojine', Phd. diss., Belgrade, 1963, pp.54–60.
80. Popović, *Die Agrarpolitik*, p.32.
81. They were used for all major works (e.g. water supply improvement), conglomeration was carried out on their goods, and they developed country paths and land consolidation measures. As a result, over 30 per cent of the acreage held as private property of individual farmers was recorded and reclaimed in the following years.
82. Popović, *Die Agrarpolitik*, pp.47f.
83. Ivan Maksimović (ed.), *Subjekti društvene svojine i njihove ekonomske funkcije*, Belgrade, 1988; Andrija Gams, *Svojina*, Belgrade, 1990.
84. Kidrič, 'O nekim principijelnim pitanjima', p.53.

PART III

PRACTICES AND MENTALITIES OF LANDOWNERSHIP

8

HOMELAND AS PROPERTY

Symbolic Ownership and the Local Heritage of the Past in Lemkowyna and the Ukraine

Jacek Nowak

In this chapter, I will explore the question of the symbolic right to manage ethnic territory in the context of ongoing debates about ownership and re-privatization. I will also discuss the value of land in the process of building social identity. Above all, I will focus on depicting the way communities remember and forget their land, and how the feeling of symbolic ownership over a territory is created.

My research in Central and Eastern Europe has repeatedly concentrated on ownership. I am mainly interested in the strategies groups adopt to maintain the privilege of deciding the factors – land, scenery, architecture or symbols – that mark the borders of a community. In this analysis I will refer to the case of the Lemkos, a regional ethnic group in the south-eastern region of Poland, showing how this community has protected its traditional space and struggled with 'strangers' who appropriated its territory. Based on my observations, I conclude that a key role and significance is ascribed to the definition of ownership and territory anchored in this community's memory, that is, the collective memory that determines the group's attitude towards ownership and land. I will share a few remarks on how such a framework of memory is stored and utilized in a multicultural setting. I will also show how communities are trying to rid their space of the markers left by other groups that, as a result of historical events, temporarily held the right to mark the same territory.

This chapter refers to a case in which different communities profess the right to one territory, showing how historical categories and rules of interpreting the past determine the dispute over space. I will depict the ways in which images of territory and ethnic homeland are created, and demonstrate how these processes tend to generate conflict.

I will only briefly mention the issue of change in the meaning of such notions as rootedness, congeniality or 'feeling at home'. One of the reasons for their redefinition is the changing attitudes people hold towards land and ownership. Anthropologists stress that such change derives from continuing modernization, especially the processes of globalization. So far, land has been perceived as one of the more important elements shaping the social framework of memory that organizes a group's identity and tradition. Currently, we are observing a process in which globalization leads to a reduction of semantic space and a destruction of the system of common meanings. New meanings and new means of interpreting social reality are in force. Traditional territories are becoming more abstract; the emotional meaning of place, names and symbols is declining. These processes lead to disconnection from territory or 'de-territorialization', which in turn leads to spatial homogenization.[1]

All this induces change in traditional systems of social organization and, in the case presented below, also a redefinition of space. In the area once reserved for a single group, new actors have appeared, changing the existing types of bonds and mutual relations. These 'new strangers' treat land as an area for their business activity, an attitude that differs decidedly from patterns previously in force. Newcomers from cities introduce new rules of spatial organization, thus changing the accepted ways of life. Methods of spatial management and perceptions of ownership of territory are changing. To a great extent, the traditional hosts are losing control over their land.[2]

In addressing the question of ownership in East Central Europe, researchers point mainly to processes connected with re-privatization. Numerous analyses refer to the social consequences of the collectivist policies once enforced by the governments of communist countries.[3] In this chapter I will primarily highlight the fact that collectivization disturbed the nature of the human relationship to land. By disrupting the networks of connections and relationships that had created a special bond between individuals, communities and the environment, collectivization had far-reaching consequences for communities' hierarchy of values, lifestyle and organization. It shattered the emotional attitude and feeling of economic interdependence built upon these relationships. Land provides meaning for people as long as work is invested in it. This work determines the significance of ownership, both of land and of what can be reaped from it. Collectivization of land dissolved these relations. Reduced to a mere natural resource, land was deprived of its meaning. I will refer to my research in western Ukraine to show that, contrary to the aforementioned Lemko case, a people might also forget its land.

The Homeland

My analysis of the issue of ownership aims to demonstrate that ethnic groups possess mechanisms and strategies for appropriating territory and subordinating it to themselves. These domesticate space and mark places that intertwine, affectively reinforcing them to make up a spatial map that enables a group to pursue identity construction. Simultaneously, the group develops a sense of possessing something unique: its own homeland.

Proxemics posits that, as a group gets to know a place and marks it, what used to be alien and undefined gradually becomes familiar. The material world becomes saturated with symbols that demarcate the context of social situations, attitudes and behaviour. Of special importance in these considerations is the fact that space consequently becomes a carrier of the collective memory of a given culture. A community's collective memory becomes inscribed in space, which itself becomes a repository providing a ready-made record when necessary. The value of this accumulated memory in the elements of space comes to the fore when a community tries to reconstruct its identity after years of crisis or tragic experiences. Then these accessible, legible signs authenticate activities and fill them with the might of ancestors who once bequeathed them to successive generations – thus we can say that existence assumes features of authenticity. These are not only sacred places, or *lieux de mémoire*, for their role and functions are self-explanatory; they are rather those elements of landscape or space that simply recollect ancestry: old households, trees, rivers – the more banal and casual, the more affectively and symbolically marked.

Such visible signs reinforce the feeling of identity and awaken awareness and loyalty towards a place. Attachment to a place can come into existence unaccompanied by great events. It may be linked to the feeling of safety and the ability to satisfy biological needs, or to memories of scents, sounds, social activity or domestic pleasures that amass with time. Such places hold familiar objects – roads, hills and buildings – that, by requiring people's physical involvement, surround them, absorb them and form part of the familiar landscape. The homely place may be a region, town or village whose denizens spend their lives making the surrounding world meaningful and inscribing themselves into it. Often they treat their native place as the centre of the world and attribute to it a unique value that they foster and hand down to future generations.

The local dimension of people's lives is a primordial frame of reference in the process of social identity construction. It is the focus of their processes of identification, and from it people depart to generalize and transfer the qualities of the immediate world to the ethnic group and nation. This is also where they form their spatial identity, which is understood as a

> mental representation, emotional and affective assessment of a given fragment of environment, which individuals add to their self-conception and perceive as part of themselves . . . It is the identity of a certain group, which perceives a given fragment of space as a constituent element of the sense of common belonging, which is functional towards group cohesion and at the same time constitutes an element of ideological representation of the concept of We.[4]

Spatial identity is inextricably related to a social network of connections. Living in or originating from the same area, people undertake activities that, by requiring cooperation or mutual help, create circles of neighbours, acquaintances and friends who provide assistance in various situations. This solidarity is especially conspicuous in mutual bonds of kinship or common ethnic descent. A symbolic community is created, providing its members with a set of symbols that instantaneously influence the social construction of reality.[5]

To build up the whole picture of the community's past, both the past and the present should be taken into account, as should certain elements of the world of symbols and things, and the ways they are interrelated. In this sense, space appears as a permanent memory of the community. Examining space draws attention not only to how the configuration of its elements changes, but also to how space is forgotten, that is, how particular forms, functions and meanings are eliminated. A community and its members are especially severely affected by the elimination of elements of space to which they are attached through special values, such as objects of the sacred sphere of symbolic space.

The environment communities inhabit is unintentionally incorporated into the consciousness of individual members of the group, and with time it takes on additional meaning. In the shape of landscape, it is remembered and transferred in time and even in space. It is often mythologized, whereupon it can endure as a myth through centuries. Under special circumstances, a landscape that is taken for granted on an everyday basis can play an important role. First and foremost, it is the simplest form of a group's identity and also a kind of spatial representation of it. It performs a few primary functions, the most essential of which appears to be to introduce the context of communication that allows mutual understanding among the members of the group. All these processes lead to the shaping of a particular kind of sense of ownership – a desire to own and be responsible for the homeland. Such a case of domesticating space and developing a sense of ownership (even if only symbolic) is described below.

The Lemkos

Here I describe the vicissitudes of a small ethnic community that continually arouses interest among anthropologists because of the complex character of its identity. Until 1944, the Lemkos lived in the south-eastern regions of Poland. This area, formerly called Galicia, was also inhabited by Jews, Ukrainians, Roma and Poles. The Lemkos numbered an estimated 150,000 people, living in rural and mountainous areas. They settled on forested land that was hard to cultivate, trees being its only natural resource. They differed from other inhabitants of Galicia in their religion, language, rituals and customs. Their language, like the whole of their culture, was the fruit of the crossing of many waves of migration. Their religion was characteristic and distinctive, and they were often viewed in terms of their Orthodoxy or Greek Catholicism. It was their particular language and religion that primarily established the cultural borders of this community.

The Second World War and the years that followed it inflicted a series of calamities upon the Lemkos. They were persecuted by the Germans, the Russians and the Poles. This period saw the beginning of a process of relocation, which was to have dire consequences for them. By 1947, they had been almost totally evicted from their territories. They were exiled initially (from 1944) to the depths of the USSR, later to Ukrainian territory and finally to the western territories of Poland taken from the Germans after the end of the war. The latter forced migration of the Lemkos, carried out by the Polish state, was called Operation Wisla. Migration had played an important role throughout the history of the Lemkos, but the one of 1944 to 1947 was decisive in that it led to the disintegration of the Lemkos as a regional ethnic group. The state authorities justified the repressive nature of their decision by claiming that the Ukrainian population was the basis for the Ukrainian Insurrectionary Army, and the Lemkos were officially considered part of the Ukrainian minority. This policy and Operation Wisla resulted in the annihilation of the structure of this local community, whose population was deliberately dispersed to different areas of Poland.

Thus the Lemko region (Lemkovyna, Lemkowszczyzna in Polish) in its old form ceased to exist. Polish settlers arrived to take the place of the Lemkos and received land under the law on the nationalization of property. Ten years later, however, political changes in Poland allowed Lemkos to return to their own region and their homelands, a process that continues to this day (though often only in a symbolic sense). Most Lemkos have nonetheless remained in the Western Territories. They colonized farms in this region and cultivated the customs and traditions of their community there, without intending to return to the land of their fathers. Yet the ethnic awakening of the 1980s resulted in the Lemkos too seeing a chance of reconstructing their ethnic identity. This is occurring in two areas: the Western Territories, where young people are actively trying to revive long-forgotten traditions, and the original Lemko region, where activists are striving to reconstruct their symbolic cultural centre. The democratization of social life in the last twenty years has encouraged these groups and given them the opportunity to revive their own identity.

The Lemkos's post-war history so undermined their ethnic self-consciousness that they came to suffer from a particular identity imbalance. The policy of ethnic cleansing after 1944 destroyed the community, and their lack of institutions of political representation hindered the process of reconstructing ethnic awareness. The communist state did not acknowledge a place for Lemkos in society, even during the period of tacit consent to ethnic minority activities in post-1945 Poland. It was much easier to regard Lemkos as Ukrainians, which in turn contributed to the group's internal disintegration. The Catholic Church treated them as an adversary, and in many instances appropriated Lemko churches and impinged on their desire to manifest their religious distinctiveness. A mechanism for negotiating an identity came into existence: present-day Lemkos either identify themselves with the Ukrainian nation (as a branch of it) or emphasize their relation to Rusyns living in Slovakia and Ukraine. It is mainly the leaders who promote the Rusyn movement, wishing to emphasize that Lemkos are different from Ukrainians. A significant number of Lemkos accentuate only their regional distinctiveness compared with Poles, without referring to any other nation. These ethnic negotiations concern not only groups but individuals as well. Still deliberating over who they are in an ethnic sense, the Lemkos thus face a dilemma of ethnic, ethical and moral choice.

The growing role of ethnic discourse that sprang from democratic changes in Eastern Europe presented Lemkos with urgent new challenges, particularly in the sphere of conflict concerning the regulation of property rights, which pits the state against minority groups. Lemkos have unsuccessfully tried to regain rights of ownership over forests (once their basic asset) that were nationalized after the war. Although this problem concerns other minority groups as well, public opinion is focused on carrying through restitutions of Jewish and German rather than Lemko property. The Lemkos still live with the impression that the Polish state denies their right to restitution, and excludes them from the process of re-privatization.

A few fundamental elements of Lemko identity determined the group's strong attachment to their territory, and created a sense of possessing Lemkovyna. The main one is the myth of common descent, which constitutes the *sine qua non* of many an ethnic group, and is a crucial component of the complex of meanings that emphasize ethnic bonds. This myth answers the questions of why we are the same, and why we create a community. Three types of myths arise from the creation of a community. Besides the myth of common descent, there are myths of a return to the land of the fathers and of the promised land (which concerns those who are unwilling or unable to return to their ethnic territory). These myths determine a group's location on a social map of the world. They describe not only the group's origins, but also its development and destiny. They mark out the will to live together and share a culture.

Participation in a culture involves the phenomenon of sharing: the members of a group have the same language, religion, symbolic space and so on. Various elements of this culture are accentuated to different extents, depending on the group's situation at a given point in time. This is the element of ethnicity, which in its greatest scope refers to the external identification of a group. Language, religion and customs, but also peculiarities of, for example, spatial organization, territorial management and architecture, are the means by which various groups tend to distinguish themselves from one another. These and other features of a culture make up the basic building blocks of ethnic boundaries that demarcate the worlds of 'us' and 'them'.

Another factor that determines the construction of identity is the ethnic link between a group and territory, which applies to both real and potential relations between a group and land. This relationship hinges on the group's needs and may constitute the fundament on which the group builds its ideology and social ties. It is also an essential aspect of a situation in which a group is undergoing a process of shaping or reconstructing its identity. A group seeks to possess or repossess the territory it needs. The groups that inhabited Galicia provide examples of different relations with territory. For Lemkos, territory (*Lemkovyna*) was and still is a basic distinguishing feature of their ethnic identity. Roma, by contrast, are a group that does not attribute meaning to this component of identity. Although the myth of descent plays a role in their identity discourse, the fact of possessing and managing a territory is of secondary (if any) importance. For Galicia's Jews, territory meant the 'promised land', which expressed the relationship with land as a symbolic one. Indeed, every group, having created its own indicators of its relationship with land, reinforces these relations with symbols of connection and unity.

Territorial factors are ascribed yet another meaning, depending on the type of a group. Their significance in peasant groups differs from that in urban communities. Emigrants relate to their lack of territory not only in its elementary understanding, but also through the notion of territory as a memorial place of a group. Cemeteries best exemplify this: the desire to be buried in a community's own land is proof of the special ethnic value attributed to territory. In this meaning, territory concentrates the aforementioned correlates of ethnicity: the myth of common ancestry, community, culture and history. Also emphasizing the salience of this ethnic determinant is the fact that it is both an external and an internal means of group identification. This is especially consequential for groups that do not possess territory. Without justification in territory, their symbolic signals are perceived from the outside as weaker and less appealing, as exemplified by the situation of the Roma. They are not 'at home' anywhere, and are regarded as intruders in most European countries.

I will adduce a few examples from my own research, in which Lemkos depicted the way in which their sense of possession of a territory arose and their awareness of a right to the land they inhabit grew. My respondents underlined the fact that the land Lemkos inhabited up to the 1940s is 'the Lemkos's sempiternal property'. To take a few examples:

> It is an autochthonous people in this area. There wasn't anybody before us here.
>
> There was nobody here before. For example, the names Uście Ruskie, Ropica Ruska, Królowa Ruska and many others prove that there were no other nationalities.
>
> We have been here since the beginning.
>
> We here are convinced that we have always been here. We did not come from anywhere.
>
> When they came, this territory was uninhabited. They deforested the area. This village was so big, so densely inhabited by Lemkos, that the housing was really congested.
>
> They have been here for a long time, because Orthodox churches and everything prove that they have.[6]

The life of this group would have continued uninterrupted, had it not been for the ethnic cleansing in the second half of the 1940s. Their eviction proved such a harrowing blow to the Lemkos that they now divide their history into 'before' and 'after' relocation. In their opinion, Operation Wisla brought a certain period in the group's history to a halt by depriving them of their territory and the property that legitimized their existence. The world of the Lemkos up until then has been mythologized, in their perception, as a 'golden age'. At the same time, they describe relocation in terms of a catastrophe and affliction. When asked 'Why were Lemkos removed?' they said:

> How do I know why? We respected one another, lived together, and then this plague came, this disease.
>
> I was born here, lived here. I got used to it, and so I think that nowhere is as good and happy as here. Now it is gone, it was lost after the eviction.[7]

Resettlement meant abrupt changes in the Lemkos's living space. Topographic, demographic, economic and cultural conditions differed considerably from those the community had previously lived in. Not only did migration radically change the life of the generation of Lemkos they directly affected, but they also influenced subsequent generations, and the results will remain noticeable for a long time to come. Another kind of change imposed by migration pertains to their mythical understanding of time.[8] A new mythical space of 'before Operation Wisla' has developed, giving new meaning to the past and influencing the future. Lemkovyna was different before this event, and is something else nowadays. Furthermore, not only did their cultural space cease to exist, but the processes of social bonding and the human ties that were characteristic of the Lemko community before its eviction disappeared. Ethnic boundaries also vanished when the group was dispersed. Moreover, the community could not be revived: Lemkos did not have the opportunity to reproduce the old patterns, but have had to modify them instead. The structures of power changed, as did the system of norms and values. The appearance of 'new strangers' produced a need to redefine identity. Ethnicity was temporarily reduced solely to the private sphere, the level of family and the individual. They were living in a new world. Individuals became defenceless in a sense, as the whole system of cultural boundaries collapsed – there were no sanctuaries, it was inadvisable to speak their language, there was no 'us'. Instead, there were 'new houses', 'different churches', 'strange people', 'odd machines', 'different air' and 'different soil'.

Only a very few Lemkos managed to stay in Lemkovyna after the eviction. A dramatic, sorrowful picture of the area after the expulsion remains in people's memory. A Lemko woman from Leszczyny recounted:

> Here in Lemkovyna everything was dilapidated, razed to the ground, houses taken apart. We stayed there, two families, so when there are no people, there is no life. My husband kept repeating that if people did not come back he would go to the west – this was not real life. Sometimes at Easter-week we both went to the Orthodox church; the church was closed, so we would walk around it, praying and weeping.

Empty houses, land laid waste and silence – this is how witnesses most often recall Lemkovyna of that time. The vacuum left by the culture that inhabited the area for so many centuries remains to this day. Yet it is the vestiges of Lemko life that leave the strongest impression on visitors to the area: traces of old, forgotten villages; scrubby fruit trees that make up a forest; the ruins of wells; remains of buildings protruding through high grass.[9]

In the Western Territories

The authorities regarded the territories the Lemkos were moved to as the spoils of war, which fostered a sense of temporariness and uncertainty. Lemkos who returned to Lemkovyna a few years later recalled their exile:

> I decided to come back, because that was never mine.
>
> I was in the west, worked in the PGR [state-owned collective farms] for ten years, but never felt secure with it; it did not work, because that used to belong to Germans. They [Poles] might have taken over, but well, we were still on foreign

> territory. And here this is mine, my property inherited from grandfathers and great-grandfathers. My father, grandfather lived there, were born there and farmed there.

The Western Territories held no ethnic value for the Lemkos, as they were not their native land – that is, not Lemkovyna, where their grandfathers lived off the land, land that later generations should have inherited. As in other peasant cultures, which prioritize the relationship with the land, they did not trust the 'gift' in the form of land allotted to them by the Polish state from formerly German territory. In their opinion, land that was not purchased from its former, rightful owner evoked uncertainty and a feeling of temporariness. (This resembles the mechanism of the 'unreciprocated gift'.) It was entirely obvious to the Lemkos that they were temporarily residing on foreign land – alien, because different from Lemkovyna; alien, because taken from other people. The uncertainty was also aggravated by the unstable political situation in Europe. Even today, when visiting these territories and seeing the ruins of households and run-down towns, one can encounter the same opinions about there being no real or rightful owners of those lands.

Also influencing this situation was the aura of estrangement the newcomers from Lemkovyna bore amidst the culture and civilization they found away from their homeland. Their war experiences engendered feelings of aversion and suspicion towards all that was formerly German. In the case of the Lemkos, it makes sense to speak simply of 'civilization shock'. The quality of the land they were to cultivate was foreign to them. They came, as they claimed, 'from the land of oats to the land of wheat', where they met a different farming culture. They moved from old, wooden huts into spacious brick houses equipped with sewerage systems and various devices that were totally new to them. As a Lemko from Leszczyny recalled:

> When we were there we did not know how the people lived. Here [in Lemkovyna] people lived in poverty. There in the west everybody was learning by observing how people lived and farmed. There everything was already mechanized; that was a German legacy. There everything was ready, you could only come and everything was done by machines . . . People learnt how to make life better.

The Lemkos also remember their inability to become acclimatized to the new territory: 'The soil did not yield anything; it was all sand. There were no individual farms, only PGR'. They disliked the climate – 'They were suffocating in this lowland air'; 'water quality was poorer' – and regretted the absence of mountains and 'their landscape'.[10]

Every diaspora has its own 'landscape', which appears in the collective consciousness of the members of a group. It teaches history, educates and justifies a group's descent – as does, for example, the Carpathian landscape in the case of Rusyns. National identities are permeated with a collective perception of landscape, notwithstanding how real or mythical it is. Natural places of a group are 'historized' and become actors in the process of the reconstruction of the past.[11] In the Lemko case, the mountains were a symbol and source of the group's ethnicity. For them, it seems, landscape was a fundamental factor in reviving the past, referring to the order of meanings and finally maintaining a symbolic connection with Lemkovyna. Reminiscing about landscape summoned the bond and ethnic identity. A mythologized depiction of Lemkovyna was present at the time when the decision to return was made, encouraged homecoming and constituted a pattern for reconstructing a given community. The Lemkos could not rebuild their community in the Western Territories – this was possible only in the territory of their 'own homeland'. The greatest role a myth played in reconstructing the past consisted in compelling the members of the group to return.

Returning

Having partially mitigated their policy, communist governments permitted returns from the mid 1950s. These, however, were undertaken only by the few who were undeterred by the new social, administrative and legal status of Lemkovyna. The authorities forced returnees to find vacant households unoccupied by Poles. They also had to procure permission from the local administration, which applied the law of not granting the restitution of farms to their evicted former owners. One returnee remembered:

> If I did not love this land, I would not have returned – never. I held the position of PGR manager in the Western Territories . . . They did not want to let me go, but I love my land, and that is why my children came here. One daughter is working in Gorlice in a design office after graduating from university; the other is working as a teacher in Gładyszów, and my son stayed to work on the farm. When I came back, there were only ashes – I had nothing, no house, nothing. My house had been taken to pieces! Most houses, there were eighty-seven altogether, only as many and some of them newly-built; all taken apart, sold as fuel or building material. Whoever came, they could buy it for a few zlotys, to make sure we were lost without a trace. They wanted to show the world that there was no other nationality, because there is Poland; but history after all is just . . . The land was partially occupied by a settler. In this house lived a Polish settler – in that one, over there [pointing to a neighbouring building]. Later on he left and deserted the land. I managed to buy it back partially, because the rest had been nationalized.[12]

Idealization of Lemkovyna was a strong stimulus encouraging return migration. This might have been because it was older Lemkos who took the initiative and who – remembering and yearning for their patrimony – were eager to return, regardless of whether it would worsen the economic condition of their families. 'The elderly wanted to come back to their nests', they would say.

> I want nothing but my patrimony, mountainous areas and forests.
>
> Where one was born, they are always attracted to the place, to their native land. I tell my children, 'This is ours!'
>
> There were some who did not have houses when they came. The houses had been taken apart and sold on a massive scale. So they built houses. They came, stayed with someone, built a house and moved in . . . The Poles inflicted serious harm on us, because they came here, and those houses were in really good condition, and they sold them for next to nothing.
>
> Only after having applied to the Ministry of Agriculture did we receive a notification that we could return, but we did not get our land, which had been settled, but a substitute . . . It was dishevelled, damaged. I lived in a building which was once a production cooperative; there was a fodder storage house, a repository and cowshed. I lived there, and later on started to build a house.
>
> Not everybody could come back, only those who managed to get an unoccupied place. Our fields were occupied. We had been expropriated. Everything was taken over by the settlers, and we had to build anew. At that time they did not welcome us when we arrived. They did not know what was happening, [they] were afraid that we would take everything back from them, but we did not do it. I lived with a settler for a year and a half, and then he found himself in the west. I paid him for it, for my own house which he gave up to me. Then I continued building.[13]

Some of the most poignant and shocking stories I heard during my research told of buying back property from Polish settlers. The negotiations with new owners resulted in unexpected outcomes in particular cases – sometimes they shared the house temporarily; sometimes conflicts arose. In interviews, the Lemkos kept repeating that the land could 'tolerate' only the Lemkos, and it forced 'the strangers' to leave. In their opinion, the Poles were unable to cultivate land that was not favourable to them.

> We came back in 1956. The Poles who lived in our house did not want to stay there any longer, so they wrote to us and my parents decided to return. The Poles did not have water in the well; a girl got killed by lightning in the fields. When they left, workmen moved in, and when we came, you could dig in mud on the floor with a spade. The walls were nailed together and everything was damaged. Then we rebuilt everything.[14]

In the process of reconstructing Lemko identity, special meaning has been attributed to this group's efforts to regain their property rights, especially to the forests they had lost in Operation Wisla. The nationalization decree of 1947 legalized the confiscation of property following this infamous action. Those who returned regained only part of their confiscated possessions. However, having undertaken the restitution of households (though in only a few cases), the authorities refused to return the forests, which by virtue of the nationalization decree were administered by the State Forests Administration. Arguing that the forests were an integral part of the confiscated farms, the Lemkos still demand that they be returned. Efforts undertaken after 1980 to achieve the restitution of forest land was halted by a martial law decree and discontinued on the grounds that they had 'no legal basis'. The only event that can be considered favourable to the Lemkos's endeavours seems to be a declaration of the Polish Senate in 1990 that condemned Operation Wisla and proclaimed measures to compensate for the harm inflicted on the Lemkos as a result of mass evictions.

According to the Lemkos, subsequent governments' lack of activity vis-à-vis the restitution of appropriated forest land is tantamount to acknowledgement of the proceedings of post-war communist governments. The Lemkos believe the provisions of Operation Wisla will remain an issue as long as the forests are not returned to their rightful owners. A Lemko from Nowica depicted the issue thus:

> We had forests, and they took everything from us, evicted people. Now they are plotting that they are going to [undertake restitution], but they do not want to do so. When they did such harm to the nation, they should give these forests back, at least to those who really deserve it. But the Polish authorities treat the Lemkos as if they were a secondary nation.

The perpetuation of this state of affairs puts the Lemkos in the position of a wronged group, and some have spoken out about the intentional economic deprivation of this community: 'They [grant restitution] to the Poles, Jews, but not us, because they do not hold us in esteem'. The effort to regain confiscated forest land is one of the few the Lemkos have undertaken as a community. Their hope of restitution of their lost property ennobles them in a unique way. Their endeavours have also created a brand-new social image of the community that is apparent in the individual stories of those who have tried to reclaim part of their patrimony, as well as current organized social initiatives. Lemko organizations created since 1989 have prioritized the issue of regaining forest land. The statutes of one of these organizations state, *inter alia*, that it seeks to 'suppress political-economic discrimination on the part of state and social authorities as regard the Lemkos, the Boikos, especially in Lemkovyna', and will work for the 'restitution to the Lemkos and Boikos of their imperishable, inalienable mortgage rights' and 'restitution of forests and other mortgage property in kind or compensation'.[15]

Until the aggrieved reclaim their lost forests, it is obvious that the state intends to continue its forestry policy, thus impoverishing Lemko forest areas. The efforts of the Lemkos are therefore also aimed at suppressing the devastating – to Lemko eyes – exploitation of the Carpathian forests. The Lemko organization has repeatedly sent petitions to state authorities at different levels. When Poland joined the European Union, the Lemkos started looking to EU institutions for allies in their struggle for the restitution of property lost sixty years ago. Difficult though it may be to find examples of social actions by the inhabitants of Lemkovyna, the pursuit of restitution mobilizes them in a special way.

To summarize, it should be emphasized that returning to Lemkovyna became the only way for this community to achieve ethnic reconstruction. As mentioned, the myth of ethnic identity was embodied in the group's ethnic territory. The process of assimilation and the disintegration of the group were to end the moment they returned to the land of their fathers, a world frozen in myth. In Lemko consciousness, the myth became muddled with their actual history. Although the myth, as is usually the case with a myth, did not entirely correspond to the new reality, in a sense it fulfilled its social function. Above all, returnees found their objective in the rebuilding of the material world. They found themselves on their land, which had to be cultivated. They started to recognize their past, and the myth led them to a defined world that, though somehow changed, was still theirs. Work in agriculture and rebuilding initiated the process of reconstructing and reinterpreting the symbolic world. Ethnic culture, encompassing the fundamental values and symbols that are the objects of human attitudes, became an attribute of the members of the group. Given their autotelic character, symbols were conducive to the group's social and ethnic integration. In this respect, autotelic values assumed a utilitarian significance. For instance, cherishing religious values was demonstrated in practice by rebuilding the Orthodox church or struggling with 'strangers' for it. Administrative names like Bielanka in original Cyrillic that reappeared in Lemkovyna concealed contents and pictures familiar only to this community. People's work on their own farms set in motion the whole process of local reintegration and the reconstruction of the 'framework of community memory'.

Remembering and Forgetting

Ethnic communities wage constant struggles over the right to manage space, most conspicuously in territories where borders have altered or mass resettlement and migration have occurred. East Central Europe contains a great many areas of this kind. These struggles frequently have a merely symbolic character, although this does not diminish their significance for the communities concerned. Fundamental to this process is the issue of historical policy towards other groups. A casual analysis reveals two mechanisms applied in disputes about the right to symbolic rule over a territory: forgetting, or cultural amnesia, and reinterpretation of the past.

To complement the picture of Lemkovyna, I will adduce a few examples from western Ukraine, where, ever since the eviction of Poles after the Second World War, the inhabitants are still noticeably struggling with the past imprinted in space. In each of these cases, the change in a given territory's ethnic composition entailed modification of the symbolic marking of space. The most legible examples applied to landscape. Some permanent elements of landscape sustain their symbolic power long after the land they are situated on has found new denizens. The Poles who were forced out of the territory of present-day Ukraine left behind churches, shrines, crosses and many other signs that prove not only that they once lived there and were sustained by these lands, but also that they managed them. Existing buildings, houses, squares and ruins confirm their presence. The Lemkos compelled to leave for the Western Territories left similar traces of the past, as outlined above. Due to the power of transmission, such carriers of memory often become targets of assaults by those who desire to efface the past, and to consign to oblivion the fact that it once was different. They want to mobilize the process of forgetting among the community now living there, erasing traces of the past. Such effacement can assume various forms, for instance, physical obliteration of churches and shrines to the point where nothing remains of them. Another method is to leave sacral objects in the church. This also ends up in destruction, although via a time-consuming process; however, in its substance it is more telling than total destruction of an object. In residents' consciousness, such memorials of the past evoke several overlapping types of meaning: symbolic, material and functional. Even if the material or functional aspect of a church is cast aside – for example, because it is damaged or cannot be adjusted to serve the community's aims – it still remains an essential symbol: a carrier of the memory of a community striving for a particular space and for symbolic dominance.

To be sure, not all traces of the past can be obliterated, nor does a group always want to wipe them from memory. The most distinguishing features of landscape are stored in the recollections of those who still want to remember the community they lived with side by side. I remember vivid stories told by a Ukrainian informant who rekindled his pre-war memories of priests' orchards in bloom around a 'Polish' church, hunting in the prefect's estate or work in the brickyard of a local manufacturer. Although hardly any physical evidence remained to confirm his words, his account of the places he depicted was like a tour through an old landscape. Every bit of long-lost scenery brought back another story. The dilapidated gravestone of the last landowner meant a several-hour story of what life used to look like. The ruins of a chapel temple revived pictures of gaudy church fairs and crowds of visitors coming from the neighbourhood, the fragrance of cooked food or even the flavour of old Polish orangeade. The scraps of a bygone landscape are amazingly powerful. Landscape may be altered, but it cannot be extirpated from the memory of those who have lived there. Remembering and forgetting is by no means a characteristic feature of one community. Run-down Orthodox churches, synagogues or Jewish cemeteries have similar appeal to Poles in Poland.

The exemplified communities seem to model the majority of mechanisms and nuances connected with the cultivation and valorization of territory. The process of appropriating a space entangles it in a cultural setting and network of social relations. Its every fragment belongs to someone in a legal sense, but that does not necessarily correspond to actual rule, especially in the symbolic sphere. The place is determined by objective coordinates, but also by its distinguishing features: past and present events, biographies, memories, graves, monuments. Absorption of space is defined as a shorter or longer location in a territory. This process consists in regarding a chosen territory as one's own to a lesser or greater extent. In this context this means the personalization of space, that is, vesting the existing place with specific features that are then associated with people and their lives. The course and character of this process is profoundly impacted upon by cultural capital, understood here as a repository of memory, knowledge and aesthetic and ethical values handed down from generation to generation.

Land and Property

Having discussed western Ukraine, I will cite an example of the question of land ownership in the context of the de-collectivization of local farms. The case of western Ukrainian villages I have examined in the former Halych region of east Galicia stands in contradistinction to the situation of the Lemko above. Owing chiefly to the relationship with land and the issue of ownership, two peasant cultures with similar ethnic backgrounds have realized the policy of private ownership in entirely different ways.

At the end of the twentieth century, all former Soviet-bloc countries in which collectivization had been in force set about the process of dismantling it. Various patterns and schemes governed efforts to restore private property. Collective farms were disassembled, and attempts were launched to find appropriate ways to cultivate neglected wasteland. The case of the Ukrainian village I have analysed seemed special to me from the very beginning. A former cooperative was being disassembled, and new forms of management were being created for this estate, but few wanted to take over the land. Soon I learnt that this was typical not only among Ukrainian peasants, but also in the majority of post-Soviet societies. Similar examples can be found in Chris Hann's work on Hungary, Deema

Kaneff's analysis of a community in Bulgaria and many other anthropologists' treatment of these issues in Central and Eastern Europe.[16] As has been noted, collectivization changed interpersonal relations in rural societies, and also altered human relations to land. In the society I studied, I noticed the understanding and value of private property had been disturbed. In a traditional understanding, private property is established by a guarantee that an individual or group can exclude others from using or benefiting from the fact of possession. Every parcel of land was assigned to a household and no one else could use it. These rights of property had been shattered, and apparently it is not easy to restore them anew. The consequences of collectivization in this regard became evident precisely when re-privatization began.

Local authorities, elected by the inhabitants, were unable to manage the territory entrusted to them. Its main wealth, land, was parcelled out to outsiders not attached to the village. These new actors treat land as fields for exploitation, and in so doing do not contribute to the village but reap the harvest themselves. Reduced to a natural resource and shorn of its significance, the land was deprived of its values, and the ethos of working it slowly vanished. Farmers have lost their emotional tie with cultivated land. Inhabitants do not say 'my field' or 'my land'. Farms have become manufacturing enterprises, impersonal factories producing corn and beetroot. Inhabitants do not even know who administers their land. What is more, they assert, land has become entangled in a set-up characterized by mafia groups, corruption and patronage. It is trafficked in an illegal manner. Few remember at all that their ancestors owned a few hectares of land. My somewhat obtrusive attempts to trace the history of a few farms were quickly extinguished by utterances to the effect that it was so long ago that people owned land that they had already forgotten it. First – they said – Polish gentry, then the kolkhoz (collective farm), then obscure and incomprehensible rules of land management by a partnership and now privately owned farms: none of it was conducive to the creation of ownership relations. A sense of ownership had been effaced from people's language too long to prompt them to deal with the issue now.

Local farmers did not feel the urge to possess this land as their own property, this special territory that their fathers and grandfathers had once cultivated. From their previous observations of the peasant community in Poland, they had extrapolated an indisputable paradigm of the struggle to own land, in which 'quarrels over the ownership of a balk' became part of the peasant ethos representing the life of people who lived from farming and fought for their property. Yet most Ukrainian agricultural workers were not at all interested in reclaiming their land and possessing it as their own property. An isolated example was the case of a museum employee in Ivano-Frankivsk whom I met during my field research. Born in 1933 in the vicinity of Marijampole, he recounted the following struggle for his land:

> We had about 10 hectares of fields, and we were well-off – till the kolkhoz was established. They deprived us of everything – machines and tools; took the barn to pieces and destroyed a lot in the meantime. Mother worked hard in the kolkhoz, and I had to help her to earn a living. I was learning, and my mother sent me to work in the city. She died in 1993. Theoretically, the land should have been parcelled out by then, but in my mother's village they started a year later for unknown reasons. I did not get a share after my mother because they said that successors were not entitled. Our house was left in the village, but I cannot sell it as the village council demanded 700 hryvnia for some documents, and I do not think I should pay anything for my own house and land. For a few years now I've been waiting for an official statement from the village mayor, but so far in vain. Neither I nor my children need this house or land, but decency and sentiment demand that I claim my patrimony, and the state does not give a damn.

Turning now to further in-depth considerations, I suggest that different social contexts determine various strategies for approaching the question of ownership and territory management. Furthermore, the case of a Ukrainian village shows that local communities utilize the heritage of the past in a number of ways. Each group, however, makes sure that their markers of symbolic management of space dominate.

In summary, when we touch upon questions of ownership, possession or re-privatization, we set in motion a series of associations with the spheres of economy or law. It is worth remembering that, in certain contexts, the symbolic dimension of these phenomena should be considered as well. A sense of ownership of a certain territory among the Lemkos demonstrates the need to treat the matter of ownership broadly. The Lemkos today, like the majority of citizens once wronged by communist governments, have undertaken to reclaim their confiscated property. They are now capable of organizing themselves and swaying the authorities in their endeavours to regain their estate. So far their ultimate goal remains out of reach, but they nevertheless persevere with symbolic rulings over their traditional territory. They have just succeeded in their quest for the right to write the name of one of the villages in their mother tongue. Such symbolic victories confirm them in their conviction that they are still at home.

Notes

1. Akhil Gupta and James Ferguson (eds), *Culture, Power, Place: Explorations in Critical Anthropology*, Durham, NC/London, 1997.
2. For more on this issue, see Andrzej Bukowski, Marcin Lubas and Jacek Nowak, *Zarządzanie przestrzenią: Globalizacja, etniczność, władza*, Kraków, 2006.
3. E.g., Hannes Grandits and Patrick Heady, *Distinct Inheritances: Property, Family and Community in a Changing Europe*, Halle, 2003; Davide Torsello, *Trust, Property and Social Change in a Southern Slovakian Village*, Halle, 2003.

4. Wojciech Łukowski, *Społeczne tworzenie ojczyzn*, Warsaw, 2002, p.83.
5. Ibid.
6. Informant statements, taken from Jacek Nowak, *Zaginiony świat? Nazywają ich Łemkami*, Kraków, 2000, p.67.
7. Informant statements, taken from ibid.
8. Zdzisław Mach, 'Myth and Cultural Construction of Time Among a Resettled Population', *Polish Sociological Bulletin* 2 (1993), pp.131–38.
9. Nowak, *Zaginiony świat?* p.78.
10. Ibid., pp.72–78.
11. Anthony D. Smith, *The Ethnic Origin of Nations*, Oxford, 1986.
12. Informant statement, from Nowak, *Zaginiony świat?* p.80.
13. Informant statements, from ibid., pp.80–100.
14. Informant statement, from ibid.
15. Ibid., pp.101–5.
16. Chris Hann, 'From Production to Property: Decollectivization and the Family–Land Relationship in Contemporary Hungary', *Man* 28/3 (1993), pp.299–320; Deema Kaneff, 'Responses to "Democratic" Land Reforms in a Bulgarian Village', in Frances Pine and Susan Bridger (eds), *Surviving Postsocialism: Local Strategies and Regional Responses in Eastern Europe and the Former Soviet Union*, London, 1996, pp.85–114.

9

Landownership in Practice
The Case of Naramice in Central Poland

Paweł Klint

> Peasants who work only to have money will never have any profit. Only peasants who work with conviction, who love this land, can form a bond with agriculture. Whoever does not love the land – has nothing . . . If somebody chooses to be a peasant, he has to be perseverant. . .
>
> —A 25-year-old farmer in 1994[1]

The issue of property has always been a challenge for government leaders and reformers in Poland. The brevity of the tradition of landownership among peasants (in parts of today's central and eastern Poland, only since 1864), together with the changing political and social systems of the twentieth century, created a certain sense of temporariness concerning one's property, and led above all to distrust among the peasantry towards the state institutions in charge of administering property. The agricultural reforms carried out in Poland during the interwar period and at the beginning of communist rule in 1944 deepened mistrust towards the rulers as big landowners lost their land, receiving little or no compensation. Recipients of expropriated land moreover often treated their new property as a temporary windfall. Poland's shifting borders significantly contributed to a sense of temporariness, and for some time displaced Poles from the eastern regions of the country regarded both their losses and their new land in the west as temporary in nature.

Therefore, it is extremely difficult to analyse the issue of property in Poland, especially when the property and inheritance are the focus. For peasants, these are very private issues. The low level of trust in state institutions is mirrored by their suspicion of a scholarly approach to property. Nonetheless, searching questions about inheritance practices, land transactions, property as patrimony and consciousness of the institution of land registration have proved particularly fruitful. This chapter is the result of research conducted among twelve farming families from Naramice, including many hours of interviews, along with observations and rather informal conversations, all conducted during householders' working hours and at other times in people's familiar surroundings (houses or fields), which is definitely the best working method for a social anthropologist.[2]

Inheritance Practices

Most of the plots owned by families in Naramice, a village in south central Poland,[3] do not exceed 20 hectares. Out of all the families I spoke to, only one has a relatively large farmstead (30 hectares). This family is an exception, given the background of the peasants from Naramice. The family only works on its own farmstead, producing vegetables, potatoes and milk. The other families own much less land: 10 to 18 hectares, and some as little as 4.7 hectares, 3 hectares and 0.48 hectares. In only two of the other families do both husband and wife work on their farmsteads, comprising 18 hectares and 16 hectares respectively. In the other families, either one or both members of the couple work in Naramice or Wieluń in other spheres of activity.[4] For example, a family comprising a farmer (husband) and a clerk (wife) own land amounting to 12 hectares, and land comprising 4.7 hectares is the property of a teacher and a housewife. In addition, most of the landowners have adult children, most of whom work in offices, markets or factories (in Wieluń or in the surrounding villages).[5] Most households in the village consist of two or three generations living together. No household I investigated had more than six members: a three-generation family usually had two grandparents, two parents and two children.[6]

In many families, the children function as adults economically, but in every case the parents work on the homestead. They acquired the land and all its property from the grandparents, who now receive agricultural pensions. Usually the grandparents transferred their homesteads to their children (the parents) ten to twelve years after the marriage of the latter, so for ten to twelve years the parents had lived in the grandparents' household without owning the homestead. Only in two cases had the grandparents given the parents relatively large plots when they married, enabling them to create their own household and little homestead. However, it was never the entire homestead. The practice of giving the complete homestead to the parents was always the same, in that it took place after several years of marriage. Everybody (both parents and grandparents) considers this a good system of inheritance. The children, who at 20 to 25 years of age are able to farm by themselves, accept having to wait a few or even a dozen years before taking over the homestead: 'It is a natural process', they explained.

However, it should be noted that most young people from the village do not remain in the village or work on their parents' homesteads.

I did not speak with any family in which a husband and wife were natives of the same village.[7] Most often the women came from other villages no more than 20 kilometres from Naramice, though one householder's wife came from a town (Kępno) situated about 40 kilometres away.[8] In two other cases, it was not the husband but the wife who was from Naramice and had inherited land from her parents, and when the man was given his parents' homestead, the couple decided to stay in Naramice and sell the land in the other village. In both cases, the plots in the other village were smaller and worse than that in Naramice, so it was an easy decision to live there.[9]

Almost every farmer knows every step of the process he must go through to transfer his land to his children – especially which office they have to go to. Even young people know and understand the procedure very well. Everybody mentions each action step by step: visiting the notary's office and obtaining the proper documents (extract from the land registry and title deed). Knowledge of these procedures is, the farmers from Naramice said, 'part of living in the countryside, of farming and of being a good farmer'; 'everybody in the country has to know every rule related to the land' (including the ways of the legal and administrative system). Anyone who has received a farm from his or her parents intends to give it to his or her children. Knowledge about how to hand a farm down to children is consolidated by information on how to change the ownership of land, transfer some property to the householder's children or sell a plot of land in the village. Every peasant claims that such activities are widely commented upon in the village, especially in order to ascertain the price of land (in case of a sale), notaries' charges or problems with civil servants at the offices in Wieluń.

However, only the parents make decisions on matters pertaining to passing land to the children. They decide when it takes place: at the moment of the child's wedding and their decision to stay in the village and to farm, or when the ageing parents have no more strength and desire to farm. Then, the parents always say, 'It is the proper time for it'. In many cases, the parents are unconvinced that the young couple will be able to manage farming, so they decide to wait a few years before giving the homestead to their children. They say that this period is meant to prepare the young couple to become individual farmers (that is, these years are like a dress rehearsal), even though all peasants raised their children as peasants and every child (even at a young age) has practised every chore on the farm, and even taken part in every bureaucratic activity related to the property. This proves that most older peasants treat farming as not only a job and a duty but also as a way of life, and one of life's most important elements, providing it with meaning.

In many cases – especially in the past – the farmers described many couples in Naramice as having married for predominantly economic reasons (*małżeństwa gospodarcze*). When both members of a young couple inherited their parents' homesteads, the resultant large property was easier to administer and maintain than a small farm was. The system of inheritance had not changed for several generations. The parents wanted to give every child an equal share of the land, but in practice usually only one or two children decided to stay in the countryside. The remaining children of larger families sought jobs in surrounding towns, and were satisfied with receiving some money to compensate for the loss of their share of their parents' land.

In a few cases, the farmers claimed that in the past it had been good to ensure that children received a higher education, which obviated the need to divide the land among all the children and thus create small farms. Nowadays, however, farmers think that too few young people want to remain in the countryside as farmers, and thus the practice of dividing the land must be changed. One or two children must be encouraged to stay in the household as peasants and be educated about farming, they said, and the parents should show young people how many opportunities and benefits are available to peasants with large farms. In this context, people emphasized: 'Farming is a laborious but permanent job, no peasant has to look for a job, he will never be unemployed, so he does not have to worry about losing a job or a pension in the future'. Of course, the practice of inheritance can be quite different in reality because so few young people want to stay in the village.

In Naramice, however, economic factors can still play an important role in a marriage. Young people in such marriages are originally from the area and – most importantly – decide to stay in the village and join their parents' homesteads to create 'thriving companies'. In these cases, the parents usually give part of their homestead to children who want to farm, so they can start farming 'from the beginning on their own land'. After about ten years, both sets of parents of the married couple give the entirety of two homesteads to these children – albeit once the parents are sure that the young farmers' work and entrepreneurship will achieve the expected results.[10]

Of course, members of the older generation, having handed their farms down to their children, remain involved in working the land and retain the option to live on the homestead and use the income from it – this is assured until the end of their lives. Very often, when parents and the children live together in a three- or even four-generation household, the elders' pensions are treated as part of the income of the entire household (which is regarded as a single economic unit).[11]

Land Transactions

Most of the people with whom I discussed the value of land have only vague ideas about the market price of agricultural land. They evaluated one hectare of land at rates between PLN 2,000 and PLN 8,000.[12] Of course, they are conscious of differences among land plots in the countryside (their location, quality and so on). Recently, however, the price of land has increased in the wake of Poland's accession to the EU, and also because many people in Poland are interested in buying not only real estate but also an agricultural plot. The price per hectare of land in the countryside is rather close to the upper limit of the evaluation mentioned by the farmers (about PLN 8,000).

There was only one distinctive problem in Naramice. A family that did not live in the village wanted to sell a relatively large tract of real estate in an attractive location by the main road. It had been on the market for a few months, and officially there was no interest in it. Yet one family did wish to buy the plot, though in their opinion the price was not especially attractive (the price was high, they claimed, in the context of its situation in the village). Above all, they wanted to keep the deal secret because they were sure that if word spread in the village about their intentions, then suddenly many more people would want to buy the plot – not because they would at once regard it as an attractive investment, but because they would feel that if someone else wanted to buy it, then it had to be quite valuable. Doubtless there were indeed people who would want to foil the plans of the family that wanted to buy the plot. In the case of such a small local community, the land market at the local level is governed not only by economic mechanisms but also by people's motives for selling or buying land: relations between inhabitants of the village, people's permanent watch on what the neighbours were doing, and so forth.

Another type of property in the village, besides private farms, are the plots owned by the church and the municipality. The (state-owned) land belonging to the municipality does not comprise a large area. A few hectares of it are mainly good land (first- or second-class). However, the forests in the surrounding area are also state property. This land is permanently leased (as is also true of the land – about 6 hectares – owned by the Catholic parish in Naramice), usually to the same leaseholders over many years. People whose own land adjoins the state-owned land often wish to lease the latter and merge the plots into a big farm, facilitating the system of work and transportation on the homestead. The rents for the land are not high – about PLN 50 to PLN 100 per year per hectare of good land – but for a large plot of land, the lessee has to pay much more per hectare than in other cases. Meanwhile, farmers have no chance to buy the land from the municipality, because – they think – tenancy is the most profitable system for the municipal budget. Before 1989 there was no state-owned farm (*Państwowe Gospodarstwo Rolne*, *PGR*) in Naramice, so unlike many Polish villages, Naramice did not have to contend with the problem of farmers taking over state-owned land in the period of transformation after the demise of communism.

Farmers in Naramice often lease plots of land to other persons. Most often the totality of a farmer's land comprises several plots, usually a few to a dozen, so they willingly lease small pieces of land located outside the village (some plots can be a few kilometres away from the rest of their property) to interested parties. Furthermore, some people in the village – as the farmers said – work in towns but also own land they are not interested in farming; they gladly lease their land as well. Most often, tenancy transactions are informal; that is, the agreement is not formally notarized. The leaseholder usually gives part of the harvest to the landlord (such as one or more sacks of potatoes) or pays a modest rent (PLN 50 to PLN 100 per hectare annually). The farmers I spoke to told me about tenancy cases in which the landlord did not charge for the leased land but instead obliged the leaseholder to pay the land tax on the plot. In these cases, the landlord wanted to obtain an EU subvention that only farmers were eligible to receive. It is necessary to not only own but farm the land in order to obtain EU subsidies. Having found a person willing to farm, the lessor could lease out the plot without charge and at the same time still obtain the money from the EU.

In another case, two villagers decided to organize a tenancy between themselves, each leasing a similar plot from the other without charge. The particular situation lent itself to this arrangement: one farmer had a plot some distance from his household property, close to the property of the other farmer, who had a similar plot far from the main portion of his land and situated on the boundary of the land belonging to the first farmer. Thus they both profit from their verbal agreement, and the tenancy has lasted for a dozen years. In this time the villagers involved have transferred their land to their children, but the arrangement persists and both families want to continue it. Naturally, they draw a clear distinction between their own and the leased property.

As I mentioned, most of the people in Naramice work in other fields of activity (especially in the towns close to the village). Herein lies the reason why their land is their only opportunity to obtain additional money. Most farmers without large landholdings claim that working the land is not profitable. Income from the farm, they say, comprises around 20 per cent of their household budget (sometimes, however, forgetting that natural products obtained from their land contribute to the household budget as well), whereas work on the farm takes three to six hours every day (including on weekends). Yet although they claim farming is not profitable, most of them do not want to sell their land. There are a few reasons for this. Their land is something like insurance for the future. One rule of the Polish pension system is that a landowner of retirement age who hands land over to the government will receive a pension in return. Of course, farmers who do not give their land to the government are still in the social insurance system and can expect a state pension upon attaining retirement age (65 years for men and 60 for women). However, those who hand their land over to the state treasury in accordance with the legal principles established in 1982,[13] receive an augmented pension (depending on the amount of land handed over), a principle that remains in effect to this day.

In village communities, however, people more often transfer their plots to their children and spend the rest of their lives living and working together with their children. Another benefit of keeping the land is the Polish social system's provision that landowners in the countryside pay lower social contributions than other employed people.

Property as Patrimony

Feelings for the land are the foremost reason why landowners do not want to sell their property. Elderly people are especially attached to it. Some old people told me that the land was their patrimony (*ojcowizna*) or fatherland (*ojczyzna*), and that was why they had never sold it.[14] Fondness for the land, attachment to it and the perception of it as patrimony are mainly associated with people who have spent all their life in the countryside as farmers ('grandparents' and also 'parents'). This attitude can also be found among young people, but it is no longer a general tendency. Younger people (even those as old as forty), tend to assign more importance to economic considerations. If a prospective purchaser of land were to appear and offer 'a very good price', in the view of the young people in Naramice, they would sell their entire homestead without hesitation.[15] In most cases, however, the homestead's owners are still of the older generation ('parents') and strongly attached to the land as their patrimony, whereas the young people who would like to sell the land are not its owners. Furthermore, public opinion in Naramice holds that it is difficult to persuade young people to stay in the village as farmers. Thus older farmers are not as worried about their own future, which is insured by means of the so-called farmer pension, as they are about the future of their homesteads.

Consciousness of the Institution of Land

Although people in Naramice do not know the value of the land, they know – as mentioned above – the practice of sale contracts. Everybody (old people and their children or grandchildren) knows where notaries' offices are situated (in the town Wieluń there are a few). The farmers know the notary's role in contracts, and are conscious of its legal importance. Almost everybody can indicate how to conclude a contract step by step. Only a few persons are confused about how it works.[16]

The process of changing the land registers (*rejestry gruntowe*) to a land registry in the modern sense (*księgi wieczyste*) started after 1989. The post-war *rejestry gruntowe*, which had been drawn up mainly out of statistical considerations, contained no information about the land's property status.[17] The communist authorities decided on an incremental replacement of the *rejestry gruntowe*, whereby a plot of land received an entry in the new land registry only at the moment when the owner changed (when the land was sold/bought or inherited). However, due to technical failures – but what is more, to the communist authorities' overall bias against private property – the land registry remained unfinished.[18] Next, the authorities decided early in the 1990s to formally establish a land registry encompassing all land in Poland. Nowadays, specialists are working to establish digital land registries and thus facilitate work in courts of land registers.

In Naramice, some old people are conscious that the practice has changed a great deal since the time of their own transactions. Every farmer I spoke to emphasized the role of the court and land registries, because nothing concerning the issue of their own property, its guarantee and its inviolability is an open subject for discussion. The farmers even think that for having a legal guarantee of their property it is worth paying a low office charge to notaries and departments of land registries. There was no need to complain, they said – they had to pay for it because it is very important for them. In a few cases – especially when the land is passed from parents to their children – they slightly understated the value of the plots in the notarial act, but 'the value of the land is always almost correct', to prevent problems with tax collectors or resale of the land to somebody else (in the course of which, the farmers say, assessing the real value of the land could be problematic). Usually the farmers understated the value of their land, valuing it at 70 to 80 per cent of the real value and – as they said – usually did so with the consent of, and even some 'encouragement' from, their friendly notary. Farmers very rarely engaged evaluation experts during transactions, and did so only when selling land to strangers.

Another problem is the peasants' lack of consciousness that the work of geodesists is necessary at all.[19] Most of the people from the village have not seen a geodesist in Naramice for some time. Some people say that the last survey was carried out twenty or even thirty years ago (one elderly lady even said that it took place in 1953). Yet most people assume that no survey is needed nowadays because each plot has its own entry in the land registers, where the correct data on the plot's surface and boundary are recorded. As the villagers said, the information about the area and boundary of a plot or homestead is only needed when selling the land or issuing inheritance documentation, as then the farmers have to fill out official forms. Of course, the farmers know the boundaries of each of their plots very well. The fields feature markers like large rocks or mounds to show the boundaries of an individual plot.

However, I was unable to obtain much information about the cadastre from villagers. Actually, nothing resembling the cadastre exists in the farmers' collective consciousness. They all say they have heard of the cadastre, but it is difficult to say anything more about it.

Conclusions

This chapter has presented various dimensions of the role of landownership in the local community of Naramice, focusing in particular on practices of inheritance, land transactions and property as an element of attachment to a place and a way of life. As we can see, land has importance beyond securing income for the owner. Landownership also determines a way of life. Being born to a landowner in the countryside leads to a moment of inheritance in the future, and then to the new owner having to reflect on what kind of a future and way of life is the best choice. Fewer and fewer young people are willing to stay in the countryside as farmers, and practices of land inheritance have changed accordingly: the landowners' children no longer inherit the land at the moment they enter adulthood, but rather when their parents become too old and weak to work as farmers. This shift is both an effect of young people's out-migration from villages to towns, and a way of postponing a final decision concerning inheritance.

What does landownership mean to the present inhabitants of Naramice? Property is certainly a natural element in the lives of present and former landowners, who were prepared to inherit the property in their youth. But nowadays there are fewer children who wish to inherit the land and remain in the countryside. Landowning thus represents a certain problem for them because, according to their parents, inheritance of the land is based on a continuation of farming. Meanwhile, young people say that immediate renunciation of landownership – for example, in favour of the state, and so that their parents can receive a pension – or sale of the land is not possible. Only when the children of the present owners become the true legal heirs of the land in the countryside – that is, after their parents die – will it be known how many of them wish to farm and care for their property.

Notes

1. Cf. Bronisław Gołębiowski, *Przełomy wieków: Od kulturozbieractwa do Internetu*, Łomża, 2002, p.152.
2. At their request, I have disguised the identities of my informants through the use of pseudonyms.
3. Naramice belongs to the commune of Biała in the district of Wieluń, which is located in the Łódź voivodeship.The village lies near the road from Wrocław to Łódź, and lies about 110 kilometres south-west of the latter.
4. In 2003, only 11.11 per cent of households consisted of persons who worked on their own land as a sole source of income. Every year the rate decreases (in 1993 it was 22.77 per cent). In comparison, people who did not have homesteads made up 23.03 per cent of households in the Polish countryside in 2003, whereas 18.97 per cent of rural households consisted of people farming and working in other spheres as well, 4.74 per cent of people had their own businesses, 36.79

per cent were simply pensioners and 5.36 per cent were unemployed. See Krystyna Hanusik and Urszula Łangowska-Szczęśniak, 'Efekt pokazowy w zachowaniach konsumpcyjnych gospodarstw domowych mieszkańców wsi', in Stanisława Sokołowska (ed.), *Wieś i rolnictwo w procesie zmian: Problemy rozwoju obszarów wiejskich*, Opole, 2006, p.166, table 1.

5. Naramice also has many unemployed people (about 10 per cent). On the mechanisms and scale of unemployment in Polish villages, see Mieczysław Kluba, 'Przestrzenne zróżnicowanie poziomu oraz struktury bezrobocia na obszarach wiejskich województwa kujawsko-pomorskiego w okresie transformacji gospodarki', in Jerzy Parysek (ed.), *Rozwój regionalny i lokalny w Polsce w latach 1989–2002*, Poznań, 2004, pp.361–73.
6. In this chapter I have assigned a name to each generation according to family members' ages and their positions in the household. Therefore the people in Naramice fell into four groups: people aged 76 years or more are 'old grandparents', those aged 51 to 75 are 'grandparents', those aged 26 to 50 are 'parents' and those aged 0 to 25 are 'children'. This shorthand precisely qualifies each group and describes each generation's various roles and duties within households and homesteads.
7. This situation differed from that in the territories joined to Poland after 1944. In villages in Lower Silesia, many farmers seek wives from their own villages (at least, this was the case until 1989); see Wanda Czapran, 'Rodziny i związki rodzinne we współczesnej wsi podwrocławskiej', in Edward Pietraszek (ed.), *Wieś dolnośląska: Studia etnograficzne*, Wrocław, 1989, pp.208–19.
8. It was strange for her to stay in the village, but she became accustomed to living there. She decided to do so because her husband's work was very important. As a teacher, he had an important reputation and position in the local community, so she thought that it would not be 'only a typical rural life'.
9. For one important social anthropological study of property in the Polish countryside (specifically, Dziekanowice in Wielkopolska) and its transformation, see Michał Buchowski, 'Property Relations and Social Identity in Rural Poland', Max Planck Institute for Social Anthropology Working Paper 83, Halle/Saale, 2006, pp.1–26 (available at www.eth.mpg.de/pubs/wps/pdf/mpi-eth-working-paper-0083.pdf).
10. Although economic considerations may still be important in marriages in Naramice, nobody decides to wed another solely in order to run a large farm that would be very attractive on the local market. Most people I spoke to claim that the work of farmers does not commonly produce the hoped for results. Yet all farmers think their homesteads are self-sufficient, even if they do not have all the machinery needed for farming. Nobody in the village expects help from other farmers. 'Neighbourly help in the direct meaning of this word appears spontaneously, it has never been forced. It is based on mutual benefits, so it has never been paid'. See Kazimiera Zawistowicz-Adamska, 'Żywe tradycje współdziałania na wsi', in Kazimiera Zawistowicz-Adamska (ed.), *Granice i horyzonty badań kultury na wsi w Polsce*, Warsaw, 1976, p.212.
11. Nevertheless, no homestead's budget consists solely of income from farming. The pensions of grandparents who now live with the householders (parents) and income from their adult children form the lion's share of the household budget. One household (of 18 hectares) consisted of people who only work on their land, but they receive remittances from their children, who work outside Poland. These, they say, are the larger part of their budget, and are crucially important when they have to make investments. The peasants also receive some money in 'subsidies' from the EU, which they believe represent about 10 per cent of their annual income from farming. On peasants' incomes, especially the proportions of income from farm work and other kinds of work, see Józef Stanisław Zegar, *Dochody ludności chłopskiej*, Warsaw, 2000; Bartosz Chorkowy, 'Zmiany w sytuacji dochodowej gospodarstw domowych związanych z rolnictwem w latach 1993–2002', in Sokołowska, *Wieś i rolnictwo w procesie zmian*, pp.177–88.
12. The figures in this chapter are from 1 June 2007, at which time the exchange rate was PLN 3.8 to €1.

13. 'Ustawa z dnia 14 grudnia 1982 r. o ubezpieczeniu społecznym rolników indywidualnych i członków ich', *Dziennik Ustaw Rzeczypospolitej Polskiej* [hereafter *Dz. U.*] 40/268, article 22.
14. Some farmers think that only land can give them a feeling of safety, and that it is an essential element of the place they live in. On land as property, a means of social prestige and a place where one can earn money, or as a patrimony or a fatherland, see Józef Styk, *Ewolucja chłopskiego systemu wartości: Analiza historyczno-socjologiczna*, Lublin, 1988, pp.122–34.
15. However, some sociological researchers hold that not many young people admit that their standard of living is very low. For example, even though most young people are unable to save any of the money they earn, about 20 per cent of young farmers in Wielkopolska – the region bordering the one where Naramice is situated – think that they have low living standards, and about 40 per cent of young people in the countryside say that the situation is satisfactory. Dorota Budyta, 'Aktywność młodych mieszkańców wsi postrzegana przez pryzmat rodziny i społeczności wiejskiej', in Maria Wieruszewska (ed.), *Samoorganizacja w społecznościach wiejskich: przejawy, struktura*, Warsaw, 2002, pp.203–5.
16. The land registries from Naramice are kept in the Department of Land Registries of the local court in Wieluń. The other court and administrative offices for Naramice are also located in Wieluń.
17. As an official document, the *rejestry gruntowe* was initiated in 1955; see 'Dekret o ewidencji gruntów z 2 II 1955 r.', *Dz. U.* 6/32.
18. This was part of the Polish communist system, in which the state cared little for private property in comparison to public or collective property. See M. Szymański and A. Soczek, 'Ewidencja gruntów', in *Służba geodezyjna i kartograficzna Głównego Urzędu Geodezji i Kartografii 1945–1980*, Warsaw, 1980, pp.98–103; *Ewidencja gruntów*, Warsaw, 1982, p.77.
19. There is no information on the cadastre for the Naramice area (Wieluń district) in the state archives in Łódź or the archives of the Department of Land Registries of the local court in Wieluń. Cadastral work began only after the Second World War, and the gathered data was to be entered into land registers (*ewidencja gruntów*). On the twentieth-century cadastre in Poland and how it changed after the Second World War, see Michał Odlanicki Poczobutt, 'Kataster gruntowy i budynkowy: Ogólne informacje o katastrze', in Michał Odlanicki Poczobutt (ed.), *Rocznik Geodezyjny*, Warsaw, 1953, pp.554–57. On the differences between cadastres in three regions in Poland – the former Prussian district (Wielkopolska, Pomorze), the former Austrian district (Galicia) and the former Russian district (Kongresówka) – see Roman Kabat, 'Kataster: Co to jest?', *Nasza Wielkopolska*, 24 January 2001, pp.29–30, which confirms that no cadastre system existed in Kongresówka before the First World War.

10

Property and Agricultural Policy in Twentieth-Century Romania

Intentions, Technical Means and Social Realities

Cornel Micu

This chapter investigates the notions, institutions and practice of landownership as both a cultural idea and a social institution from 1917, when Romanian legislation first mentioned agrarian reform, to the 2000s. On a general level, I examine the possibility of modernizing a given society from above, exclusively through politics and with very general aims designed by policy makers. Attempting to go beyond the limits of a specific case study, I will explain the long-term evolution of landownership mainly in terms of economic, social and political factors, focusing less on the specific cultural traits of the local communities. Because the area examined contained enough land to distribute to both local peasants and incoming colonists, it makes for a case study that should be able to explain the positive and negative results of agricultural policy without having to account for land scarcity. Therefore this study not only represents the regional situation in Brăila county, but also contributes to the general discussion of modernization in rural areas.

With these purposes in mind, I analyse three distinct actors directly implicated in agricultural policy: national elites, who formulate general policy programmes mainly in the area of legislation; the administration, whose task it is to implement the elites' projects; and peasants, those affected directly by the implemented measures. Therefore I will address specific questions regarding each type of actor.

In the case of the elites, the main problem is to determine to what extent they really wanted rural areas to be modernized by means of programmes with long-term objectives, and to what extent their strategies were only intended to calm the discontented peasant masses and gain their political support by redistributing land. The ideological perspective on land reform is also relevant here. Were the elites able to formulate viable long-term solutions addressing the backwardness of rural areas, or did they mainly act to achieve short-term goals, such as pacifying discontented peasants or gaining their support for other political programmes?

The main problem facing the rural administration was its own development during the twentieth century. Both quantitative and qualitative data prove that, at least during the 1920s, civil servants were rather poorly trained.[1] So how did they carry out their tasks, especially at the sensitive village level, where they were in direct contact with local realities?

Finally, the peasants themselves are the most important subject of this chapter. The question here is to what extent they were willing to support the more or less idealistic modernization programmes of the elites, taking into account that socio-economic relations at the village level remained more or less pre-modern. To generalize this problem, it becomes meaningful to ask to what extent land distribution itself can catalyse the transformation of rural areas, or whether it needs to be accompanied by other measures to be effective.

The research is based on archival documents (especially for the interwar period), field interviews and data collected by means of a questionnaire to which ninety-six households responded. My historical sources were mostly documents from the archive of the Bordei Verde mayoralty. However, administrative reorganization over time necessitates occasional reference to reports from the mayoralties of the communes of Lişcoteanca, Filiu and Constantin Gabrielescu, to which Bordei Verde belonged at different times during the twentieth century. Most of the information was gathered through fifty-one interviews with different categories of informants. I interviewed a member of each generation in ten three-generation families for a total of thirty interviews, and separately interviewed elderly people, who are interesting from a historical perspective, and employees of state and private institutions relevant to the project.

Historical Overview

The area of what is now Brăila county was under Ottoman administration from the sixteenth century until 1829, a situation that affected the property structure in the nineteenth century. Since property rights were unclear, great areas of land were distributed to different autonomous establishments such as Eforia Spitalelor Civile, the foundation behind the hospital system in nineteenth-century Romania. At the county level in 1905, estates of more than 100 hectares held 73.2 per cent of the total arable land; those between 10 and 100 hectares, 0.7 per cent, and those with up to 10 hectares, 26.1 per cent.[2] The region's high ratio of large units can also be explained by its low population. In-migration spiked after 1829, and by the end of the century 67 per cent of its inhabitants were migrants, mostly from Transylvania.[3] In most cases they did not acquire land, which remained concentrated in large estates.

Ottoman domination had lent the area a certain strategic importance. Military maps of the area thus appeared earlier than those of the rest of the Old Kingdom (comprising Wallachia and Moldavia). The first was an Austrian map of 1789, followed by a Russian one in 1835 that was revised by 1853. The Romanian government, for its part, started its initial cartographic works in the late nineteenth century (1890 to 1900).[4] The slow progress of cartographic projects could explain why, as late as 1919, all three documented cases of expropriated estates in the examined area had no cadastral plans.

The Interwar Period

State and Elite Perspectives

The land reform at the end of the First Word War radically changed the property structure in Greater Romania. The 'agrarian problem' was hardly a recent phenomenon in Romanian society; land redistribution among peasants had first been attempted in 1864. However, land distribution was still a problem at the beginning of the twentieth century. In 1907 the deterioration of social conditions in the rural area culminated in a peasants' uprising whose violent quelling resulted in a high number of victims among the insurgents. Yet no clear initiative tackled this issue before 1917.[5]

At first glance, the year 1921 can be considered the date of the Romanian equivalent of Western Europe's first wave of land appropriation of the late eighteenth and early nineteenth centuries. This large, ambitious project sought to reorganize society through a project that regarded landownership as aiming at emancipation and individual freedom, and as triggering progress and development.[6] Indeed, since the peasantry comprised around 80 per cent of the population,[7] reform affected the entire society and, according to a political pamphlet of the National Liberal Party dated 1913, it was intended to vigorously spur the country's modernization. The land redistribution process was expected to increase overall agricultural production, ensure adequate living standards for peasants and transform them into economically independent owners, and thus responsible citizens and trustworthy soldiers. Former landowners were supposed to invest the money received in compensation for their land in the development of national industry, and the peasantry would become their customers.[8]

However, a closer look at the context in which the reform was enacted and implemented proves that it had little to do with the classical liberal concept of property. The first legislative text to address the problem was a constitutional amendment legalizing the expropriation of land for the purpose of its redistribution to peasants.[9] The law was promulgated in the summer of 1917, in the context of the First Word War, the Romanian defeats of 1916 by the Central Powers and the Russian Revolution, whose ideas were spreading among the peasantry, and who formed the backbone of the Romanian army.

Even under these circumstances, though, the legislative process was rather slow. Between 1918 and 1919, three laws on expropriation affecting the territory of the Old Kingdom were promulgated.[10] The most important was that of December 1918,[11] which regulated the administrative implementation of this action. It stipulated that compensation be paid for lost land, and defined two forms of expropriation: total and partial. Three categories of property were subject to total expropriation: the estates of foreigners (non-Romanian citizens), the estates of citizens living outside Romania (the so-called *absenteişti*) and the lands of legal persons, corporations and charitable associations. Privately owned lands were subject to partial expropriation based on a progressive scale, allowing the owner to keep a minimum of 100 hectares per estate. To carry out the process, it established three levels of control by local, county and regional commissions respectively. Expropriated and allocated land was to be paid for partly by the peasants and partly by the state, in instalments over a period of fifty years.

The Agrarian Reform Law of 1921 was the main legislative text regulating the land distribution process.[12] Indeed, it recapitulated the problem of expropriation, granting it a whole chapter and trying to allocate expropriated land among private owners. Other provisions aimed to regulate economic aspects of the process: owners who had invested in their land, had a degree in agronomy or had children who either held such a degree or were studying at a school of agronomy were entitled to keep a further 50 hectares. The expropriated land was used for establishing communal pasture and land redistribution. It would be allocated not only to peasants but also to certain institutions – schools, churches, mayoralties – as sites for village cultural centres and other such projects. The distribution order favoured veterans of the First Word War and, among them, veterans with war injuries. Next in line were war widows and orphans, landless peasants and finally the rest.

Actually, these provisions prove that the main reasons behind the reform were socio-political. Granting land primarily to people crippled during the war was not conducive to the establishment of economically viable households, a conclusion somewhat applicable to war widows and orphans as well, since Romanian agriculture in the 1920s used little or no machinery, and the physical work of farming, a critical element of rural life, was mainly the province of men. Further sale of the newly granted land (or any other form of land alienation) was strictly prohibited for a period of five years, under penalty of the seizure of the newly gained property. Land mortgaging was possible only at the 'popular banks' of the Central House of Land Distribution or other state institutions, which restricted peasants' ability to obtain agricultural loans.

Another important chapter of the law addressed the issue of colonization. The state offered colonists a settlement credit, to be paid back over a period of forty years, but they were obliged to settle no farther than 15 kilometres from the granted plots. The reasons for colonization were both economic and political. Agrarian reform led to land shortages in densely populated areas and labour shortages in under-populated areas. Some analysts indicate that 600,000 hectares of expropriated land remained uncultivated in the years just after the agrarian reform,[13] and population transfer seemed like a possible way to make such land productive. From a political viewpoint, colonization was a way of 'adjusting' the proportion of Romanians in newly acquired territories. For this reason, the state held the right of pre-emption over land sales throughout the interwar period, and wielded it especially in cases of transactions between ethnic non-Romanians.

The Process of Land Distribution in Brăila County

The low population density and concentration of land in the hands of great estates were key factors in land redistribution and the evolution of property in the examined area. Before the expropriation of 1918, most estates were owned by Eforia Spitalelor Civile. The inhabitants of Bordei Verde commune were now granted land on the 5,925 hectares of Bordei Verde estate,[14] and denizens of Filiu commune received plots on the Filiu estate, which previously belonged to the Eforia Spitalelor Civile, and which had an area of 3,100 hectares.[15] The only private estate expropriated in the area was the roughly 1,000 hectare Spiru M. Stilu estate near Lişcoteanca village (belonging to the commune of Filiu), around 600 hectares of which was expropriated.[16] In at least two of these well-documented expropriations, the estate had no cadastral plan, and the area was actually estimated, not measured.

Land distribution statistics prove that before 1921, the area owned by peasants was rather insignificant. According to the 1919 budget of the commune of Bordei Verde, 1,349 inhabitants (261 families) in the villages of Bordei Verde and 776 inhabitants (197 families) in Constantin Gabrielescu owned land.[17] Tables 10.1 and 10.2 summarize the numbers of people entitled to receive land in 1921.[18]

As the area of expropriated land was greater than that needed for land redistribution, the remainder was reserved for colonization. In the particular case of Bordei Verde, colonists came mostly from the neighbouring counties of Buzău and Vrancea, where land was in short supply. The colonists' situation in the village was not an easy one. Although officially the law granted them some financial aid to establish new households, this never materialized.[19] And it was documented that, at the county level, land granted to colonists was qualitatively inferior to that granted to locals.[20]

Table 10.1 Land recipients, Bordei Verde village, 1921

Inhabitants	Number	Owned land (ha)	Area of land required for distribution (ha)
Owners of plots measuring less than 5 ha	46	60	170
Landless peasants	274	–	1,370 (including the school plot)
Total	321		1,540

Source: Direcţia Judeţeană a Arhivelor Statului Brăila, Primaria Bordei Verde, file no. 1/1921: Tablou cu locuitorii ce deţin şi nu deţin pământ, p.40.

Table 10.2 Land recipients, Constantin Gabrielescu village, 1921

Inhabitants	Number	Owned land (ha)	Area of land required for distribution (ha)
Owners of plots measuring less than 5 ha	27	32	103
Landless peasants	144	–	720 (including the school plot)
Total	171		823

Source: Direcţia Judeţeană a Arhivelor Statului Brăila, Primaria Bordei Verde, file no. 1/1921: Tablou cu locuitorii ce deţin şi nu deţin pământ, p.40.

Aside from administrative problems, the colonists also had to deal with the hostility of the locals. A monograph on the commune attributes the conflict between the two groups to the allocation to colonists of plots previously used by locals.[21] However, according to interviews with the colonists' descendants, the problems tended instead to be culturally defined: 'Yes, the *cojans* [locals] were bearing us a grudge, because the *munteni* [colonists] came here, to live . . . They were richer. They had land here . . . here was their native village, it was their village . . . We came here as aliens, as they would say. We came from over there, here, to them'.[22] After the Second Word War, the Communist Party exploited this situation by using colonists as agents of the new regime, a practice that exacerbated tensions between the two communities. Friendly relations slowly developed between the groups as members of the two groups intermarried, and collectivization brought people together on the collective farm. However, certain distinctions were maintained even in the communist era, which opened with the creation of two collective farms – one for *cojani* and one for *munteni*. Only in the 1960s were the two farms united, and even then, different brigades of *cojani* and *munteni* continued to work separately: 'They had their brigadier, we had ours . . . They [the *munteni*] had their collective farm there in the beginning. And only afterwards, in time, did they unite with the *cojani*'.[23]

Local Administration and Land Registration

Before the reform the land was concentrated in large estates, most of whose owners were unaccustomed to land transactions. Cadastral maps were useful only when it came to land transactions, so owners were uninterested in measuring the land precisely.[24] When an estate was sold, it was sold as a whole, and the prospective buyer paid a price based on its productivity, location and other factors unrelated to its exact size. In the particular case of the examined region, boundary conflicts between different estate owners were rare because most of the land had the same owner (Eforia Spitalelor Civile). Even so, boundaries tended to be clearly delimited by roads or tree lines.[25]

The state was arguably the main actor interested in the registration and clear measurement of proprieties, because it collected taxes from the owners. In the early twentieth century, however, the state had not yet completed its cartographic mapping of the region, let alone cadastral mapping. Landowners' position in the political system before the First Word War was also an obstacle to land registration. Due to the census system, they were among the few able to directly vote and vie for political positions. These men wielded great power and influence; hence the local administration had difficulty controlling them. The Spiru M. Stilu estate in Lişcoteanca village, for example, had no cadastral plan, and its area – registered in different reports as comprising 1,000 hectares, 1,081.5 hectares and 1,076.5 hectares – was uncertain at the time of expropriation.[26]

This situation changed radically after agrarian reform. Suddenly the number of landowners exploded, creating problems at the administrative and judicial levels. Meanwhile, conflicts often arose between small owners, since clearly delimiting plots meant losing a significant percentage of land to the demarcation of the boundary. Furthermore, the skyrocketing number of owners rendered insufficient the number of professionals competent to handle land transactions, such as lawyers (private practitioners) and public notaries. The answer was to delegate the problem of land registration to the local administration via the agricultural registers of mayoralties, an idea that seemed realistic in theory but proved problematic in practice.

First of all, the local administration's professionalism was rather questionable. A decision by the prefecture of Brăila county on the qualifying examination for the position of public notary stipulated that actually providing a certificate of primary school education was not compulsory.[27] The 'professionals' in charge of land distribution and plot measurement were often similarly unprepared. The registration of plots distributed to peasants from the commune of Filiu, signed by the representative of the cadastral office, contains several elementary mistakes in calculation.[28]

Second, the bureaucracy lacked sufficient personnel. The centralized Romanian administration was (and still is) organized into different levels.

Those directly affecting the village are the mayoralty, represented by the civil servants it employs, and the level above it, consisting of professionals operating in districts encompassing several communes (or *plăşi* in the interwar period). According to the local budget for 1919, the clerks in the Bordei Verde mayoralty numbered six, with an extra chief gendarme; these served a population of 2,125 inhabitants.[29] One of the clerks acted simultaneously as postal agent and telephone operator, and was also responsible for public announcements. In 1947, nine clerks (including the priest and the schoolteacher) were registered to serve the 668 denizens of Filiu commune.[30]

National-level statistics show that this was a normal situation during the interwar period, as in 1948 only 0.5 per cent of the rural population worked in public administration.[31] Normally, the small number of office workers would not have been problematic, given the existence of an infrastructure of liberal professionals such as private notaries and lawyers. But the liberal professions were also underrepresented, at least at the village level, as proven by communal statistics from 1919 that list only five tavern owners under this category.[32] Seen in comparison, by 1948 the percentage of the population working in the sector of public administration and the liberal professions had reached 4.3 per cent in Romania, whereas it had amounted to 10.1 per cent in Germany in 1939.[33]

Third, most civil servants were recruited from the important families that made up the local elite, who wished both to keep their position as state representatives and to preserve good relations with the peasantry. For instance, in 1919 the mayor of the village was Milea Manta; a different Manta owned a local tavern,[34] and, according to an interviewee, in the later 1940s another Manta was one of the local leaders of the Ploughmen's Front (Frontul Plugarilor), a political organization that worked closely with the Communist Party: 'And those joined the Ploughmen's Front, here all those who were rich, the kulaks, these, the priests, the schoolteachers, who had land, because they were natives from here. And as mayor we had someone who was the son of Ion Manta, a great tavern keeper here, he had land, he had around 50 hectares of land'.[35] Another example is the Motoc family, which provided a village mayor in the late nineteenth century, a series of candidates for the status of kulak in the 1950s and a chief of police in the neighbouring town of Ianca and later in the county capital Brăila in the 1980s and 1990s.

Administrative powers were limited at the village level since they were, in theory, subject to the control of the central administration through the institution of the county prefect, a government appointee. Yet local public servants had some power when it came to applying state decisions because, given all the problems of registration and documentation, they were the only ones who knew what was actually happening in the village. The modernization of a society implies growing economic and cultural differentiation, and in backward societies, creating this differentiation is the task of the state or of the controlling elites.[36] From this point of view, the task of the local bureaucracy or administration was not to keep records, but rather to create them by including the peasantry in different categories, such as, in the case of agrarian reform, landless peasants, war veterans or war widows. Creating the records gave the individuals in charge more power than just simply keeping them. Local clerks tended to use the administrative chaos to their own advantage, and consequently had little interest in ending it.

Land Transactions as Part of Village Social Relations

The state's economic policy also influenced people's willingness to register land. The National Liberal Party, which governed for more than half of the interwar era, supported the idea of industrialization, but at the same time it did everything possible to prevent the penetration of foreign capital in Romania. In the long run, rural areas became the only suitable source of capital, a situation that continued unchanged throughout the communist era. Under these circumstances, not registering one's property allowed one to avoid being excessively taxed.

However, state policy deserves only half the blame for the deficient level of property registration. As my interviews show, other factors hindered the registration process as well. The general economic situation, and specifically price fluctuations on the agricultural markets, restricted the area of land that peasants were willing to work. The majority of my interviewees said the land they had was enough, and they were unwilling to buy more because the expense of working an additional area exceeded their capacities. Even today, as my field questionnaire reveals, landowners tend to invest money from other sources in agriculture, and to consume the products obtained rather than sell them. Only 27 out of 96 respondents mentioned agriculture as their primary source of income. The overwhelming majority earned more from pensions (45), wages (18) or other sources (6).

Similar conditions prevailed in the interwar period, especially after agricultural prices began to plummet in 1928. One interviewee told me that his father had bought just enough land to allow his children to inherit 3.5 hectares each.[37] More land meant more paid labourers, and hence more risk. Of course, a certain amount of the harvest was sold, since to some extent the peasants used money, either to buy products they were unable or unwilling to produce themselves (sugar, textiles, alcohol and so on) or to pay taxes, but to quote one interviewee: 'The taxes were not so high, but money was expensive back then'.[38]

Another factor limiting land transactions was a general tendency not to sell land: 'I don't sell it [the land] because I have children ... How could I sell it? How should they [the children] live? They also have children! They are young!'[39] Such an explanation was typical throughout the interviews. In quantitative terms, the field questionnaire showed that out of 93 respondents, 61 were opposed to land transactions. Of these, 28 saw the land as their children's inheritance, and another 19 as their sole source of survival. Viewing the land as a source of survival is quite logical, taking into account the fact that finding a job and a wage was and still is very difficult in rural areas. The best decision under these circumstances might be to migrate to the cities, but this implies both a certain youth (by the age of fifty or so, people would rather stay in the village than move to the city) and the availability of work in urban areas, which is closely linked to the lacklustre industrialization rate, a problem solved only briefly, by the communist regime in the 1950s and 1960s.

More interesting is the specific idea of 'inheritance'. The key to explaining this is the lack of a viable social insurance system until the second half of the twentieth century. At the state level, the first pension system developed in the communist era, but after 1989 it collapsed due to the general inflation that followed. In these circumstances, the only element of 'social security', especially for old or disabled people, remained the community and the family.

To a certain extent, community support was, and still is, non-existent. Villages have no homes for the disabled or the poor, and even in cities only a small percentage of the local budget goes towards maintaining such establishments. Inter-generational relations were based on splitting land among inheritors, especially at the moment of marriage. According to some of interviewees, land was a girl's most important asset when it came to marriage:

> The land itself was highly desired. Indeed. Because when I was around seventeen or eighteen I had no land, I had nothing and the boys were telling me: 'You, M., why don't you have at least one *pogon* [half a hectare] of land? Because I would like to marry you, I would . . . but since you don't have![40]

This was a way of ensuring some economic stability for the young married couple, which had no prospects of a livelihood other than working the land. But this situation also provided social security for the parents, since children were supposed to take care of them when they grew old. Neither party to this arrangement had any interest in registering the land. The parents were best served by keeping the land in their names as insurance that the children would keep their promise of caring for them. The children tended to see family relations as more important than those with the state: the family could provide support in emergencies, whereas the state was no more than a tax collector.

On top of this was the problematic notion of property as defined by the Agrarian Reform Law. The peasantry had no right to transactions – that is, sale or donation of the land – for a period of five years. Interestingly, at least in the case of the Gabrielescu village, the ban on land transactions was announced directly to the peasantry without any mention of the five-year limit in 1924. Upon the conclusion of agrarian reform in the village, the agronomist in charge of land redistribution informed the peasants: 'The agrarian law, under the punishment of dispossession, prevents the person who was granted land to alienate his plot, either by selling or by donating it'.[41]

The interdiction on land transactions led to a situation in which neither of the parties directly involved in them – the state and the peasantry – was eager to formalize marriage-related land transactions. For the state, this was in theory a way of alienating the land plots, but at the local administrative level the problem was well known, and no mayor would risk his position in the community by attempting to prohibit such transactions. In fact, some of them were registered at the mayoralty as a way of proving who had to actually pay the land taxes.

The Communist Period

The Agrarian Reform of 1945

Continuous population growth and the slow pace of industrialization in the interwar period led the land problem to resurface within a generation.[42] Like its predecessor, the reform of 1945 was an attempt to gain the peasantry's political support. However, there is an important difference between the two actions: whereas the agrarian reform of 1918 to 1921 aimed to eliminate the revolutionary potential of the peasants, the 1945 reform was intended to mobilize it.

For that reason, the legislative basis of the 1945 reform consists of a single law addressing both expropriation and land distribution, and regulating their implementation.[43] It stipulated that private estates were to be expropriated up to a limit of 50 hectares, with the exception of those defined as 'model farms'. Owners who were leasing their estate or fell into the category of 'Nazi collaborator' were to be fully expropriated. An interesting distinction from the interwar laws was that the expropriation of agricultural inventory was proportional to the expropriated area. The law was vague on the subject of land redistribution: it did not establish a standard plot area but instead left the dimensions of this unit to the discretion of local committees and regional commissions. Prioritized recipients included veterans of the western campaign during the Second Word War, landless peasants and peasants with less than 5 hectares. The land granted was to be paid for over a period of ten to twenty years, at a price equivalent to 1 tonne of wheat or 1.2 tonnes of maize per year per hectare.

However, unlike in 1921, there was not much land to redistribute. In the commune of Bordei Verde, 240 persons obtained land totalling only 309.5 hectares.[44] This was because there was so little to expropriate: only two estates, of 100 and 244.5 hectares each.[45] My interviews prove that splitting property among children, sometimes even before they married, nullified the validity of land registers and entitled everybody to receive land. Not only peasants but also estate owners had recourse to this strategy of dividing property among family members in an attempt to keep more land. This was the case for the Concăl family (which had an estate in Lişcoteanca village), three members of which asked the mayoralty in 1945 to exempt them from expropriation of tracts of 10, 50 and 30 hectares respectively, as this land had been inherited from the previous estate owner.[46]

Meanwhile, the chaos again profited those in charge of land distribution. A striking example would be the head of the communal land-granting committee and village mayor of Lişcoteanca, Chiriţă Costin, who was granted 4 hectares, although allocations in the village averaged 3 hectares. He was, in fact, one of only two persons who received 4 hectares of land in the village, the second being someone with the same family name: Petre Costin.[47]

The agrarian reform intensified the chaos of the land registering process, but only when it came to private land. National-level data show that a considerable share of the land entered into state possession and became the nucleus of the future collective state farms. From the total expropriation of 1,468,946 hectares, 450,000 hectares remained state property.[48] Later on, in 1948, Crown domains and Church lands that had not been subject to the 1945 land expropriation also became state property. Finally, on 1 March 1949, the remaining estates were definitively expropriated, further augmenting the state's total landholdings. The state also took control of the expropriated agricultural inventory, which was to form the core of the agricultural machine stations (*Staţiune de Maşini Agricole*). Ostensibly created to provide small households with cheap technology, they proved really valuable later, during collectivization. Since the new collective farms had priority access to their services and technology, the stations quickly turned into efficient propaganda tools.

Collectivization

Starting in 1949, the collectivization of agriculture solved the land registration problem – at least theoretically. To avoid joining the collective farms, peasants used the same strategy of not declaring all their land. Dividing the land between inheritors or not declaring it could also keep a landowner from being categorized as a kulak (peasant proprietor). But these tactics proved of no use in the thoroughgoing collectivization process that swept the area examined. All the villagers were included in the collective farms, and the remaining land, officially considered unused, was taken over by the state farms.

At the legal level, collectivization also meant the development of new legal definitions of property. The three constitutions promulgated between 1948 and 1989 (of 1948, 1952 and 1965) marked the gradually increasing importance of socialist property. While the 1948 Constitution was the legal instrument that suppressed the inviolability of private property,[49] thus paving the way for state control of the economy, the 1952 Constitution defined collective property for the first time and emphasized the state's role in supporting it.[50] Finally, the Constitution of 1965 openly defined socialist property and its two forms, state and collective, as the basis of the economy, with private landownership considered acceptable solely in regions where collectivization was not possible.[51]

However, a legal problem appeared when it came to defining collective farms. Initially, a distinction was drawn between 'collective agricultural farmsteads' (*Gospodării Agricole Colective*) and other types of associations for working the land. In the former case, the land was legally defined as collective property, whereas in the latter the members retained their private property rights but worked the land together. The compromise solution came in September 1956 with the publication of a model statute of a third type of association, the 'agricultural production cooperative' (*Cooperativă Agricolă de Producţie*). In this new legal form of organization, the peasants were still the landowners, but their property rights were reduced to merely possessing the land, whereas all disposal rights shifted to the collective farm. The basic nature of these property rights made it possible to turn associations for working the land into production cooperatives, which eventually, via the 1965 Constitution, became the only legally recognized type of collective farm.[52]

The Struggle to Control Collective Farms

Whatever the legal definition of property, Communist Party control over the collectivization process remained problematic. Whereas the existence of two collective farms in Bordei Verde – one for the locals and another for the colonists – was easily explicable, one interviewee mentioned attempts to establish a third one: 'And then came someone from the regional administration, from the party, from wherever he came, and we formed another collective farm, a third one . . . There were already two collective farms; we were setting up the third one!'[53] This statement seems to indicate that, at some point, competition between different party representatives in the village, each with its own group of adherents, resulted in the founding of more collective farms in one village.

State efforts to control the collective farms continued, even after collectivization had ended. Beginning in 1965, they were grouped into the National Assembly of Agricultural Production Cooperatives,[54] and the Communist Party's policy at the time seems to have been to reduce their number as much as possible by uniting many of them. In 1989, the Bordei Verde commune had only two collective farms: one in Bordei Verde, for the villages of Bordei Verde and Constantin Gabrielescu, and one in Lişcoteanca.

At the social level, collectivization did not lead to the achievement of egalitarianism. It was backed, at least in the early stages, by an ideological programme emphasizing class struggle through the mobilization of poor peasants against rich kulaks (*chiaburi* in Romanian). However, the regime preferred a more realistic approach based on a 'minimum usage of symbolic violence'.[55] According to the local monograph of the examined area, five people were arrested in Bordei Verde during the collectivization period. Two of them returned home after spending around a year in prison, but the other three died in detention.[56] To be sure, not all of the kulaks were arrested. The category 'kulak' itself generally proved to be quite vague, since some people were placed in it only to be withdrawn later, usually with the help of a combination of bribery, nepotism and personal relations. The economic pressures manifested through the so-called quotas played a more important role than repression: 'Quotas! Compulsory quotas! As time was passing by, oh another series came, and then another, until . . . And this is how the situation was. Back then it was the milk quota, the cereals quota, the meat quota. You gave . . . for everything'.[57]

Meanwhile, the Communist Party's control over the whole process remained inefficient, at least in the initial stages. In some cases, former clerks and members of the local elite worked willingly with the party, trying to maximize the effects of collectivization in their favour: 'My father told me that, when the communists came, there was someone here in the village, one named Niţă Butuc, who had a shop, and he used to say that since that time he was always with the sickle and the hammer'.[58] In other cases, the party tried to instrumentalize poor men from the villages or from different subordinate groups (such as the colonists), an approach that proved questionable at the least, since a person's educational level was usually directly proportional to family wealth and social position: 'We had [as mayor] a boy from here, from the village [Vintileşti, the part of the village where colonists lived] . . . one with four years of school. An uneducated one, one of us . . . He stayed for a year and then came [another] one from among the workers'.[59] In the end, when it came to administration of the collective farms, the local elite, thanks to the knowledge and social relations it had developed in the area, proved more reliable than the poor peasants.

Changes in Social Relations

An important change during the communist era concerned social relations. Under the pressure of urban migration, the idea of children taking care of their parents in their old age lost its basis. The delocalization of family members led many to question the traditional notion of family insurance. The new wage and pension systems also contributed to this process. In certain respects, the collective farm tended to take over the role of the family by providing the elderly with special assignments that they were able to carry out: 'The third brigade was with *diribau*, this was how it was named, because they were older. They don't . . . They were working only there, in the collective farm [i.e., easier work in the village, not in the fields]'.[60]

Some progress was also made in terms of inserting peasants into the market, as it seems to have been state policy to turn peasants into 'consumers'. The collective farms paid workers partly in products and partly in money, which was, of course, to be spent at a market, usually one representing the local stores, or 'cooperatives'. The general idea of progress emphasized by communist ideology also contributed to this process. Rural electrification, for example, a core policy of the communist regime, also meant that people would have to pay for the new services provided.

State control over the collective farms remained a delicate problem, since peasants had the right to choose their leaders at the collective farm's general assembly. However, state control over the means of production through machine and tractor stations, its monopoly position as both customer of and provider to the collective farms, and strict price controls nullified any form of collective property rights for the peasants. A more subtle form of control was based on the communist system's characteristic mixture of politics and administration. Officially, the president of the collective farm was elected by the general assembly of the collective, but often only a single candidate, approved by the regional party organization, stood for office: 'No, he [the president] was not elected by the people – let's be serious. He was not . . . He was coming . . . It was established . . . When I gave up the post of president, for two months I took candidates to the County Party Committee, for interviews'.[61]

The Post-communist Period

The Legislative Basis of De-collectivization

After the communist regime collapsed, property rights were restored, at least in theory. The process was rather inevitable, as in many cases peasants took the initiative to divide the assets of the collective farms. The first decree addressing this problem, enacted in January 1990,[62] gave peasants from collective farms the right to lease and work a plot of a maximum 0.5 hectares. However, the basic legislative text regulating the process was Law 18/1991, which dissolved the collective farms and restored property rights up to a limit of 10 hectares for every owner who had brought land into the cooperative.[63] The heirs of deceased owners would together receive no more than 10 hectares, which they were to divide among themselves. The eventual surplus of land was to be distributed to landless peasants who had worked on the collective farms, to young married couples or to anyone at hand. As in 1921 and 1945, alienation of the granted land was forbidden, this time for ten years. The state farms remained in place, and the former landowners became shareholders in them. A law of 1997 extended the reconstitution of property rights to up to 50 hectares of land.[64] This generated a new wave of property restoration requests that have prolonged the retrocession of land property to this day. However, because surplus land was distributed among landless peasants and former workers on the collective farms in 1991, by 1997 little remained to be distributed. The legal solution was to compensate owners for their lost land, but some of my interviewees were still waiting for this compensation in 2007.

The Problematic Process of Property Restoration

The difficult process of restitution lasted until the end of the 1990s, and the delay complicated it even further. To some extent, the registers for 1945 were of little use, but by turning to village elders who were able to remember who used to own how much land, and using the land register for corroboration, the local administration established some control over the restoration of property rights. This time the chaos in the land registers was, at least in this region of low population density, to the peasants' advantage. Such transactions as dowries were not registered, so some of them could claim all the land of their parents and, separately, the land that they had received upon marrying.[65]

Land distribution complicated matters even further. The unclaimed land in the area was sufficient for use as a source of political capital, and the local bureaucracy took its share of it. The field questionnaires registered two persons with the family name 'X'. One was mayor between 1996 and 2000. Living in Gabrielescu, he was granted 3 hectares, and today he owns a total area of 9.5 hectares.[66] Of the twenty-four people questioned in Gabrielescu, he tops the quantitative list of land redistributions. The other member of this family, from Bordei Verde, also received 3 hectares – the largest area granted, the next largest having gone to three persons who each received 1.5 hectares. Here it is worth mentioning that he had only 1 hectare of land prior to the land distribution process. This was possible because, according to the law, the area of the land grant depended on the period in which the recipient had worked in the collective farm. Meanwhile, the location of the documents that prove this is uncertain. Some interviewees in Bordei Verde told me that the collective farm's archive, where the records were kept, was deliberately burned by a former accountant. According to the mayor, the archive was only partially lost in uncertain circumstances.

The 1990s were a transitional period in which no property titles existed. People knew how much land they had, but not exactly where it was. Throughout this period, the land was worked by different types of associations formed according to Law 36/1991.[67] My interviews generally confirm that the new association leaders had been important figures on the former collective farms. In the case of Lişcoteanca village, for example, the leaders of the three agricultural associations formed immediately after the law's promulgation were none other than the former collective farm's accountant, agronomist and warehouse keeper. In Bordei Verde, apparently the mayor instructed people who had held different positions in the collective farm administration to take the lead in the new associations: 'It was difficult. At the beginning it was difficult. This is why Mr B. [the mayor from 1990 to 1996] told us: "You, you take over [the leadership], the ones who have been in the collective farms, you have experience"'.[68]

My interlocutors often emphasized the expertise of the specialists, but their 'know-how' should be considered with great caution. Of the two agronomists I spoke with, only one claimed to have taken courses in management (of socialist enterprises, of course) during his university studies. The other specialized strictly in growing fruit trees. However, they and the other collective farm staff had developed a network of personal relations with members of the state bureaucracy. These relations were important because the Land Fund Law of 1991 gave the land to the peasants and leased the agricultural inventory to its old owners, that is, the state farms and agricultural machine stations. Creation of certain specific structures, such as rural credit programmes or private enterprises engaged mainly with the inputs and outputs of agricultural production, was delayed.[69] Under these circumstances, the association leaders' role was to negotiate better agricultural conditions with the state, and in this endeavour the network of personal relations was crucial.

Adjusting Local Social Relations to New Realities

The agricultural associations did not last long. Conflicts between the membership and leadership, the impossibility of establishing clear labour contracts and dependency on the state contributed to their disintegration. But perhaps most important were changes in legislation. The Leasing Law of 1994 regulated agricultural contracts, and many association chiefs turned into landlords.[70] In 1998, another legislative text regulated land transactions, opening the possibility of creating larger, economically more viable farms.[71] In at least one registered interview, the speaker admitted buying land in the early 1990s, when such a purchase was theoretically unregulated by any law. The transaction was apparently made legal when the seller, a former police officer, used his connections to smooth things out:

> I bought [the land] from a colonel, who was from here, from the village; he retired, he sold . . . But we found this lawyer, she didn't know he was a police colonel, he was dressed as a civilian, and she began to ask questions . . . With whom did he speak in Bucharest? – because she did the papers on the spot, she said nothing more. He just phoned once![72]

Finally, a law of 2000 reconstituted property rights to the land included in the state farms,[73] and in 2005 legislation was passed permitting the sale of land to foreigners.[74]

Nowadays, according to the field questionnaires, younger people tend to work the land on their own, whereas older owners tend to lease it or have it worked by the associations. The average age of all questioned persons was 54, and the average age of a land tenant was 53; the average age of persons leasing their land to others was 62 (far above the average); the average age of those with mixed property (partly self-worked, partly worked by tenants) was 57; and of people farming on their own, 53. The type of lease may differ from case to case – based on the evidence of the field questionnaires, official contracts are not the rule. Out of 43 persons not farming on their own (partially or totally), 29 admitted having no legal contract. At the same time, the market insertion of households is still problematic. As mentioned above, the situation is better than in the interwar period, when goods were seldom bought on the market. And modern technology has become commonplace, especially when it comes to agriculture.[75] Of the 96 persons questioned, 43 spent money mainly on technology, and 19 on both human labour and technology.

When asked what kind of property rights they had, 37 persons admitted having titles for which the partition between the inheritors had not been carried out. Formal land transactions, at least among peasants, seem to be rare. Only 6 respondents said they owned certificates of land purchase or sale. The interviews indicate that efforts to regulate property rights have been rather inefficient. The fees for issuing the documents play an important role here: 'I bought 0.2 hectares, and only the paperwork cost me 4 million Lei and something . . . I bought it at 16 million per hectare, so 0.2 hectares cost me, let's say 3 million. So I paid 3 million to the owner and 5 million to the notary'.[76] Nevertheless, in many cases the respondents admitted they were uninterested in proper property registration and had no idea of the costs.

The European Union as a New Actor in the Process

The interviews show that, in the last few years at least, the situation has tended towards change due to two main factors. Firstly, a 1997 law on the sale of land plots enabled the emergence of a land market, and thus called attention to the problem of ownership documents, as land brokers are unwilling to buy or sell land that lacks clear property status. The second factor is the European integration process, which has had a rather strange effect.

Generally, attempts to reform Romanian agriculture during the pre-accession period were fairly ineffective. State institutions adjusted slowly to the new context, and the Special Accession Programme for Agriculture and Rural Development (SAPARD) was under-advertised, bureaucratically complicated and financially accessible to only a small percentage of peasants. Private consultancy firms noticed this new market opportunity too late and failed to take over the role of state institutions in offering expertise to eventual SAPARD project candidates: 'At this moment there are so many projects on the Romanian market to be done, that there are not enough specialized consultants'.[77]

However, EU integration has acted as something of a guarantee that the development path Romania chose was the right one. Foreign land investors were the first to seize the opportunity, and their capital, together with the 1998 law as a framework for land transactions, rapidly boosted the value of land. After several years, people realized that although a hectare of land would fetch a good price on the market, it was almost impossible to sell it without proper documentation of ownership. In at least three of the ten families studied, heirs have engaged in disputes over the area of land they are entitled to. This development has thus put an end to the peaceful coexistence of several heirs on the same land.

Finally, since the 2007 integration, direct subsidies have also influenced people's view of property registration. For the first time, declaring possession seems a good idea, now that one can profit by doing so. The same holds true for land, especially affecting the practice of leasing it without papers. Since the person working it is entitled to receive the subsidy it is in their interest to obtain the necessary papers to prove the identity of the lessee. Overall, this is perhaps the first time in history that it pays for Romanian peasants to unambiguously declare and register their property. The main reasons for doing so lie in state (or in this case, European) policy and economic gain.

Conclusion

Several factors contributed to the slow development of modern landowning practices in twentieth-century Romania. Historically, the modern notion of property appeared in Western European societies in the eighteenth century, in a specific socio-economic context. The expansion of capitalism led to the generalization of economic transactions between individuals, and under these circumstances documents proving property rights backed by the state functioned as insurance that the object of transaction was not subject to third-party rights.

The different socio-economic conditions in interwar Romania were unsuited to development of the modern notion of property, which anyway lost any sense under the communist regime, when the state consolidated its control over the economy. However, the social changes that took place in the communist period, together with the redefinition of the concept of property after 1989 and the influence of the European Union in the 2000s, are a foundation for the eventual development of a property concept very close to the 'modern' one.

Linking these conclusions with this chapter's initial hypotheses, I suggest that modernizing rural areas from above – that is, exclusively through land expropriation and redistribution – was actually the wrong answer to the Romanian rural question. The shortfalls of this approach become visible at the point of intersection between the general political reform programmes, the administration's inefficient implementation of them and the social context of Romanian villages. Changes in attitudes towards property since 1989 are due less to the Romanian state or the new actor, the European Union, than to the social transformations that took place in villages during the communist period and to foreign investors' direct involvement as agents of modernization.

Notes

This chapter summarizes the results of six months of fieldwork at the Bordei Verde commune, Brăila county, rural eastern Romania. The research took place over two periods: August–September 2006 and March–June 2007. The research was conducted as part of the project 'Land Law, Cadastre and Land Registers in Eastern Europe, 1918–1945–1989: Poland, Romania and Yugoslavia in Comparison', financed by Volkswagen Stiftung and partially through a PhD grant from the University of Jena (Graduate College 1412).

1. Romania's first civil service statute was not introduced until 1923. This initial legislative text established the compulsory examination of candidates for civil service and a minimum educational requirement of a high school certificate. However, art. 122 specified that if no high school graduates were available in the area, persons with a primary school certificate could hold office, a situation that seems to have been normal in rural areas. For the text of the statute, see George Alexianu, *Statutul Funcţionarilor Publici (Lege şi Regulament) din 19 iulie 1923 cu toate legile modificatoare (1923–1937), adnotat cu jurisprudenţă, Ediţia a III-a*, Bucharest, n.d.
2. Data from Victor Axenciuc, *Evoluţia economică a României: cercetări statistico-istorice; 1859–1947*, vol. 2, Bucharest, 1996, pp.126f.
3. Gheorghe Mihăilescu, 'Note asupra populaţiei şi satelor din Câmpia Brăilei', *Analele Brăilei* 2–3 (1932), p.89.
4. Ibid., p.87.
5. Philip Gabriel Eidelberg, *The Great Romanian Peasant Revolt of 1907: The Origins of a Modern Jacquerie*, Leiden, 1974.
6. See the introduction to this volume.
7. Actually, 87.7 per cent according to the 1912 census, and 78.9 per cent according to that of 1930. Data from Ion Alexandrescu, Ion Bulei, Ion Mamina and Ioan Scurtu, *Enciclopedia de istorie a României*, Bucharest, 2000.
8. Vintilă I. Brătianu, *Foloasele exproprierii*, Bucharest, 1914.
9. 'Lege pentru introducere in Constituţie a exproprierii proprietătii rurale pentru împroprietărirea sătenilor, 20 July 1917', *Monitorul Oficial* [hereafter M. O.] 93, pp.947f.
10. Romania gained new provinces after the First Word War. Specific laws for expropriation and land distribution were passed for each of them. However, since the examined area is situated in the Old Kingdom, only legislative texts applicable to this region are cited in this chapter.
11. 'Decret-lege pentru executarea exproprierii, 16 December 1918', M.O. 215, pp.3845–49.
12. 'Lege pentru reforma agrară din Oltenia, Muntenia, Moldova şi Dobrogea, 17 July 1921', M.O. 82, pp.3054–76.
13. Constantin Garoflid, 'Regimul Agrar în România', in *Enciclopedia României*, vol. 1, Bucharest, 1938–1943, p.581.
14. Direcţia Judeţeană a Arhivelor Statului Brăila [hereafter DJASB], Comisia Judeţeană de Expropriere şi Improprietărire a Judeţului Brăila [hereafter CE], file no. 1/1922: Dosar de împroprietărire în comuna Constantin Gabrielescu, p.29.

15. DJASB/CE, file no. 35/1919: Exproprierea moşiei Filiu, proprietatea Eforiei Spitalelor Civile, p.1.
16. DJASB/CE, file no. 34/1919: Dosar de expropriere a moşiei Spiru M. Stilu, comuna Filiu, Lişcoteanca, p.5 (the data are approximate; different expropriation reports indicate different land areas with discrepancies of up to 81.5 hectares).
17. DJASB, Primăria Bordei Verde [hereafter PBV], file no. 1/1919: Bugetul Ordinar al Primăriei, p.34.
18. DJASB/PBV, file no. 1/1921: Tablou cu locuitorii ce deţin şi nu deţin pământ, p.40. Interpreters of these data should take into account that the land was granted only to the adult, male population – in most cases, either heads of families or young, unmarried men. The standard for measuring the extent of the land distribution process is in this case families rather than individuals. Another element proving the scarcity of peasants' land is the ratio of owned land to people, which in both cases was less than 1.5 hectares per person.
19. Maria Puia, *Viaţa agrară a judeţului Brăila în perioada interbelică*, Brăila, 1995, pp.42f.
20. Colonization records for the nearby commune of Batogu reveal that one of the colonists received 5 hectares of land in two plots of 2.5 hectares, one of which was uncultivable, and the other flooded. Arhivele Naţionale ale României, Oficiul Naţional al Colonizării [hereafter ANIC], vol. 2, Judeţul Brăila, comunele Bordei Verde şi Batogu, file 90/1932: Toader D. Neculai, comuna Batogu, p.19. Actually, it seems that whereas land grants to colonists were common, at least 2.5 hectares of the granted area was unproductive land. See also ibid., file 50/1931.
21. Ion Bănică, *Monografia comunei Bordei Verde, Judeţul Brăila*, n.p., n.d., p.87.
22. J.I. (b. 1929), a man from Bordei Verde and a descendant of colonists.
23. F.M. (b. 1941), a local woman from Bordei Verde and pat of a three-generation household.
24. According to the Brăila County Land Board (Direcţia Funciară), a total of nine estates were either sold or exchanged between 1924 and 1926: ANIC, Ministerul Agriculturii şi Domeniilor, Direcţia Funciară Brăila, dossier 190/1924, p.4, and 287/1926, p.1.
25. The expropriation documents for the Filiu estate, property of Eforia Spitalelor Civile, mention compensation for eighty-four poplar and acacia trees. DJASB/CE, file no. 35/1919: Exproprierea moşiei Filiu, proprietatea Eforie Spitalelor Civile, p.7.
26. DJASB/CE, file no. 34/1919: Dosar de expropriere a moşiei Spiru M. Stilu, comuna Filiu, Lişcoteanca, pp.1, 3.
27. DJASB/PBV, file no. 2/1920: Decizie a Prefecturii Judeţului Brăila, Serviciul Administrativ, privind examenul de notar din februarie 1920, p.207.
28. DJASB/CE, file no. 8/1920: Memoriu descriptiv privind parcelarea cadastrală în comuna Filiu, pp.147, 149.
29. DJASB/PBV, file no. 1/1919: Bugetul General al Administraţiei Comunei Bordei Verde, p.80.
30. DJASB, Primăria Filiu, file no. 9/1944,1947: Chestionar despre viaţa sătească, p.86.
31. Axenciuc, *Evoluţia economică a României*, p.40.
32. DJASB/PBV, file no. 1/1919: Tabel cu profesioniştii şi comercianţii din comună, p.71.
33. Axenciuc, *Evoluţia economică a României*, p.42.
34. DJASB/PBV, file no. 1/1919: Tabel cu profesioniştii şi comercianţii din comună, p.71.
35. D.G. (b. 1918), a male colonist from Bordei Verde and member of a three-generation household.
36. Holm Sundhaussen, 'Wandel ohne Modernisierung: Theorien nachholender Entwicklung unter besonderer Berücksichtigung Südosteuropas', in Krista Zach and Cornelius R. Zach (eds), *Modernisierung auf Raten in Rumänien: Anspruch, Wirkung*, Munich, 2004, pp.28f. On the state as an agent of identification and categorization, see Rogers Brubaker, *Ethnicity without Groups*, Cambridge, MA, 2004, pp.42f.
37. A.M. (b. 1923), an elderly man from Lişcoteanca.
38. D.G. (b. 1918), an elderly male colonist from Bordei Verde, and member of a three-generation household.

39. B.F. (b. 1942), a woman from Constantin Gabrielescu, and member of a three-generation household.
40. Z.M. (b. 1925), a local woman from Bordei Verde, and member of a three-generation household.
41. DJASB/CE, file no. 1/1922, Dosar de împroprietărire în comuna Constantin Gabrielescu: Proces verbal de punere în posesie, p.51.
42. The annual growth rate of the rural population in the interwar period was approximately 1.5 per cent. Anton Golopenţia and D.C. Georgescu, *60 sate româneşti cercetate de echipele studenţeşti în vara 1938*, Bucharest, 1941, vol. 1, p.94.
43. 'Lege nr. 187 din 23 martie 1945 pentru înfăptuirea reformei agrare, 23 May 1945', M.O. 68, pp.2205–8.
44. DJASB/PBV, file no. 15/1945, 'Proces verbal de definitivare a reformei agrare', p.65.
45. Ibid., p.38.
46. DJASB, Primăria comunei Lişcoteanca [hereafter PCL], file no. 7/1945, 'Cereri de exceptare de la expropriere', pp.41, 43, 45.
47. DJASB/PCL, file no. 7/1945, 'Lista definitivă a împroprietăriţilor and Proces Verbal de încheiere a lucrărilor de împroprietărire', pp.12–17.
48. Costin Scorpan, *Istoria României, Enciclopedie*, Iaşi, 1997, p.515.
49. Eleodor Focşăneanu, *Istoria constituţională a României (1859–1991)*, Bucharest, 1998, p.117.
50. Angela Banciu, *Istoria vieţii constituţionale în România (1866–1991)*, Bucharest, 1996, p.224.
51. Constituţia Republicii Socialiste România din 1965 (republicată). Retrievable from: www.constitutia.ro/const1965.htm.
52. Linda Miller, 'Drept şi propagandă: posesia asupra terenurilor agricole, colectivizarea şi proprietatea socialistă', in Dorin Dobrincu and Constantin Iordachi (eds), *Ţărănimea şi puterea: Procesul de colectivizare a agriculturii în România (1949–1962)*, Iaşi, 2005, pp.69, 144f.
53. J.I. (b. 1929), a male colonist from Bordei Verde, and member of a three-generation household.
54. Uniunea Cooperativelor Agricole de Producţie din R.S.R., *Statutul Uniunilor Cooperativelor Agricole de Producţie din Republica Socialistă România*, Bucharest, 1972.
55. Katherine Verdery, *Transylvanian Villagers: Three Centuries of Political, Economic and Ethnic Change*, Berkeley, 1983, p.39.
56. Bănică, *Monografia comunei Bordei Verde, Judeţul Brăila*, pp.122f.
57. D.G. (b. 1918), a male colonist from Bordei Verde, and member of a three-generation household.
58. A.M. (b. 1923), an old man from Lişcoteanca.
59. D.G. (b. 1918), a male colonist from Bordei Verde, and member of a three-generation household.
60. N.R. (b. 1928), a woman from Lişcoteanca, and member of a three-generation household.
61. C.M. (b. 1948), a man from Lişcoteanca, formerly an agronomist and collective farm president, now a land agent.
62. 'Decret-Lege nr. 42 din 29 ianuarie 1990, privind unele măsuri pentru stimularea ţărănimii, 30 January 1990', M.O. 17. Retrievable from: www.cdep.ro/pls/legis/legis_pck.frame.
63. 'Lege nr. 18 din 19 februarie 1991, Legea Fondului Funciar, 20 February 1991', M.O. 37, pp.1–15, republished 5 January 1998, M.O. 1. www.cdep.ro/pls/legis/legis_pck.frame.
64. 'Lege nr. 169 din 27 octombrie 1997 pentru modificarea şi completarea Legii Fondului Funciar nr.18/1991, 4 November 1997', M.O. 299. Retrievable from: www.cdep.ro/pls/legis/legis_pck.frame.
65. M.R. (b. 1933), an old woman from Lişcoteanca.
66. He could have purchased land after the land distribution, but stated that he had not done so.
67. 'Lege nr. 36 din 30 aprilie 1991 privind societăţile agricole şi alte forme de asociere în agricultură, 6 May 1991', M.O. 97. Retrievable from: www.cdep.ro/pls/legis/legis_pck.frame.
68. D.T. (b. 1931), a local from Bordei Verde, a specialist, former brigadier and president of the collective farm.

69. Gheorghe Socol, *Evoluţie, involuţie şi tranziţie în agricultura românească*, Bucharest, 1999, p.36.
70. 'Lege nr. 16 din 5 Aprilie 1994, Legea Arendarii, 7 April 1994', M.O. 91, pp.1–3. Retrievable from: www.cdep.ro/pls/legis/legis_pck.frame.
71. 'Lege nr. 54 din 2 martie 1998 privind circulaţia juridică a terenurilor, 3 April 1998', M.O. 102. Retrievable from: www.cdep.ro/pls/legis/legis_pck.frame.
72. D.N.(b. 1948), a male colonist of Bordei Verde, and member of a three-generation family.
73. 'Lege nr.1 din 11 ianuarie 2000 pentru reconstituirea dreptului de proprietate asupra terenurilor agricole şi celor forestiere, solicitate potrivit prevederilor Legii Fondului Funciar nr.18/1991 şi ale Legii nr.169/1997, 1 December 2000', M.O. 8, pp.1–6.
74. 'Lege nr. 247 din 19 iulie 2005 privind reforma în domeniile proprietăţii şi justiţiei, precum şi unele măsuri adiacente, 22 July 2005', M.O. 653, pp.3–195. This law made the sale of land to non-Romanian citizens theoretically possible; however, the actual process is to be regulated through a specific law that was still unpublished in 2006.
75. Technology implies tractors for ploughing the land, selected seeds and so on. However, on small plots, such as those in yards, horses are still used, and some activities, such as corn harvesting, are still done by hand.
76. C.D. (b. 1951), a man from Gabrielescu, and a SAPARD programme beneficiary. The high costs of land registration are also due to property fragmentation. The cadastral registration of every plot of land is taxed, so it costs more to register a hectare fragmented into several plots than an undivided one.
77. B.C. (b. 1981), a professional man from Brăila, manager in a consultancy firm specializing in SAPARD projects.

11

Contemporary Notions and Practices of Landownership in Central Serbia

The Case of Mrčajevci

Srđan Milošević

Introduction

Ownership of land in Serbia has so far not been a common topic of research in the social sciences, particularly not in historiography or historical anthropology. Although a handful of works deal with this topic, knowledge of the issue is still particular and fragmented.[1] Yet a whole range of very interesting phenomena and specific attitudes and practices related to landownership deserve and demand historical, legal, sociological and anthropological analysis.

Numerous questions are of major importance. For instance, how do normative and factual dimensions of different aspects of owning land (possession, use, sale) interrelate? How is it possible that some properties are listed in land registers under the names of people who passed away decades ago? What explains the vast number of protracted, vigorous legal proceedings and informal disputes and feuds over boundaries between properties? What makes people believe that the institution of *zadruga*, whose very substance is patriarchal collectivism, is a traditional institution, something which is deserving of glorification and to which many people feel strongly attached?[2]

These questions call for more profound, exhaustive research than just the study presented in this chapter. Here I will only suggest some answers, based mostly on experiences of the recent past. My general hypothesis is that the end of the communist regime in Yugoslavia and Serbia did not in itself represent a decisive step towards mastering the basic problems of Serbian society, which predate the communist regime: a low level of legal consciousness, patriarchal collectivism, reluctance to adopt the values of a liberal society and, not uncommonly, an arrogant sense of self-confidence, particularly the belief that 'our' authentic values and practices are 'better' than those found in other Western and Central European societies and countries. The latter runs up against another, opposing but also false idea, namely, that 'up-to-date' European values and institutions prevailed in modern Serbia before the 'communist dictatorship'.

Different issues of landownership are highly interrelated in this context, as well as in many paradigmatic aspects of the structural characteristics of society. This chapter thus treats the contemporary situation from the perspective of one particular aspect of social life: notions and practices related to the ownership of land in a central Serbian village. Taking the historical context into consideration, I aim to elucidate the present-day lack of firmly established and regulated property relations, especially in practice. I begin with a short description of the chief regional differences in modern Serbia, outlining particular differences between the two regions that were the special focus of my research: central Serbia – more precisely, Šumadija – and the northern part of contemporary Serbia, known as Vojvodina.[3] Then I provide a general historical overview of state policies regarding landownership in Serbia before presenting the results of my field research.

Historical Context

Historical Regions in Serbia

From the broadest and most general perspective, Serbia appears to consist of three areas that I would describe as historical regions. The first, and historically the most important (as it was the birthplace of the modern Serbian state) is central Serbia, particularly its largest region, Šumadija. From the mid fifteenth to the early nineteenth century, this part of Serbia was under Ottoman rule. Only after two insurrections against the Ottomans, in 1804 and 1815, did the first elements of modern state organization appear among the Serbs of the region. This was achieved through the establishment of an autonomous principality, still officially part of the Ottoman Empire but enjoying considerable autonomy. Major social change occurred in the principality in the years between 1830 and 1833, when feudalism was officially abolished. After two wars against the Ottoman Empire (from 1876 to 1878), Serbia had expanded its territory somewhat, and was declared independent by the great powers gathered at the Congress of Berlin in 1878.[4] As both an autonomous province of the Ottoman Empire and an independent state, Serbia set out on a path to modernization and Westernization, with controversial and debatable results. As barely a third of all Serbs in southeastern Europe lived within the borders of independent Serbia, throughout the nineteenth century Serbia's national aspirations stretched beyond the borders of the autonomous province and independent Serbian state, ambitiously aiming to unite all Serbs in a single, independent nation-state. Thus Serbia systematically prepared itself for wars 'to liberate and unify' Serbs and, more ambitiously, all Southern Slavs.

The second historical region comprises so-called Old Serbia and Macedonia – or more specifically, remnants of this region that remain within contemporary Serbia.[5] Old Serbia and Macedonia were incorporated into Serbia after the Balkan Wars of 1912/13. During the decisive decades of the development of the principality and, after 1882, the kingdom of Serbia, that is, from the 1830s to the early twentieth century, processes of modernization and Westernization were under way – including the abolition of the feudal system early in the 1830s; the passage of the first Constitution, also in the 1830s; the establishment of private property rights; the organization of political parties and so on. At the same time, the southern parts of what the Serbs regarded as their ethnic and historical territory (namely the territory of the *sanjak* of Novi Pazar, Kosovo and Macedonia), which had remained within the Ottoman Empire, stood apart from those processes. Those regions were incorporated into the Serbian state following the Balkan Wars of 1912/13. This was actually a new wave of wars that the Balkan states fought against the Ottoman Empire, and resulted in the considerable territorial expansion of Serbia and the other victorious Balkan states.[6] Unlike central Serbia, inhabited almost exclusively by Serbs, the southern regions of Novi Pazar, Kosovo and Macedonia had no clear Serb ethnic majority outside certain areas; rather, the whole region was characterized by a mixed ethnic structure. When this territory became part of Serbia in 1912/13, important differences came to light, to be overcome only after the next wave of war, suffering and conflict started in 1914.

Finally, the third historical region is Vojvodina, a province in the north of contemporary Serbia that was part of the Dual Monarchy of Austro-Hungary until 1918. As part of Hungary and the Habsburg Empire, the territory of contemporary Vojvodina also experienced Ottoman rule from the mid sixteenth to the end of the seventeenth century, but Ottoman Empire had no lasting impact. Colonization in Vojvodina, undertaken over centuries by the Habsburg state, resulted in a multiethnic population with almost thirty ethnic groups, among whom Serbs are the majority.

After the First World War, a new state emerged in the Balkans, namely the Kingdom of the Serbs, Croats and Slovenes, also called Yugoslavia. Its territory included an enlarged Serbia, Montenegro and the Southern Slavic regions of the Austro-Hungarian Dual Monarchy, one of which was Vojvodina. The country did not manage to attain internal stability in the interwar period, and after suffering monumental destruction in the Second World War, Yugoslavia became a communist federation. Serbia was now one of the six federal republics of socialist Yugoslavia, which subsequently disintegrated in another wave of wars and violence in the first half of the 1990s. In 1945, Vojvodina was made an autonomous province within the Republic of Serbia, a status it retains to this day. Each of the three regions treated here is characterized by its own historical legacies, including different legal traditions and – particularly in Vojvodina – the impact of different civilizations.

Two Traditions: A Frame for Comparative Research (Šumadija and Vojvodina)

The differences resulting from the very different historical experiences of Šumadija and Vojvodina are the reason behind the division in my research on landowning in Serbia. Unlike Vojvodina, Šumadija has never been primarily an administrative unit. The name Šumadija has been used to designate administrative units no larger than a district (*Šumadijska oblast*), which is a much smaller area than what Šumadija encompasses geographically or, and especially, as a 'mental construct'.

Whereas Šumadija is a geographical entity, it is primarily an ideological concept. Geographically, it lies at the very centre of Serbia. This geographical location lends the notion of 'Šumadija' a more important connotation: that of an idealized area of insurrections and rebellions against foreign oppressors – the most Serbian part of Serbia and Serbdom. In his famous book *Kneževina Srbija* (1876), the author Milan Milićević begins his account of Šumadija with the following words: 'We love Šumadija as we love our own mother, and with conceivable passion we enter into research about Šumadija and a review of her beauties'.[7]

In a latent but permanent disputatious rivalry that pits Šumadija against Vojvodina, Šumadija has always prevailed politically as the centre of the unification of Serbs and Yugoslavs. But in terms of cultural life and economy, Vojvodina has always been more developed than Šumadija and, without intending to elaborate upon the topic, I will briefly note that this discrepancy has proved problematic for the functioning of the state. It was somewhat muted during the process of establishing the first Yugoslav state in 1918, a time when the idea of national unity was paramount. This was a period of the unanimous glorification of Šumadija, which hinged mainly on its role in the First World War, an image that Šumadija preserved, more or less and in many ways, for the next few decades.[8] Furthermore, in the early 1930s the opinion emerged that the whole purpose of Vojvodina's cultural and economic development was to prepare the ground for Šumadija to assume a leading role amongst the Southern Slavic peoples.[9]

The name Šumadija derives from the noun *šuma* (forest), but this is no longer adequate to describe the region. Today, Šumadija boasts highly developed agricultural and cattle-raising sectors. I conducted my field research in Mrčajevci, a village at the very edge of the Šumadija region in central Serbia's Čačak municipality. Geographically speaking, Čačak municipality does not lie entirely within the Šumadija region, but people who live in Čačak consider themselves Šumadinci (a Šumadinac is someone who comes from Šumadija). Mrčajevci itself belongs to Šumadija, since the settlement is on the left bank of the Morava River and therefore within the boundaries of Šumadija.

Another preliminary remark will assist in a better understanding of the practices related to owning land in Šumadija: unlike in Vojvodina, where title to land has been regulated for centuries, central Serbian landholdings were literally seized during the national revolution at the beginning of the nineteenth century.[10] The peasants occupied as much land as they could, thus dispossessing their former masters, soldiers who had been granted feudal privileges for military service in the sultan's army – the Ottoman *spahijas*. This origin of landownership likely influenced the proprietary notions and practices that I study in this chapter.

The Development of Property Relations and Land Surveying in Central Serbia

A brief review of the development of the question of landownership in modern Serbia reveals a specific, interesting and somehow controversial evolution.[11] Peasants in Serbia became full owners of the land they worked and lived on in the early 1830s, as a result of liberation from Ottoman rule.[12] All nineteenth-century Serbian constitutions (the first of which, passed in 1835, was very short-lived) protected private property, and in this respect it appears that the notion of private property was fully respected formally.[13] However, the difference – indeed, the irreconcilability – between norms and practice is key to understanding many aspects of Serbian history, especially the history of institutions.[14] This certainly includes the institutions related to property.

The small size of land plots (most less than 5 hectares) caused a whole range of problems for peasants, whose insufficient income from the land they lived on rendered them dependent on the state, thus structurally diminishing their economic independence – the key to freedom in modern society.[15] Few doubt that throughout Serbian history, notions and institutions of landowning were accepted and introduced only superficially, mostly at a normative level. The system of *okućje* ('house surrounding'), elaborated in Serbia since the mid 1830s,[16] prescribed a minimum area of inalienable land, limiting the owner's rights to sell his property. That is, the house and a certain portion of the land surrounding it (generally not larger than 1 hectare) were not alienable and could not be sold.[17] This was how the state 'protected' the peasantry.

Another important process related to landownership involved agrarian reforms, which took place both in interwar and socialist Yugoslavia.[18] However, those agrarian reforms, especially the former, were of minor importance to the region of Šumadija, where there were few of the large landed estates that the reforms mainly affected. Agrarian reforms in interwar and socialist Yugoslavia alike nonetheless violated citizens' proprietary rights, and promoted an idea of land as something that is not bound to the market or the principle of the 'sanctity' of private property.

On the other hand, the state very early on recognized the need to develop modern institutions dedicated to landowners' property relations, such as the cadastral service. The idea of surveying and registering landholdings in modern Serbia originated in the 1830s, when Prince Miloš Obrenović (who ruled from 1815 to 1839 and from 1858 to 1860) realized the utility of introducing a modern system of surveying and classifying land in the autonomous principality of the Ottoman Empire, and of training experts in the field.[19] Over the next few decades, however, little was accomplished to this end, with the notable exception of the state's capital city, Belgrade. Although the legal base was established, serious setbacks plagued the whole process.[20]

In 1856, Prince Miloš Obrenović ordered the Ministry of Finance to survey the 'fatherland' and compile topographic and cadastral maps, as well as land registers. The metric system was introduced in Serbia in 1873, and in 1878 the geographical section was organized as a distinct department of the army general staff tasked with surveying and classifying the land for military and civil purposes. In parallel, that same year a department of the Ministry of Civil Engineering was set up to survey the land and regulate geodetic issues. The staff were largely engineers from Serbia, educated abroad on state scholarships, then hired by the government after finishing their studies and returning to their country.[21] In the meantime, Serbia had begun educating experts by introducing geodesy into the curricula of higher education institutions.[22]

In 1884, a law on direct taxation passed in the newly independent state prescribed a census of owned land. According to this law, landowners were to declare all their property, but the system failed as soon as it was introduced because peasants boycotted the census.[23] A new law in 1889 introduced the cadastral system, and in 1890 the first survey took place, based on the German model. In accordance with the new law, a cadastral department was founded at the Ministry of Finance. Again in parallel, a section with similar duties was established within the Ministry of Civil Engineering eight years later. Surveying and classification of the land was carried out in Serbia until 1894, when it was interrupted because the state could not afford the expenses it entailed.[24] In 1900, the system of triangulation was introduced, and land was surveyed according to this method until 1912.[25] The first results of this cadastral surveying were destroyed during the First World War.

After the war, the leadership of the new Kingdom of the Serbs, Croats and Slovenes did not neglect cadastral surveying. The work resumed in 1919 with the establishment of the General Cadastral Direction, which founded a specialized school for geodesists in 1924. However, different systems of cadastral surveying continued to coexist in the new state until 1924, when one projection (Gaus-Krieger's) was adopted for the entire state; it is still in use in Serbia today. The law on cadastral surveying finally passed in 1929, followed by a whole range of related ordinances and regulations. The General Cadastral Direction was replaced by a new department at the Ministry of Finance – the Department of Cadastre and Public Property – and an organized, fully regulated form of surveying began. In the period from 1931 to 1941, surveying of some 4.12 million hectares (out of a total 6.6 million hectares) was completed, but the Second World War annihilated the greater part of this work. After the war, the work continued, or in some regions began from scratch, but deficits of interest, money and experts have prevented its completion to the present day.

In 1947, the decree on the organization of the Geodetic Authority of the People's Republic of Serbia was passed. The most important change after this was a law passed in 1992 providing for the consolidation of data from the cadastres and land registers into the so-called United Register of Real Estate. Work on this consolidation is still ongoing. The survey of the land in Čačak, the site of my field research, started between 1931 and 1934 and continued after 1945.

Owning Land in Mrčajevci: Contemporary Practices and Attitudes

Here I will present the main aspects of practices related to owning land in Mrčajevci. It is important to emphasize that Mrčajevci, like the other villages in Šumadija, does not and never did have many large landowners, so the agrarian reforms – aimed primarily at expropriating large landed estates and redistributing the land among poor peasants, in both interwar and in socialist Yugoslavia – did not affect many households. Family stories and collective memories of violations of property rights to land during the agrarian reforms in Yugoslavia, especially in the socialist period (1945 to 1948 and 1953),[26] are neither vivid nor traumatic. The oldest people I talked to during field research mostly mention general fears and concern about their land in the process of agrarian reform, rather than concrete examples of expropriation or specific violations of their property rights or those of their parents, relatives or neighbours.

The Dismemberment of the Zadruga and the Issue of Landowning

The households I visited during my field research had their origins in the *zadruga*. The final demise of the *zadruga* coincided with the socialist period, when its ongoing process of disintegration accelerated as a result of communist social and agrarian policies. People themselves attribute the dismemberment of the institution of the *zadruga*, as my oldest informants state, to communist agrarian policy, mostly overestimating its influence on a process that was already occurring. The younger generations repeat the same story, but their knowledge is mostly limited to myths about the *zadruga*. Besides, the majority of my informants share the opinion that the largest evil for Serbian villages was the division and partitioning of households and estates amongst heirs, which gradually diminished the extent of their properties. According to my informants, this partitioning of land has two strong connections to the communist system. First, it forced the *zadruga* to dismember in order to preserve the land in the hands of one core family, which was the first 'blow to the Serbian peasantry'. Secondly, households abandoned the custom whereby the oldest son (or the one remaining in the household) inherited most of the land, while the others were usually sent to obtain higher education and find jobs outside agriculture. That was the case, for instance, in the Erić family household: the older brother was sent to university in Belgrade and became a dentist, while the younger stayed to run the household and, by family agreement, inherited the land, his older brother having unofficially renounced his rights.

No one who blames communism for today's generally unsatisfactory conditions in Serbia's villages offers an alternative solution that they would consider righteous and just, especially regarding rules governing the inheritance of land. Still, the common opinion amongst those who support the *zadruga* system – inevitably as a memory of 'good old days' – is presumably that whoever stays on the land should inherit it, which they believe was almost exclusively the custom during the pre-socialist period. Of course, those who support such a solution are greatly interested in it precisely because they stayed on their parents' land. The wife of one of the men I interviewed, who had not inherited part of the land of her parents but renounced it in favour of her brother, also supports the idea that the land belongs to whoever stays on the land, as her husband did.[27] So in most cases, personal interest biases the evaluation of the inheritance rules of one or another system of property relations.

Some informants consider the *zadruga*, as an organization in which everybody knows and respects the rules, the best solution to property issues. Many of those I talked to on the subject, particularly the men, shared this opinion. Furthermore, the former mayor of the village stated for the local TV station that it was a real pity that the *zadruga*, the symbol of 'our' people and village, no longer existed, owing to communist politics. But knowledge of the real conditions in the *zadruga* during its period of existence is mostly lacking, especially among the post-1945 generation.

The oldest informants I talked to were women, who related their memories of life at the time of the *zadruga*. All of them had lived in the *zadruga*, but, threatened by nationalization, the members of the *zadruga* had divided their estates between 1945 and 1949 and for a while continued living as before, though officially the institution was dismantled. Some families left the *zadruga* well into the first half of the 1950s.

Women who lived in the *zadruga* talk about it with a mixture of nostalgia and scorn. Unlike those who never lived in the *zadruga* or did so for only a short period in early childhood, they do not idealize the *zadruga* system. Regarding the matter of landed property, the topic I insisted on was the matter of inheritance and dowry. Maidens were commonly given a dowry, which sometimes was a portion of land that fell short of the real portion of the land they ought to be given as an inheritance. The two oldest informants told me that their dowries had not been registered under their names 'in the books',[28] and they were not entitled to own that land. The dowry of one of them ultimately remained her father's property, since the two families, hers and her husband's, made another arrangement: instead of giving a dowry for his daughter, her father bought the tiles for the roof of her new father-in-law's stable. The other woman had been given the land as a dowry, but it was registered under the name of her father-in-law. 'I was stupid', she stated. 'I didn't know anything'. Her dowry was sold, but not, she said, against her will; she had agreed to the sale. 'What could I do? At least they asked me', she concluded.[29]

Thus, the renewed memory of the *zadruga* and the widespread glorification of the *zadruga* system is not only an outcome of the breakdown of socialism, but also the traditional answer to the challenges of transition, not in accordance with individualistic, liberal notions of property but rather with the collectivistic, patriarchal past, reinvented and reshaped to suit an idealized image of previous times. The main argument for glorifying the *zadruga* is the idea that the *zadruga* is bound up with Serbian identity, which was, allegedly, doomed to disappear under the communists. That the communists also tried to replace the *zadruga* system by organizing cooperatives was apparently, as many people believe, the best proof that the *zadruga* was a successful, prosperous institution that was nonetheless destroyed because of communist politics in the village.[30]

Cooperatives and Landed Property in Mrčajevci

After the Second World War, a socialist agricultural policy was implemented in Mrčajevci as well as other parts of the country. From the mid 1940s onwards, cooperatives existed in the village, but only the largest estates were nationalized.[31] Other households joined the cooperative system in another way, for instance by entering into sales contracts. Since the idea of collectivisation and formation of the *kolhoz*-type peasant cooperatives had failed in Yugoslavia by the beginning of the 1950s, people mostly remember another type of cooperative: consumer-supplying cooperatives.

People in Mrčajevci express mixed, confused feelings when talking about cooperatives. They mostly consider cooperatives to have been a positive aspect of socialist agricultural politics. The general opinion is that it was better back when the cooperatives organized the processes of agriculture, from tilling the soil to buying and selling produce. That is to say, cooperatives had machines to rent to producers for all necessary work, and also bought peasants' products.

Most people have an idyllic, idealized image of this kind of cooperative. They admit that many people suffered because of the cooperative system, if not in Mrčajevci then in other places, but they generally do not differentiate between different types of cooperatives, only one of which entailed forced collectivization.[32] A majority of informants stated that it was better than the contemporary free-market system, especially for small landowners. One of the informants nostalgically recalls a period when numerous combines dotted the fields in summertime. This is no longer the case. 'Nobody sows anymore. The village is dying'.[33]

On the other hand, rich families, prosperous households and owners of larger estates are not positively inclined towards the system of cooperatives, which they never (or only partly) took part in. They refer to the cooperatives exclusively as a system of exploitation and involving the forced expropriation of estates. Nonetheless, some other well-to-do families still believe that the cooperative system was better than the free market in terms of the distribution of products: 'It was up to you to produce, and the cooperative was here to buy everything'.[34]

Meanwhile, it should be stressed that some strongly anti-communist informants also acknowledge that it was obviously better for the farmers when the state was in charge of buying and selling agricultural products. They talk about the need for a new type of association of agricultural producers, although some express serious doubts about the organizational capacities of 'our people'. For instance, one informant who still believes in the values of the former socialist system said: 'Nothing can be done without state intervention. Private intermediaries are unreliable and they are interested only in profit, not in the quality of the products'.[35]

Most informants in Mrčajevci seem to share the opinion that the cooperatives were useful and prosperous, and particularly the cooperatives that specialized in buying products from the farmers and offering them different kinds of support: mechanization, credit, seeds and so on. Not having suffered expropriation or collectivization, they do not much dwell on this aspect of communist agrarian politics but just generally condemn the communist regime, including agricultural politics. On the other hand, the communist policy of *otkup*, a compulsory sale of products to state agencies to fixed and lower than market prices, left very unpleasant memories and even today elicits negative comments in discussions of this aspect of communist agrarian politics. The belief that Serbia suffered the greatest hardship from *otkup* is also widespread.

Owning the Land: Informal Practices

One of the most noticeable characteristics of landed property practices in Mrčajevci is the omnipresent confusion about the most fundamental question for any activity on the land: ownership of it. This confusion is due in part to people's very low level of legal consciousness, but also to the state's lack of perseverance in regulating property relations. The juncture of these two aspects led, for instance, to numerous households being registered in land registers under the names of people who had died years or even decades ago, but whose heirs did not initiate the legal procedure to officially transfer the property title to themselves. State authorities also failed to initiate the procedure, so these estates have been the property of dead people for years now.

The first step in the inheritance procedure is the only thing that must be done ex officio by the court upon the death of the landowner: the heirs must be assembled to formally state that they accept 'ideal portions' of the inheritance. For example, if there are three heirs, each of them receives an 'ideal third'. But almost nobody bothers to define which third, and very few register the change in the land registers. For a long time, nothing else happens. Usually only one of the heirs actually uses the land, paying all necessary taxes and so forth, but all of the heirs legally hold their 'ideal portion' for a very long period.

The heirs have a few reasons for accepting a situation in which the land remains registered under the names of deceased former owners. The most common one is to avoid the taxes normally incurred by transferring titles and other legal costs. Sometimes, however, when the context is more complicated, the main problem is again a dearth of legal consciousness and a sort of inertia rooted in a superficial understanding of the importance of legally regulating property relations. That is, some heirs are uninterested in the inheritance proceedings because they have moved out of the household, mostly while their parents were still alive, leaving a brother (or, though rarely, a sister) in the parents' household. This means that they have practically, though of course not legally, renounced their right to inherit the land. Whoever stays on the land pays the taxes due, works the land, lives in the parents' house and takes care of the parents. Then, once the parents die, nobody initiates the above-mentioned proceedings because nobody is interested: neither the person remaining in the household, nor the person who moved out, nor the state. The person living on and using the land has no problem with it being registered under their father's or mother's name and does not wish to change anything, as a change could mean legal proceedings that would require the land to be divided among the heirs, only one of whom actually uses the land. The heir who has moved out of the parents' household is not interested either, and refrains from declaring openly that they do not wish to take their own share of the inheritance. The state receives the tax from the heir who has stayed on the parents' land, in hopes that remaining there will in time entitle them to inherit all or at least the lion's share of it. So the state's viewpoint is that everything can last this way for decades, so long as it receives the necessary taxes. In sum, therefore, it is considered better not to initiate anything.

Once the issue of ownership has been resolved – which has occurred more frequently over the past decade – a different set of problems appears: most plots in Mrčajevci have been inherited by at least two heirs. This means that each individual portion of land – each cadastral unit, in real-estate terms – is divided amongst the heirs so that each receives the 'ideal portion' (a half, third, quarter or whatever) of each particular cadastral unit. The inheritance proceedings usually stop there. It is easy to imagine how complications can arise in a situation where there is no agreement about what belongs to whom.

Another reason not to register land under one's own name, dating back to a prior era, was the system of social care under socialism. Because people who did not own property had the right to receive allowances for their children, for instance, or certain other benefits such as 'solidarity flats' and so on, landholders had no interest in being registered as the owners of the land. Many people who claimed these allowances were the actual owners and users of land that was legally owned by other persons, usually their close relatives.

The Y. family, for example, had the following recent experience of inheritance proceedings upon the death of the landowner, Miloje Y., in April 2006. The land Miloje had owned passed to his heirs: one third to his wife, Živana; one third to his daughter, Miojla; and one third to his son, Milan. Miojla, who does not live in Mrčajevci, sent a letter to the court stating that she accepted the inheritance. Legally, this meant that one third went to her. The letter was not formulated properly, however, and did not adequately convey the fact that she intended to accept only the small inheritance that the family had previously agreed upon: 0.3 hectares of the entire land area (3 hectares).[36] The proceedings ground to a halt, and now the case is awaiting appeal, which will incur costs prior to completion. Moreover, Milan regards the situation as time-consuming and annoying. The first step has been taken, but the most important thing – registering him as the owner of the land in 'the books' – is still on hold. The only thing that has been resolved is that his mother and sister have renounced their right to their portions. To satisfy the court, however, the proceedings must go forward; meanwhile, nobody wants to go through with the entire affair because the costs are prohibitive.

There are further aspects of interest regarding landed property in Mrčajevci. First of all, farmers who are suspicious about the state's motives reject the option of registering their land as agricultural estates. The state, for its part, tries to financially stimulate the farmers to register their land by promising a subsidy of €100 per hectare of arable land. When farmers arrive at local authorities' offices to ask for the money, they find out about unexpected conditions: to receive the prescribed amount of money, a farmer must register the estate as arable land under grain or vegetable crops. Farmers usually understand the state's promise of

€100 per hectare and take only this into account, but it is not enough that the land is used for arable: it must also be registered as arable land, not as a meadow, forest or orchard. Many farmers, although they have changed the way they use their land – by, for instance, converting meadows into ploughed land – have not registered the change in the type of land usage with the cadastral service. This is why, upon discovering that this form of registration is required, they believe that the state lied to them when promising subsidies.

In response to this and other problems related to unregistered property, in 2007 the highest Serbian authority for issues related to land, the State Geodetic Authority (Republički Geodetski Zavod), organized and launched a campaign promoting property registration under the slogan 'Registered property has higher value!' TV advertisements encouraged people to register their property, stating, 'Safeguard your children's future!'[37]

But even as the authorities see registering land in Serbia as a matter of national interest, their aims remain ambiguous, so to speak. 'Modernize but preserve the substance unchanged' is a simplified but adequate phrase to describe the essence of the state authorities' actions in this respect. For instance, one pamphlet, issued by the Ministry of Agriculture to encourage farmers to register their land as agricultural estates and their households as agricultural households, reads:

> Serbia, as a small European country, exhausted by wars, isolation and poverty, has nevertheless succeeded in preserving her values. An abundant cultural and natural heritage, together with human resources, has enabled Serbia to survive all the critical periods of her history. At all times, when lacking other solutions, agriculture was the only way to endure the moments of crisis . . . We want our villages to be revived and to be one of the foundations in preserving a recognizable identity for Serbia.[38]

This expresses an orientation towards perpetuating an approach in which agriculture is not only a branch of the economy but also a matter of identity. Registering the land becomes a national task that should be fulfilled for patriotic reasons. That is, it is a renewal of the same old approach that makes almost every activity part of the discourse of identity, national interests and so on, rather than an approach underlining the citizen's individual interest or their legal duty.

A similar situation concerns the informal, non-contractual leasing of land: a farmer who works leased land but lacks the proper contract with the owner is unable to receive the state subsidy granted to support agricultural production under a formal lease. The motive for avoiding a formalization of land leasing is again obvious: to be free of tax obligations. Yet the situation did not change, even after it became permissible to state in contracts that the land was leased without material compensation. Suspicious of the state, farmers still avoid legal leases, even though they have nothing to lose and would otherwise be eligible for state subsidies. One of the most prosperous farmers in Mrčajevci, who owns around 10 hectares and leases another 10 hectares of land, strongly opposes the idea of concluding formal contracts. With a mischievous facial expression, he states: 'I do not trust the state' – at least, certainly not in this case, as long ago he was actually the chief of the cooperative in Mrčajevci.[39]

One of the most important aspects of landowning practices concerns lawsuits brought over disputed boundaries between estates. In this regard some comments on my methodology for this part of the research are warranted. My experience suggests that a more productive approach to such problematic issues is to collect data in passing during discussions that do not resemble formal interviews. I gathered a great deal of interesting information from certain short conversations, which I later tried to corroborate. While fully understanding the disadvantages of this approach, I sometimes used it because it proved quite useful in relation to statements and data that people provided about other people they knew. It was how I was able to find out, for instance, that Mr A. is a quarrelsome person who was or still is engaged in disputes about land with almost all his neighbours and relatives. There being a great many people like Mr A., this gossip inspired me to carry out a little inquiry among households that revealed that more than 70 per cent of them were involved in some kind of legal proceedings concerning their property, apart from inheritance proceedings. This percentage is approximate but, I believe, reliable: I selected twenty households and visited them with only one question: whether they were involved in any lawsuits concerning land with their neighbours or relatives. Fifteen of the households answered the question, and of these, eleven stated that they had had or were still engaged in lawsuits related to landownership, that these proceedings take too much time, that they are too expensive and so on. Some of these trials last for more than a decade. Furthermore, the disputed plots are sometimes very small (3 square metres, for example). This provoked the question of whether such disputes reflect the depth of attachment to private property, or whether there are other aspects more relevant to the matter. A lawyer specializing in land-related lawsuits informed me that approximately 50 per cent of all cases brought before the courts concern property rights.[40] One of the problems that complicate boundary disputes is that people sometimes, as the local geodesist informed me, purposely remove the stones used in geodetic practice to mark the boundaries between estates.

Interestingly, nobody considers it wise or useful not to regulate property relations. But at the same time, nobody considers unregulated relations a serious problem either. People are used to regarding the issue as something charming and somehow 'specific to us'. It is a problem, of course, and in the end it is important to regulate property relations, but it takes too much time, the state is uninterested in this regard, it is expensive, it require many people's involvement, someone must start it, someone must pay for the whole procedure and so on.

Attitudes towards the Land

People in Mrčajevci talk about land with respect mixed with dissatisfaction, and in their opinion the local and central government authorities both neglect agriculture. They share the general impression that the state has left them alone and unprotected to face the challenges of the market. They may refer to the socialist period as 'damned communism', but they also talk about the advantages of the cooperative system, in which, as mentioned already, they were able to sell everything they produced.[41] One can conclude overall that the attitude of most of my informants is essentially that they were dissatisfied with the communists' national policy, but not with the economic system itself. They generally believe that, for farmers, the period of socialist economy and agriculture was better.

This disappointment frequently emerged in expressions of resignation about landed property and agriculture. One informant stated, 'Land is not to be sold', but her mother-in-law later said: 'I would sell it only if I could find someone who would pay properly. But land is cheap'.[42] Another informant stated, in the course of repeating a story I had heard innumerable times about the futility of working the land in the total absence of state support, that the land was merely a burden on him: 'I would even sell it to an Albanian'.

When any kind of sentimental understanding of landed property is found, it is among the older people. It is not clearly identifiable, however. For instance, one of my oldest informants said that her father 'had liked to buy the land', but she does not remember him having an emotional relation towards the land.[43] On the other hand, her father-in-law had wanted to sell his land and to emigrate to America, but his wife stopped the whole process by brandishing an axe to chase away both the husband and the buyer. Some informants, while discussing nationalization, remarked with a certain irony or even a 'mystical' sense of predestination that people who were granted land that had been taken away from the real owners seized the advantage to sell it as soon as possible. 'They did not earn that land on their own – that is why they sold it so easily', one person stated.

During my field research I realized that Mrčajevci is part of a region where raising cattle is more important than farming. Thus older people usually refer to cattle, not landed property, as an indicator of fortune. They speak about their or their fathers' oxen and cows with stronger emotion than arises in talk of land.

The younger generations I met in local cafés are uninformed about anything relating to their family history, to the legal aspects of owning the land and so forth. For them, staying on the land and working is an unattractive prospect. Most younger informants may have heard mention of the cadastre, for instance, but they usually have no idea of the formal aspects of landed property relations. The great majority of them dream of moving to town or at least finding a job in a sector other than agriculture.

An exception to this tendency (though I would not call it a rule) is that of the rich and prosperous households, whose members clearly consider land to be a value in itself. Their property relations are in order: documents, registration, contracts – everything is more or less regulated. Nevertheless, they do whatever is possible to avoid taxation, for instance, when selling their products. Their attitude suggests a kind of pride in owning a large estate, but like other locals they are dissatisfied with the state's agricultural policy, and complain about its neglect of agricultural production.

Conclusion

This chapter aimed to describe and explain how landed property relations function in contemporary Serbia – that is, how a society deals with the implementation of liberal, capitalist notions and institutions in a sphere that experienced fifty years of socialist policy regarding property. The results of the study reveal that, in many respects, neither values nor practices in contemporary Serbia correspond to the system that is accepted at the state level, namely, liberal capitalism, in the broadest sense. The whole context is further complicated by the fact that liberal institutions, far from being 'reintroduced' or 'revived' in Serbia after the breakdown of communism (as some would argue, and as is true at the most formal level of analysis), still remain to be almost literally introduced into Serbian society, where there is no, or at least no relevant and 'effective', liberal tradition to rely upon. Meanwhile, it is important not to oversimplify by regarding the socialist period as a complete deviation from the legal traditions of previous periods and from the common European property system of civil law. Many elements of those legal traditions survived throughout the socialist period of Eastern European history.[44]

Another critical observation is that a chief characteristic of Serbian society that widely affects property relations regarding land is a permanent lack of the rule of law, combined with a very low level of legal culture. That the law 'fails' in post-communist countries has been generally accepted, but some clarifications are still expected.[45] With regard to landownership, undefined or blurred property relations could be depicted as a manifestation of the 'failed' or at least 'contested' modernization of Serbian society. However, the main problem in this respect emphatically is not that Serbian practices differ from those in Central and Western Europe, but that Serbian practices do not accord with the positive legal solutions actually existing in Serbia itself, which, since the fall of socialism, have mostly developed along the lines of European models. By the terms 'failure of law' and 'failed/contested modernization', I therefore wish to describe a particular situation in which different attempts to introduce modern Central or Western European systems of landowning relations still face obstacles and suffer setbacks, despite the existence of a general and elaborated legal framework.

The notions and practices of owning property in Serbia cover a broad range of ideas and experiences, and reveal a remarkable variety of changes. Notwithstanding efforts to unify conditions in the sphere of property rights (normative unification, above all), different parts of the country have retained their own informal practices, which differ more or less from the stipulated rules.

In Serbia, the idea of property is still not perceived as a basic value of modern society. Considering the atmosphere during legal proceedings that I witnessed in court as a representative of the public, hoping to better understand people's attitudes, it appears that property rights are somehow being protected 'instinctively', rather than as a result of an established legal consciousness and culture. Some people, as was mentioned, find it hard to accept that all heirs have equal inheritance rights in their parents' property. In particular, some see the right of daughters to inherit the same amount of land as their brothers as a basis for the destruction of Serbian villages through the diminishment and partition of estates. Even today, most people I interviewed who expressed any stance on this issue consider it blasphemous for a sister or even a brother who has moved out of the household to demand their share of the land. This usually happens during personal feuds between relatives.

Otherwise, the practice is that whoever remains on the land uses that land, though without becoming the sole proprietor. Officially, all heirs remain proprietors, but only one of them really owns and uses the land. In addition, a lingering, albeit not prevalent, custom dictates that family members who leave the household renounce their right to inherit an equal share of the estate, with inheritance rights favouring those who continue to live on the land. This is sometimes the reason why probationary proceedings are postponed: one person renounces their right unofficially, but once it comes before the court, they could 'change their mind'.

There is a strong conviction that people who are able to move out of households have already been compensated by way of family support throughout their education. The heir who stays on the land 'inherits', by informal family agreement, at least the majority of that land, and regardless of the official position that all heirs have the same rights, some of them, especially women, usually renounce their inheritance rights. It is considered a just and reasonable act.

The glorification of the *zadruga* is mostly the result of dissatisfaction with socialism and the communist period. People perceive the *zadruga* as having been an authentic Serbian institution that communists destroyed as part of a project of 'breaking the spine of the Serbian nation' – that spine being the Serbian village. Yet when it comes to the economic results delivered by communist agrarian policies, criticism is almost entirely lacking. Moreover, if there is one aspect of socialist agrarian policy that nearly all informants view favourably, it is the highly rated institution of the cooperative system – that is, of course, the consumer-supplying type of cooperative that prevailed after 1953.

Although people understand the need to regulate property relations, a sort of lethargy persists in this respect, with the consolation that most people have the same problems with their property, namely, that they all share the same conditions. The famous interwar Serbian historian Slobodan Jovanović wrote that Prince Miloš, in his own businesses, was 'like a real peasant, who besides making mockery of the law has a pious respect for the documents that certify something in his favour'.[46] That spirit of 'pious respect' for documents, even when they certify something in someone's favour, is quite scarce in Serbia today. But this does not mean that mid-nineteenth-century Serbians had a more developed legal consciousness. 'Pious respect for the documents that certify something in one's favour' obviously differs from anything understandable as a modern notion of legal consciousness, which in the terms used above would probably be expressed as a 'respect for documents', no matter whom they favour.

Taken together at a broader level, these characteristics of Serbian society periodically produce an almost revolutionary atmosphere resulting in the violent change of regimes, but not of the substance of the structures that actually generate crises and cause Serbian society to permanently oscillate between revolution and counter-revolution, between anarchy and autocracy, resulting in disorder and the absence of the rule of law.[47] This is why one type of collectivism or oppressive ideology is periodically replaced by another. This is why almost all discussions within and about Serbian society, on any topic of certain importance, circle endlessly around references to ideology, great narratives on identity and the nation, national interests, the state, corruption, internal or external enemies and so forth. Serbian society lacks the traditions that influenced the establishment of the modern principles of liberal individualistic society along with the range of institutions and values that undergird this type of society. Attempts at modernization across two centuries of modern Serbian history created a specific atmosphere that has pointedly been described as comprising 'modern institutions in a pre-modern society'. In this context, the landed property issue, being of utmost importance in any society, is also discussed from a perspective that widely transcends its purely economic and social dimensions.

Appendix: Key Informants

During my field research in Mrčajevci, I visited three households of different social and economic backgrounds. I also carried out short interviews with their neighbours, relatives and friends, who provided certain information and observations, lending insight into general attitudes towards landed property. I therefore had contact with more than twenty-five people, including representatives of local government.

The Y family, the first I visited, had a mixed structure, combining both agriculture and outside work. In this four-member family, the oldest person was Živana (b. 1935), followed by her son Milan (b. 1956), his wife Danica (b. 1959) and their son Goran (b. 1979). Their daughter Gordana (b. 1977) left the household after marrying. None of them had any formal agricultural education. Živana completed four years of elementary school, Milan and Danica attended school for eight years and Goran has a secondary education. They lived on a very modest income drawn from both their employment and their land. They owned 3 hectares, which they mostly used to meet their own needs, and did not sell their produce on the market. Their land mostly consisted of pasture for the cattle they raised. Like the majority of households in Mrčajevci, they worked the land without mechanization.

The Z family was agricultural and very prosperous. The members of this household were Branko, the grandfather (b. 1933), his son Živojin (b. 1956) and Dragica, his wife (b. 1957), and their son Ivan (b. 1982). They made a good living from agriculture. Their highly mechanized farmstead possessed all the machines necessary for the full range of farming activity, from breaking land to distributing produce. Their home was modernized and affluent. They owned many animals, and had 10 hectares of leased land and 10 hectares of their own.

Finally, the X family was the smallest, and had only two members: Dušanka (b. 1922) and her son Milivoje (b. 1946). Agriculture was also their livelihood. They owned 5 hectares of land, and their main income came from selling products from the cattle they raised.

In addition to the people in these three households, I met and had short interviews with their relatives and neighbours, as well as representatives of the local authorities in both the municipality and the village. In the municipality of Čačak I met the officers Zorica R., in charge of demography, and Milka K., in charge of agriculture. In Mrčajevci I met the village agronomist (a post introduced in spring 2006), Bojan T. The local geodesist Staniša L. gave me important data on organizing land measurement, and on certain other aspects of his activity as a geodesist.

Notes

This chapter is the result of field research conducted in the central Serbian village of Mrćajevci in 2007. The research was conducted as part of the project 'Land Law, Cadastre and Land Registers in Eastern Europe, 1918–1945–1989: Poland, Romania and Yugoslavia in Comparison', financed by Volkswagen Stiftung. I also wish to express my sincere and profound gratitude to my informants in Mrčajevci and Čačak, and to everyone else who helped in the research on which this chapter is based.

1. Sreten Vukosavljević, *Istorija seljačkog društva*, 3 vols, Belgrade, 1953–1983; Branko Peruničić, *Zemljišna svojina u Srbiji 1815–1845*, Belgrade, 1977; Borislav Dimković, *Promene u zemljišnoj svojini individualnih poljoprivrednih gazdinstava i njihov odnos prema zemljoradničkim zadrugama*, Sremska Mitrovica, 1964; Sreten Vukosavljević, 'Postanak privatne zemljišne svojine u nas', *Arhiv za pravne i društvene nauke* 30/1 (1940), pp. 91–100; Abadin Palošević, 'Zemljišni maksimum i promene u agrarnoj strukturi', *Ekonomika poljoprivrede* 4 (1987), pp.233–38.
2. The *zadruga* is, in the broadest sense, an extended family, a type of community that lives in one household and is characterized by the shared life and work of its members, most usually of the same family – for instance, a father and his sons together with their wives and children. There was also a type of *zadruga* whose members did not belong to the same family, but it was not very common. On this topic, see Aleksa Jovanović, *Istorijski razvitak srpske zadruge*, Belgrade, 1896; Stojan Novaković, *Selo*, Belgrade, 1912; Živojin Perić, *Zadružno pravo u Građanskom zakoniku Kraljevine Srbije*, Belgrade, 1920; Milenko Filipović, *Nesrodnička i predvojena zadruga*, Belgrade, 1945; Dragana Stjepanović-Zaharijevski, 'Porodična zadruga kao tradicija porodičnog života balkanskih naroda', in Ljubiša Mitrović, Dragana Stjepanović-Zaharijevski and Vjekoslav Butigan (eds), *Strategije razvoja i procesi regionalne saradnje na Balkanu*, Niš, 2000, pp.257–64; Nikola Pavković, 'Porodična zadruga u srpskom građanskom zakoniku', in Miodrag Jovičić (ed.), *Sto pedeset godina od donoševa Srpskog građanskog zakonika 1844–1994*, Belgrade, 1996, pp.329–36; Karl Kazer, *Porodica i srodstvo na Balkanu*, Belgrade, 2003 (in German: K. Kaser, *Familie und Verwandtschaft auf dem Balkan*, Vienna, Cologne and Weimar, 1995); Robert Byrnes, *Communal Families in the Balkans: The* Zadruga, Notre Dame/London, 1976; Ruth Trouton, *Peasant Renaissance in Yugoslavia, 1900–1950*, New York, 1952; Jochen George Hiany, *Kinship and Modernization in Mediterranean Society*, Hanover, New Hampshire, 1976.
3. My fieldwork entailed research on attitudes and practices related to the phenomenon of landownership in Šumadija in central Serbia; meanwhile a colleague of mine addressed the same issues in Vojvodina, another part of Serbia. See the chapter by Jovana Diković (this volume).
4. For a general perspective on Serbian history, see Sima Ćirković, *The Serbs*, Malden/Oxford/Calton, 2004; Holm Sundhaussen, *Geschichte Serbiens. 19.–21. Jahrhundert*, Vienna/Cologne/Weimar, 2007.
5. I am speaking here of the *sanjak* (an administrative unit of Ottoman Empire) of Novi Pazar, Kosovo and Macedonia. Macedonia is now an independent state, and Kosovo – the most important part of so-called Old Serbia – also declared independence from Serbia in February 2007. At the time of writing, Kosovo's independence remained unrecognized by Serbia.
6. The Second Balkan War, fought between Bulgaria and Serbia in 1913, was started by the Bulgarians, who demanded correct execution of the agreement between Bulgaria and Serbia on territorial arrangements achieved before the war against the Ottomans, that is, the First Balkan War of 1912. Forbidden to annex parts of north Albania as had been planned, Serbia annexed some territories that, according to the agreement, were to be annexed by Bulgaria. Serbia argued in favour of this action on the basis of the Bulgarians' failure to fulfil their part of the alliance agreement. The Bulgarian army attacked and very shortly thereafter suffered defeat, which enabled Serbia to annex almost all of northern Macedonia. See Grupa Autora, *Istorija srpskog naroda*, vol. 6, Belgrade, 1993.
7. Milan Milićević, *Kneževina Srbija*, Belgrade, 1876, p.1.
8. On this topic, see e.g. Mira Radojević, *Naučnik i politika. Politička biografija Božidara V. Markovića (1874–1946)*, Belgrade, 2007, pp.25–28.
9. Veljko Petrović, *Šumadija i Vojvodina*, Belgrade, 1930.

10. Vukosavljević, 'Postanak privatne zemljišne svojine u nas'; Jovan Erdeljanović, *Etnološka građa o Šumadincima*, Belgrade, 1951, p.100.
11. The territory of the nineteenth-century autonomous province and later of the independent state (from 1878) of Serbia covered most of what today is central Serbia.
12. See Radoš Ljušić, *Kneževina Srbija 1830–1839*, Belgrade, 2004.
13. Miodrag Jovičić, *Ustavi Kneževine i Kraljevine Srbije*, Belgrade, 1988.
14. See Olga Popović-Obradović, *The Parliamentary System in Serbia 1903–1914*, Belgrade, 2013, retrievable from: http://www.helsinki.org.rs/doc/parliamentary%20system%20in%20serbia.pdf.
15. See Života Đorđević, 'Zemljišni minimum i zemljišni maksimum kao ograničenja razvoja Srbije u novo doba', in Latinka Perović (ed.), *Srbija u modernizacijskim procesima XX veka*, Belgrade, 1994, pp.113–21; Momčilo Isić, 'Sitno posedništvo kao kočnica ekonomske modernizacije Srbije u prvoj polovini XX veka', in Perović, *Srbija u modernizacijskim procesima XX veka*, pp.101–11; Ljubodrag Dimić, 'Srbija 1804–2004 (suočavanje sa prošlošću)', in Ljubodrag Dimić, Dubravka Stojanović and Miroslav Jovanović (eds), *Srbija 1804–2004: Poziv na dijalog*, Belgrade, 2005, p.43.
16. The minimum of arable land called *okućje*, protected and inalienable by law, had been established for the first time in 1836, then abolished in 1838, and reintroduced with some changes in 1873.
17. On this, see Jelenko Petrović, *Okućje ili Zaštita zemljoradničkog minimuma*, Belgrade, 1930.
18. On the agrarian reforms in Yugoslavia see Nikola Gaćeša, *Agrarna reforma i kolonizacija u Banatu: 1919–1941*, Novi Sad, 1972; Nikola Gaćeša, *Agrarna reforma i kolonizacija u Bačkoj: 1918–1941*, Novi Sad, 1968; Nikola Gaćeša, *Agrarna reforma i kolonizacija u Sremu: 1919–1941*, Novi Sad, 1975; Nikola Gaćeša, *Agrarna reforma i kolonizacija u Jugoslaviji: 1945–1948*, Novi Sad, 1984; Bogdan Lekić, *Agrarna reforma u Jugoslaviji 1918–1941*, Belgrade, 2002; Bogdan Lekić, *Agrarna reforma i kolonizacija u Jugoslaviji: 1945–1948*, Belgrade, 1997; Milivoje Erić, *Agrarna reforma u Jugoslaviji 1918–1941. god.*, Sarajevo, 1958; Marijan Maticka, *Agrarna reforma i kolonizacija u Hrvatskoj 1945–1948*, Zagreb, 1990.
19. Aleksandar Živković, 'Nastajanje i razvoj geodetske delatnosti u Srbiji', in Petar Miljanić (ed.), *Putevi srpskog inženjerstva tokom XIX veka*, Belgrade, 1994, pp.29–43.
20. For a short and useful review of the legal documents related to the development of the normative side of the landed property issue, see Anka Čkrebić (ed.), *150 godina geodetske službe Beograda 1839–1989*, Belgrade, 1989, pp.49–53.
21. See Ljubinka Trgovčević, 'Srpski inženjeri na studijama u inostranstvu do 1918. godine', in Miljanić, *Putevi srpskog inženjerstva tokom XIX veka*, pp.148–67.
22. Natalija Bratuljević-Mašanović, 'Geodetska nauka i praksa u Srbiji', in Miodrag Sekulović (ed.), *Razvoj nauke u oblasti građevinarstva i geodezije u Srbiji*, Belgrade, 1996, pp.337–55.
23. Živković, 'Nastajanje i razvoj geodetske delatnosti u Srbiji', p.32.
24. Ibid.
25. Dragoljub Vujović, 'Geopremer u Moravičkom okrugu (Čačak, Gornji Milanovac, Lučani i Ivanjica) i osnivanje katastra zemljišta', *Zbornik radova Narodnog muzeja u Čačku* 36 (2005), p.175.
26. Ibid.
27. Interview with Danica Y., 27 July 2007.
28. 'The books' is the most frequently used term for all kinds of official registers.
29. Dušanka Y., 27 November 2007.
30. The most explicit accusation of this kind about the communists was during an interview with Milivoje Erić, 27 July 2007.
31. For example, the roughly 20 hectare estate of Rajko Erić, as my oldest informants stated.
32. For a description of the different types of cooperatives, see Desimir Tošić, *Snaga i nemoć: naš komunizam 1945–1990*, Belgrade, 2001; Desimir Tošić, *Kolektivizacija u Jugoslaviji*, Belgrade, 2002; Vera Gudac, *Agrarna politika FNRJ i seljaštvo u Srbiji 1949–1953*, Belgrade, 1999.

33. Interview with Milan Y., 19 July 2007.
34. Dragan J. (b. 1955), former director of the communal service in the village, informed me about local gossip about the fate of the cooperative's machinery: one former manager took one machine, and the second another; thus was the property of the cooperative alienated. Interview with Dragan J., 15 May 2007.
35. Interview with Dragan J., 15 May 2007.
36. Milan Y. said, 'I gave my sister one portion of the land'. From his viewpoint, it is totally understandable that he is the only legitimate heir of the whole estate since he lives there, pays the taxes, etc. His sister is married, and it is a matter of her own conscience to renounce her right.
37. See *Politika* (Belgrade), 27 June 2007; retrieved 15 January 2009 from: www.rgz.sr.gov.yu/template1.asp?PageName=2007_06_27_4&MenuID=none&LanguageID=2.
38. This text is from the cover page of a document issued by the Ministry of Agriculture in 2007 that contains the form for registering agricultural land.
39. Interestingly, an important archive related to the cooperative in Mrčajevci is in this man's possession.
40. I requested information on this matter from the court, but received no response.
41. In Yugoslavia, the concept of working peasant cooperatives failed until the early 1950s. The cooperatives that survived and dominated until the late 1980s were consumer-supplying type, which did not entail collectivization of the land but rather enabled producers to buy or rent technical materials, machinery and so on at reduced prices and also to sell their products.
42. Interview with Danica Y. and Živana Y. respectively, 6 June 2007.
43. Interview with Dušanka X., 27 November 2007.
44. Cf. Gianmaria Ajani, 'By Chance and Prestige: Legal Transplants in Russia and Eastern Europe', *American Journal of Comparative Law* 43/1 (1995), p.94.
45. Denis James Galligan, 'Legal Failure: Law and Social Norms in Post-communist Europe', in Denis James Galligan and Mary Kurkchiyan (eds), *Law and Informal Practices: The Post-communist Experience*, Oxford/New York, 2003, pp.1–23.
46. Slobodan Jovanović, *Druga vlada Miloša i Mihaila*, Belgrade, 2005, p.90.
47. For this interpretation, see Latinka Perović, *Između anarhije i autokratije: Srpsko društvo na prelazima vekova (XIX–XXI)*, Belgrade, 2007; L. Perović, M. Obradović and D. Stojanović, (eds), *Srbija u modernizacijskim procesima 20. veka*, Belgrade 1994; Latinka Perović (ed.), *Srbija u modernizacijskim procesima 19. i 20. veka 2. Položaj žene kao merilo modernizacije*, Belgrade, 1998; Latinka Perović (ed.), *Srbija u modernizacijskim procesima 19. i 20. veka 3: Uloga elita*, Belgrade, 2003; Latinka Perović (ed.), *Srbija u modernizacijskim procesima 19. i 20. veka 4: Žene i deca*, Belgrade, 2006; Olga Popović-Obradović, *The Parliamentary System in Serbia 1903–1914*, Belgrade, 2013; Olga Popović-Obradović, *Kakva ili kolika država*, Belgrade, 2009; D. Stojanović, *Srbija i demokratija 1903–1914*, Belgrade 2003; D. Stojanović, *Ulje na vodi. Ogledi iz istorije sadašnjosti*, Belgrade 2010. I mention here only major works of Serbian historians dealing with the problem of modernization. For the socio-economic context, see Mari Žanin Čalić, *Socijalna istorija Srbije 1815–1941*, Belgrade, 2004 (Marie-Janine Calic, *Sozialgeschichte Serbiens, 1815–1941. Der aufhaltsame Fortschritt während der Industrialisierung*, München, 1994).

12

The Practices of Landownership in Vojvodina

The Case of Aradac

Jovana Diković

Introduction

The question of the peasantry and its future seems more topical than ever, whether due to rapid social and political change and the disappearance of the traditional village in some parts of the world, or to widespread professionalization in almost every field of human activity. These continuously challenging, provocative subjects therefore require fresh evaluation in accordance with current social, cultural and political conditions at national and international levels.

The concepts of social determinism, as advocated by Henri Mendras in his study of peasant societies – namely, the fact that a peasant is any person who belongs to peasant society, regardless of whether they are actively involved in agriculture – are inapplicable to post-socialist countries.[1] Under socialism in Eastern Europe, the main motive of various social and political reforms was to significantly restrict private property, and the repercussions of this ideology were deeply felt in rural areas. Therefore, although I disagree with Mendras, I believe that in this part of the world there exists a specific type of property determinism in which a peasant is determined by the condition of having their ancestors' land as property. A peasant cultivates this land, lives on it and bequeaths it to the next generation.[2] This involves a chain of specific, complex relationships that very often are more symbolic than economically profitable. Recent research on these processes has relied especially on approaches from social anthropology, which I too will draw on.[3]

In contrast to post-socialist states, market-oriented societies with regulated property rights that are accepted and implemented tend to perceive land as a material and economic asset. In this chapter I argue that, despite the social and political changes from 2000 to the present in Serbia, and particularly in Vojvodina, land is still understood much more as an immaterial category than in economic terms – it is perceived in relation to an unreliable livelihood and way of life rather than as anything worthy of investment for the future.

In the case of Vojvodina and the sub-region of Banat, seventy years of failed agrarian politics[4] and a decade of industrial isolation at the end of the twentieth century meant that agriculture did not follow a linear, progressive path of development in any significant respect.[5] This was due to various factors, such as the impossibility of enlarging individual property for several decades, the maintaining of 'mixed' worker-agricultural households,[6] the demographic predominance of older people in Vojvodina's villages and the outflow of the younger part of the population, outdated machinery and cultivation techniques on farms, and state encroachments on peasants' property rights. Yet despite this negative record, and contrary to all economic ideas of progress, agricultural households in Banat did not disappear.

In this chapter I therefore try to show at least two aspects of property at different times. On the one hand, I treat property with regard to its institutional – that is, state-regulated – dimension, by considering various property-related legal acts concerning the first and second agrarian reforms and the restitution law, as well as those valid at present. Such an approach can reveal different perceptions of notions of property inspired over time by the state's various political, economic and social evolution. In other words, it can explain how during the twentieth century private property was – as a result of ideological indoctrination – increasingly conceived as a state possession, and how today, after property restitution, it has become one of the basic preconditions for market liberalization.

Meanwhile, I will treat personal and family relationships with land from my informants' perspective, in terms of livelihood and the symbolic dimension of land. These relationships imply symbolically motivated investments in farms, resulting in an array of reasons for maintaining rural households. Accordingly, land figures as a symbolic element of family history, family inheritance and people's experiences of running a farm, something which is passed on from one generation to another. Land is not simply part of a farm but, in a broader sense, part of a family biography that represents a sort of symbolic real estate.

My research focused on four families from Aradac, two Serb (P. and K.) and two Slovak (L. and Z.).[7] The younger members of the P. and L. families live in cities, whereas the Z. and K. families reside permanently in Aradac. Each of these families, including their oldest members, forms one household. Their households can be considered medium-sized agricultural households whose land encompasses an area of between 3 and 15 hectares. What they have in common is their experience, albeit in different ways, of measures implemented during agricultural reforms, and their categorization as 'mixed' worker-agricultural households throughout the socialist period until the 1980s. Nowadays the situation has changed: some of the family members are retired, and some work in the agricultural sector only as a secondary occupation. Only the Z. family, consisting of five members, is registered as an agricultural producer; the other families are listed only as property owners.

Perceptions of land and land ownership differed across generations in the twentieth century. Different generations within one household were torn between old and new social and cultural patterns, the burdens of history, patriarchal attitudes and emotional and economic views of the land. In a broader sense, then, land and property have many meanings dependent on manifold political, economic, social and personal transformations.

Agrarian Policy, Agricultural Organization and Agrarian Reform

The chronological framework of this chapter aims to show how state regulation of agriculture influenced the development of individual households. I will relate historical data and personal and family experiences to the periods of the first and second agrarian reforms – 1919 to 1941, and 1945 to 1953 respectively – while also investigating the current situation in several rural households and the effects of state agricultural policies on individual households.[8] Combining the study of the agrarian reforms in Vojvodina with analyses of personal accounts of the devastation – or survival – of agricultural households provides a more complete insight into processes of adaptation to the changing circumstances peasants were subjected to.

The Impact of the First Agrarian Reform and Colonization, 1919–1941

According to Milivoje Erić, 38.3 per cent of the population in Vojvodina had no land in 1910,[9] which obviously made the issue of landownership the most significant socio-economic problem in this region.[10] During the first agrarian reform in the Kingdom of Yugoslavia, and especially in Vojvodina, riots and spontaneous attacks on state property and the private estates of the rich reflected the revolutionary spirit of the times.[11] People expressed their dissatisfaction by burning down municipal buildings (where ownership documents were kept), trespassing and confiscating landlords' land and giving it to the poor. The rebels were particularly aggravated by the ethnic distribution of landed estates in Vojvodina, where non-Slavic people of Hungarian and German origin were landowners with huge properties. Of the 87 landowners in Banat who owned more than 1,000 cadastral acres (575 hectares) just before the implementation of the first agrarian reform, 81 were Hungarians and 6 were Germans. Out of 3,456 landowners with more than 100 cadastral acres, 391 were Hungarian, 1,300 German, 160 Romanian, 148 Slovak and 1,458 Serb, alongside a few Croats, Russians and others.[12]

Ethnic and socio-economic differences in Vojvodina and Banat reached their culmination during and after the First World War, when the ruling political powers conducted a new socio-economic programme for agrarian reform meant to satisfy the angry peasantry's call for the sub-division of great estates. By parcelling out estates belonging to owners of non-Serb nationality, the Kingdom of Yugoslavia attempted to implement its national politics in Vojvodina and thus dominate the area politically, while also responding to the social demands of poor peasants. Therefore, agrarian reform in Vojvodina was both socio-political and nationalist. Further, it assumed the form of 'Slavicization' by sending colonists from economically less developed (passive) areas of Yugoslavia to Vojvodina.[13]

From 1919 to 1929, the Ministry of Agrarian Reform in Belgrade was responsible for enforcing agrarian policies; then, from 1929 to 1941, this duty fell to the Ministry of Agriculture, also situated in Belgrade.[14] The eminent Marxist scholar Nikola Gaćeša characterized Yugoslavia's agrarian reform as follows:

> The agrarian reform between the wars doubtless had a civil [in the modern sense] character, which is understandable if we bear in mind that: 1) its legal standardization was enforced in regional offices; 2) its realization was in the hands of the state; 3) its enforcement represented an elimination of the remains of feudal agrarian ownership structures on the one hand, and easily made possible the extension of capitalist production relationships in the agricultural sphere on the other hand.[15]

Supporters of the first agrarian reform believed that smaller country farms were more efficient than large estates, due to the greater diligence of peasants working their own land in comparison with agricultural workers on big estates. In their opinion, this peasantization of agriculture would unleash hitherto dormant potential, leading to a competitive atmosphere and more goods on the market.

Landless peasants and those owning less than 10 cadastral acres, disabled people, families of soldiers killed in the war, former soldiers and volunteers who had fought for the freedom of Serbs, Croats and Slovenes: these were the beneficiaries of the reform.[16] The regulation on four-year lease holding precisely defined the duties of the peasants. Further on, it stated the main criteria for maximum and minimum land ownership, which governed decisions on whether or not someone could claim the right to own land. A rule in the regulation held that every allotted farm had to be adequately cultivated, and that the holder could not sell it to a third party. An additional, quite important stipulation was that land could be given only to families whose members were citizens of the

Kingdom of Yugoslavia and permanent residents of one of its municipalities. This regulation legally did not disqualify citizens of the Kingdom of Yugoslavia of foreign nationality (mainly Hungarians and Germans) as would-be beneficiaries, but in practice such a discriminatory policy was enacted nevertheless.[17]

The agrarian reform potentially targeted all larger cultivable estates of between 100 and 500 cadastral acres, depending on the quality of the land and the local situation. Expropriated land was distributed among the peasantry, who had to pay their share of compensation payments along with the state, which paid compensation to the original owners in cash or bonds. The properties of the Habsburg dynasty and owners who had obtained land from the dynasty were expropriated without compensation. However, political misuse and bribery resulted in many large estates in Vojvodina being exempt from agrarian reform during this period.

At the beginning of the agrarian reform, Aradac was divided into two municipalities: Serb Aradac and Slovak Aradac. In Serb Aradac, 43 cadastral acres of land owned by Pavle Galambos (a Hungarian landowner) were given to landless people and poor peasants. His property, known as Vrbica, was near the Tisa River, and crossing the river was the only way to reach it. Galambos decided to outmanoeuvre the recipients by offering to sell his ferryboat to the municipality for 30,000 Austro-Hungarian crowns. The municipality could not come up with this sum, so he banned use of his ferryboat; meanwhile, the municipality could not afford a new one. In this way he kept his land, leaving the aspiring new owners landless.[18]

In Slovak Aradac, the situation was much worse. Because the village had no uncultivated arable land suitable for division, only a few meadows were given to the peasants. Numerous people were interested in land, but there was so little land to redistribute that two to six peasants wound up sharing each allotted cadastral acre. Slovak Aradac had a territory of approximately 1,860 cadastral acres, while Serb Aradac comprised 1,534 cadastral acres, meaning that the combined area of the two municipalities could satisfy the needs of all the Slovak peasants as well. Accordingly, the agrarian administration was instructed to treat the estate of Aradac as a single entity.

The administrative unit of Dunavska Banovina decided to merge the two municipalities of Aradac in 1932.[19] Thus, in the unified municipality there were 521 cadastral acres of productive soil, the rest being evaluated as unproductive. According to the decision, 388 cadastral acres of the entire area of Aradac were to be expropriated for the needs of Slovak peasants. However, this decision was not carried out because the two municipalities separated again in 1934. Aradac's potential Slovak beneficiaries of land distribution thus lost more than 500 cadastral acres. In the end following the decision of Dunavska Banovina, only 56 cadastral acres of the area of Slovak Aradac was allotted to Slovak peasants.[20]

Other sources at the time indicate that 300 households in Slovak Aradac were home to more than 700 taxpayers.[21] Almost two thirds of these peasants had no land at all. Families with seven or eight members received 3 to 4 cadastral acres (or a maximum of 5) of land under lease. However, Germans, Hungarians and Romanians, like all other non-Slavs, received no land, which provoked much anger. Very often, applicants for land allotments from Aradac and other villages could neither redeem the land they had received from large landowners nor cultivate the soil with modern techniques. Therefore, most of those who did not manage to redeem the land were then forced to sell the land to wealthier peasants. Only those who had owned some land before the reform and thus possessed the necessary tools kept the land. This starkly divided the village into wealthy landowners on the one hand and poor peasants on the other. Many of the latter group left Aradac in pursuit of work and land, and settled in nearby villages, usually finding work on the estates of wealthy landowners.[22]

The four families I interviewed were not among the wealthy agricultural households whose property structure was affected by the first agrarian reform. Pavel L'.s father, as a Slovak beneficiary of the first agrarian reform, had received 2 cadastral acres of land. However, in that same period the forefathers of both Serb families received 8 cadastral acres of first-class land because they had been volunteers on the Salonika Front between 1915 and 1918. As one of them said, 'People did not go to war for patriotic reasons, but for the land that was guaranteed to them in return'.[23]

The last decade of the first period of agrarian reform (1931 to 1941) was marked by efforts to close the issue of the agrarian reform with a law on 'liquidating' the agricultural reform as a tool.[24] Most of the peasants who had received landowners' property were unable to redeem it completely, so the Ministry of Agriculture opted to enforce the principle of facultative redemption of the land, whereby the price of the land was mutually agreed upon between owner and leaseholder. This favoured landowners and wealthy peasants, who could determine the price on their own. Facultative redemption was suitable only for those peasants who could afford the redemption and enter the process of 'liquidating' agrarian reform by becoming owners of an estate. Nevertheless, unsettled tax bills issued by the so-called 'agrarian communities' prolonged the 'liquidation' process of agrarian reform from 1931 to 1941, as official ownership was conditional on settled bills.[25] Meanwhile, the 'liquidation' of the agrarian reform was necessary to enact files on land ownership, without which it was impossible to either speed up agricultural production or achieve a market surplus.

We should bear in mind that this process changed the landownership structure in Banat to some degree. A certain number of poor peasants, due to the elimination of remains of feudal property relations, had become landowners; prior to the agrarian reform, they had been only leaseholders. Nevertheless, a significant number of peasants remained dissatisfied, especially among ethnic minorities who had not received any land. The unsatisfactory distribution of land thus became one of the main reasons for the second agrarian reform.

The Impact of the Second Agrarian Reform and Colonization after 1945

Just after the Second World War,[26] the Yugoslav Communist Party began enacting an agrarian policy that can be characterized as a radicalized extension of interwar agrarian reform and colonization.[27] The commonalities of the two reforms consist, first, in the state's pivotal role in prescribing the size of agrarian property that could be legally owned, and determining the benefits peasants could reap from their land when selling goods on the market. Second, despite provisions for the legal equality of all citizens in both the constitutions and agrarian reforms of the First and Second Yugoslavia, an obvious bias favoured members of the titular nations.[28]

There were certain differences, however. The first agrarian reform had been undertaken by the leading political powers with the aim of thwarting communist notions concerning property that had been spreading all over the country,[29] and a certain number of capitalist agricultural landowners were exempted from expropriation. The new agrarian policy featured the same land-to-the-tiller ideology as the interwar agrarian reform, stating in the first paragraph of the Law on the Agrarian Reform and Colonization of August 1945: 'The land belongs to those who till it'.[30] The law contained no explicit ethnic determination of those who were entitled to obtain land, but it singled out German citizens and Germans from Yugoslavia as people to be expropriated.[31] In general, land was expropriated from big landowners, banks, joint-stock companies, churches and monasteries and wealthy peasants, as well as from smaller and middling landowners who did not cultivate their property. Thus the aim of the second agrarian reform was hardly to quell communist ideology but rather to fortify medium-sized peasants' property and increase agricultural production based on agricultural cooperatives. Finally, this reform resulted in the creation of 'mixed' worker-agricultural households, which went hand in hand with the industrialization of the country and the glorification of the working class.

Regulations with the force of law determined the maximum area of property for both peasants' and non-peasants' families. In Banat, peasants could own a maximum of 36 hectares. Any land exceeding this limit was to be included in the property fund and later given to people who did not have enough land. The Law on Agricultural Reform and Internal Colonization of November 1945, stipulated in Article 36 that the distributed land should become the 'private property' of the peasants and be entered as such in the land register.[32] This very reform (whose effects lasted in some respects until the 1980s) established the absolute prevalence of medium-sized peasant properties and agricultural cooperatives, and the state's dominant position as the major holder of agricultural machinery, seeds and technical knowledge.[33] As Mirko Joksimović notes, just after the implementation of the agrarian reform and colonization law, the Serb part of Aradac was home to thirty-two families with 2 hectares or less of land, some without any.[34] Twenty-nine of these families were Serb, two were Slovak and one Roma. These families owned a combined total of 23 hectares of land. In the Slovak part of Aradac, eighty-five households (two Hungarian, one German, and the rest Slovak) had no land at all. They lived in an area comprising 1,880 hectares; thus, in the Serb and Slovak parts of Aradac, a total of 117 families were landless or had less than 2 hectares. By contrast, thirty-three households had over 40 hectares. The remaining households lived on farms ranging from 3 to 39 hectares. Data from the Aradac agricultural office indicate that potential beneficiaries of land distribution in Aradac altogether, Slovaks and Serbs, totalled 223.

In Vojvodina, the consequences of the second agrarian reform were several. First, it eliminated a considerable number of interwar agricultural producers who had carried out intensive cultivation. Second, landless people disappeared and colonists settled in Vojvodina. Third, hired agricultural workers vanished completely. A fourth consequence was that farms were reduced by up to 5 hectares. A final consequence was the creation of state property and peasant cooperatives as the main agents of agricultural production, which made the state a majority owner of a considerable portion of the country's machinery, seeds and technical knowledge.[35]

From 1945 to 1948, citizens were permitted to own a maximum of 36 hectares of land. Below I analyse how the state stipulated the extension of peasants' property and how my informants from Aradac recall those times. It is especially important to note that during the period from the first to the second agrarian reform, the four households examined did not extend their property through purchases, but mostly by inheritance.

Given the fact that the beneficiaries of land distribution were very poor and tilled the soil under poor conditions, peasants started to organize work cooperatives in Aradac after the Second World War. Their earliest members were poor peasants who entered the cooperatives with their land and inventory. The mandatory repurchase of crops by the state obliged every household that owned up to 36 hectares to deliver to the state, at a price set by the state, a requisite quantity of crops determined according to its plans for acreage under cultivation, under penalty of legal prosecution in case of refusal.[36] According to my informants, people coped with the situation in different ways, often going to nearby villages to buy such quantities of crops as they were forced to give to the cooperatives. Persons who were unwilling or unable to fulfil the quotas were arrested and punished, and their assets confiscated and handed over to the cooperatives.[37] According to Pavel L., 'property would be confiscated if the owners openly declared their opposition to the communist regime'.[38] There were altogether three such families in Aradac, two Slovak and one Serb, who were given the pejorative nickname 'wheaters'.

From 1945 to 1948, there were two types of cooperative. The first included landless peasants without the means of cultivation, and the second was made up of those whose land had been confiscated to augment the cooperatives, whose members they became by way of punishment.[39] The cooperatives were based on common investment and labour, and the gains were shared equally. This kind of agricultural cooperative existed until peasant cooperatives were reformed in 1953; thereafter, everyone joining a cooperative did so voluntarily, and those who wanted to leave the cooperatives received their invested property – tools and/or land – if the cooperatives were willing to return it.

After the first phase of the second agrarian reform (1945 to 1948), the planned execution of agrarian policy continued, aimed at strengthening cooperatives and collective property. As Desimir Tosić claims, peasant work cooperatives were merely a means, not the objective, of the socialist transformation. 'Instead of increasing agricultural production and helping the peasants of the lower and middle economic classes, the objective seems to be that of bringing a profound social transformation to the villages, of economically ruining the private landowners, and of creating the socialist sector in agriculture by means of state-ownership and peasant work cooperatives'.[40] The Law on the Agrarian Land Fund of Common People's Property, passed in 1953,[41] represented a new stage in the collectivization of property and the creation of 'mixed' worker-agricultural households. This phase of agricultural regulation lasted until the restitution law that was proclaimed in 1991 took effect. During the state's promotion of intensive industrialization, the law established a new maximum area of land owned by peasants and non-peasants – that is, industrial workers – who represented a growing socio-economic category. To foster medium-sized peasant properties, the maximum land area was set at 17 hectares for peasants; meanwhile, non-peasants were allowed only 5 hectares. All expropriated land was handed over to state agricultural organizations, mainly cooperatives and so-called state farms. Thus 'a period in the history of the Yugoslavian village began, a period that resulted in a cancellation of the agrarian reform and the disinheriting of direct agricultural producers by enforcing the development of peasants' work cooperatives'.[42]

During this period, the L. family household was listed as a 'mixed' household, and according to the aforementioned regulation, property exceeding 5 hectares was confiscated from Pavle L. Not even his wife, who came from an agricultural family, was allowed to inherit more than 20 hectares from her parents and cousins, because she was married to a worker. The remaining three households were also listed as 'mixed' households. In this group, only the P. family lost land – 6 hectares – under the regulation of maximum landownership. During this period, the Z. family had 10 hectares and the K. family had just 7 hectares, which allowed them to buy more land after 1953. All confiscated land went to the property fund, and from there to the cooperatives. The state repaid the land in bonds, which meant a loss for the peasants (all my informants agreed on this) because the state-assessed price of the land was lower than its real value.

To maintain their farms and cultivate more land than the prescribed maximum, peasants very often organized 'artificial' households, meaning that one real household split itself in two or more, each of which could have 10 hectares – for example, a father and a son living in the same house and cultivating the same land would nominally list their land as two farms under their respective names. In addition, it often happened that families with members in both peasant and worker categories would list the whole farm under the names of those who were agricultural producers; the others could then buy land using their maximum quota and thus extend the family land fund.

After 1953, one contractual relationship remained between peasants and peasant cooperatives: the buyer–seller relationship, based on which the cooperatives had the right to buy peasant land at considerably reduced prices. Meanwhile, peasants who owned the prescribed maximum were not allowed to lease land. As George Hoffman has stated, this and similar factors induced instability in agricultural society because 'the private peasant felt insecure regarding the permanency of his holding and therefore lost any incentive to work and improve his property'.[43]

In the 1960s, great numbers of people renounced their land in favour of the state. Often, they ceded land of the worst quality (seventh class), as Adam Z. did to be free of a tax obligation. In addition, households whose members were employed often renounced their land to obtain the right to child allowances, or they would, for the same purpose, transfer land to the names of brothers or sisters. Heavy taxes on livestock deterred all but a few people from being involved keeping a herd.

Whilst the 10 hectare limit was still in force, people were usually able to afford tractors only by getting together to buy them. Peasant cooperatives had the most up-to-date machinery, so many people used their services. According to my informants, from the beginning of the 1970s to the 1980s, peasants' standards of living and the state of agriculture improved noticeably, and the state exerted less pressure than before on farmers. Only then did peasant households start to mechanize independently, and thus achieve larger harvests.

With the end of the socialist system in 1991, changes in the political system brought a new law on property restoration into effect.[44] Land that had been confiscated and included in the land fund in 1953 was returned, even though the state had compensated the injured parties. Nonetheless, peasants remained uncompensated for the land confiscated during the second agrarian reform of 1945 to 1948. Thanks to the new law, however, the informants finally, after several decades, had the right to expand their agricultural households without impediment.[45]

From land restitution in 1991 until today, state agricultural strategies have been oriented towards privatizing state-owned enterprises, creating conditions for foreign investment, preparing Serb agrarian products for export to the European Union, abolishing mixed agricultural households and increasing the number of registered agricultural producers. Efficient regulation of legal property relationships is a key precondition for development in agriculture. Therefore, the restitution legislation can be said to provide the institutional basis for the new agricultural strategy.

However, even though there is no real need to pass any radical agricultural measures today, transition still inspires real fear, as was the case in the past. Peasants believe that agricultural reorganization threatens small and medium-sized farms. The agricultural market is becoming more open, the state is retreating from agriculture, and the principle of supply and demand is becoming the leading principle of agricultural politics. Small and medium-sized producers reckon that they will be pushed out of the market upon the entrance of major 'players', namely, large private agricultural companies, which would radically change established agricultural relationships as well as the structure of new agricultural holdings.

Registering, Buying and Selling: The Institutional and Informal Organization of Property

Above, I presented the development of agricultural households in the interwar and socialist periods and the political, economic and social conditions of agricultural organization. I described the institutional framework of agricultural households, that is, the laws and regulations regarding agriculture. Now I turn my focus to the period after the federal state fell apart, that is, from the moment of land restitution up to the present day. I consider this a crucial period because of the turbulent processes of denationalization involved – particularly the restitution of individual property and de-collectivization in the case of Aradac – as well as the implementation of governmental agrarian policy, the tendency to transform the socialist economy into a market economy and the transformation of 'mixed' worker-agricultural households into professional agricultural households. Below I present different aspects of registering, buying and selling practices – both the institutional aspects established by the state, and the informal aspects related to the everyday needs of ordinary rural people.

Cadastral Records of Estates and Unregulated Ownership Issues

The first point that should be addressed here is the important difference between land registers and cadastres.[46] Land registers are public registers that keep records of the real rights inhering in real estate. By enrolling in land registers, property owners acquire, abolish, transfer or restrict these rights. In other words, land registers keep records of proprietorship over estates. The records in a land cadastre, by contrast, concern the position, shape, area, land use practices, land quality (classes) and users of estates. Because the cadastre was the basis for setting taxes, it was unpopular among peasants – in contrast to the land register. In recent years, older people from Vojvodina have tended to refer to the land register (*gruntovnica*) to establish or confirm documentation of landownership, likely because they are convinced that it is more reliable than the cadastres.[47]

However, the legal practice of land register use lasted until 1988, when a new law marked the merger of the land register with the cadastre.[48] Nonetheless, this measure did not (clearly) distinguish between certain legal property relationships in Serbia, especially in Banat. It is especially problematic that the land changes resulting from agricultural reforms and colonization in Vojvodina were not recorded in the cadastres, primarily because poorly qualified staff had been assigned to huge administrative areas. Furthermore, lost documentation and outdated land registers for the period from the Second World War to the present pose great obstacles in the regulation of property relationships.

Today, despite the land restitution of 1991, a significant number of people from Aradac still have not been given back their land. The roots of property confusion lie in changes in properties and their ownership that were not recorded in either the land registers or the cadastres, due to villagers joining peasant work cooperatives en masse. That is to say, the property peasants usually brought to the cooperatives was unregistered in land registers. They saw no reason to register their ownership of their allotted land, since joining a cooperative automatically meant that the cooperative became the owner of the land. On the other hand, many peasants who did not join cooperatives leased out their allotted land to cooperatives and thus ceased to cultivate the land themselves.[49]

Numerous attempts to privatize cooperatives to date have revealed a significant proportion of unregulated legal property relationships. These pose an obstacle to the process of privatization because investors are unwilling to make capital investments in this sector due to the lack of legal security or guarantees that their property cannot be claimed by a third party. The state has not yet resolved the overriding problem that state-owned companies use property belonging to other owners.[50]

Informal (Family) Management of Property

As my informants claim, peasants nowadays realize that the possibility of receiving state subsidies[51] makes it more important to be listed in the cadastre than in the land register, which was not the case in the past.[52] A relevant peculiarity regarding cadastres and land registers is that whereas land registers list property owners, cadastres record only users of the estate. Consequently, land that is registered in a cadastre alone can be leased out but not sold. Anyone who wants full rights over the land therefore needs to be listed in both a cadastre and land register.

According to the informants, buyers are very careful during the process of legal purchase and sale. Nobody wants to buy estates that are not listed in the land register. In recent years, no land has been bought from peasants previously categorized as 'landless people', who due to specific circumstances did not become landowners but were listed in the cadastre only as users of an estate. Furthermore, at present no one is buying cooperative land because property relationships are not clearly distinguished in the sense of what remains state-owned property and what has become private property again.

Informants believe that the bureaucratic procedure has not changed much, and that the owner of a larger plot abutting a property for sale enjoys the right of pre-emption. Today, standard forms are in use; both interested parties need only verify them. Based on this verification, the transfer of property is carried out later, as is payment of the property taxes the new owner owes. In practice, according to informants, the property transfer (including the payment of property taxes) takes place 'at some point', and people seldom avoid this kind of legal obligation, especially when registered agricultural estates are in question. Wealthy peasants increasingly resort to legal assistance in the process of buying and selling, and with the associated bureaucratic procedures. In addition to traditional means of announcing the sale or purchase of land, peasants now also use other media (the press, internet, TV). The value of land is negotiable among villagers, whereas the price for non-peasants is significantly higher.

The standard answer to the question 'When do you buy land?' is 'Always!' But land is not sold as it was before. Ljubomir P. claims: 'Serbs do not often buy and sell land. Everyone keeps his land because the price is low, so it is not profitable to sell it, and moreover there are some family and emotional reasons which make it difficult to part from one's land'.[53] Another major obstacle to selling a farm are patriarchal patterns and village gossip, and there is usually disapproval of the sale of complete estates, this being one reason why it is so rare in Aradac.[54] One gains the impression that land is sold only when its owner is in need, or when the proceeds will be invested in children or in the purchase of real estate or machinery. Slovaks often decide to sell a couple of hectares to invest in their children's education. According to informants, Serbs also invest heavily in their children's education to provide them with a more comfortable life in the city, whilst Slovaks try to keep their children on the land. Nevertheless, sales of inherited farms are rare even among educated Slovaks and educated Serbs who do not live in the village; instead, the land is mostly leased to peasants and thus is seen as a source of additional income.

According to Radovan K., 'there is an open secret in the village that Serbs will never buy land from Slovaks, but Slovaks will buy land from Serbs'.[55] He believes that if Slovaks are selling land, they are doing so only because it is of poor quality; therefore it is not worth buying.

Evidently, village buying and selling practices have not changed greatly over the years, except that peasants try to keep as much land as they can. In the socialist period, land was very often perceived merely as a source of survival, mostly because the state prohibited extension of landownership. Now, however, land seems to be the mainstay of a peasant's social and economic security.

Property as an Economic Resource and as a Category of Wealth

Today's agricultural production is characterized by several different organizational aspects, some of which the state regulates to a greater or lesser extent. The most common concern private cultivation of the land, leasing land and the merging of agricultural households. *Arenda*, a type of land lease under which the lessor receives a certain amount of money after the harvest as payment, is one of the most interesting aspects and the dominant pattern of contractual relationships between owners and leaseholders. In former times, land was provided for tenants' use on the basis of mutual trust, but this is not the case anymore. With this leasing contract peasants may apply for the state subsidies and refunding for seeds, gas and fertilizers. Both parties fill out standard forms containing information on cadastral and property rights, as well as on the leaseholder, which are verified at the municipal court. An *arenda* is often signed for a period of several years because this favours both parties by strengthening their commitment to cultivating the land. The leaseholder pays for the usage of the land in money or grain. However, one of the more important reasons for the increasing number of leaseholders is that the proprietor pays the taxes. In other words, the tax obligations for leased land are not transferred to the tenant.

Association of households is very frequent in Aradac, and for now it is practised mostly by wealthier peasants, who thereby enjoy to a certain extent economies of scale. My informants claim that the Ministry of Agriculture stimulates this strategy of land mergers based on voluntary association of households, known as *komasacija*. In Aradac, however, it has often led to the indignation of poorer peasants, who feel the associations' main intention is to disadvantage small peasants. Since the quality of land around Aradac varies, associations of agricultural households buy up large areas of land, even those of poor quality, where they can obtain considerable profit thanks to mechanization.

Nowadays cultivation implies many risks for small and average peasants, but it can also, with reasonable investment, generate profits. Although it might not turn a profit in the end, peasants are still unwilling to alienate the land. The feeling of belonging attached to property that in previous decades was taken away from them due to repressive agrarian policies might point towards a reconceptualization of land as a reliable source of livelihood and a permanent kind of real estate.

Indeed, my informants claim that, in Aradac, wealth is still measured in terms of land, which represents both symbolic and economic capital. The wealthiest are those who have 'old capital', meaning high-quality land that was returned to them. They have thus regained the symbolic reputation of old and wealthy families, as well as the real economic potential of the returned land.[56] 'Land is a certain way of saving', says Adam Z. 'Whether the people live in the village or not, they have an investment that pays off'.[57] It seems that for younger members of households, the symbolic dimension of land is a less important factor than the knowledge that the land is an economic resource. Therefore, even when they do not regard land cultivation as profitable, young people do not want to sell it either, because they realize it has economic potential.

Inheritance Practices

Overall, perhaps the most important aspect of property relationships is the process of inheritance, which is how most of my informants acquired their households. According to them, property inheritance used to differ between Serb and Slovak families, in that before the Second World War, female children in Serb families had the right to inherit up to one third of the land if there were male heirs. The child who took care of the parents usually received more land. These were mostly male children who stayed in their parents' households after founding their own families. After the Second World War and the organization of cooperatives, more land was given to a male child who did not want to become a member of the cooperative. Furthermore, when property was divided, wage-working children received less land than those who lived on the estate. As in the past, a strong rule dictates that arrangements with children about who receives what are made during the parents' lives, and only after their death is the land actually transferred. In most cases nowadays, property is shared equally between male and female children in Slovak and Serb families alike. People in Aradac still seldom have formal wills; only childless people do so, in order to share the property among relatives or villagers.

Slovak families have typically always maintained equality among children in inheritance matters. However, according to Pavel L., before the Second World War a certain unusual phenomenon appeared in order to maintain family property, whereupon the living standards of Slovak households rose, leading to a decreased birth rate that fell still further after the occupation and liberation of the country. Wealthier Slovaks in Aradac wanted fewer children in order to maintain their capital, rather than spend it. Therefore, relatives (for example, first cousins) would marry each other to keep the property in one household. Some of the children born to these families had deformities attributed to incest, and some of them still live in Aradac today. In every decade since, cases like this have existed among wealthy families. The phenomenon is less common today, but it has not disappeared entirely. Other Slovaks disapproved of such marriages. Nevertheless, the phenomenon could not be stopped because the Slovaks and Serbs who disapproved of it were poor and at the mercy of the wealthy peasants who entered into this kind of relationship.

With no exceptions, every interviewed family showed a certain level of respect towards inherited land, and towards the means of acquiring and maintaining it. Therefore, land represents a category of symbolic wealth and an immobile document of the existence and lifetime of a family tree.

Conclusion

Agricultural relationships in Vojvodina, especially in Banat, cannot be understood without a complete description of the historical and political context of this region. After Vojvodina joined the Kingdom of the Serbs, Croats, and Slovenes in 1918 it became an important part of Yugoslavian and Serbian politics, and remains so until this day. Without intending to minimize the dimensions of agricultural policy in other former Yugoslavian republics, I consider the most obvious consequences and losses incurred after the first and second agrarian reforms to have been felt in Vojvodina – mostly because of its national and ethnic mixture, great agricultural potential and high proportion of rural inhabitants who were, to a greater or lesser degree, accommodated by the system of agricultural reforms.

From the Second World War to the present, agricultural households have endured several transformations, going from small or medium-sized 'mixed' worker-agricultural households to professional agricultural households with the possibility of unrestricted expansion of their estates following the restitution law of 1991 and subsequent democratic changes in 2000. Peasant livelihoods themselves have also undergone transformations relative to state regulation, from 'mixed' worker-agriculturist and inhibited independent peasants in communist Yugoslavia, to stimulated professional agricultural producers after 2000.

Information provided by my informants shows that land is not just an economic resource but also a complex of symbolic potentials that prolong the continuity of family history. In this regard, I emphasize two important dimensions of landownership relevant to different generations. The first applies to the youngest family members. Having no experience of the agrarian reforms, and at best remembering only the restitution of land starting in the 1990s, they mostly have an instrumental attitude towards land. From their point of view, land is a source of livelihood and should be alienated only if necessary. In other words, the younger rural population that is planning life in the village is mostly market- and profit-oriented. This attitude might indicate a developing class of peasant-entrepreneurs (farmers) long known in Western societies, who in Eastern Europe have been increasingly evident since the late 1990s.

The second dimension concerns the oldest family members. In the past they invested in land both emotionally and economically. Today they cannot profit much from the land because they cannot cultivate it and will not sell it, but they still enjoy memories of the land as symbolic property. Therefore, one informant's statement that 'the peasant is never free' seems to contain an important semantic denotation. Land, its maintenance and various economic and political factors keep peasants dependent on land. However, this dependency is also connected to a special form of duty towards the family past and family heritage, which cannot be disposed of easily.

Although these generational dimensions seem to be in conflict, I prefer to place the issue the other way round. According to Chris Hann, 'all societies have property relations that transcend their individual members, i.e. they imply some sort of integrated collectivity'.[58] The youngest and the oldest family members both perceive the land as a most precious thing, but in different ways. They are unaware that they are already integrated in their different attachments to the land, because the common, essential element of their allegedly different reasons for attachment is nothing other than the land. In other words, as long as land continues to have a profound significance in rural people's life, it incorporates generational splits, different meanings and old and new patterns of economic and emotional investment. The notion of land therefore functions above individuals, making them peasants and uniting them as a peasantry.

Notes

1. See Henri Mendras, *Seljačka društva – Elementi za jednu teoriju seljaštva*, Zagreb, 1986.
2. Joel M. Halpern defines a peasant culture as a 'subculture, the essential feature of which is a territorial based relationship between familial units either nuclear or extended and the land they cultivate mainly with their own labor'. Joel M. Halpern, 'Yugoslav Peasant Society in Transition: Stability in Change', *Anthropological Quarterly* 36/3 (1963), p.156.
3. See e.g. Chris M. Hann (ed.), *Property Relations: Renewing the Anthropological Tradition*, Cambridge, 1998; Chris Hann et al. (eds), *The Postsocialist Agrarian Question: Property Relations and the Rural Condition*, Münster, 2003; Deema Kaneff, *Who Owns the Past? The Politics of Time in a 'Model' Bulgarian Village*, New York, 2004.
4. According to Nikola Gaćeša, both agrarian reforms (after 1918 and after 1945) neglected the interests of the peasantry: he characterized the reforms as 'the most unsuccessful points in

seven decades of social development'. Nikola Gaćeša, *Agrarna reforma i kolonizacija u Jugoslaviji 1945–1948*, Novi Sad, 1984, p.113. On the different political implications of the two agrarian reforms, see Nikola Gaćeša, 'Agrarna politika prve i druge Jugoslavije', in Nikola Gaćeša, *Radovi iz agrarne istorije i demografije*, Novi Sad, 1995, pp.111–14.

5. The Ministry of Agriculture report on the development of households in Vojvodina over the last ten years can be found at: www.mpt.gov.rs.
6. The term 'mixed' household, referring to households whose members were at the same time industrial workers and peasants, emerged after 1953, when the Law on the Agrarian Land Fund of Common People's Property ('Zakon o poljoprivrednom fondu opštenarodne imovine') was passed.
7. The main fieldwork was conducted in October 2007. Informants' statements, taken from informal talks and recorded interviews, are quoted in the text, and their abbreviated names and the interview dates are provided in the notes.
8. For an overview of agrarian policy and land reforms, see Jozo Tomasevich, *Peasants, Politics and Economic Change in Yugoslavia*, New York, 1975 [1955]; John B. Allcock, *Explaining Yugoslavia*, London, 2000, pp.101–44. For a recent analysis and the laws and regulations of the interwar agrarian reform and colonization, see Bogdan Lekić, *Agrarna reforma i kolonizacija u Jugoslaviji 1918–1941*, Belgrade, 2002.
9. The Kingdom of Serbs, Croats and Slovenes (SCS) – after 1929 the Kingdom of Yugoslavia – consisting mainly of these three nationalities, was established in December 1918. The People's Parliament of Vojvodina, situated in Novi Sad, passed legislation on Vojvodina's secession from the Kingdom of Hungary and its merger with SCS. Vojvodina became a part of Serbia for the first time in modern history on 25 November 1918. To avoid misunderstanding in the following pages, I generally use the term Kingdom of Yugoslavia, since it represented a form of territorial and political continuity with the previous SCS.
10. Milivoje Erić, *Agrarna reforma u Jugoslaviji 1918–1941*, Sarajevo, 1958, p.52.
11. See Danilo Kecić, 'Oktobarska Revolucija i agrarno-seljački pokret u Vojvodini tokom 1918. i početkom 1919. godine', *Zbornik za društvene nauke* 49 (1968), pp.26–68.
12. Erić, *Agrarna reforma u Jugoslaviji*, p.53.
13. Among the huge amount of contemporaneous literature on agrarian reform and colonization as a means of ethno-politics, see e.g. Milorad Zebić, 'Unutrašnja kolonizacija u vezi agrarne reforme', in *Almanah Udruženja Pravnika Kraljevstva Srba, Hrvata i Slovenaca*, Belgrade, 1920, pp.287–314; Fedor Nikić, 'Revizija naše politike u Vojvodini', *Letopis Matice Srpske* 104/2 (1929), pp.252–67; Vladan Jojkić, *Nacionalizacija Bačke i Banata: Etno-politička studija*, Novi Sad, 1931. For the interwar minority policy of Yugoslavia, see Zoran Janjetović, *Deca Careva, pastorčad Kraljeva: Nacionalne manjine u Jugoslaviji 1918–1941*, Belgrade, 2005.
14. For an official account of the agrarian reform, see Đoko Bogojević: 'Agrarna reforma', in *Jubilarni Zbornik života i rada Srba, Hravata i Slovenaca1918–1928*, vol. 1, Belgrade, 1928, pp.299–316.
15. Nikola Gaćeša, 'Opšta obeležja agrarne reforme i kolonizacije u Vojvodini 1919–1941', in Gaćeša, *Radovi*, p.238.
16. Volunteers had a privileged position, since one of the agrarian reform provisions guaranteed them 8.5 cadastral acres of land (civilians received 5 cadastral acres), as well as financial and material assistance to build houses and acquire tools. See Erić, *Agrarna reforma u Jugoslaviji*, pp.235–55; Nikola Gaćeša, *Agrarna reforma i kolonizacija u Banatu 1919–1941*, Novi Sad, 1972, pp.33–97.
17. Erić, *Agrarna reforma u Jugoslaviji*, p.239; Nikola Gaćeša, 'Nemci u agrarnoj reformi i vlasništvu obradivog zemljišta u Vojvodini 1919–1941', in Gaćeša, *Radovi*, p.290. For Germans in general, see Zoran Janjetović, *Between Hitler and Tito: The Disappearance of the Vojvodina Germans*, Belgrade, 2005.

18. Gaćeša, *Agrarna reforma i kolonizacija u Banatu*, pp.41f.
19. Dunavska Banovina was established by a law proclaimed by King Aleksandar Karadjordjević in October 1929 (this being the 'Zakon o nazivu i podeli kraljevine na upravna područja'). Dunavska Banovina comprised Vojvodina (Banat, Bačka, Baranja), the greater part of Srem and the whole of Šumadija, Požarevačka Morava and Stig.
20. However, not all the data on the number of beneficiaries and the distribution of land among households have been preserved. On the distribution of agrarian estates to the Slovaks from Vojvodina during the first agrarian reform, see Nikola Gaćeša, 'Vojvođanski Slovaci u agrarnoj reformi posle prvog svetskog rata', in Gaćeša, *Radovi*, pp.270–86.
21. See Mirko Joksimović, *Hronika Aradca*, Zrenjanin, 1981, pp.26–36.
22. In Vojvodina, several new villages (e.g. Aleksandrovo, Stajičevo) emerged as a result of internal colonization of dissatisfied peasants.
23. Radovan V. also holds that 'Serb soldiers could not have had any patriotic feelings for the Kingdom of Yugoslavia' because they (and their forefathers) had been in the service of the Austro-Hungarian army for hundreds of years. Radovan V., October 2007.
24. This law was the 'Zakon o likvidaciji agrarne reforme' (19 June 1931).
25. During the first agrarian reform, so-called 'agrarian communities' were in charge of all matters of land distribution.
26. After the Second World War, the state of Yugoslavia became the Federal People's Republic of Yugoslavia, proclaimed under the leadership of the Communist Party. Six republics entered the union: Serbia, Croatia, Slovenia, Bosnia and Herzegovina, Macedonia and Montenegro. This Second Yugoslavia existed until 1992.
27. For the uneasy relation between the Communist Party of Yugoslavia and the peasantry, see Melissa K. Bokovoy, 'Peasants and Partisans: The Politics of the Yugoslav Countryside, 1945–1953', in Melissa K. Bokovoy, Jill A. Irvine and Carol S. Lilly (eds), *State–Society Relations in Yugoslavia, 1945–1992*, Houndmills, 1997, pp.115–38; Melissa K. Bokovoy, 'Peasants and Partisans: A Dubious Alliance', in Norman Naimark and Leonid Gibianskii (eds), *The Establishment of Communist Regimes in Eastern Europe, 1944–1949*, Oxford, 1997, pp.167–89.
28. For a comparison of the first and second agrarian reforms in Romania and Yugoslavia, see Dietmar Müller, 'Landreformen, *Property rights* und ethnische Minderheiten: Ideen- und Institutionengeschichte nachholender Modernisierung und Staatsbildung in Rumänien und Jugoslawien 1918–1948', in Karl-Peter Krauss (ed.), *Agrarreformen und ethnodemographische Veränderungen: Südosteuropa vom ausgehenden 18. Jahrhundert bis in die Gegenwart*, Stuttgart, 2009, pp.207–34.
29. The ideas of the Bolshevik October Revolution of 1917 had spread through the activity of the Communist Party of Yugoslavia, established in 1919 as an opposition party in the SCS. The Russian law on land – a response to the needs of peasants throughout Russia, who took private land and shared it among themselves – exerted significant influence on dissatisfied peasants in Vojvodina.
30. See 'Zakon o agrarnoj reformi i kolonizaciji' (28 August 1945), in Vladimir Todorović, *Denacionalizacija između nacionalizacije i privatizacije*, Belgrade, 2001, p.107. See also Gaćeša, *Agrarna reforma i kolonizacija u Jugoslaviji*, pp.140–50.
31. 'Zakon o agrarnoj reformi i kolonizaciji', art. 10. Like the Germans, the Hungarians in reality were also excluded from the land reform.
32. See 'Zakon o agrarnoj reformi i unutrašnjoj kolonizaciji' (24 November 1945), in Todorović, *Denacionalizacija*, p.126.
33. According to Nikola Gaćeša, these factors later influenced the failure of agricultural production, which could barely achieve simple reproduction, as its manageable capacities were divided into

small parts that could afford only basic needs. Gaćeša, *Agrarna reforma i kolonizacija u Jugoslaviji*, p.372.

34. Joksimović, *Hronika Aradaca*, pp.26–36. The law in question is 'Zakon o agrarnoj reformi i kolonizaciji' (28 August 1945).
35. Gaćeša, *Agrarna reforma i kolonizacija u Jugoslaviji*, p.207.
36. This process is analysed in depth in Jelena Popov, *Drama na Vojvodjanskom selu (1945–1952): Obavezi otkup poljoprivrednih proizvoda*, Novi Sad, 2002. For Serbia in general, see Momčilo Pavlović, *Srpsko selo 1945–1952: Otkup*, Belgrade, 1997.
37. There were several cases of punishing households consisting of old people who could not cultivate the land on their own, and therefore could not provide the cooperatives with the requisite quotas of crops.
38. Pavel L., October 2007.
39. For a study on the use of violence and its effectiveness during collectivization in two European villages, and as a means of interrupting social continuity and influencing the reshaping of social relationships in local communities, see Tatjana Thelen, 'Violence and Social (Dis)continuity: Comparing Collectivization in Two East European Villages', *Social History* 30/1 (2005), pp.25–44.
40. Desimir Tochitch, 'Collectivization in Yugoslavia', *Journal of Farm Economics* 41/1 (1959), p.27. For a more detailed account of collectivization, see Desimir Tosić, *Kolektivizacija u Jugoslaviji 1949–1953*, Belgrade, 2002.
41. 'Zakon o poljoprivrednom zemljišnom fondu opštenarodne svojine i dodeljavanju zemlje poljoprivrednim organizacija' (1953), in Ratomir M. Slijepčević and Ilija Babić, *Real Property Rights in Serbia*, Vienna/Graz, 2005, p.32.
42. Gaćeša, *Agrarna reforma i kolonizacija u Jugoslaviji*, p.375.
43. George W. Hoffman, 'Yugoslavia: Changing Character of Rural Life and Rural Economy', *American Slavic and East European Review* 18/4 (1959), p.570.
44. 'Zakon o načinu i uslovima priznavanja i vraćanja zemljišta . . .' (1991); see Slijepčević and Babić, *Real Property Rights*, p.36.
45. After 1991, the confiscated land was returned to Ljubomir P., who today owns only 23 hectares of first- and second-class land. The L. family was returned a total of 10 hectares of land of varying quality, which had been obtained by inheritance. Since property restoration, they have not enlarged their property but invested in viniculture. The K. family had not fulfilled the old 10 hectares land maximum, so they had the right to successively enlarge their property. Today, they own 12 hectares of land of varying quality and cultivate another 4 hectares under the *arenda* system using their own machinery. Since the 1990s, the Z. family have been registered as agricultural producers. Besides the land they had before, they have extended their property by buying land and through inheritance, so now they own 15 hectares of land with all the necessary machinery.
46. On the history of cadastres in Serbia, see Ivan Obradović, 'Final Report on the Cadastres and Land Registries', unpublished research report for the project 'Land Law, Cadastre and Land Registers in Eastern Europe 1918–1945–1989', pp.1–10. For the legal aspects, see Slijepčević and Babić, *Real Property Rights*, pp.169–209.
47. According to accessed documentation, the condition of cadastres is worst in Banat. Until 1946, the municipality of Aradac was divided into Serb and Slovak municipalities that collected cadastral data separately. For Slovak Aradac, the old survey was valid from 1911 until the new survey was carried out in 1938. In Serb Aradac, the new survey was carried out in 1955.
48. The new law is 'Zakon o premeru i katastru i upisima prava na nepokretnostima' (27 April 1988), 'Sluzbeni glasnik SRS', no. 17/88. Access to data on cadastres and land registers in Banat was provided by Ilonka J., a clerk in the Department of Real Estate Cadastres of Zrenjanin.

49. Gaćeša, *Agrarna reforma i kolonizacija u Jugoslaviji*, pp.176–212.
50. The L. family recounted an example of a state-owned company's abuse of private property. This family has been in legal conflict for many years with the state-owned firm Srbijašume, which usurped about 8 hectares of the forest their son had inherited. Srbijašume has been using this land illegally for years, since the adoption of the legal act on land restitution in 1991. The L. family pursued the firm through the courts from 1991, and all arbitration was in their favour. Eventually, Srbijašume was obliged to return the land or provide compensation by providing other land of the same quality, or a monetary payment if land restitution was not possible. In the end, Srbijašume was ordered to pay for the land, which it never did.
51. Obvious reasons to register as agricultural producers, in people's opinion, include state subsidies and stimulants, as well as favourable rates for insurance and loans to buy land and livestock. Records of paid property tax show that certain registered peasants have access to subsidized fuel, first-class seed, fertilizer, seedlings and so on. Two age groups have access: peasants younger than forty years old, to increase the number of young agricultural workers, and retired peasants who are no longer capable of cultivating land on their own and therefore rent it to younger people.
52. This was so because unpredictable, insecure socio-political conditions lent significant import to the ownership of land, whereas today ownership of land is largely guaranteed.
53. Ljubomir P., October 2007.
54. The most vivid example is the fate of a young man from Aradac who fell in love with a girl from another village. When the time for the wedding came, the girl made him sell his whole estate in order to move to her village. Everyone criticized him, especially the younger men, first because such an act was contrary to established patriarchal norms, and second because he had sold land inherited from his grandfather, which, apart from other things, had huge symbolic value.
55. Radovan K., October 2007.
56. Moreover, in Chris Hann's opinion, 'a radical attack on the old class structure was accompanied by decline in civic and political rights'. Chris Hann, 'Land Tenure and Citizenship in Tazlar', in Ray Abrahams (ed.), *After Socialism: Land Reform and Social Change in Eastern Europe*, Oxford, 1996, p.35. In accordance with this statement, these families appear to have regained not just their land but also something more important, their civic and political rights.
57. Adam Z., October 2007.
58. Chris Hann, 'Introduction: The Embeddedness of Property', in Chris Hann (ed.), *Property Relations*, p.6.

Select Bibliography

Academia de Agricultură din România. *Reforma Agrară*, Bucharest, 1945.

Agrigoroaiei, Ion. 'Problema reformelor agrară şi electorală din România între anii 1916 şi 1918', *Cercetări Istorice* 1 (1975), pp.179–94.

Ajani, Gianmaria. 'By Chance and Prestige: Legal Transplants in Russia and Eastern Europe', *American Journal of Comparative Law* 43/1 (1995), pp.94–117.

Alexandrescu, Ion, Ion Bulei, Ion Mamina and Ioan Scurtu. *Enciclopedia de istorie a României*, Bucharest, 2000.

Alexianu, George. *Statutul Funcţionarilor Publici (Lege şi Regulament) din 19 iulie 1923 cu toate legile modificatoare (1923–1937), adnotat cu jurisprudenţă, Ediţia a III-a*, Bucharest, n.d.

Allcock, John B. *The Collectivisation of Yugoslav Agriculture and the Myth of Peasant Resistance*, Bradford, 1981.

——— *Explaining Yugoslavia*, London, 2000.

Anderson, R. Jerome, Igor A. Rumyantsev and Larisa G. Sudas. 'Path Dependence in Russian Land Relations: An Analysis of Recent Legislation through an Historical Perspective', *Journal of Eurasian Law* 2/2 (2009), pp.1–22.

Antal, Endre. *Beteiligung der RGW-Länder am Weltagrarhandel in den achtziger Jahren*, Berlin, 1992.

Antohi, Sorin, Balázs Trencsényi and Péter Apor (eds). *Narratives Unbound: Historical Studies in Post-communist Eastern Europe*, Budapest/New York, 2007.

Ausrottung der Ukrainer in Polen, Prague, 1930.

Axenciuc, Victor. *Evoluţia economică a României. Cercetări statistico-istorice 1859–1947*, vol. 2, Bucharest, 1996.

——— *Introducere în istoria economică a României. Epoca modernă*, Bucharest, 1997.

Baberowski, Jörg. 'Stalinismus und Nation: Die Sowjetunion als Vielvölkerreich 1917–1953', *Zeitschrift für Geschichtswissenschaft* 54/3 (2006), pp.199–213.

Bachmann, Hanns. *Das Buch von Kramsach*, Innsbruck/Munich, 1972.

Baikalov, Anatole. 'Bolshevist Agrarian Policy', *Slavonic and East European Review* 8 (1929/30), pp.533–47.

Bairoch, Paul. *L'agriculture des pays développés, 1800 à nos jours: Production – Productivité – Rendements*, Paris, 1999.

Balcerowicz, Leszek. *Socialism, Capitalism, Transformation*, Budapest, 1995.

Ballerstedt, Kurt. *Erbrecht, Erbsitten und Grundbesitzzersplitterung in Polen*, Stuttgart/Berlin, 1939.

Banaszak, Bogusław. *Prawo konstytucyjne*, Warsaw, 2001.

Banciu, Angela. *Istoria vieţii constituţionale în România (1866–1991)*, Bucharest, 1996.

Bănică, Ion. *Monografia comunei Bordei Verde, Judeţul Brăila*, n.p, n.d.

Bauerkämper, Arnd. *Ländliche Gesellschaft in der kommunistischen Diktatur: Zwangsmodernisierung und Tradition in Brandenburg 1945–1963*, Cologne/Weimar/Vienna, 2002.

Beauvois, Daniel. *Trójkąt ukraiński: Szlachta, carat i lud na Wołyniu, Podolu i Kijowszczyźnie, 1793–1914*, Lublin, 2005.

Begović, Vlajko. 'Naša poljoprivreda i pitanje njenog preobražaja', *Komunist* (1949), pp.83–111.

Bender, Gerd and Ulrich Falk (eds). *Recht im Sozialismus. Analysen zur Normdurchsetzung in osteuropäischen Nachkriegsgesellschaften (1944/45–1989)*, vol. 1, Frankfurt am Main, 1999.

Benecke, Werner. *Die Ostgebiete der Polnischen Republik. Staatsmacht und öffentliche Ordnung in einer Minderheitenregion 1918–1939*, Cologne/Weimar, 1999.

Bilandžić, Dušan. *Historija Socijalističke Federativne Republike Jugoslavije: Glavni procesi 1918–1985*, Zagreb, 1985.

Bockenförde, Ernst-Wolfgang. 'Eigentum, Sozialbindung des Eigentums, Enteignung', in Ernst-Wolfgang Bockenförde (ed.), *Staat, Gesellschaft, Freiheit. Studien zu Staatstheorie und Verfassungsrecht*, Frankfurt am Main, 1976, pp.318–35.

Boeckh, Katrin, and Natali Stegmann (eds). 'Veterans and War Victims in Eastern Europe during the Twentieth Century: A Comparison', *Comparativ* 20/5 (2010), special issue.

Bogojević, Đoko. 'Agrarna reforma', in *Jubilarni Zbornik života i rada Srba, Hrvata i Slovenaca 1918–1928*, vol. 1, Belgrade, 1928, pp.299–316.

Bokovoy, Melissa K. 'Peasants and Partisans: The Politics of the Yugoslav Countryside, 1945–1953', in Melissa K. Bokovoy, Jill A. Irvine and Carol S. Lilly (eds), *State–society Relations in Yugoslavia, 1945–1992*, Houndmills, 1997, pp.115–38.

——— 'Peasants and Partisans: A Dubious Alliance', in Norman Naimark and Leonid Gibianskii (eds), *The Establishment of Communist Regimes in Eastern Europe, 1944–1949*, Oxford, 1997, pp.167–89.

——— *Peasants and Communists: Politics and Ideology in the Yugoslav Countryside, 1941–1953*, Pittsburgh, 1998.

Bold, Ion, Vasile Niţă and Petre Săbădeanu. *Revoluţia industrială în agricultura României*, Bucharest, 1980.

Bonkowicz-Sittauer, Jerzy. *Osadnictwo wojskowe*, Rowne, 1933.

Bookmann, Milica Zarkovic. *Economic Decline in the Balkans*, New York, 1994.

Borodziej, Włodzimierz, and Hans Lemberg. *'Unsere Heimat ist uns ein fremdes Land geworden . . .': Die Deutschen östlich von Oder und Neiße 1945–1950. Dokumente aus polnischen Archiven*, 4 vols, Marburg, 2000–2004.

Boş, Nicolae. *Cartea funciară şi expertiza tehnică topo-cadastrală*, Bucharest, 2003.

Bozga, Vasile. *Criza agrară în România dintre cele două războaie mondiale*, Bucharest, 1975.

Brabant, Jozef M. *Privatizing Eastern Europe: The Role of Markets and Ownership in the Transition*, Dordrecht/Boston/London, 1992.

Brădeanu, Salvator A. *Către o nouă legislaţiune funciară*, Bucharest, 1938.

Brandes, Detlef. *Der Weg der Vertreibung 1938–1945. Pläne und Entscheidungen zum 'Transfer' der Deutschen aus der Tschechoslowakei und aus Polen*, Munich, 2001.

Brandt, Reinhardt. *Eigentumstheorien von Grotius bis Kant*, Stuttgart, 1974.

Brashich, Ranko M. *Land Reform and Ownership in Yugoslavia, 1919–1953*, New York, 1953.

Brătianu, Vintilă I. *Foloasele exproprierii*, Bucharest, 1914.

Bratuljević-Mašanović, Natalija. 'Geodetska nauka i praksa u Srbiji', in Miodrag Sekulović (ed.), *Razvoj nauke u oblasti građevinarstva i geodezije u Srbiji*, Belgrade, 1996, pp.337–55.

Brauneder, Wilhelm. 'Europas erste Privatrechtskodifikation: Das Galizische Bürgerliche Gesetzbuch', in Heinz Barta, Rudolf Palme and Wolfgang Ingenhaeff (eds), *Naturrecht und Privatrechtskodifikation*, Vienna, 1999, pp.303–20.

Breidenbach, Stephan (ed.). *Handbuch Wirtschaft und Recht in Osteuropa*, vol. 2, Munich, 1997.

Breuilly, John. *Nationalism and the State*, Chicago, 1994.

——— 'Approaches to Nationalism', in Gopal Balakrishnan (ed.), *Mapping the Nation*, London/New York, 1996, pp.146–74.

Brock, Peter. 'The Politics of the Polish Peasant', *International Politics of Social History* 1/2 (1956), pp.210–22.

Bronikowski, Wiktor. *Drogi postępu chłopa polskiego*, Warsaw, 1934.

Brubacker, Rogers. *Ethnicity without Groups*, Cambridge, MA, 2004.

Brunnbauer, Ulf (ed.). *(Re)Writing History: Historiography in Southeastern Europe after Socialism*, Münster, 2004.

Brunner, Georg. 'Verfassungsrechtlicher Eigentumsschutz und Restitution enteigneten Vermögens in Osteuropa', in Gerrit Manssen and Boguslaw Banaszak (eds), *Wandel der Eigentumsordnung in Mittel- und Osteuropa*, Berlin, 1998, pp.29–68.

——— 'Rechtskultur in Osteuropa: Das Problem der Kulturgrenzen', in Georg Brunner (ed.), *Politische und ökonomische Transformation in Osteuropa*, Berlin, 2000, pp.111–32.

Brunner, Georg, and Dieter Pfaff (eds). *Wandlungen in der Eigentumsverfassung der sozialistischen Länder Südosteuropas*, Munich, 1990.

Brzozowski, Czesław. 'Akcja osadnictwa wojskowego na Kresach Wschodnich 1920–1931', PhD diss., Warsaw, 1938.

Buchowski, Michał. *Property Relations and Social Identity in Rural Poland*, Max Planck Institute for Social Anthropology Working Paper 83, Halle/Saale, Halle.

Buckley, Peter J., and Pervez N. Chauri (eds). *The Economics of Change in East and Central Europe: Its Impact on International Business*, London, 1994.

Budyta, Dorota. 'Aktywność młodych mieszkańców wsi postrzegana przez pryzmat rodziny i społeczności wiejskiej', in Maria Wieruszewska (ed.), *Samoorganizacja w społecznościach wiejskich: przejawy, struktura, zróżnicowania*, Warsaw, 2002, pp.203–5.

Bukowski, Andrzej, Marcin Lubas and Jacek Nowak. *Zarządzanie przestrfpzenią: Globalizacja, etniczność, władza*, Krakow, 2006.

Bulgaru, Valeriu. *Câtre o nouă reformă agrară?* Iaşi, 1936.

Byrnes, Robert. *Communal Families in the Balkans: The Zadruga*, Notre Dame/London, 1976.

Calic, Marie-Janine. *Sozialgeschichte Serbiens, 1815–1941: Der aufhaltsame Fortschritt während der Industrialisierung*, Munich, 1994.

Carli, Johann R. *Maylands Steuerverfassung*, Vienna, 1818.

Cartwright, Andrew L. *The Return of the Peasant: Land Reform in Post-communist Romania*, Aldershot, 2001.

Chiari, Bernhard. '"Nationale Renaissance", Belorussifizierung und Sowjetisierung. Erziehungs- und Bildungspolitik in Weißrußland 1922–1944', *Jahrbücher für die Geschichte Osteuropas* 42/4 (1994), pp.521–40.

Chomać, R. *Struktura agrarna Królestwa Polskiego na przełomie XIX i XX w.*, Warsaw, 1970.

Chorkowy, Bartosz. 'Zmiany w sytuacji dochodowej gospodarstw domowych związanych z rolnictwem w latach 1993–2002', in S. Sokołowska (ed.), *Wieś i rolnictwo w procesie zmian. Problemy rozwoju obszarów wiejskich*, Opole, 2006, pp.177–88.

Ciesielski, Stanislaw. *Umsiedlung der Polen aus den ehemaligen polnischen Ostgebieten nach Polen in den Jahren 1944–1947*, Marburg, 2006.

Ćirković, Sima. *The Serbs*, Malden/Oxford/Calton, 2004.

Čkrebić, Anka (ed.). *150 godina geodetske službe Beograda 1839–1989*, Belgrade, 1989.

Clemens, Elizabeth S., and James M. Cook. 'Politics and Institutionalism: Explaining Durability and Change', *Annual Review of Sociology* 25 (1999), pp.441–66.

Codul General al României, vol. 9/10, Bucharest, n.y.

Colbourn, Forrest D. (ed.). *Everyday Forms of Peasant Resistance*, Armonk, 1989.

Colomy, Paul. 'Neofunctionalism and Neoinstitutionalism: Human Agency and Interest in Institutional Change', *Sociological Forum* 13/2 (1998), pp.265–300.

Confiscarea pădurilor particulare din Basarabia, n. p., 1922.

Congost, Rosa. 'Property Rights and Historical Analysis: What Rights? What History?' *Past and Present* 181 (2003), pp.74–106.

Conquest, Robert. *The Harvest of Sorrow: Soviet Collectivisation and the Terror-famine*, New York/ Oxford, 1986.

Constantinescu, Nicolae N. *Istoria economică a României*, vol. 2, Bucharest, 2000.

Conte, Èdouard. 'Land und "ethnische Reinheit" im polnisch-ukrainischen Grenzgebiet', in Èdouard Conte and Christian Giordano (eds), *Es war einmal die Wende . . . Sozialer Umbruch der ländlichen Gesellschaften Mittel- und Südosteuropas*, Berlin, 1999, pp.35–82.

Cosma, I.T. 'Problema notariatul public', *Notariatul Public* 2/8 (1938), pp.141–44.

Costin, Alexandru. 'Concepţiile actuale ale proprietăţii şi constituţia', in *Noua Constituţia din 1923 în dezbaterea contemporanilor*, pp.356–80, Bucharest, 1990.

Cozloschi, Orest I. *O interpelare: Fraudele dela cadastru*, Roman, 1933.

Crawford, Beverly (ed.). *Markets, States, and Democracy: The Political Economy of Post-communist Transformation*, Boulder/San Francisco/Oxford, 1995.

Csaba, László (ed.). *Systemic Change and Stabilization in Eastern Europe*, Dartmouth, 1991.

Čulinović, Ferdo. 'O upisima u zemljišne knjige', *Arhiv za pravne i društvene nauke* 39/5–6 (1931), pp.360–72, 447–61.

Czapran, Wanda. 'Rodziny i związki rodzinne we współczesnej wsi podwrocławskiej', in Edward Pietraszek (ed.), *Wieś dolnośląska. Studia etnograficzne*, Wroclaw, 1989, pp.208–19.

Czechowski, Pawel. 'Die Sonderrolle landwirtschaftlich genutzten Bodens am Beispiel Polens', in Christian Tomuschat (ed.), *Eigentum im Umbruch. Restitution, Privatisierung und Nutzungskonflikte im Europa der Gegenwart*, Berlin, 1996, pp.165–78.

Dąbrowska, Maria. *Rozdroże: Studium na temat zagadnień wiejskich*, Warsaw, 1937.

Daniel, Ute. *Kompendium Kulturgeschichte: Theorien, Praxis, Schlüsselworte*, Frankfurt am Main, 2001.

Darkó, Eugen. 'Die rumänische Agrarreform und die ungarischen Kirchen', in Emerich Lukinich (ed.), *Die Siebenbürgische Frage. Studien aus der Vergangenheit und Gegenwart Siebenbürgens*, Budapest, 1940, pp.366–80.

Das Eigentum im Ostblock, Berlin, 1958.

Das Schicksal der Deutschen in Jugoslawien, Munich, 2004.

David, Thomas. *Nationalisme économique et industrialization: L'expérience des pays de l'est (1789–1939)*, Geneva, 2009.

Davies, Norman. *White Eagle, Red Star: The Polish–Soviet War 1919–1920 and 'the Miracle on the Vistula'*, London, 1972.

Davies, Robert W. *The Soviet Collective Farm, 1929–1930*, Basingstoke, 1989.

de Soto, Hernando. *Freiheit für das Kapital! Warum der Kapitalismus nicht weltweit funktioniert*, Berlin, 2002.

de Vries, Tina. 'Die Eigentumsgarantie in Polen', *WGO-Monatshefte für Osteuropäisches Recht* 42 (2000), pp.173–81.

Dichmann, Werner, and Gerhard Fels (eds). *Gesellschaftliche und ökonomische Funktionen des Privateigentums*, Cologne, 1993.

Die Agrarreformen im Königreich der Serben, Kroaten und Slowenen und ihre Folgen, Novi Sad, 1924.

Die neue Verfassung der Republik Polen: Nach dem amtlichen Text vom Sejmabgeordneten Eugen Franz, Katowice, 1935.

Diemer-Benedict, Tanja. 'Die Grundrechte in der neuen polnischen Verfassung', *Zeitschrift für ausländisches öffentliches Recht und Völkerrecht* 58 (1998), pp.205–38.

Dimić, Ljubodrag. 'Srbija 1804–2004 (suočavanje sa prošlošću)', in Ljubodrag Dimić, Dubravka Stojanović and Miroslav Jovanović (eds), *Srbija 1804–2004: Poziv na dijalog*, Belgrade, 2005, pp.13–114.

Dimković, Borislav. *Promene u zemljišnoj svojini individualnih poljoprivrednih gazdinstava i njihov odnos prema zemljoradničkim zadrugama*, Sremska Mitrovica, 1964.

Diner, Dan. *Das Jahrhundert verstehen: Eine universalhistorische Deutung*, Munich, 1999.

Djelic, Marie-Laure, and Sigrid Quack (eds). *Globalization and Institutions: Redefining the Rules of the Economic Game*, Cheltenham, 2003.

Djilas, Milovan. *The New Class: An Analysis of the Communist System*, New York, 1957.

——— *Der Krieg der Partisanen: Memoiren 1941–1945*, Vienna, 1978.

Dobrogeanu-Gherea, Constantin. *Neoiobăgia: Studiu economico-sociologic al problemei noastre agrare*, Bucharest, 1910.

Dołęga-Mostowicz, Tadeusz. *Kariera Nikodema Dyzmy*, n.p., 1932.

Doliesen, Gerhard. *Die polnische Bauernpartei 'Wyzwolenie' in den Jahren 1918–1926*, Marburg, 1996.

Đorđević, Života. 'Zemljišni minimum i zemljišni maksimum kao ograničenja razvoja Srbije u novo doba', in Latinka Perović (ed.), *Srbija u modernizacijskim procesina XX veka*, Belgrade, 1994, pp.113–21.

Drinóczi, Tímea. *Gazdasági alkotmány és gazdasági alapjogok*, Budapest/Pécs, 2007.

Dziewicka, Maria. *Chłopi-robotnicy*, Warsaw, 1968.

Dziurżyński, Patrycy. 'Udział Wojska Polskiego w zasiedlaniu i zagospodarowaniu Ziem Odzyskanych', *Przegląd Zachodni* 23/1 (1967), pp.74–88.

Eichenberg, Julia. 'Stiefsöhne des Vaterlands: Die polnischen Veteranen des Ersten Weltkriegs und die Debatte um ihre Versorgung 1918–1939', *Nordost-Archiv* 17 (2008), pp.176–94.

——— *Kämpfen für Frieden und Fürsorge: Polnische Veteranen des Ersten Weltkriegs und ihre internationalen Kontakte, 1918–1939*, Munich 2011.

Eidelberg, Philip Gabriel. *The Great Romanian Peasant Revolt of 1907: The Origins of a Modern Jaquerie*, Leiden, 1974.

Eisenstadt, Shmuel. 'Multiple Modernities', *Daedalus* 129/1 (2000), pp.1–29.

Erdeljanović, Jovan. *Etnološka građa o Šumadincima*, Belgrade, 1951.

Erić, Milivoje. *Agrarna reforma u Jugoslaviji 1918–1941*, Sarajevo, 1958.

Esch, Michael G. *'Gesunde Verhältnisse': Deutsche und polnische Bevölkerungspolitik in Ostmitteleuropa 1939–1950*, Marburg, 1998.

Evans, Ifor E. *The Agrarian Revolution in Roumania*, Cambridge, 1924.

Ewidencja gruntów, Warsaw, 1982.

Expunerea de motive şi proectul de lege pentru Cartea Funciară alcătuite de Consiliul Legislativ, Iaşi, 1938.

Federico, Giovanni. *Feeding the World: An Economic History of Agriculture, 1800–2000*, Princeton/Oxford, 2005.

Feldbrugge, Ferdinand (ed.). *Law in Transition*, The Hague/London/New York, 2002.

Ficker, Adolph. 'Die Statistik der Bodenpreise und der bisherigen Methoden ihrer Ermittlung', *Mitteilungen aus dem Gebiete der Statistik* 15 (1869), pp.31–33.

Filipović, Milenko. *Nesrodnička i predvojena zadruga*, Belgrade, 1945.

Fischer, Wolfram. *Handbuch der europäischen Wirtschafts- und Sozialgeschichte*, vol. 6, Stuttgart, 1987.

Fitzgerald, Deborah. *Every Farm a Factory: The Industrial Ideal in American Agriculture*, New Haven/London, 2003.

Focşeneanu, Eleodor. *Istoria constituţională a României (1859–1991)*, Bucharest, 1998.

Frank, Susanne, and Thomas Wachter (eds). *Handbuch Immobilienrecht in Europa: Zivil- und steuerrechtliche Aspekte des Erwerbs, der Veräußerung und der Vererbung von Immobilien*, Heidelberg, 2004.

Freudenstein, Roland, and Hennig Tewes. 'Stimmungstief zwischen Deutschland und Polen: Für eine Rückkehr zur Interessengemeinschaft', *Internationale Politik* 2 (2000), pp.49–56.

Freund, Rudolf. 'Die polnische Agrarreform', *Weltwirtschaftliches Archiv* 24/2 (1926), pp.308–20.

Frevert, Ute. 'Neue Politikgeschichte. Konzepte und Herausforderungen', in Ute Frevert and Heinz-Gerhard Haupt (eds), *Neue Politikgeschichte: Perspektiven einer historischen Politikforschung*, Frankfurt/New York, 2005, pp.7–26.

Fritscher, Ludwig. 'Die südslawische Agrarverfassung und die Agrarverordnungen von 1919/21', PhD diss., Berlin, 1922/23.

Frydman, Roman, Andrzej Rapaczynski and John S. Earl. *The Privatization Process in Central Europe*, Budapest, 1993.

Gaćeša, Nikola. *Agrarna reforma i kolonizacija u Bačkoj 1918–1941*, Novi Sad, 1968.

——— *Agrarna reforma i kolonizacija u Banatu 1919–1941*, Novi Sad, 1972.

——— *Agrarna reforma i kolonizacija u Sremu 1919–1941*, Novi Sad, 1975.

——— 'Koncepcija Komunističke partije Jugoslavije o agrarnom pitanju i seljaštvu tokom narodnooslobodilačkog rata i socijalističke revolucije', *Zbornik za istoriju Matice Srpske* 19 (1979), pp.9–48.

——— *Agrarna reforma i kolonizacija u Jugoslaviji 1945–1948*, Novi Sad, 1984.

——— 'Agrarna politika prve i druge Jugoslavije', in Nikola Gaćeša (ed.), *Radovi iz agrarne istorije i demografije*, Novi Sad, 1995, pp.111–14.

——— 'Vojvođanski Slovaci u agrarnoj reformi posle prvog svetskog rata', in Nikola Gaćeša (ed.), *Radovi iz agrarne istorije i demografije*, Novi Sad, 1995, pp.270–86.

——— 'Nemci u agrarnoj reformi i vlastništvu obradivog zemljišta u Vojvodini 1919–1941', in Nikola Gaćeša (ed.), *Radovi iz agrarne istorije i demografije*, Novi Sad, 1995, pp.286–308.

——— 'Delatnost Sretena Vukosavljevića kao ministra kolonizaciju od marta 1945. do februara 1946. g.', in Nikola Gaćeša (ed.), *Radovi iz agrarne istorije i demografije*, Novi Sad, 1995, pp.413–23.

Galligan, Denis James. 'Legal Failure: Law and Social Norms in Post-communist Europe', in Denis James Galligan and Mary Kurkchiyan (eds), *Law and Informal Practices: The Post-communist Experience*, Oxford/New York, 2003, pp.1–23.

Gams, Andrija. *Svojina*, Belgrade, 1990.

Gardó, Sándor. 'Rumänien: Wirtschaft in Transformation', in Thede Kahl, Michael Metzeltin and Mihai-Răzvan Ungureanu (eds), *Rumänien*, Vienna, 2006, pp.655–92.

Garlicki, Lech. *Polskie prawo konstytucyjne*, Warsaw, 2002.

Garoflid, Constantin. 'Regimul Agrar în România', in *Enciclopedia României*, vol. 1, Bucharest, 1938–1943, pp.577–85.

Gärtner, Wolfram. 'Die Eigentumsgarantien in den Verfassungen Polens, Ungarns, der Tschechischen und der Slowakischen Republik: Verfassungsrechtliche Grundlagen und Verfassungspraxis', in Herwig Roggemann (ed.), *Eigentum in Osteuropa. Rechtspraxis in Ost-, Ostmittel- und Südosteuropa mit Einführungen und Rechtstexten*, Berlin, 1996, pp.219–31.

Gavrilović, Žarko. *Osnovne odlike telesnog razvoja prve generacije doseljenika iz Hercegovine u Vojvodinu*, Novi Sad, 1970.

Gawryszewski, Andrzej. *Ludność Polski w XX wieku*, Warsaw, 2005.

Gay, Peter. *Der Begriff des Eigentums bei Karl Marx: Zur Kritik des klassischen Eigentumsparadigmas von Locke, Smith und Hegel*, Frankfurt am Main, 1981.

Georgescu, Mircea. *Principii şi metode în legiuirile Române pentru reforma agrară*, Bucharest, 1943.

Gersković, Leon. *Dokumenti o razvoju narodne vlasti*, Belgrade, 1948.

Gieysztorowa, Irena. 'Ludność', in Antoni Mączak (ed.), *Encyklopedia historii gospodarczej Polski do 1945 r.*, vol. 1, Warsaw, 1981, pp.429–41.

Giordano, Christian. 'Agrarreformen als Potential ethnischer Spannungen in Osteuropa: Das Beispiel Jugoslawiens. Das Prinzip der Staatsnation und der Mythos der ethnischen Reinheit', in Catherine Bosshart-Pfluger (eds), *Nation und Nationalismus in Europa: Kulturelle Konstruktion von Identitäten*, Frankfurt am Main, 2002, pp.463–80.

Glass, Jakub, Alfred Kraus and Fryderyk Zoll. *Instytcja ksiąg gruntowych na ziemiach polskich*, Warsaw/Krakow, 1921.

Głowacka, Lidia, and Andrzej Czesław Żak. 'Osadnictwo Wojskowe na Wołyniu w latach 1921–1939 w świetle dokumentów Centralnego Archiwum Wojskowego', *Biuletyn Wojskowej Służby Archiwalnej* 28 (2006), pp.140–64.

Gönczi, Katalin. *Ungarisches Stadtrecht aus europäischer Sicht. Die Stadtrechtsentwicklung im spätmittelalterlichen Ungarn am Beispiel Ofen*, Frankfurt am Main, 1997.

Gołębiowski, Bronisław. *Przełomy wieków: Od kulturozbieractwa do Internetu*, Łomża, 2002.

Golopenţia, Anton, and D.C. Georgescu. *60 sate româneşti cercetate de echipele studenţeşti în vara 1938*, vol. 1, Bucharest, 1941.

Górny, Maciej. 'From the Splendid Past into the Unknown Future: Historical Studies in Poland after 1989', in Sorin Antohi, Balázs Trencsényi and Péter Apor (eds), *Narratives Unbound: Historical Studies in Post-communist Eastern Europe*, Budapest/New York, 2007, pp.101–72.

Goruneanu, Octav I. *Regimul circulaţiunii pământurilor rurale: Studiu economico-juridic. Legislaţie – doctrină – jurisprudenţă*, Constanţa, 1932.

Gosewinkel, Dieter, and Stefan Meyer. 'Citizenship, Property Rights and Dispossession in Post-war Poland (1918 and 1945)', *European Review of History* 16/4 (2009), pp.575–95.

Grabski, Władysław. *Rocznik statystyczny Królestwa Polskiego*, Warsaw, 1914.

——— 'Parcelacja agrarna wobec struktury, koniunktury i chwili dziejowej Polski', *Ekonomista* 36/4 (1936), pp.16–52.

Gralak, Bronisław. 'Miejsce osadnictwa wojskowego w planach zasiedlania i zagospodarowania ziem zachodnich w latach 1945–1947', *Śląski Kwartalnik Historyczny Sobótka* 29/2 (1974), pp.220–25.

Gralla, Erhardt. 'Immobilienerwerb und -nutzung in Polen', *Jahrbuch für Ostrecht* 2 (1996), pp.303–34.

Grandits, Hannes, and Patrick Heady. *Distinct Inheritances: Property, Family and Community in a Changing Europe*, Halle, 2003.

Grigorescu, Constantin. *Nivelul dezvoltării economico-sociale a României în context european, 1989*, Bucharest, 1993.

Grimm, Dieter. *Recht und Staat der bürgerlichen Gesellschaft*, Frankfurt am Main, 1987.

Groniowski, Krzysztof. *Uwłaszczenie chłopów w Polsce*, Warsaw, 1978.

Grün, Beate. 'Transformation spezifischer DDR-Sachenrechtsinstitute in das Recht des BGB durch die Sachenrechtsbereinigung', in Gerrit Manssen and Boguslaw Banaszak (eds), *Wandel der Eigentumsordnung in Mittel- und Osteuropa*, Berlin, 1998, pp.85–106.

Grzybowski, Konstanty. *Historia państwa i prawa Polski*, vol. 4, Warsaw, 1982.

Gudac, Vera. *Agrarna politika FNRJ i seljaštvo u Srbiji 1949–1953*, Belgrade, 1999.

Gupta, Akhil, and James Ferguson (eds). *Culture, Power, Place: Explorations in Critical Anthropology*, Durham, NC/London, 1997.

Guzina, Ružica. 'Regulisanje svojinskih odnosa u Srbiji XIX veka na bazi običajnog prava', in SANU (ed.), *Obicajno pravo i samouprave na Balkanu i u susednim zemljama*, Belgrade, 1974, pp.455–66.

Häberle, Peter. 'Vielfalt der Property Rights und der verfassungsrechtliche Eigentumsbegriff', in Manfred Neumann (ed.), *Ansprüche, Eigentums- und Verfügungsrechte*, Berlin, 1984, pp.63–102.

Hackl, Berhard. *Die Theresianische Dominikal- und Rustikalfassion in Niederösterreich 1748–1756: Ein fiskalischer Reformprozess im Spannungsfeld zwischen Landständen und Zentralstaat*, Frankfurt/Vienna, 1997.

Hadaczek, Bolesław. *Kresy w literaturze polskiej: Studia i szkice*, Gorzów Wielkopolski, 1999.

Hadler, Frank, and Matthias Middell (eds). 'Verflochtene Geschichten: Ostmitteleuropa', *Comparativ* 20/1–2 (2010), special issue.

Halpern, Joel M. 'Yugoslav Peasant Society in Transition: Stability in Change', *Anthropological Quarterly* 36/3 (1963), pp.156–82.

Hann, Chris. 'From Production to Property: Decollectivization and the Family–land Relationship in Contemporary Hungary', *Man* 28/3 (1993), pp.299–320.

——— 'Land Tenure and Citizenship in Tazlar', in Ray Abrahams (ed.), *After Socialism: Land Reform and Social Change in Eastern Europe*, Oxford, 1996, pp.23–49.

——— 'Introduction: The Embeddedness of Property', in Chris Hann (ed.), *Property Relations: Renewing the Anthropological Tradition*, Cambridge, 1998, pp.1–47.

——— 'Propertization und ihre Gegentendenzen: Beispiele aus ländlichen Gebieten Europas', in Hannes Siegrist (ed.), *Entgrenzung des Eigentums in modernen Gesellschaften und Rechtskulturen*, Leipzig, 2007, pp.84–98.

Hann, Chris (ed.). *Property Relations: Renewing the Anthropological Tradition*, Cambridge, 1998.

Hann, Chris (ed.). *Postsozialismus: Transformationsprozesse in Europa und Asien aus ethnologischer Perspektive*, Frankfurt am Main, 2002.

Hann, Chris, et al. *The Postsocialist Agrarian Question: Property Relations and the Rural Condition*, Münster, 2003.

Hanusik, Krystyna, and Urszula Łangowska-Szczęśniak. 'Efekt pokazowy w zachowaniach konsumpcyjnych gospodarstw domowych mieszkańców wsi', in Stanisława Sokołowska (ed.), *Wieś i rolnictwo w procesie zmian. Problemy rozwoju obszarów wiejskich*, Opole, 2006, pp.163–76.

Harrison, Mark (ed.). *The Economics of World War II: Six Great Powers in International Comparison*, Cambridge, 1998.

Haupt, Heinz-Gerhard, and Jürgen Kocka (eds). *Geschichte und Vergleich: Ansätze und Ergebnisse international vergleichender Geschichtsschreibung*, Frankfurt/New York, 1996.

Hausleitner, Mariana. *Die Rumänisierung der Bukowina: Die Durchsetzung des nationalstaatlichen Anspruchs Großrumäniens 1918–1944*, Munich, 2001.

Havlan, Petr. 'Das Eigentum der kommunalen und regionalen Selbstverwaltungen im tschechischen Recht', *Jahrbuch für Ostrecht* 2 (2004), pp.351–61.

Hazard, John N. *Communists and Their Law: A Search for the Common Core of the Legal Systems of the Marxian Socialist States*, Chicago/London, 1969.

Hein, Heidi. *Der Piłsudski-Kult und seine Bedeutung für den polnischen Staat 1926–1939*, Marburg, 2002.

Hellwege, Friedrich. 'Agrarverfassung und Agrarreform in Polen', in Max Sering (ed.), *Die agrarischen Umwälzungen im außerrussischen Osteuropa. Ein Sammelwerk*, Berlin, 1930, pp.154–204.

Henschel, Christhardt. 'Der Erste Weltkrieg zwischen Erinnerungskultur und Politik in Polen am Beispiel der Stadt Lublin (1918–1939)', *Nordost-Archiv* 17 (2008), pp.201–11.

Herbert, Ulrich. 'Europe in High Modernity: Reflections on a Theory of the 20th Century', *Journal of Modern European History* 5/1 (2007), pp.5–21.

Herlea, Alexandru. *Cărţile de proprietate în Transilvania*, Braşov, 1945.

——— 'Organizarea şi principiile publicităţii imobiliare reale în România după Unirea din 1918', in Alexandru Herlea (ed.), *Studii de istorie a dreptului*, vol. 2, Cluj-Napoca, 1985, pp.160–96.

Hertz, Frederick. *The Economic Problems of the Danubian States: A Study in Economic Nationalism*, London, 1947.

Hitchins, Keith. *The Identity of Romania*, Bucharest, 2003.

Hoffmann, Alfred. 'Grundlagen der Agrarstruktur der Donaumonarchie', in Alfred Hoffmann and Roman Sandgruber (eds), *Österreich-Ungarn als Agrarstaat: Wirtschaftswachstum und Agrarverhältnisse im 19. Jahrhundert*, Vienna, 1978, pp.11–65.

Hoffman, George W. 'Yugoslavia: Changing Character of Rural Life and Rural Economy', *American Slavic and East European Review* 18/4 (1959), pp.555–78.

Hoffmann, Manfred. 'Bodenrecht und Bodenrechtspolitik in kommunistisch regierten Ländern unter dem Einfluß der Marx'schen Variante der Arbeitswerttheorie, *Recht in Ost und West* 33/2 (1989), pp.97–104.

Hoffmann, Walter. *Südost-Europa: Bulgarien – Jugoslawien – Rumänien. Ein Querschnitt durch Politik, Kultur und Wirtschaft*, Leipzig, 1932.

Hollmann, Anton Heinrich. 'Die polnische Agrarreform', *Berichte über Landwirtschaft* 5/1 (1926), pp.125–38.

Horak, Stephan. *Poland and Her National Minorities, 1919–39: A Case Study*, New York, 1961.

Horvat, Branko. *Die jugoslawische Gesellschaft: Ein Essay*, Frankfurt am Main, 1971.

Inglot, Stefan (ed.). *Historia chłopów polskich*, vols. 1–3, Warsaw, 1970–1980.

Innerhofer, Ian. 'Agrarische Überbevölkerung. Zur Konstruktion eines Problems bei Otto Frangeš und Rudolf Bićanić', in Carola Sachse (ed.), *'Mitteleuropa' und 'Südosteuropa' als Planungsraum: Wirtschafts- und kulturpolitische Expertisen im Zeitalter der Weltkriege*, Göttingen, 2010, pp.262–89.

Ionescu, Cristian. *Dezvoltarea constituţională a României: Acte şi documente 1741–1991*, Bucharest, 2000.

Isić, Momčilo. 'Sitno posedništvo kao kočnica ekonomske modernizacije Srbije u prvoj polovini XX veka', in Latinka Perović (ed.), *Srbija u modernizacijskim procesima XX veka*, Belgrade, 1994, pp.101–11.

Izdebski, Hubert. 'Ownership in "People's Poland": Shaping, Growth, and Decomposition of the Theory of Socialist Ownership in the Years 1944–1990', in Gerd Bender and Ulrich Falk (eds), *Recht im Sozialismus: Analysen zur Normdurchsetzung in osteuropäischen Nachkriegsgesellschaften (1944/45–1989)*, vol. 1, Frankfurt am Main, 1999, pp.57–72.

Jabłonowski, Marek. *Sen o potędze Polski . . . Z dziejów ruchu byłych wojskowych w II Rzeczypospolitej (1918–1939)*, Olsztyn, 1998.

Janjetović, Zoran. 'Die Konflikte zwischen Serben und Donauschwaben', *Südost-Forschungen* 58 (1999), pp.119–68.

——— *Between Hitler and Tito: The Disappearance of the Vojvodina Germans*, Belgrade, 2005.

——— *Deca Careva, pastorčad Kraljeva: Nacionalne manjine u Jugoslaviji 1918–1941*, Belgrade, 2005.

Jarosz, Dariusz. *Polityka władz komunistycznych w Polsce w latach 1918–1956 a chłopi*, Warsaw, 1998.

Jasiewicz, Krzysztof. *Zagłada polskich Kresów*, Warsaw, 1998.

Jojkić, Vladan. *Nacionalizacija Bačke i Banata: Etno-politička studija*, Novi Sad, 1931.

Joksimović, Mirko. *Hronika Aradca*, Zrenjanin, 1981.

Jovanović, Aleksa. *Istorijski razvitak srpske zadruge*, Belgrade, 1896.

Jovanović, Slobodan. *Druga vlada Miloša i Mihaila*, Belgrade, 2005.

Jovanović, Vladan. *Jugoslovenska država i Južna Srbija 1918–1929: Makedonija, Sandžak, Kosovo i Metohija u Kraljevini SHS*, Belgrade, 2002.

Jovanović, Žarko. *KPJ prema seljaštvu 1919–1941*, Belgrade, 1984.

Jovičić, Miodrag. *Ustavi Kneževine i Kraljevine Srbije*, Belgrade, 1988.

Józewski, Henryk. 'Zamiast pamiętnika (2)', *Zeszyty Historyczne* 60 (1982), pp.65–157.

Judt, Tony. *Postwar: A History of Europe since 1945*, London, 2005.

Jurecka-Krzyżanowska, Renata. *Mój ojciec: Wspomnienia rodziny wojskowej z Brzeżan od roku 1923 do 1945 roku*, Krakow, 1997.

Kabat, Roman. 'Kataster: Co to jest?', *Nasza Wielkopolska*, 24 January 2001, pp.29–30.

Kaczmarczyk, Zdzisław. *Historia państwa i prawa Polski*, vol. 2, Warsaw, 1971.

Kaelble, Hartmut, and Jürgen Schriewer (eds). *Vergleich und Transfer: Komparatistik in den Sozial-, Geschichts- und Kulturwissenschaften*, Frankfurt am Main, 2003.

Kaindl, Raimund Friedrich. *Das Unterthanswesen in der Bukowina: Ein Beitrag zur Geschichte des Bauernstandes und seiner Befreiung*, Vienna, 1899.

Kamenik, Walter. 'Katastralvermessung, historische Kontinuität und zeitgenössische Aspekte', in Robert Messner (ed.), 'Der Franziszeische Grundsteuerkataster', *Jahrbuch des Vereins für Geschichte der Stadt Wien*, Wien, 1967, pp.81–89.

Kamler, Marcin. 'Folwark', in Antoni Mączak (ed.), *Encyklopedia*, Warsaw, 1981, p.176.

Kaneff, Deema. 'Responses to "Democratic" Land Reforms in a Bulgarian Village', in Frances Pine and Susan Bridger (eds), *Surviving Postsocialism: Local Strategies and Regional Responses in Eastern Europe and the Former Soviet Union*, London, 1996, pp.85–114.

——— *Who Owns the Past? The Politics of Time in a 'Model' Bulgarian Village*, New York/Oxford, 2004.

Kardelj, Edvard. *Problemi socijalističke politike na selu*, Belgrade, 1959.

Kaser, Karl. *Familie und Verwandtschaft auf dem Balkan*, Vienna/Cologne/Weimar, 1995.

Kataster gruntowy w świetle cyfr i rzeczywistości, Lviv, 1933.

Kautsky, Karl. *Die Agrarfrage: Eine Übersicht über die Tendenzen der modernen Landwirthschaft und die Agrarpolitik der Sozialdemokratie*, Stuttgart, 1899.

Kecić, Danilo. 'Oktobarska Revolucija i agrarno-seljački pokret u Vojvodini tokom 1918. i početkom 1919. godine', *Zbornik za društvene nauke* 49 (1968), pp.26–68.

Kempner, Stanisław A. *Dzieje gospodarcze Polski porozbiorowej w zarysie*, Warsaw, 1922.

Kempter, Dorota. *Der Einfluss des europäischen Rechts auf das polnische Zivilgesetzbuch*, Baden-Baden, 2007.

Kersten, Krystyna. 'Osadnictwo wojskowe w 1945 roku: Próba charakterystyki', *Przegląd Historyczny* 55/4 (1964), pp.640–59.

——— *The Establishment of Communist Rule in Poland, 1943–1948*, Berkeley/Los Angeles/Oxford, 1991.

Kęsik, Jan. *Zaufany komendanta: Biografia polityczna Jana Henryka Józewskiego 1892–1981*, Wroclaw, 1995.

Kidrič, Boris. 'O nekim principijelnim pitanjima naše privrede', *Komunist* 2/2 (1947), pp.47–58.

Kieniewicz, Stefan. *The Emancipation of the Polish Peasantry*, Chicago/London, 1969.

K.K. Finanzministerium. *Instruktion zur Ausführung von Vermessung mit Anwendung des Messtisches behufs Herstellung neuer Pläne für die Zwecke des Grundsteuerkatasters (sog. Grüne Instruktion)*, Vienna, 1907.

K.K. Generaldirektion der direkten Steuern. *Instruction zur Ausführung der in Folge der allerhöchsten Patente vom 23. XII. 1817 und 20. X. 1849 angeordneten Katastralvermessung*, Vienna, 1865.

Klein, Gustav Adolf. *Soziale und nationale Probleme der Agrarreform in Siebenbürgen*, Hermannstadt, 1927.

Klein, Wilhelm. 'Die Liquidierung des siebenbürgisch-sächsischen Nationalvermögens', *Nation und Staat* 10 (1936/37), pp.721–30.

Kluba, Mieczysław. 'Przestrzenne zróżnicowanie poziomu oraz struktury bezrobocia na obszarach wiejskich województwa kujawsko-pomorskiego w okresie transformacji gospodarki', in Jerzy Parysek (ed.), *Rozwój regionalny i lokalny w Polsce w latach 1989–2002*, Poznan, 2004, pp.361–73.

Knell, Mark (ed.). *Economics of Transition: Structural Adjustment and Growth Prospects in Eastern Europe*, Cheltenham/Brookfield, 1996.

Kochanowicz, Jacek. 'The Peasant Family as an Economic Unit in the Polish Feudal Economy of the Eighteenth Century', in Richard Wall, Jean Robin and Peter Laslett (eds), *Family Forms in Historic Europe*, Cambridge, 1983, pp.153–66.

——— 'La théorie économique . . . après vingt ans', *Acta Poloniae Historica* 56 (1987), pp.187–211.

——— 'L'exploitation paysanne en Pologne a la charnière des XVIIIė et XIXė siècles: Théorie, histoire, historiographie', *Acta Poloniae Historica* 57 (1988), pp.203–37.

——— 'Stato e contadini: La politica agraria polacca negli anni 1956–1970', *Studi Storici* 3 (1988), pp.759–85.

——— 'The Polish Economy and the Evolution of Dependency', in Daniel Chirot (ed.), *The Origins of Backwardness in Eastern Europe.: Economics and Politics from the Middle Ages until the Early Twentieth Century*, Berkeley, 1989, pp.92–130.

Kocka, Jürgen. *Civil Society and Dictatorship in Modern German History*, Waltham, MA/ London, 2010.

——— 'Zivilgesellschaft in historischer Perspektive', in Jürgen Kocka (ed.), *Arbeiten an der Geschichte: Gesellschaftlicher Wandel im 19. und 20. Jahrhundert*, Göttingen, 2012, pp.191–202.

Komadinić, Milan J. *Problem seljačkih dugova*, Belgrade, 1934.

Konrád, György, and Ivan Szelenyi. *The Intellectuals on the Road to Class Power: A Sociological Study of the Role of the Intelligentsia in Socialism*, Harcourt, 1979.

Konstantinović, Mihajlo. 'Pitanje svojine: Od svojine individualnog prava ka svojini socialnoj funkciji', in Mijo Mirković and Mihajlo Arsić (eds), *Generacija pred stvaranjem: Almanah jedne grupe*, Belgrade, 1925, pp.7–16.

Kopczyński, Michał. *Wielka transformacja: badania nad uwarstwieniem społecznym i standardem życia w Królestwie Polskim 1866–1913 w świetle pomiarów antropometrycznych poborowych*, Warsaw, 2006.

Köpeczi, Béla. *Kurze Geschichte Siebenbürgens*, Budapest, 1990.

Korioth, Stefan. 'Der Eigentumsschutz in den europäischen Verfassungsordnungen in historischer Sicht', in Gerrit Manssen and Boguslaw Banaszak (eds), *Wandel der Eigentumsordnung in Mittel- und Osteuropa*, Berlin, 1998, pp.9–27.

Kornai, János. *The Socialist System: The Political Economy of Communism*, Oxford, 1992.

Kosanović, Djordje. 'Uloga fondova narodnooslobodilačkih odbora u materijalnom obezbedjenju odluka od 1941 do početka 1944', *Vojno-istorijski glasnik* 5 (1957), pp.30–49.

Kossewska, Elżbieta. *Związek Legionistów Polskich 1922–1939*, Warsaw, 2003.

Kostić, Darinka. *Promene u društvenom životu kolonista*, Belgrade, 1963.

Kovačević, Ivan. *Istorija srpske etnologije II: Pravci i odlomci*, Belgrade, 2001.

Kowalik, Tadeusz. *Spory o ustrój gospodarczy w Polsce: lata 1944–48*, Warsaw, 2006.

Kowalski, Tadeusz Antoni. *Mniejszości narodowe w siłach zbrojnych Drugiej Rzeczypospolitej Polskiej (1918–1939)*, Toruń, 1998.

Kowecka, Elżbieta. *W salonie i w kuchni: Opowieść o kulturze materialnej pałaców i dworów polskich w XIX w.*, Warsaw, 1984.

Kraft, Claudia. *Europa im Blick der polnischen Juristen: Rechtsordnung und juristische Professionen in Polen im Spannungsfeld zwischen Nation und Europa 1918–1930*, Frankfurt am Main, 2002.

Krenzlin, Anneliese, and Ludwig Reusch. *Die Entstehung der Gewannflur nach Untersuchungen im nördlichen Unterfranken*, Frankfurt am Main, 1961.

Kretschmer, Ingrid. '150 Jahre Österreichischer Grundsteuerkataster', *Mitteilungen der Österreichischen Geographischen Gesellschaft* 110/1 (1968), pp.63–71.

——— 'Die Entwicklung der österreichischen Katastralmappen und ihre Bedeutung für die Geographie', *Mitteilungen der Österreichischen Geographischen Gesellschaft* 116 (1974), pp.206–18.

Krisań, Maria. *Chłopi wobec zmian cywilizacyjnych w Królestwie Polskim w drugiej połowie XIX – początku XX wieku*, Warsaw, 2008.

Krstić, Đorđe. *Kolonizacija u Južnoj Srbiji*, Sarajevo, 1928.

Kubů, Eduard, Torsten Lorenz, Uwe Müller and Jiří Šouša (eds). *Agrarismus und Agrareliten in Ostmitteleuropa*, Berlin/Prague, 2013.

Küpper, Herbert. 'Rechtskultur(en) in Ostmitteleuropa: Hemmschuh oder Quelle der Hoffnung auf dem Weg ins 21. Jahrhundert?', *Berichte und Beiträge des Geisteswissenschaftlichen Zentrums Geschichte und Kultur Ostmitteleuropas e.V. 1999, Öffentliche Vorträge 1998/99*, Leipzig, 1999, pp.331–77

——— *Autonomie im Einheitsstaat: Geschichte und Gegenwart der Selbstverwaltung in Ungarn*, Berlin, 2002.

——— *Einführung in die Rechtsgeschichte Osteuropas*, Frankfurt am Main, 2005.

——— *Die ungarische Verfassung nach zwei Jahrzehnten des Übergangs: Einführung mit Textübersetzung*, Frankfurt am Main, 2007.

——— 'Sozialistische Überreste in den Verfassungen der neuen EU-Mitgliedstaaten im Lichte des gemeinschaftsrechtlichen Homogenitätsgebots', *Jahrbuch für Ostrecht* 2 (2007), pp.203–61.

Kula, Witold. *An Economic Theory of the Feudal System*, London, 1976.

Kuljić, Todor. *Umkämpfte Vergangenheiten. Die Kultur der Erinnerung im postjugoslawischen Raum*, Berlin, 2010.

Landau, Ludwik, Jerzy Pański and Edward Strzelecki, *Bezrobocie wśród chłopów*, Warsaw, 1939.

Lapenna, Ivo. 'Die Rechtsnatur des gesellschaftlichen Eigentums in Jugoslawien', *Osteuropa-Recht* 8 (1962), pp.216–36.

——— *State and Law: Soviet and Yugoslav Theory*, New Haven, 1964.

Łappo, Henryka, Danuta Gradosielska and Bronisława Kacperek (eds). *Z kresów wschodnich Rzeczpospolitej: Wspomnienia z osad wojskowych 1921–1940*, London, 1998.

L'Association de l'Ukraine Occidentale pour la Société des Nations, *La situation de la population ukrainienne en Pologne: Irredentist and Nationalist Questions in Central Europe, 1913–1939*, vol. 2, Nendeln, 1973.

Latawski, Paul (ed.). *The Reconstruction of Poland, 1914–23*, Houndmills/London, 1992.

Lavigne, Marie. *The Economics of Transition*, Houndmills/London, 1995.

Lazarević, Adam. 'Stari i novi zakon o izdavanje tapija', *Arhiv za pravne i društvene nauke* 41/4 (1932), pp.296–307.

Leblang, Stanislawa. 'Polnische Bauernparteien', in Heinz Gollwitzer (ed.), *Europäische Bauernparteien im 20. Jahrhundert*, Stuttgart/New York, 1977, pp.271–322.

Le cadastre, le livre foncier et la reforme agraire en Yugoslavie, Belgrade, 1936.

Lego, Karl. *Geschichte des Österreichischen Grundkatasters*, Vienna, 1968.

Lekić, Bogdan. *Agrarna reforma i kolonizacija u Jugoslaviji 1945–1948*, Belgrade, 1997.

——— *Agrarna reforma i kolonizacija u Jugoslaviji 1918–1941*, Belgrade, 2002.

Lenin, Vladimir Iljitsch Uljanov. *Über das Bündnis der Arbeiterklasse mit der werktätigen Bauernschaft: Eine Sammlung ausgewählter Aufsätze und Reden*, East Berlin, 1961.

Liebscher, Marc, and Fryderyk Zoll. *Einführung in das polnische Recht*, Munich, 2005.

Lifszyc, Isaj. *Die Agrarfrage in Polen*, Lodz, 1928.

Linden, Joseph. *Die Grundsteuerverfassung in den deutschen und italienischen Provinzen der österreichischen Monarchie, mit vorzüglicher Berücksichtung des stabilen Katasters*, Vienna, 1840.

Lippert, A. Joseph. 'Die Entwicklung des Grundsteuerwesens im Herzogthume Bukowina unter österreichischer Herrschaft', *Czernowitzer Zeitung* 1 (1868) 1 (6.1.); 13 (28.1.); 17 (4.2.); 20 (9.2.), 27 (21.2.); 61 (22.4.).

Lippott, Joachim. 'Das Eigentum in den osteuropäischen Verfassungen der Gegenwart', *Zeitschrift für Vergleichende Rechtswissenschaft* 95 (1996), pp.227–60.

Litzinger, Heike Kathrin. *Juristen und die Bauernfrage: Die Diskussion um das bäuerliche Grundeigentum in Russland von 1880 bis 1914*, Frankfurt am Main, 2007.

Ljušić, Radoš. *Kneževina Srbija 1830–1839*, Belgrade, 2004.

Ludkiewicz, Z. 'Land Reform in Poland', *Slavonic and East European Review* 8 (1929/30), pp.315–30.

Łukasiewicz, Juliusz. 'Drogi rozwojowe rolnictwa na ziemiach polskich', in Stefan Kieniewicz (ed.), *Polska XIX w. Państwo, społeczeństwo, kultura*, Warsaw, 1977, pp.13–55.

——— 'Agrarna struktura', in Antoni Mączak (ed.), *Encyklopedia historii gospodarczej Polski do 1945 r*, vol. 1, Warsaw, 1981, pp.10–12.

Lukić, Radomir. 'Notions de la propriété dans l'Europe socialiste et dans les États capitalistes', *Rabels Zeitschrift für ausländisches und internationales Privatrecht* 26/2 (1961), pp.238–54.

Łukowski, Wojciech. *Społeczne tworzenie ojczyzn*, Warsaw, 2002.

Macdonnell, A.G. 'East Poland after Ten Years', *Fortnightly Review* 33 (1933), pp.492–502.

Macpherson, Crawford B. *The Political Theory of Possessive Individualism: Hobbes to Locke*, Oxford, 1962.

Mach, Zdzisław. 'Myth and Cultural Construction of Time among a Resettled Population', *Polish Sociological Bulletin* 2 (1993), pp.131–38.

Madajczyk, Czesław. *Burżuazyjno-obszarnicza reforma rolna w Polsce, 1918–1939*, Warsaw, 1958.

——— *Polityka III Rzeszy w okupowanej Polsce*, vol. 2, Warsaw, 1979.

Madgearu, Virgil. *Evoluţia economiei româneşti: După războiul mondial*, Bucharest, 1995.

Maksimović, Ivan (ed.). *Subjekti društvene svojine i njihove ekonomske funkcije*, Belgrade, 1988.

Malcolm, Noel. *Kosovo: A Short History*, London/New York, 1998.

Mannori, Luca. *Kataster und moderner Staat in Italien, Spanien und Frankreich (18. Jh.)*, Baden-Baden, 2001.

Marković, Predrag, Miloš Ković and Nataša Miličević. 'Developments in Serbian Historiography since 1989', in Ulf Brunnbauer (ed.), *(Re)Writing History. Historiography in Southeastern Europe after Socialism*, Münster, 2004, pp.277–316.

Marx, Karl. 'Kritik des Gothaer Programms', in *Marx-Engels-Werke*, vol. 19, East Berlin, 1973, pp.11–31.

Maticka, Marijan. *Agrarna reforma i kolonizacija u Hrvatskoj 1945–1948*, Zagreb, 1990.

Matl, Josef. *Die Agrarreform in Jugoslavien*, Berlin/Wroclaw, 1927.

Matwiejew, Aleksander. *Die Agrarreformen Polens im XX. Jahrhundert*, Kiel, 1958.

Maurer, Andrea, and Michael Schmid (eds). *Neuer Institutionalismus: Zur soziologischen Erklärung von Organisation, Moral und Vertrauen*, Frankfurt am Main, 2002.

Meissner, Otto. *Die Rechtsverfassung*, Berlin, 1919.

Mendras, Henri. *Seljačka društva – Elementi za jednu teoriju seljaštva*, Zagreb, 1986.

Merl, Stephan. 'Einstellungen zum Privateigentum in Rußland und in der Sowjetunion', in Hannes Siegrist and David Sugarman (eds), *Eigentum im internationalen Vergleich*, Göttingen, 1999, pp.135–59.

Messner, Robert. *150 Jahre österreichische Grundkataster*, Vienna, 1967.

——— 'Der Franziszeische Grundsteuerkataster: Ein Überblick über seinen Werdegang und sein Wirken', *Jahrbuch des Vereins für Geschichte der Stadt Wien* 28 (1972), pp.62–105; 29 (1973), pp.88–141.

Meusburger, Peter. 'Subjekt – Organisation – Region: Fragen an die subjektzentrierte Handlungstheorie', in Peter Meusburger (ed.), *Handlungsorientierte Sozialgeographie: Benno Werlens Entwurf in kritischer Diskussion*, Stuttgart, 1999, pp.95–132.

Meyer, John W., and W. Richard Scott (eds). *Organizational Environments: Ritual and Rationality*, Beverly Hills, 1983.

Mieszczankowski, Mieczysław. *Struktura agrarna Polski międzywojennej*, Warsaw, 1962.

Mihăilescu, Gheorghe. 'Note asupra populaţiei şi satelor din Câmpia Brăilei', *Analele Brăilei* 2–3 (1932), pp.83–93.

Milewski, Jan Jerzy. 'Osadnicy wojskowi na Kresach', *Biuletyn Instytutu Pamięci Narodowej* 12 (2004), pp.44–50.

Milićević, Milan. *Kneževina Srbija*, Belgrade, 1876.

Miller, Linda. 'Drept şi propagandă: posesia asupra terenurilor agricole, colectivizarea şi proprietatea socialistă', in Dorin Dobrincu and Constantin Iordachi (eds), *Ţărănimea şi puterea: Procesul de colectivizare a agriculturii în România (1949–1962)*, Iaşi, 2005, pp.136–56.

Mirković, Mijo. 'Regulisanje seljačkih dugova', *Arhiv za političke i društvene nauke* 33 (1936), pp.347–52.

——— *Agrarna politika*, Belgrade, 1940.

——— *Ekonomska historija Jugoslavije*, Zagreb, 1958.

Misiło, Eugeniusz. *Repatriacja czy deportacja: Przesiedlenie Ukraińców polskich do USRR*, Warsaw, 1996.

Mitrany, David. *The Land and the Peasant in Rumania: The War and Agrarian Reform (1917–21)*, New York, 1968 [1930].

Moody, V. Alton. 'Agrarian Reform before Post-war European Constituent Assemblies', *Agricultural History* 7/2 (1933), pp.81–95.

Morawiec, Małgorzata. 'Antemurale christianitatis: Polen als Vormauer des christlichen Europa', *Jahrbuch für europäische Geschichte* 2 (2001), pp.249–60.

Moritsch, Andreas. 'Der franziszeische Kataster und die dazugehörigen Steuerschätzungsoperate als wirtschafts- und sozialhistorische Quellen', *East European Quarterly* 3 (1970), pp.438–48.

Müller, Dietmar. 'Wirtschaftsprogrammatik und -politik für den ländlichen Raum Rumäniens: Zwischen Agrarpopulismus und bäuerlichem Mittelstandsdenken', *Zeitschrift für Siebenbürgische Landeskunde* 23/1 (2000), pp.6–23.

——— *Agrarpopulismus in Rumänien: Programmatik und Regierungspraxis der Bauernpartei und der Nationalbäuerlichen Partei Rumäniens in der Zwischenkriegszeit*, St Augustin, 2001.

——— *Staatsbürger auf Widerruf: Juden und Muslime als Alteritätspartner im rumänischen und serbischen Nationscode. Ethnonationale Staatsbürgerschaftskonzeptionen, 1878–1941*, Wiesbaden, 2005.

——— 'Die Gouvernementalität des Bodeneigentums im östlichen Europa', *Comparativ* 16/5–6 (2006), pp.112–29.

——— 'Landreformen, Property Rights und ethnische Minderheiten: Ideen- und Institutionengeschichte nachholender Modernisierung und Staatsbildung in Rumänien und Jugoslawien 1918–1948', in Karl-Peter Krauss (ed.), *Agrarreformen und ethnodemographische Veränderungen: Südosteuropa vom ausgehenden 18. Jahrhundert bis in die Gegenwart*, Stuttgart, 2009, pp.207–34.

——— 'Vorarbeiten zu einer Begriffs- und Kulturgeschichte des Eigentums in Rumänien, 1746 bis 2009', in Vasile Dumbrava (ed.), *Geschichte politisch-sozialer Begriffe in Rumänien und Moldova*, Leipzig, 2010, pp.185–214.

——— 'The Governmentality of Land Ownership in South-eastern Europe: Romania and Yugoslavia, a Comparison', in Rosa Congost and Rui Santos (eds), *Contexts of Property in Europe: The Social Embeddedness of Property Rights in Land in Historical Perspective*, Brepols, 2011, pp.211–27.

Müller, Dietmar, and Alina Bojincă. 'Die juristische und geodätische Administration des Eigentums an Grund und Boden in Rumänien im 20. Jahrhundert', in Dietmar Müller and Angela Harre (eds), 'Transforming Rural Societies: Agrarian Property and Agrarianism in East Central Europe in the Nineteenth and Twentieth Centuries', *Jahrbuch für Geschichte des ländlichen Raumes* 7 (2010), pp.26–54.

Müller, Dietmar and Andrei Florin. 'Sora Notarul comunal în România: Cadrul normativ al unei instituţii moderne (1864–1940)', *Arhivele Olteniei* 25 (2011), pp.369–85.

Müller, Uwe. 'Landreformen und Wirtschaftsnationalismus in Ostmitteleuropa', in Dagmara Jajeśniak-Quast (ed.), *Soziale Konflikte und nationale Grenzen in Ostmitteleuropa*, Berlin, 2006, pp.171–87.

——— 'Modernisierung oder Diskriminierung? Siedlungspolitik in den preußischen Ostprovinzen zwischen nationalitäten- und agrarpolitischen Zielen', in Uwe Müller (ed.), *Ausgebeutet oder alimentiert? Regionale Wirtschaftspolitik und nationale Minderheiten in Ostmitteleuropa (1867–1918)*, Berlin, 2006, pp.147–65.

Murgescu, Bogdan. 'The Economic Performance of Interwar Romania: Golden Age Myth and Statistical Evidence', *Jahrbücher für Geschichte und Kultur Südosteuropas* 6 (2004), pp.43–64.

——— *România şi Europa: Acumularea decalajelor economice (1500–2010)*, Iaşi, 2010.

Naszkowska, Krystyna, and Paweł Wroński. 'Chłopi w czasach ludowych', *Gazeta Wyborcza*, 25–26 May 2002, p.10.

Nikić, Fedor. 'Revizija naše politike u Vojvodini', *Letopis Matice Srpske* 104/2 (1929), pp.252–67.

Nitschke, Bernadetta. *Vertreibung und Aussiedlung der deutschen Bevölkerung aus Polen 1945–1949*, Munich, 2003.

North, Douglass C. *Structure and Change in Economic History*, New York, 1981.

——— *Institutions, Institutional Changes and Economic Performance*, Cambridge, 1990.

Novaković, Stojan. *Selo*, Belgrade, 1912.

Nove, Alec. *An Economic History of the USSR*, Harmondsworth, 1986.
Nowak, Jacek. *Zaginiony świat? Nazywają ich Łemkami*, Krakow, 2000.
Obradović, Milovan. *Agrarna reforma i kolonizacija na Kosovo (1918–1944)*, Prishtina, 1981.
Offe, Claus. *Der Tunnel am Ende des Lichts: Erkundungen der politischen Transformation im Neuen Osten*, Frankfurt/New York, 1994.
——— *Varieties of Transition*, Cambridge, 1996.
Ogrodowczyk, Arakadiusz. *Nad Odrą i Bałtykiem: Osadnictwo wojskowe na zachodnich i północnych ziemiach Polski po II wojnie światowej*, Warsaw, 1979.
Osmani, Jusuf. 'Zakonski propisi o agrarnoj reformi i kolonizacija na Kosovo između dva svetska rata', *Vjetar i arkivit të Kosovës* 20 (1985), pp.169–89.
Otiman, Ion Păun. *Viaţa rurală a României în secolul al XX-lea: Un secol de iluzii, dezamăgiri şi speranţe (sau drama satului şi a ţăranului roman)*, Timişoara, 2005.
Paldus, J. 'Die Einverleibung Galiziens und der Bukowina in die österreichische Monarchie im Jahre 1772 und die Landesaufnahme durch den k.k. Generalquartiermeisterstab 1775–1783', *Mitteilungen der Geographischen Gesellschaft Wien* 59 (1916), pp.417–55.
Palošević, Abadin. 'Zemljišni maksimum i promene u agrarnoj strukturi', *Ekonomika poljoprivrede* 4 (1987), pp.233–38.
Paneyko, Basil. 'Galicia and the Polish-Ukrainian Problem', *Slavonic and East European Review* 9 (1930), pp.567–87.
Parnreiter, Christof. *Historische Geographie: Verräumlichte Geschichte. Mexico-City und das mexikanische Städtenetz von der Industrialisierung bis zur Globalisierung*, Stuttgart, 2007.
Pasvolsky, Leo. *Economic Nationalism of the Danubian States*, New York, 1928.
Pătrăşcanu, Lucreţiu. *Probleme de bază ale Romîniei*, Bucharest, 1946.
Paul, Ellen Frenkel, Fred D. Miller and Jeffrey Paul (eds). *Liberalism and the Economic Order*, Cambridge, 1993.
Paunović, Živojin M. 'Svojina i njena ograničenja u srpskom zakonodavstvu', *Arhiv za pravne i društvene nauke* 12/1 (1926), pp.40–52; 12/2 (1926), pp.112–32; 12/3 (1926), pp.209–21.
Pavković, Nikola. 'Porodična zadruga u srpskom građanskom zakoniku', in Miodrag Jovičić (ed.), *Sto pedeset godina od donoševa Srpskog građanskog zakonika 1844–1994*, Belgrade, 1996, pp.329–36.
Pavlović, Momčilo. *Srpsko selo 1945–1952: Otkup*, Belgrade, 1997.
Perić, Živojin. *Zadružno pravo u Građanskom zakoniku Kraljevine Srbije*, Belgrade, 1920.
Peristiany, Jochen George. *Kinship and Modernization in Mediterranean Society*, Hanover, New Hampshire, 1976.
Perović, L., M. Obradović and D. Stojanović (eds). *Srbija u modernizacijskim procesima 20. veka*, Belgrade, 1994.
Perović, Latinka. *Između anarhije i autokratije: Srpsko društvo na prelazima vekova (XIX – XXI)*, Belgrade, 2007.
Perović, Latinka (ed.). *Srbija u modernizacijskim procesima 19. i 20. veka 2: Položaj žene kao merilo modernizacije*, Belgrade, 1998.
——— *Srbija u modernizacijskim procesima 19. i 20. veka 3: Uloga elita*, Belgrade, 2003.
——— *Srbija u modernizacijskim procesima 19. i 20. veka 4: Žene i deca*, Belgrade, 2006.
Peruničić, Branko. *Zemljišna svojina u Srbiji 1815–1845*, Belgrade, 1977.
Petrescu, Christina, and Dragoş Petrescu. 'Mastering vs. Coming to Terms with the Past: A Critical Analysis of Post-communist Romanian Historiography', in Sorin Antohi, Balázs Trencsényi and Péter Apor (eds), *Narratives Unbound: Historical Studies in Post-communist Eastern Europe*, Budapest/New York, 2007, pp.311–408.
——— 'The Piteşti Syndrom: A Romanian Vergangenheitsbewältigung', in Stefan Troebst (ed.), *Postdiktatorische Geschichtskulturen im Süden und Osten Europas: Bestandsaufnahmen und Forschungsperspektiven*, Göttingen, 2010, pp.502–618.

Petrétei, József. *Magyar alkotmányjog*, vol. 3, Pécs/Budapest, 2004.

Petrović, Jelenko. *Okuće ili zaštita zemljoradničkog minimuma*, Belgrade, 1930.

Petrović, Veljko. *Šumadija i Vojvodina*, Belgrade, 1930.

Pießkalla, Michael. *Goldene Aktien aus EG-rechtlicher Sicht*, Hamburg, 2006.

——— '"Goldene Aktien": Ungarisches Privatisierungsgesetz geändert', *Wirtschaft und Recht in Osteuropa* 16/7 (2007), pp.193–97.

Piirainen, Ilpo Tapani. *Das Stadt- und Bergrecht von Kremnica/Kremnitz*, Heidelberg, 1983.

Pijade, Moša. 'O seljačkim radnim zadrugama', in Moša Pijade (ed.), *Izabrani spisi*, vol. 1, book 4, Belgrade, 1966, pp.169–76.

——— 'O predlogu Opšteg zakona o narodnim odborima', in Moša Pijade (ed.), *Izabrani spisi*, vol. 1, book 4, Belgrade, 1966, pp.182–210.

Piłsudski, Józef. *Pisma zbiorowe: Wydanie prac dotychzas drukiem ogłoszonych*, vol. 5, Warsaw, 1937.

Pipes, Richard. *Die Russische Revolution*, vol. 1, Berlin, 1992.

Poczobutt, Michał Odlanicki. 'Kataster gruntowy i budynkowy: Ogólne informacje o katastrze', in Michał Odlanicki Poczobutt (ed.), *Rocznik Geodezyjny*, Warsaw, 1953, pp.554–57.

Polek, Johann. 'Joseph's II. Reisen nach Galizien und der Bukowina und ihre Bedeutung für letztere Provinz', *Jahrbuch des Bukowiner Landesmuseums* 3 (1895), pp.25–140.

——— 'Die Bukowina zu Anfang des Jahres 1801', *Jahrbuch des Bukowiner Landesmuseums* 15 (1907), pp.3–76.

Polonsky, Antony. *Politics in Independent Poland 1921–1939: The Crisis of Constitutional Government*, Oxford, 1972.

Poniatowski, Juliusz. *Przeludnienie wsi i rolnictwa*, Warsaw, 1935.

Popov, Jelena. *Drama na Vojvodjanskom selu (1945–1952): Obavezi otkup poljoprivrednih proizvoda*, Novi Sad, 2002.

Popović, Svetolik. *Die Agrarpolitik in Jugoslawien*, Belgrade, 1964.

Popović-Obradović, Olga. *The Parliamentary System in Serbia 1903–1914*, Belgrade, 2013.

——— *Kakva ili kolika država*, Belgrade, 2009.

Portmann, Michael. *Die kommunistische Revolution in der Vojvodina 1944–1955: Politik, Gesellschaft, Wirtschaft, Kultur*, Vienna, 2008.

Powell, Walter W. and Paul J. DiMaggio, (eds). *The New Institutionalism in Organizational Analysis*, Chicago, 1991.

Predlog slobodne i kraljevske varoši Novog Sada u predmetu sprovađanja agrarne reforme, Novi Sad, 1920.

Primas, Georg. 'Die Staatsintervention auf dem polnischen Agrarmarkt', *Berichte über Landwirtschaft* 22/1 (1937), pp.41–82.

Proect de lege pentru Expropriere şi Împroprietărire: Lupta Partidului Naţional-Ţărănesc pentru reformele agrare, Bucharest, 1945.

Programul Partidului Comunist Român de făurire a societăţii socialiste multilateral dezvoltate şi înaintare a României spre communism, Bucharest, 1975.

Pryor, Frederic L. *The Rise and Fall of Collectivized Agriculture in Marxist Regimes*, Princeton, 1992.

Puia, Maria. *Viaţa agrară a judeţului Brăila în perioada interbelică*, Brăila, 1995.

Puşcaşiu, I.C. *Agricultura, reforma agrară, colonizările, cadastrul şi cartea funduară*, Satu-Mare, 1931.

Radojević, Mira. *Naučnik i politika: Politička biografija Božidara V. Markovića (1874–1946)*, Belgrade, 2007.

Rădulescu, Andrei. *Publicitatea drepturilor reale imobiliare şi registrele de proprietate*, Bucharest, 1923.

Ránki, György. *The Economics of the Second World War*, Vienna/Cologne/Weimar, 1993.

Reformele agrare din 1920 şi 1945, Bucharest, 1945.

Regele, Oskar. *Beitrag zur Geschichte der staatlichen Landesaufnahme und Kartographie in Österreich bis zum Jahre 1918*, Vienna, 1955.

Rehberg, Karl-Siegbert. 'Institutionen, Kognitionen und Symbole: Institutionen als symbolische Verkörperungen', in Andrea Maurer and Michael Schmid (eds), *Neuer Institutionalismus: Zur soziologischen Erklärung von Organisation, Moral und Vertrauen*, Frankfurt am Main, 2002, pp.39–56.

Resich, Zbigniew. 'Kodeks cywilny: Komentarzs', in *Wydawnictwo Prawnicze*, vol. 1, Warsaw, 1972.

Restabilirea Adevărului asupra situaţiunei dela Direcţiunea Cadastrului, n.p., n.d.

Rifkin, Jeremy. *The Age of Access: How the Shift from Ownership to Access is Transforming Capitalism*, Harmondsworth, 2000.

Rittstieg, Helmut. *Eigentum als Verfassungsproblem: Zur Geschichte und Gegenwart des bürgerlichen Verfassungsstaates*, Darmstadt, 1975.

Roberts, Henry L. *Rumania: Political Problems of an Agrarian State*, London/Oxford, 1951.

Roggemann, Herwig. 'Wandel der Eigentumsordnung in Osteuropa', *Recht in Ost und West* 37/11 (1993), pp.321–31.

——— 'Eigentum in Ost und West: Zur Entwicklung eines Rechtsinstituts aus rechtsvergleichender Sicht', in Herwig Roggemann (ed.), *Eigentum in Osteuropa: Rechtspraxis in Ost-, Ostmittel- und Südosteuropa mit Einführungen und Rechtstexten*, Berlin, 1996, pp.17–58.

Roggemann, Herwig (ed.). *Eigentum in Osteuropa: Rechtspraxis in Ost-, Ostmittel- und Südosteuropa mit Einführungen und Rechtstexten*, Berlin, 1996.

Rohlack, Momme. *Kriegsgesellschaften (1914–1918): Arten, Rechtsformen und Funktionen in der Kriegswirtschaft des Ersten Weltkrieges*, Frankfurt am Main, 2001.

Rose, W.J. 'Wincenty Witos', *Slavonic and East European Review* 25 (1946/47), pp.39–54.

Roszkowski, Wojciech. *Gospodarcza rola większej prywatnej własności ziemskiej w Polsce 1918–1939*, Warsaw, 1986.

——— *Land Reforms in East Central Europe after World War One*, Warsaw, 1995.

Rottleuthner, Wilhelm Johann. *Die alten Localmasse und Gewichte nebst den Aichungsvorschriften bis zur Einführung des metrischen Mass- und Gewichtssystems und der Staatsaichämter in Tirol und Vorarlberg*, Innsbruck, 1883.

Roux, Michel. *Les Albanais en Yougoslavie: Minorité nationale et développment*, Paris, 1992.

Ruchniewicz, Krzysztof. 'Die polnische Geschichtspolitik der Nach-"Wende"-Zeit am Scheideweg', in Stefan Troebst (ed.), *Postdiktatorische Geschichtskulturen im Süden und Osten Europas: Bestandsaufnahmen und Forschungsperspektiven*, Göttingen, 2010, pp.307–29.

Rumpler, Helmut. *Eine Chance für Mitteleuropa: Bürgerliche Emanzipation und Staatsverfall in der Habsburgermonarchie*, Vienna, 1997.

Sandgruber, Roman. 'Österreichische Agrarstatistik 1750–1918', in Alfred Hoffmann, Herbert Matis and Michael Mitterauer (eds), *Materialien zur Wirtschafts- und Sozialgeschichte*, vol. 2, Vienna, 1978.

——— 'Der Franziszeische Kataster als Quelle für die Wirtschaftsgeschichte und historische Volkskunde', *Mitteilungen des Niederösterreichischen Landesarchivs* 3 (1979), pp.16–28.

——— *Ökonomie und Politik: Österreichische Wirtschaftsgeschichte vom Mittelalter bis zur Gegenwart*, Vienna, 1995.

Şandru, Dumitru. *Reforma agrară din 1921 în România*, Bucharest, 1975.

——— *Creditul agricol în România (1918–1944)*, Bucharest, 1985.

——— *Reforma agrară din 1945 în România*, Bucharest, 2000.

Sapa, Dorota. *Między polską wyspą a ukraińskim morzem: Kresy południowo-wschodnie w polskiej prozie 1918–1988*, Krakow, 1998.

Scharr, Kurt. 'Erfolg oder Misserfolg? Die Durchsetzung des modernen Territorialstaates am Beispiel des Ansiedlungswesens in der Bukowina von 1774–1826', in Hans-Christian Maner (ed.), *Grenzregionen der Habsburgermonarchie im 18. und 19. Jahrhundert. Ihre Bedeutung und Funktion aus der Perspektive Wiens*, Münster, 2005, pp.51–87.

——— 'Die innere Verwaltungsentwicklung der Bukowina 1775–1918: Beharrlichkeit alter und Heranwachsen neuer politischer Strukturen', *Jahrbücher für Geschichte Osteuropas* 55/2 (2007), pp.178–209.

Scheer, Tamara. *Zwischen Front und Heimat: Österreich-Ungarns Militärverwaltungen im Ersten Weltkrieg*, Frankfurt am Main, 2009.

Scheuermann, Martin. *Minderheitenschutz contra Konfliktverhütung? Die Minderheitenpolitik des Völkerbundes in den zwanziger Jahren*, Marburg, 2000.

Schivelbusch, Wolfgang. *Entfernte Verwandtschaft: Faschismus, Nationalsozialismus, New Deal, 1933–1939*, Munich/Vienna, 2005.

Schlau, Wilfried. 'Die Agrarreformen und ihre Auswirkungen', in Hans Lemberg (ed.), *Ostmitteleuropa zwischen den beiden Weltkriegen. Stärke und Schwäche der neuen Staaten, nationale Minderheiten*, Marburg, 1997, pp.145–59.

Schlesinger, Rudolf. 'Diversity and Unity in the Socialist Law of Property', *Soviet Studies* 15/4 (1964), pp.474–85.

Schlucher, Wolfgang. 'Interessen, Ideen und Institutionen: Schlüsselbegriffe der an Max Weber orientierten Soziologie', in Steffen Sigmund (ed.), *Soziale Konstellationen und historische Perspektive*, Wiesbaden, 2008, pp.57–80.

Schultz, Helga, and Angela Harre (eds). *Bauerngesellschaften auf dem Weg in die Moderne: Agrarismus in Ostmitteleuropa 1880 bis 1960*, Wiesbaden, 2010.

Schultz, Helga, and Eduard Kubů (eds). *History and Culture of Economic Nationalism in East Central Europe*, Berlin, 2006.

Schwab, Dieter. 'Eigentum', in Otto Brunner, Werner Conze and Reinhart Koselleck (eds), *Geschichtliche Grundbegriffe: Historisches Lexikon zur politisch-sozialen Sprache in Deutschland*, vol. 2, Stuttgart, 1975, pp.65–115.

Scorpan, Costin. *Istoria României: Enciclopedie*, Iaşi, 1997.

Scott, James C. *Weapons of the Weak: Everyday Forms of Peasant Resistance*, New Haven, 1985.

——— *Seeing Like a State: How Certain Schemes to Improve the Human Condition Have Failed*, New Haven, 1998.

Scott, W. Richard. *Institutions and Organizations*, London/New Delhi, 1995.

Šećerov, Slavko. *Iz naše agrarne politike*, Belgrade, 1930.

Sering, Max (ed.). *Die agrarischen Umwälzungen im außerrussischen Osteuropa: Ein Sammelwerk*, Berlin, 1930.

Siegrist, Hannes. 'Die Advokaten auf dem Land', in Wolfgang Jacobeit, Josef Mooser and Bo Stråht (eds), *Idylle oder Aufbruch? Das Dorf im bürgerlichen 19. Jahrhundert. Ein europäischer Vergleich*, Berlin, 1990, pp.169–80.

——— 'Juridicalisation, Professionalisation and the Occupational Culture of the Advocate in the Nineteenth and the Early Twentieth Centuries: A Comparison of Germany, Italy and Switzerland', in David Sugarman and Wesley Pue (eds), *Lawyers and Vampires: Cultural Histories of Legal Professions*, Oxford/Portland, 2003, pp.123–50.

——— 'The Professions in Nineteenth-century Europe', in Hartmut Kaelble (ed.), *The European Way: European Societies during the Nineteenth and Twentieth Centuries*, New York, 2004, pp.68–88.

——— 'Comparative History of Cultures and Societies: From Cross-societal Analysis to the Study of Intercultural Interdependencies', *Comparative Education* 42/3 (2006), pp.377–404.

——— 'Die Propertisierung von Gesellschaft und Kultur: Konstruktion und Institutionalisierung des Eigentums in der Moderne', in Hannes Siegrist (ed.), *Entgrenzung des Eigentums in modernen Gesellschaften und Rechtskulturen*, *Comparativ* 16/5–6 (2006), pp.9–52.

Siegrist, Hannes and Isabella Löhr. 'Intellectual Property Rights between Nationalization and Globalization', in Hannes Siegrist and Isabella Löhr (eds), 'Intellectual Property Rights and Globalization', *Comparativ* 21/2 (2011), pp.7–28.

Siegrist, Hannes, and David Sugarman. 'Geschichte als historisch-vergleichende Eigentumswissenschaft: Rechts-, kultur- und gesellschaftsgeschichtliche Perspektiven', in Hannes Siegrist and David Sugarman (eds), *Eigentum im internationalen Vergleich*, Göttingen, 1999, pp.9–30.

Sienkiewicz, Witold. *Wysiedlenia, wypędzenia i ucieczki 1939–1959: Atlas ziem Polski: Polacy, Żydzi, Niemcy, Ukraińcy*, Warsaw, 2008.

Skowrońska-Bocian, Elżbieta. *Kodeks cywilny: Komentarz do artykułów 1-44911*, ed. Krzysztof Pietrzykowski, Warsaw, 2005, art. 140/4–13.

Słabek, Henryk. *Polityka agrarna PPR*, Warsaw, 1967.

Slezkine, Yuri. 'The USSR as a Communal Apartment, Or How a Socialist State Promoted Ethnic Particularism', *Slavic Review* 53/2 (1994), pp.414–52.

Slijepčević, Ratomir M., and Ilija Babić. *Real Property Rights in Serbia*, Vienna/Graz, 2005.

Smith, Anthony D. *The Ethnic Origin of Nations*, Oxford, 1986.

Snyder, Timothy. *Sketches from a Secret War: A Polish Artist's Mission to Liberate Soviet Ukraine*, New Haven, 2005.

Sobczak, Tadeusz. *Przełom w konsumpcji spożywczej w Królestwie Polskim*, Wroclaw, 1968.

Socol, Gheorghe. *Evoluţie, involuţie şi tranziţie în agricultura românească*, Bucharest, 1999.

Spickermann, Alexander. *Agrarfrage und neustaatliche Bodenreformbestrebungen in Polen*, Lodz, 1928.

Srokowski, Stanislaw. 'The Ukrainian Problem in Poland: A Polish View', *Slavonic and East European Studies* 9 (1930/31), pp.588–97.

Srpski ustavi od 1835. do 1990. godine sa ustavima Kraljevine SHS i Kraljevine Jugoslavije, Belgrade, 2004.

Stachura, Peter D. 'National Identity and the Ethnic Minorities in Early Inter-war Poland', in Peter D. Stachura (ed.), *Poland between the Wars, 1918–1939*, London/New York, 1998, pp.60–86.

Stały Kataster w Galicyi, Lvov, 1866.

Staniewicz, Witold. 'The Agrarian Problem in Poland between the Two World Wars', *Slavonic and East European Review* 43 (1964), pp.23–33.

Stark, David, and László Bruszt (eds). *Postsocialist Pathways: Transforming Politics and Property in East-Central Europe*, Cambridge, 1998.

Starowieyski, Franciszek. *Franciszka Starowieyskiego opowieść o końcu świata, czyli Reforma rolna (pisała Krystyna Uniechowska)*, Warsaw, 1994.

Stauter-Halsted, Keely. 'The Moral Community and Peasant Nationalism in Nineteenth-century Poland', in Judith Pallot (ed.), *Transforming Peasants: Society, State and Peasantry, 1861–1930*, Houndmills, 1998, pp.73–89.

——— *The Nation in the Village: The Genesis of Peasant National Identity in Austrian Poland, 1848–1914*, Ithaca/London, 2001.

Stjepanović-Zaharijevski, Dragana. 'Porodična zadruga kao tradicija porodićnog života balkanskih naroda', in Ljubiša Mitrović, Dragana Stjepanović-Zaharijevski and Vjekoslav Butigan (eds), *Strategije razvoja i procesi regionalne saradnje na Balkanu, Socio-kulturni odnosi na Balkanu*, Niš, 2000, pp.257–64.

Stobniak-Smogorzewska, Janina. *Kresowe osadnictwo wojskowe 1920–1945*, Warsaw, 2003.

——— 'Osadnicy wojskowi a ludność żydowska na Kresach Wschodnich 1920–1940', in Krzysztof Jasiewicz (ed.), *Świat niepożegnany: Żydzi na dawnych ziemiach wschodnich Rzeczypospolitej w XVIII-XX wieku*, Warsaw, 2004, pp.559–69.

Stojanović, Dragoljub. 'Pozitivno-pravna ograničenja privatne svojine', PhD diss., Belgrade, 1963.

Stojanović, Dubravka. *Srbija i demokratija 1903–1914*, Belgrade, 2003.

——— *Ulje na vodi: Ogledi iz istorije sadašnjosti*, Belgrade, 2010.

Stokes, Gale. *Politics as Development: The Emergence of Political Parties in Nineteenth-century Serbia*, Durham, NC/London, 1990.

Stolberg-Rilinger, Barbara. 'Was heißt Kulturgeschichte des Politischen. Einleitung', in Barbara Stolberg-Rilinger (ed.), *Was heißt Kulturgeschichte des Politischen?* Berlin, 2005, pp.9–24.

Struve, Kai. *Bauern und Nation in Galizien: Über Zugehörigkeit und soziale Emanzipation im 19. Jahrhundert*, Göttingen, 2005.

Styk, Józef. *Ewolucja chłopskiego systemu wartości: Analiza historyczno-socjologiczna*, Lublin, 1988.

Styś, Wincenty. *Wpływ uprzemysłowienia na ustrój rolny*, Lviv, 1936.

——— *Drogi postępu gospodarczego wsi*, Wroclaw, 1947.

Suchon, Aneta, and Jan Schürmann. 'Grundstücksverkehr mit landwirtschaftlichen Grundstücken in der Republik Polen', *Agrar- und Umweltrecht* 34/6 (2004), pp.169–74.

Sundhaussen, Holm. 'Die "Transformation" Osteuropas in historischer Perspektive oder: Wie groß ist der Handlungsspielraum einer Gesellschaft?' in Hellmut Wollmann, Helmut Wiesenthal and Frank Bönker (eds), *Transformation sozialistische Gesellschaften: Am Ende des Anfangs, Leviathan* 15 (1995), pp.77–92.

——— 'Wandel ohne Modernisierung: Theorien nachholender Entwicklung unter besonderer Berücksichtigung Südosteuropas', in Krista Zach and Cornelius R. Zach (eds), *Modernisierung auf Raten in Rumänien: Anspruch, Umsetzung, Wirkung*, Munich, 2004, pp.27–32.

——— *Geschichte Serbiens. 19.–21. Jahrhundert*, Vienna/Cologne/Weimar, 2007.

Surd, Vasile. 'Ein Teil von Europa wird ausgegrenzt', *Tübinger Geographische Studien* 128 (2000), pp.139–47.

Synadino, P.V. *Memoriul agricultorilor având peste 25 hectare pământ din Basarabia*, Chisinau, 1921.

——— *Însemnătatea reformei agrare în Basarabia*, n.p., 1926.

Szczepański, Janusz. *Społeczeństwo Polski w walce z najazdem bolszewickim 1920 roku*, Warsaw, 2000.

Szemberg, Anna. *Przemiany struktury agrarnej w świetle narodowych spisów powszechnych 1960 i 1970*, Warsaw, 1973.

Szladits, Károly. *Magyar Magánjog*, Budapest, 1939–1942.

Szlajfer, Henry (ed.). *Economic Nationalism in East-Central Europe and South America, 1918–1939*, Geneva, 1990.

Szymański, M., and A. Soczek. 'Ewidencja gruntów', in *Służba geodezyjna i kartograficzna Głównego Urzędu Geodezji i Kartografii 1945–1980*, Warsaw, 1980, pp.98–103.

Tafeln zur Statistik der österreichischen Monarchie 1855–57, vol. 3, Vienna, 1857.

Taşcă, Gheorghe. *Reforma Agrară*, n.p., 1945.

Teichova, Alice. *Kleinstaaten im Spannungsfeld der Großmächte: Wirtschaft und Politik in Mittel- und Südosteuropa in der Zwischenkriegszeit*, Munich, 1988.

Tepicht, Jerzy. *Marxisme et Agriculture: Le Paysan Polonais*, Paris, 1973.

——— 'A Project for Research on the Peasant Revolution of Our Time', *Journal of Peasant Studies* 2/3 (1975), pp.257–69.

Thelen, Tatjana. 'Violence and Social (Dis)Continuity: Comparing Collectivization in Two East European Villages', *Social History* 30/1 (2005), pp.25–44.

Tito, J. Broz. 'Mi nismo stvarali zadruge samo za tri godine', *Socijalistička poljoprivreda* 2/11 (1951), pp.1–6.

Tkaczyński, Jan Wiktor. *Polen im Umbruch: Skizzen aus Geschichte, Wirtschaft und Politik*, Berlin, 1997.

Tochitch, Desimir. 'Collectivization in Yugoslavia', *Journal of Farm Economics* 41/1 (1959), pp.26–42.

Todorović, Vladimir. 'Zakon o agrarnoj reformi i kolonizaciji', in Vladimir Todorović (ed.), *Denacionalizacija između nacionalizacije i privatizacije*, Belgrade, 2001, pp.107–16.

Tomasević, Jozo. 'Postwar Foreign Economic Relations', in Robert J. Kerner (ed.), *Yugoslavia*, Berkeley/Los Angeles, 1949, pp.387–426.

——— *Peasants, Politics, and Economic Change in Yugoslavia*, Stanford, 1955.

Tomuschat, Christian. *Eigentum im Umbruch: Restitution, Privatisierung und Nutzungskonflikte im Europa der Gegenwart*, Berlin, 1996.

Torsello, Davide. *Trust, Property and Social Change in a Southern Slovakian Village*, Halle, 2003.

Tošić, Desimir. *Snaga i nemoć: naš komunizam 1945–1990*, Belgrade, 2001.

——— *Kolektivizacija u Jugoslaviji 1949–1953*, Belgrade, 2002.

Trgovčević, Ljubinka. 'Srpski inženjeri na studijama u inostranstvu do 1918. godine', in Petar Miljanić (ed.), *Putevi srpskog inženjerstva tokom XIX veka*, Belgrade, 1994, pp.148–67.

Trkulja, Jovica. 'Der Realsozialismus und der Rechtsstaat', *Rechtstheorie* 24 (1993), pp.33–53.

Trouton, Ruth. *Peasant Renaissance in Yugoslavia, 1900–1950*, New York, 1952.

Tudor, Constantin. 'Aspecte din activitatea de măsurări terestre şi cadastru', *Geodezie, cadastru şi organizarea teritoriului* 15/4 (1971), pp.4–14.

Ţurcanu, Ion. *Relaţii agrare din Basarabia în anii 1918–1940*, Bucharest, 1991.

Turnock, David. *The Economy of East Central Europe, 1815–1989: Stages of Transformation in a Peripheral Region*, London/New York, 2006.

Turnock, David (ed.). *Privatization in Rural Eastern Europe: The Process of Restitution and Restructuring*, Cheltenham/Northampton, MA, 1998.

Tyszka, Kryzsztof. *Nacjonalizm w komunizmie: Ideologia narodowa w Związku Radzieckim i Polsce Ludowej*, Warsaw, 2004.

Uniunea Centrale a Sindicatelor Agricole din România. *Memoriu prezentat Comisiei de Studii pentru Reforma Agrară*, n.p., 1945.

Uniunea Cooperativelor Agricole de Producţie din R.S.R. *Statutul Uniunilor Cooperativelor Agricole de Producţie din Republica Socialistă România*, Bucharest, 1972.

Vasić, Velimir. *Putevi razvitka socijalizma u poljoprivredi Jugoslavije*, Belgrade, 1960.

Veljković, Ljubomir. 'O uzrocima i borbi protiv kolebanja u seljačkim radnim zadrugama', *Socijalistička poljoprivreda* 2/11 (1951), pp.7–15.

Verdery, Katherine. *Transylvanian Villagers: Three Centuries of Political, Economic and Ethnic Change*, Berkeley, 1983.

——— *What Was Socialism, and What Comes Next?* Princeton, 1996.

——— *The Vanishing Hectare: Property and Value in Postsocialist Transylvania*, Ithaca/London, 2003.

Vereinigung des deutschen Volkstums in Polen and Deutschtumsbund Polen e.V. *Die Verfassung der Polnischen Republik vom 17. März 1921*, Bromberg/Posen, 1921.

Vilfan, Sergij. 'Jugoslawien', in Helmut Coing (ed.), *Handbuch der Quellen und Literatur der neueren europäischen Privatrechtsgeschichte*, vol. 3(5), Munich, 1988, pp.324–470.

von Benda-Beckmann, Franz. 'Propertization in Indonesien: Parallele und gegenläufige Entwicklungen', in Hannes Siegrist (ed.), *Entgrenzung des Eigentums in modernen Gesellschaften und Rechtskulturen*, Leipzig, 2007, pp.99–111.

von Benda-Beckmann, Franz, Keebet von Benda-Beckmann and Melanie S. Wiber. 'The Properties of Property', in Franz von Benda-Beckmann, Keebet von Benda-Beckmann and Melanie S. Wiber (eds), *Changing Properties of Property*, New York/Oxford, 2006, pp.1–39.

von Bieberstein, Christoph Freiherr Marschall. *Freiheit in der Unfreiheit: Die nationale Autonomie der Polen in Galizien nach dem österreichisch-ungarischen Ausgleich 1867. Ein konservativer Aufbruch im mitteleuropäischen Vergleich*, Wiesbaden, 1993.

von Chlupp, Chlonau Johann Moritz. *Systematisches Handbuch der direkten Steuern im Kaisertum Österreich*, Prague, 1874.

von Eyberg, Karl. *Chronologisches systematisches Compilationswerk über das Steuer- und Peräquationswesen Tyrols*, Innsbruck, 1793.

von Frangeš, Otto. *Die sozialökonomische Struktur der jugoslawischen Landwirtschaft*, Berlin, 1937.

von Harnier, Alexander. *Entwicklung und Ergebnisse der Agrarreform in Polen*, Danzig, 1931.

von Schullern zu Schrattenhoven, Hermann. *Geschichtliche Darstellung der Besteuerung der Land- und Forstwirtschaft*, Vienna, 1899.

Vučković, Mihajlo. *Zadrugarstvo*, Belgrade, 1947.

Vujović, Dragoljub. 'Geopremer u Moravičkom okrugu (Čačak, Gornji Milanovac, Lučani i Ivanjica) i osnivanje katastra zemljišta', *Zbornik radova Narodnog muzeja u Čačak* 36 (2005), pp.175–90.

Vukosavljević, Sreten. 'Postanak privatne zemljišne svojine u nas', *Arhiv za pravne i društvene nauke* 30/1 (1940), pp.91–100.

——— 'Zajednički radovi na selu', *Arhiv za pravne i društvene nauke* 1/1–2 (1945), pp.30–35.

——— 'Zajednička zemljišna svojina', *Pravna Misao* 11/1–4 (1945), pp.17–29.

——— *Istorija seljačkog društva*, 3 vols, Belgrade, 1953–1983.

Vultur, Smaranda. 'New Topics, New Tendencies and New Generations of Historians in Romanian Historiography', in Ulf Brunnbauer (ed.), *(Re)Writing History: Historiography in Southeastern Europe after Socialism*, Münster, 2004, pp.236–76.

Wädekin, Karl-Eugen. *Agrarian Policies in Communist Europe*, The Hague/London, 1982.

Wagner, Rudolf. *Die Reisetagebücher des österreichischen Kaisers Franz I. in die Bukowina (1817 und 1823)*, Munich, 1979.

Warriner, Doreen. *Economics of Peasant Farming*, Oxford, 1939.

——— *Jugoslavia Rebuilds*, Neudeln/Lichtenstein, 1979.

Weber, Eugene. *Peasants into Frenchmen*, Stanford, 1976.

Weichhart, Peter. 'Vom "Räumeln" in der Geographie und anderen Disziplinen: Einige Thesen zum Raumaspekt sozialer Phänomene', in Jörg F. Mayer (ed.), *Die aufgeräumte Welt: Raumbilder und Raumkonzepte im Zeitalter globaler Marktwirtschaft*, Rehburg-Loccum, 1993, pp.225–41.

Weiske, Julius. 'Bemerkungen über das Brünner Schöffenbuch', *Zeitschrift für deutsches Recht und deutsche Rechtswissenschaft* (1853), pp.113–54.

Wesel, Uwe. *Geschichte des Rechts: Von den Frühformen bis zum Vertrag von Maastricht*, Munich, 1997.

Wessely, Josef. 'Österreichisches Grundsteuerkataster', *Österreichische Revue* (1865), pp.147–78.

Westen, Klaus, Georg Brunner and Friedrich-Christian Schroeder. *Sozialistisches Wirtschaftsrecht zwischen Wandel und Beharrung*, Berlin, 1988.

Wiese, Willy. *Die polnische Bodenbesitzpolitik: Untersuchungen auf dem Gebiete der Agrarreform und der landwirtschaftlichen Organisationen in Polen während der Jahre 1919 und 1926*, Berlin, 1928.

Winczorek, Piotr. 'Die neue Verfassung der Republik Polen – ein Streit um Werte', in *Forschungsstelle Osteuropa an der Universität Bremen: Recht und Kultur in Ostmitteleuropa*, Bremen, 1999, pp.279–95.

Winsch, M.B. 'Scenes in Eastern Poland', *Contemporary Review* 146 (1934), pp.472–79.

Wróbel, Piotr. 'Kombatanci kontra politycy: Narodziny i początki działania Związku Legionistów Polskich 1918–1925', *Przegląd Historyczny* 76/1 (1985), pp.77–111.

Zaborski, Bogdan. *Les nationalités et les confessions en Pologne d'après le recensement de 1931: Remarques générales*, Warsaw, 1937.

Zagoroff, S.D. *The Agricultural Economy of the Danubian Countries, 1935–45*, Stanford, 1955.

Zaitseff, Leo. 'Das Eigentumsrecht im Sovietstaate', *Zeitschrift für Osteuropäisches Recht* 2/4 (1926), pp.425–35.

Zaitsev, Cyril. 'The Russian Agrarian Revolution', *Slavonic and East European Review* 9 (1930/31), pp.547–66.

Zakon o izdavanju tapija na području Kasacionog Suda u Beogradu i Velikog Suda u Podgorici, Belgrade, 1931.

Zaremba, Marcin. *Komunizm, legitymacja, nacjonalizm*, Warsaw, 2001.

Zawistowicz-Adamska, Kazimiera. 'Żywe tradycje współdziałania na wsi', in Kazimiera Zawistowicz-Adamska (ed.), *Granice i horyzonty badań kultury na wsi w Polsce*, Warsaw, 1976, pp.189–243.

Zebić, Milorad. 'Unutrašnja kolonizacija u vezi agrarne reforme', in *Almanah Udruženja Pravnika Kraljevstva Srba, Hrvata I Slovenaca*, Belgrade, 1920, pp.287–314.

Zegar, Józef Stanisław. *Dochody ludności chłopskiej*, Warsaw, 2000.

Zerilli, Filippo M. 'Sentiments and/as Property Rights: Restitution and Conflict in Postsocialist Romania', in Maruška Svašek (ed.), *Postsocialism: Politics and Emotion in Central and Eastern Europe*, Oxford/New York, 2008, pp.74–94.

Živković, Aleksandar. 'Nastajanje i razvoj geodetske delatnosti u Srbiji', in Petar Miljanić (ed.), *Putevi srpskog inženjerstva tokom XIX veka*, Belgrade, 1994, pp.29–43.

Zlinszky, János. 'Superflua lex? Non loquitur?' *Magyar Jog* (2007), pp.724–28.

Zloch, Stefanie. 'Nationsbildung und Feinderklärung: "Jüdischer Bolschewismus" und der polnisch-sowjetische Krieg 1919–1920', *Jahrbuch des Simon-Dubnow-Instituts* 4 (2005), pp.279–302.

Zur Grundsteuerregulierung in der Bukowina: Denkschrift der Vertreter der Bukowinaer Grunndsteuerträger, Vienna, 1880.

Notes on Contributors

Jovana Diković is a PhD candidate in the Department of Social and Cultural Anthropology at the University of Zurich, and has been a junior researcher at the Institute of Ethnography, the Serbian Academy of Sciences and Arts since 2010. She received her BA in social anthropology from the Faculty of Philosophy, University of Belgrade, and an MA in political sciences from the Faculty of Political Sciences, University of Belgrade. Apart from political anthropology, her main interests are economic and legal anthropology, especially regarding property issues, access to resources and the post-socialist transformation of rural livelihoods. The area of her fieldwork research is south-eastern Banat in Vojvodina (Serbia).

Christhardt Henschel studied medieval and modern history, eastern and south-eastern European studies and musicology at the University of Leipzig. Since 2008, he has been a doctoral student at the Simon Dubnow Institute for Jewish History and Culture, where he has been working on a project on Jews and the Polish military during the interwar period. He has edited and co-edited the special issues *Juden im Militär. Erfahrung und Erinnerung im 19. und 20. Jahrhundert* in *Simon Dubnow Institute Yearbook* 12 (2013), and co-edited together with Stephan Stach the volume *Pragmatismus. Staatliche Institutionen und Minderheiten in Polen 1918–1939*, *Zeitschrift für Ostmitteleuropaforschung* (2013).

Paweł Klint holds a doctorate from the Institute of History, Faculty of Historical and Pedagogical Sciences, University of Wrocław (Poland). His research focuses on the social and economic history of Poland in the seventeenth century, especially the testaments of members of the gentry, the trade in nobility-owned land, as well as social conflicts and crimes among the Polish nobility. He is author of *Testamenty szlacheckie z ksiąg grodzkich wielkopolskich z lat 1631–1655* (2008), *Testamenty szlacheckie z ksiąg grodzkich wielkopolskich z lat 1657–1680* (2011) and *Szlachecki obrót ziemią w powiecie kcyńskim w latach 1626–1655* (2012).

Jacek Kochanowicz is professor of economic history at Warsaw University and visiting professor of history at the Central European University, Budapest. His current research interests include economic and social change in East Central Europe from the eighteenth to the twentieth century. His publications include two books on peasant economy and a collection of essays, *Backwardness and Modernization: Poland and Eastern Europe in the Sixteenth to the Twentieth Centuries* (2006). His latest publication is 'Private Suffering, Public Benefit: Market Rhetoric in Poland, 1989–1993', *Eastern European Politics and Societies* 28/1 (2014), pp. 103–18.

Herbert Küpper studied law in Cologne and London, and pursued his practical legal education in Cologne and Budapest. Since 2003 he has been senior research fellow in Hungarian law at the Institute for Eastern European Law, Munich, of which he has been managing director since 2004. He is a Professor honoris causa at Andrássy Gyula University, Budapest, and regularly teaches at the universities of Budapest (ELTE), Pécs, Szeged, Vienna and Munich (LMU). Among his recent publications are *Einführung in die Rechtsgeschichte Osteuropas* (2005), *Einführung in das ungarische Recht* (2011) and *Ungarns Verfassung vom 25. April 2011: Einführung – Übersetzung – Materialien* (2012).

Jovica Luković is a PhD candidate in south-east European history at the Free University of Berlin, where he is studying processes of social differentiation among the peasantry of Yugoslavia between the world wars. His research interests and publications have focused on topics such as agrarian reform, peasant knowledge, property rights and economic and scientific relations between south-east European countries and Germany. Publications include 'Sozialismus als bäuerliche Zukunft. Ideologische Grundlagen des linken Agrarismus in Jugoslawien in der Zwischenkriegszeit', in Müller and Harre (eds), *Transforming Rural Societies* (2010) and 'Developing the "Bread-Basket". Agricultural Politics of the German Occupying Forces in Yugoslavia and their Impact on Rural Development' available at http://www.kuleuven.be/icag/files/Jovica_Lukovic.pdf.

Cornel Micu is assistant professor in the Faculty of Communication and International Relations at 'Danubius' University, Galaţi, Romania. His fields of interest are social and economic history, the transformation of social structures following Europeanization, urbanization from a historical perspective and agricultural history. He graduated in history and political sciences from University of Bucharest, Romania, and has a PhD from the University of Jena. He has worked on several research projects in Romanian history, and has been a fellow of New Europe College, Bucharest (2011/12) and Imre Kertész Kolleg, Jena (2012). He authored the book *From Peasants to Farmers? Agrarian Reforms and Modernisation in Twentieth Century Romania. A Case Study: Bordei Verde Commune in Braila County* (2012).

Srđan Milošević is a research assistant in the Institute for Recent History of Serbia, and PhD candidate in the Faculty of Philosophy in Belgrade. His research interests cover the agrarian question in twentieth century, the history of historiography and the problem of historical revisionism (including the juridical rehabilitation of persons declared war criminals after the Second World War in Yugoslavia). He is the author of the book *Istorija pred sudom* (2013) and of several articles and book chapters, among them 'The Agrarian Reform – A "Divine Thing". Ideological Aspects of the Interwar Agrarian Reform in the Kingdom of the Serbs, Croats and Slovenes', in Müller and Harre (eds), *Transforming Rural Societies* (2010).

Bogdan Murgescu is professor of history and director of the Council for Doctoral Studies at the University of Bucharest; since 2011 he has also been president of the Romanian Society for Historical Sciences. He has previously been Roman Herzog Fellow of the Alexander von Humboldt Foundation, as well as visiting professor at the University of Pittsburgh and at the Central European University, Budapest. He has conducted and/or coordinated several national and international research projects focusing mostly on economic and social history. Among his publications is the recent book *România şi Europa: Acumularea decalajelor economice (1500–2010)*, a comparative analysis of the relative economic backwardness of Romania. He contributed to collected volumes, such as Helga Schultz and Angela Harre, *Bauerngesellschaften auf dem Weg in die Moderne. Agrarismus in Ostmitteleuropa* (2010); Victor Neumann and Armin Heinen, *Key Concepts of Romanian History* (2103); Günther Heydemann and Karel Vodička, *Vom Ostblock zur EU. Systemtransformationen 1990–2012 im Vergleich* (2013).

Dietmar Müller received his PhD in history from the Free University of Berlin. In 2012/13 he was a fellow at Imre Kertész Kolleg, Jena. He has conducted and coordinated research projects on land ownership and legal culture in East Central Europe at the University of Leipzig and at the Centre for the History and Culture of East Central Europe at the same university. Among his property-related publications are the co-edited volumes *Transforming Rural Societies* (2010) (ed. with Angela Harre), *Institutionen und Kultur in Südosteuropa* (2014) (ed. with Wim van Meurs) and *Professionen, Eigentum und Staat. Europäische Entwicklungen im Vergleich – 19. und 20. Jahrhundert* (2014) (ed. with Hannes Siegrist) and contributions to collected volumes: Rosa Congost and Rui Santos, *Contexts of Property in Europe* (2010); Hannes Siegrist and Stefan Troebst, *Institutionenwandel und Rechtstransfer im 20. Jahrhundert* (special issue of *Zeitschrift für Ostmitteleuropa-Forschung* 61 [2012] 3) and Victor Neumann and Armin Heinen, *Key Concepts of Romanian History* (2103).

Jacek Nowak is a scholar in the Department of Social Anthropology, Institute of Sociology, Jagiellonian University, Krakow. His teaching, research and publications focus on identity issues, social space, collective memory and ethnic and religious minorities. He is the author of the books *Zaginiony świat? Nazywają ich* Łemkami (2000), *Social Rules of Remembrance: Anthropology of Collective Memory* (2011) and co-author of *Zarządzanie przestrzenią. Globalizacja, etniczność, władza* (2006), and of articles including 'Reorganisation of Ethnic Space in the Context of the Challenges of Globalization', in *Polish Sociological Review* (2010), 'Collective Memory and Religious Transmission: A Greek Catholic Example in Western Ukraine', in Mahieu and Naumescu (eds), *Churches in-between. The Greek Catholic Churches in Postsocialist Europe* (2008).

Kurt Scharr received his PhD from Innsbruck University in 2000, and currently works as a senior researcher at the Austrian Academy of Sciences. His historical and geographical focus on the border areas of the eastern Alps (Tyrol, south Tyrol) and those of the Carpathians (Romania, Ukraine). From 2008 to 2011 he co-directed a research project on the Franciscan Cadastre with Helmut Rumpler (University of Klagenfurt/Austrian Academy of Sciences), and he is currently engaged on a project on the Greek Orthodox Church foundation of Bukovina from the late eighteenth to the first half of the twentieth century. Among his publications is *'Die Landschaft Bukowina': Das Werden einer Region an der Peripherie 1774–1918* (2010).

Hannes Siegrist is professor of the social and cultural history of modern and contemporary Europe at the Faculty of Social Sciences and Philosophy, University of Leipzig. He is a member of the Saxonian Academy of Science and stands on the advisory board of the Centre for the History and Culture of East Central Europe at the University of Leipzig. He is currently co-editor of *Comparativ: Zeitschrift für Globalgeschichte und Vergleichende Gesellschaftsforschung* and of the book-series 'Moderne europäische Geschichte' with Wallstein Verlag, Göttingen. His publications include: 'Intellectual Property Rights and Globalization', special issue of *Comparativ*, 21 (2011) 2; *Eigentum im internationalen Vergleich (18.-20. Jahrhundert)* (1999) (ed. with David Sugarman); *Professionen, Eigentum und Staat. Europäische Entwicklungen im Vergleich – 19. und 20. Jahrhundert* (2014) (ed. with Dietmar Müller); 'Bourgeoisie, Middle Classes, History of', in Neil J. Smelser und Paul B. Baltes (eds), *International Encyclopedia of the Social and Behavioral Sciences* (IESBS), (2001) vol. 2.

Index